Advances in
LIBRARIANSHIP

Volume 8

Advances in LIBRARIANSHIP

Edited by

MICHAEL H. HARRIS
University of Kentucky
Lexington, Kentucky

Volume 8

ACADEMIC PRESS   New York San Francisco London   1978
A Subsidiary of Harcourt Brace Jovanovich, Publishers

COPYRIGHT © 1978, BY ACADEMIC PRESS, INC.
ALL RIGHTS RESERVED.
NO PART OF THIS PUBLICATION MAY BE REPRODUCED OR
TRANSMITTED IN ANY FORM OR BY ANY MEANS, ELECTRONIC
OR MECHANICAL, INCLUDING PHOTOCOPY, RECORDING, OR ANY
INFORMATION STORAGE AND RETRIEVAL SYSTEM, WITHOUT
PERMISSION IN WRITING FROM THE PUBLISHER.

ACADEMIC PRESS, INC.
111 Fifth Avenue, New York, New York 10003

United Kingdom Edition published by
ACADEMIC PRESS, INC. (LONDON) LTD.
24/28 Oval Road, London NW1 7DX

LIBRARY OF CONGRESS CATALOG CARD NUMBER: 79–88675

ISBN 0–12–785008–2

PRINTED IN THE UNITED STATES OF AMERICA

Contents

Contributors ix
Preface xi
Contents of Previous Volumes xv

Collection Development in Large University Libraries
ROSE MARY MAGRILL AND MONA EAST
    I. Introduction 2
   II. Acquisition Trends in the 1960s 3
  III. Acquisition Environment in the 1970s 7
  IV. Adjustments in Selection Priorities 20
   V. Special Problems and Responses 24
  VI. Cooperative Programs 32
 VII. Quantitative Approaches to Control and Evaluation 37
VIII. Conclusion 39
      References 40

The Library of Congress in American Life
JOHN Y. COLE
   I. Introduction 55
  II. The Legislative and the National Roles 57
 III. Disagreements Concerning the Library's Role 63
  IV. The Task Force on Goals, Organization, and Planning 68
   V. The Task Force Recommendations 71
      References 78

Affirmative Action and American Librarianship
ELIZABETH DICKINSON AND MARGARET MYERS
- I. Introduction 82
- II. Affirmative Action and Librarianship 83
- III. Prospects for the Future 121
- IV. Conclusion 127
- References 128

American Indian Library Service
CHARLES T. TOWNLEY
- I. Introduction 136
- II. Indian America in the 1970s 137
- III. American Indian Library Service to 1973: Defining the Domain 142
- IV. American Library Service since 1973: Demonstration and Testing 149
- V. Findings: The Knowledge Base of American Indian Library Service 168
- VI. Implementing American Indian Library Service: The Next Five Years 172
- References 174

Advances in American Library History
DAVID KASER
- I. Recent Attention to American Library History 181
- II. Survey of Recent Research 184
- III. Some General Observations 193
- References 196

Trends in Library Education—Canada
JOHN P. WILKINSON
- I. Introduction: The Canadian Milieu 201
- II. Perspective: A Comparison with Education for Librarianship in Britain and Canada 204
- III. Regional and National Needs 206
- IV. Curricular Responses 209
- V. Stratification 216
- VI. Librarianship as an Academic Discipline 219

VII. Practice Work in Libraries 222
VIII. Continuing Education 224
IX. Harmonization of Qualifications 226
X. The Research Component 229
XI. Canadian Library Associations and Education for Librarianship 231
XII. Extrapolation 233
References 236
Appendix 238

Continuing Education for Librarians in the United States
ELIZABETH W. STONE

I. Introduction 242
II. Definitions: Distinctions 243
III. Factors Affecting the Design of Continuing Education Systems 255
IV. Responsibility for Continuing Education of Librarians .. 271
V. The Continuing Library Education Network and Exchange (CLENE) 314
VI. Looking toward the Future 322
References 323

Subject Index 333

Contributors

Numbers in parentheses indicate the pages on which the authors' contributions begin.

John Y. Cole (55), Library of Congress, Washington, D.C.

Elizabeth Dickinson (81), Broward County Division of Libraries, Fort Lauderdale, Florida

Mona East (1), University Library, University of Michigan, Ann Arbor, Michigan

David Kaser (181), Graduate Library School, Indiana University, Bloomington, Indiana

Rose Mary Magrill (1), School of Library Science, University of Michigan, Ann Arbor, Michigan

Margaret Myers (81), American Library Association, Chicago, Illinois

Elizabeth W. Stone (241), Graduate Department of Library and Information Science, The Catholic University of America, Washington, D.C.

Charles T. Townley (135), School of Library Science, University of Michigan, Ann Arbor, Michigan

John P. Wilkinson (201), Faculty of Library Science, University of Toronto, Toronto, Ontario, Canada

Preface

For the past decade librarians have been preoccupied with the implications that the coming of the "post-industrial age" might have for society, and more specifically for libraries within society. Especially disconcerting has been the rapid and inchoate rise of new technology touted by commercial entrepreneurs as the panacea for the problems facing the library profession. This concern was only intensified with the publication of the Report of the National Commission on Library and Information Science, which argued relentlessly for the application of sophisticated new technology to library operations and ignored most of the human problems involved.

While the new technology and its role in library service are clearly of great interest, we have recently witnessed a new awareness among librarians of the many social, economic, and political problems that must be dealt with before information professionals can make sensible use of the new technology to improve and extend library service. Volume 8 of *Advances in Librarianship* focuses on some of the major nontechnological problems currently facing the profession. Problems which, while exacerbated or even stimulated by the rise of the new technology, clearly are not dependent upon this technology for solution. These problems now appear to be central to the operation of libraries, and the way in which librarians deal with them will have long-range consequences for the delivery of library services.

In the opening paper, two specialists in library collection development examine the momentous changes evident in that area over the past decade. In the mid-sixties vastly increased budgets, a prodigious growth in publication rates, and the emergence of comprehensive blanket-order plans persuaded many academic librarians to enter into arrangements with book jobbers, which allowed them to diminish the size of their professional acquisition staffs, while at the same time keeping abreast of their burgeoning collections. In the second half of the period covered in this paper, book budgets declined rapidly, in some cases disastrously, and the comprehensive blanket-order plans—represented most graphically by the Richard Abel Co. —ran into serious problems, leaving those libraries that had become dependent on them in chaos. Magrill and East thoroughly examine the steps taken by large academic libraries to attempt to cope with the drastically altered conditions of the mid-seventies. In so doing, they clearly demonstrate the significance of the well-trained and imaginative professional in the matrix of the collection development programs of contemporary academic libraries.

The Library of Congress, the Nation's largest and most influential library, has always been central to the thinking of librarians in this country and abroad. But this interest has been heightened recently by (1) the controversial appointment of historian Daniel Boorstin as the new Librarian of Congress, (2) the basic role assigned to the Library by the National Commission on Library and Information Science, and (3) the completion of the Report of the Library of Congress Task Force on Goals, Organization, and Planning. John Y. Cole, the Chairman of the Task Force, has written a timely assessment of the Library of Congress and the Nation, which not only summarizes and evaluates the Task Force Report but also examines the emergence of the Library of Congress' "dual role" and the difficulties this conflict of interest has caused for those attempting to administer the Nation's largest library.

Affirmative action in libraries, the topic of the third paper in this volume, represents yet another problem that would appear to owe little to the technological concerns of librarians. And yet, the question—given the intense pressure to comply with the complex and frequently conflicting laws and regulations—is of great interest to librarians everywhere. Further, while the topic has obvious importance for the administration of libraries, it rests at the very heart of any consideration of the direction and nature of the library profession itself. For the clear evidence of discrimination against women, Blacks, and others in the library field runs counter to not only the law of the land but also the professional credo of librarians. This situation has forced librarians to deal with the problem on two levels: the purely administrative and the philosophical. In their paper, Dickinson and

Preface xiii

Myers provide the essential groundwork for any attempt to intelligently grapple with what appears to be one of the most serious issues facing the profession today.

Directly related to the librarian's concern for the question of affirmative action, but a topic deserving full-scale treatment in itself, is the matter of library service to American Indians. Charles T. Townley, a principal figure in the effort to extend library service to this long-neglected segment of American society, assesses the progress made to date and delineates the future direction of the American Indian library service. Presenting the first detailed and critical evaluation of the recent experimental programs designed to extend library service to America's Indian population, he unflinchingly addresses the shortcomings of the programs as well as their strengths.

Together with the bicentennial of the United States, 1976 represented the centennial of the American Library Association. This event focused the attention of the library profession, for a brief time at least, on the evolution and present status of librarianship in America. The resultant interest in library history generated a flurry of historical research uncommon to our professional literature. It thus seems appropriate to examine the nature and value of historical research in a profession not prone to historical introspection and to assess the implications this research might have for contemporary librarianship. David Kaser, widely recognized as an authority in the field of present-day librarianship, has undertaken this difficult task. His paper emphasizes the solid, thoroughly documented contributions to the literature of library history and cautiously reads their "lessons" for modern librarians.

The final two papers in this volume deal with library education. The first, a detailed analysis of Canadian library education, continues a series of studies of the condition of library education in various parts of the world. Professor J. P. Wilkinson has prepared a thoughtful and carefully documented study that will be of interest to educators everywhere. Combining, as it does, features of both the English and American systems of library education, the Canadian system might be considered derivative by the casual observer. However, the Canadians have evolved a unique brand of library education—especially with their emphasis on a two-year program of theoretical instruction combined with practical field work—that promises to be a highly influential model for library educators in the United States and elsewhere.

The second paper on library education deals with continuing education for librarians in the United States. This subject, which has gained considerable recent attention, is both controversial and confused. Librarians and library educators appear to be unable to agree on a definition of continuing education, let alone arrive at any systematic plan for the future. One thing is clear, as Elizabeth Stone so forcefully insists, information professionals faced with a rapidly evolving body of professional knowledge and ever-increasing demands for public accountability must move quickly to provide for the systematic and continuing education of practicing librarians. Dr. Stone's detailed paper outlines the nature of continuing education, discusses the conflicts over content and method, and fully analyzes the responsibilities of the various organizations and groups who must involve themselves in this aspect of library education; thus encouraging further discussion designed to refine and improve our emerging system of continuing education for librarianship.

Michael H. Harris

Contents of Previous Volumes

Volume 1

The Machine and Cataloging
  George Piternick

Mechanization of Acquisitions Processes
  Connie R. Dunlap

Mechanization and Library Filing Rules
  Kelley L. Cartwright

Standards for Technical Service Cost Studies
  Helen Welch Tuttle

The Undergraduate Library Trend at Large Universities
  Robert H. Muller

The Changing School Library: An Instructional Media Center
  Chase Dane

Reference Service to Children—Past, Present, and Future
  Lillian K. Orsini

Progress in Bibliotherapy
  Ruth M. Tews

Effectiveness in Cooperation and Consolidation in Public Libraries
  Ralph Blasingame and Ernest R. DeProspo, Jr.

Library Planning: The Challenge of Change
  Robert E. Kemper

Acceleration of Library Development in Developing Countries
  Carl M. White

SUBJECT INDEX

Volume 2

Access to Information
  William S. Budington

Control and Dissemination of Information in Medicine
  David Bishop

The Computer in Serials Processing and Control
  Don L. Bosseau

Micropublication
  Allen B. Veaner

The Changing Role of the State Library
  Kenneth E. Beasley

Censorship, Intellectual Freedom, and Libraries
  Edwin Castagna

Reader Services to the Disadvantaged in Inner Cities
  Margaret E. Monroe

Oral History: Problems and Prospects
  Louis M. Starr

Armageddon in International Copyright: Review of the Berne Convention, the Universal Convention, and the Present Crisis in International Copyright
  Dorothy M. Schrader

AUTHOR INDEX—SUBJECT INDEX

Volume 3

On Beyond 999Z—Patterns of Library Service to Children of the Poor
  Binnie L. Tate

Youth as a Special Client Group
  James W. Liesener and Margaret E. Chisholm

The Emergence of the Community College Library
  Harriett Genung and James O. Wallace

Teaching Library Skills to College Students
  Miriam Dudley

Academic Library Buildings in the United Kingdom
  H. Faulkner Brown

Academic Library Buildings in the United States
  Ralph E. Ellsworth

Federal Grants and Public Libraries
  James G. Igoe

Anglo-American Code Implementation
  Elizabeth L. Tate

Catalog Use Studies and Their Implications
  James Krikelas

Converting Bibliographic Data to Machine Form
  Don Sherman

Archive and Manuscript Collections
  Robert L. Brubaker

AUTHOR INDEX—SUBJECT INDEX

Volume 4

MARC and Its Application to Library Automation
  Roy B. Torkington

Selective Dissemination of Information
  Georg R. Mauerhoff

Circulation Automation
  Hugh C. Atkinson

Social Responsibility and Libraries
  Arthur Curley

Women in Librarianship
  Anita R. Schiller

The Use of Resources in the Learning Experience
  Johnnie Givens

Reading as Information Processing
  John J. Geyer and Paul A. Kolers

SUBJECT INDEX

Volume 5

International Information Systems
  Jacques Tocatlian

National Planning for Library and Information Services
  Foster E. Mohrhardt and Carlos Victor Penna

Statistics That Describe Libraries and Library Service
  Thomas Childers

Coordination of the Technical Services
  Helen Welch Tuttle

Trends in Library Education—United States
  Lester Asheim

The Technologies of Education and Communication
  Gerald R. Brong

Audiovisual Services in Libraries
  Irving Lieberman

Sound Recordings
  Gordon Stevenson

Joint Academic Libraries
  Richard D. Johnson

AUTHOR INDEX—SUBJECT INDEX

Volume 6

Performance Measures for School Librarians; Complexities and Potential
  Evelyn H. Daniel

Productivity Measurement in Academic Libraries
  Thomas J. Waldhart and Thomas P. Marcum

Relevance: A Review of the Literature and a Framework for Thinking on the Notion in Information Science
  Tefko Saracevic

The Impact of Reading on Human Behavior: The Implications of Communications Research
  Roger Haney, Michael H. Harris, and Leonard Tipton

Trends in Library Education—Europe
  Donald Davinson

The Role of Middle Managers in Libraries
  Beverly P. Lynch

AUTHOR INDEX—SUBJECT INDEX

Volume 7

Vocabulary Control in Information Retrieval Systems
  F. W. Lancaster

Major Developments in Classification
  Ingetraut Dahlberg

National Libraries in Developing Countries
  Simeon B. Aje

The American Library Association and the Library Association: Retrospect, Problems, and Prospects
  W. A. Munford

Popular Culture and the Public Library
  Gordon Stevenson

Public Library Use, Users, Uses: Advances in Knowledge of the Characteristics and Needs of the Adult Clientele of American Public Libraries
  Douglas Zweizig and Brenda Dervin

Personal Roles and Barriers in Information Transfer
  Anne Wilkin

The Applications of Citation Analyses to Library Collection Building
  Robert N. Broadus

AUTHOR INDEX—SUBJECT INDEX

Collection Development in Large University Libraries

ROSE MARY MAGRILL

School of Library Science
University of Michigan

and

MONA EAST

University Library
University of Michigan

I.	Introduction	2
II.	Acquisition Trends in the 1960s	3
	A. Introduction	3
	B. Growth Rates	3
	C. Expansion of Foreign Acquisitions	4
	D. Subject Bibliographers	5
	E. Blanket Orders and Approval Plans	6
III.	Acquisition Environment in the 1970s	7
	A. Economic Realities	7
	B. Other Aspects of the Academic Environment	10
	C. Administrative Adjustments to Changing Acquisitions Environment	12
IV.	Adjustments in Selection Priorities	20
	A. Review of Previous Commitments	20
	B. Emphasis on Current Domestic Publications	21

		C.	Conflicts between Research and Teaching Needs	22
		D.	Competition among Various Subject Fields and Forms of Publication	23
	V.		Special Problems and Responses	24
		A.	Serials	24
		B.	Gifts and Gift Funds	26
		C.	Exchanges	27
		D.	Replacement and Duplication	28
		E.	Variations in Funding	28
		F.	Weeding and Storage	29
		G.	Conservation	30
	VI.		Cooperative Programs	32
		A.	Increased Interest in Long-Standing Arrangements	33
		B.	Development of Newer Arrangements	35
	VII.		Quantitative Approaches to Control and Evaluation	37
	VIII.		Conclusion	39
			References	40

I. INTRODUCTION

This review will be devoted to recent activities in collection development in large university libraries, with emphasis on research libraries meeting the qualifications for membership in the Association of Research Libraries (ARL). After a summary of developments during the 1960s, the changing situation of the 1970s will be described. The downward trend in library funding and the shifting academic environment have led to administrative adjustments such as formal statements of policy, formulas for budget allocations, long-range planning statements, and establishment of staff committees to share responsibility and increase staff awareness of policies and procedures. As budgets have declined, selection priorities have been adjusted by reviewing previous commitments, emphasizing current domestic publications, and attempting to determine a fair balance among subject fields and forms of publication and between research needs and teaching needs. The difficult financial situation in all of higher education and the inflation in the publishing industry have led to new problems or aggravated old ones, particularly in regard to serial publications. Cooperative arrangements are being widely discussed as one solution to some of the collection development problems of the 1970s; quantitative methods to control and evaluate collections are also gaining in popularity. Outlined in the following pages are the ways in which collection development has changed in large university libraries during the past ten years.

II. ACQUISITION TRENDS IN THE 1960s

A. Introduction

At some time during the 1960s, most large university libraries encountered problems of increase: the need for more books in more fields, for more copies of frequently used materials, for careful selection from an increasing volume of publication, for more staff time devoted to straightforward collecting as well as to collection development, and, eventually, for the wise spending of much larger funds than had previously been available. The effects of these increases could be observed in the amount of foreign acquisitions, the use of standing orders and blanket plans, and the appointment of subject specialists to assume much of the responsibility for collection development and evaluation. These developments are discussed in articles in the October 1966 and July 1970 issues of *Library Trends* (Babb, 1966; Chapin and McCoy, 1966; Coney and Michel, 1966; Downs, 1966; McCarthy, 1966; Miller and Moriarity, 1966; O'Brien, 1966; Orne and Powell, 1966; Skipper, 1966; Wilson, 1966; Archer, 1970; Downs, 1970; Dudley, 1970; Gregory, 1970; Huff, 1970; Paulson, 1970; Reichmann, 1970; R. D. Stevens, 1970; R. E. Stevens, 1970; Thompson, 1970; Tuttle, 1970), as well as in certain other articles (Haro, 1967, 1969b; Kraft, 1967; Blanchard, 1968; Lane, 1968; Schad and Adams, 1969; Voigt, 1969; White, 1969; Kosa, 1972a; Edelman and Tatum, 1976).

B. Growth Rates

The high growth rates of large university library collections and materials budgets during the 1950s and 1960s have been extensively documented (Baumol and Marcus, 1973; Downs, 1974; Dunn *et al.*, 1973; Leach, 1976). Downs (1974) noted that the national average for percentage of increase of volumes held in research libraries was 332 percent between 1955 and 1973. Percentages of increase tended to be higher for libraries which had smaller collections at the beginning of the expansion period, but even some of the research libraries with the largest collections in 1950 had recorded increases of over 100 percent in library holdings by 1968–1969.

The annual statistics compiled by the Association of Research Libraries give some indication of how the rate of acquisitions varied for individual libraries, beginning in the late 1960s. Between the academic years of 1965–1966 and 1968–1969, at least 85 percent of the ARL libraries enjoyed annual increases in the amount of money spent for library materials. In 1969–1970, more than one fourth of the ARL members experienced a decrease from the previous year's expenditures. In 1970–1971 and 1971–1972, more than 40 percent of the libraries suffered annual decreases. For the academic years of 1972–1973, 1973–1974, and 1974–1975, the percentage of libraries suffering annual decreases ranged from 20 to 30 percent.

Owing to rising prices and inflation, percentage increases in rate of volumes added (gross) were not as high as increases in expenditures. However, annual reports on the total number of volumes added to all ARL libraries, as well as the median number of volumes added (gross) for the group, showed no decreases between 1965–1966 and 1970–1971. But beginning with the 1970–1971 academic year, the total volumes added (gross) for all libraries and the median number of volumes added (gross) decreased each year. In 1971–1972 and 1973–1974, almost 60 percent of the ARL libraries added fewer volumes than they had added the year before.

C. Expansion of Foreign Acquisitions

In the 1950s, encouraged by activities of professional societies and grants from foundations, major universities began to establish area studies programs. As curricular offerings and research in these areas expanded in the 1960s, university libraries were faced with increased demands for material in non-Western languages and from countries which lacked an organized book trade and systematic bibliographic coverage. The Farmington Plan, the Latin American Cooperative Acquisitions Project, the Public Law 480 programs of the Library of Congress and later the National Program for Acquisitions and Cataloging brought a flood of materials into many of the largest libraries but did not supply materials from all countries whose publications were needed.

Problems of selection, acquisition, processing, and bibliographic control of materials published in other parts of the world were discussed at several institutes and conferences, such as the 1965 annual conference of the University of Chicago Graduate Library School (Tsien and Winger, 1966) and the Institute on the Acquisition of Foreign Materials, held at the University of Wisconsin–Milwaukee in 1971 (Samore, 1973). A variety of articles on foreign acquisitions appeared in the *Farmington Plan Newsletter* (since 1970, the *Foreign Acquisitions Newsletter*) and in other journals (Downs, 1971; Edelman, 1973; Jay and McGowan, 1969; McNiff, 1963; Skipper, 1966; Stevens, 1968; R. D. Stevens, 1963, 1970; Vosper, 1967). Public Law 480 and its impact on foreign acquisitions in libraries in the United States were discussed at a 1967 conference at the University of Wisconsin–Madison (Williamson, 1968) and in a dissertation at Columbia (El-Erian, 1972). Acquisition of Latin American materials was covered in the numerous working papers presented at the annual meetings of the Seminar on the Acquisition of Latin American Library Materials, begun in 1956, and in other publications by Shepard (1962, 1969) and Savary (1968). If the space devoted to a topic in the professional literature is any indication of the amount of interest the topic holds for librarians, then foreign materials were clearly a concern of the 1960s.

D. Subject Bibliographers

The acquisition environment of the 1960s—increasing rate of publication, rapid growth of book budgets, expansion of collections to materials and languages not previously covered, and decline of faculty participation in selection—encouraged the addition of subject/area bibliographers to university library staffs. In most libraries the move toward subject bibliographers began with the employment of specialists familiar with the languages of the areas in which intensive and interdisciplinary studies were beginning or were being greatly increased. The success of bibliographers in those areas prompted the appointment of specialists in more traditional areas or the assignment of members of the library staff to spend part of their time in current selection or more thorough collection development in a particular area or field.

The professional literature of the 1960s and early 1970s furnishes many expressions of opinion about the role of the subject bibliographer, some descriptions of experiences in individual libraries, but little that would qualify as research or evaluation. Danton (1963, 1967), Humphreys (1967), Haro (1969a), Harrer (1969), Lopez (1969), Steele (1970), Edelman (1972), and Coppin (1974) all discuss qualifications and responsibilities of the subject bibliographer, while Tuttle (1969a) warns against expecting too much of the subject bibliographer. Experiences in one library are described by Byrd (1966) and Kosa (1972b, 1975) and can also be found in annual reports of libraries employing subject bibliographers.

Two surveys (Smith, 1972; Stueart, 1971) offer broader views of the changing role and organizational placement of the subject bibliographer. The subject bibliographer of the 1960s seems to have been assigned primarily to collection development activities, but Smith (1972, 1974) and others (Gration and Young, 1974; Michalak, 1976) note a tendency for specialists to expand the range of their activities. The new emphasis is on serving in a variety of ways as a link between the faculty and students and the library, somewhat in the manner of subject specialists in British universities (Crossley, 1974; Guttsman, 1965, 1973; Holbrook, 1972; Woodhead, 1974). The knowledge gained from increased contact with the library's users will presumably improve the performance of collection development activities by the specialists, although less time will be devoted to such activities.

E. Blanket Orders and Approval Plans

The rise of various kinds of blanket plans usually has been credited to the sudden expansion of book budgets between the late 1950s and mid-1960s, but other factors deserve consideration as well. While book budgets were increasing at a rapid rate, acquisitions staffs were growing at a somewhat lower rate. The apparent shortage of staff, coupled in some cases with poor business techniques and inefficient procedures in technical services, placed additional stress on those responsible for acquisitions. Other pressures came from the revised expectations of library service on the part of the increasing numbers of faculty members and students who were involved in new programs of teaching and research and who wanted easy access to comprehensive collections. When librarians promised comprehensiveness and began to lower criteria for selection, jobbers (including several international booksellers who wanted to maintain and enlarge the business created by the Farmington Plan) set up plans to exploit the situation.

The advantages and drawbacks of such plans have been widely discussed. In addition to the papers from three International Seminars on Approval and Gathering Plans in Large and Medium Size Academic Libraries (Spyers-Duran, 1969; Spyers-Duran and Gore, 1970, 1972), a steady stream of publications has appeared. Some emphasize the blanket orders and approval plans as selection devices (Dobbyn, 1972; Dudley, 1970; Lane, 1969; Merritt, 1968; Meyer and Demos, 1970; Morrison, 1968; Rouse, 1970), while others stress the effective organization of procedures (Gamble, 1972; McCullough, 1972; Rebuldela, 1969; Rouse, 1970; Taggart, 1970; Thom, 1969). Other aspects also are covered in the literature: DeVolder (1972) reviews early attempts at blanket plans; Wedgeworth (1970) reports on a survey of foreign language plans; and Wilden-Hart (1970b) warns of long-term effects. In 1972, McCullough identified and reviewed more than 60 books, articles, papers, reports, and letters-to-the-editor that discussed blanket orders and approval plans between 1958 and 1972.

Most of the earlier papers on the subject of blanket orders and approval plans were informal and enthusiastic case studies of the operation of specific plans in individual libraries. Eventually, studies were made to compare collections built in the traditional way with those produced by the newer methods (DeVilbiss, 1975; Evans, 1969, 1970; Evans and Argyres, 1974; Maher *et al.*, 1969; Raney, 1972). Among recent cost studies of blanket orders and approval plans are those by Axford (1971) and McCullough (1975). In general, the amount and tone of the professional writing about blanket plans has changed since the 1960s. Unqualified enthusiasm has given place, in most large university libraries, to the belief that these methods are of value in certain circumstances and should be used with care in those circumstances: they are methods, not panaceas.

III. ACQUISITION ENVIRONMENT IN THE 1970s

A. Economic Realities

The most striking difference between the acquisition environment for large university libraries in the 1960s and that of the 1970s is the economic setting in which these libraries operated. The relationship between the economic situation and research library acquisition is a serious one, since "research" materials are the ones most likely to be considered expendable by the general public (Tolman, 1971). Increasingly during the 1970s, librarians' concerns have been directed chiefly toward maintaining and developing library collections within budgets which may have continued to increase slightly, but which furnished decreased purchasing power.

1. SUPPORT OF HIGHER EDUCATION

Overall support for higher education increased significantly during the past decade, but the rate of growth has now started to decline rapidly. According to the *Chronicle of Higher Education* (October 25, 1976), a state-by-state analysis of appropriations for higher education during the decade ending with the 1976–1977 academic year showed ten-year increases (minus inflation) ranging from a low of 32 percent (Louisiana) to a high of 375 percent (Alaska), with a total increase of 111 percent in the United States. However, a similar analysis for the two years of 1974–1976 indicated that changes (minus inflation) ranged from a decrease of 17 percent (Maine) to an increase of 55 percent (Alaska). The total change in the United States between 1974 and 1976 was an increase of 7 percent in appropriations to state-supported institutions; however, twelve states suffered decreases. Comparable figures for private institutions are not easy to find, but according to a *Chronicle of Higher Education* (December 8, 1975) report on a study sponsored by the Association of American Colleges, the resources of private universities and colleges, after allowance for inflation and enrollment growth, have increased only slightly since 1970.

Voluntary support of colleges and universities in 1975 dropped about $80 million from the 1974 level, according to estimates of the Council for Financial Aid to Education reported in the *Chronicle of Higher Education* (March 29, 1976). Within the overall 1975 decline of 3.6 percent, private universities experienced an 8 percent drop. Gifts from business corporations increased slightly in 1975, but gifts from other groups—private foundations, alumni, and other individuals—declined. Gifts from individuals, in fact, have been decreasing since 1972–1973. In general, the Council has noted that drops in giving by individuals and private foundations tend to accompany general economic recessions.

2. APPROPRIATIONS TO ACADEMIC LIBRARIES

Estimates published in *Bowker Annual* of aggregate U.S. statistics on college and university libraries show an increase during the last ten years in library expenditures as a percentage of the total education and general expenditures (3.3 percent in 1965; 4.7 percent in 1975). However, the estimates also indicate that, during the same period, the expenditures for books and other library materials as a percentage of operating expenditures rose from 34.2 percent in 1965 to 38.4 percent in 1970 and then declined steadily, reaching a low of 29.9 percent in 1975. Binding expenditures as a percentage of operating expenditures also fell, from a high of 3.5 percent in 1965 and 1966 to a low of 2.2 percent in 1975.

3. DECREASES IN FEDERAL FUNDING

While state appropriations and voluntary giving to universities were slowing down, federal funds for library materials also were being cut. Appropriations for fiscal year (FY) 1966 under Title II-A of the Higher Education Act were $10 million; for each of the next three fiscal years the appropriation was $25 million. In FY 1970 the appropriation was half that of the previous year, and in FY 1971 it was down even more (to $9.9 million). In FY 1972 the appropriation was increased slightly, and in FY 1973 it was raised to the amount appropriated in FY 1970 ($12.5 million); FY 1974 saw another decrease to slightly under $10 million, which remained the appropriation level for FY 1975 and FY 1976. Beginning in 1970–1971, annual reports reflect the concern of ARL library directors about the decline in available book funds from federal sources, often accompanied by a stable or declining library materials appropriation from university general funds.

4. INFLATION, RISING PRICES, DEVALUATION

Three problems—inflation, rising prices, and devaluation—are mentioned repeatedly in annual reports by library directors who are trying to explain why the previous year's materials budget was inadequate. According to *Publishers Weekly* figures, the average price in the United States of a hardcover trade-technical book in 1975 was more than 80 percent higher than in the base years 1967–1969.

Studies based on actual volumes purchased by research libraries have tended to support an inflation rate of 80 percent or greater for that period. In the same period of time, the average price of a selected group of periodicals published in the United States increased by 130 percent. Each group of scientific and technical periodicals listed in the U.S. periodical price indexes rose at least 100 percent between 1967–1969 and 1975. Most scientific-technical categories rose 150 percent, and one (chemistry and physics) rose over 200 percent.

While prices rose, production of new titles also rose. American title output, as reported in *Publishers Weekly,* increased 38 percent between 1969 and 1974 (from a total of 29,579 new books and new editions in 1969 to a total of 40,846 in 1974). Part of this increase was due to improvement in the listing procedures for the "Weekly Record," but most of it represents real growth in research and publication. In 1975, for the first time in many years, American publishers' overall output decreased by about 3.6 percent from the 1974 figure. Unfortunately for book budgets, several of the subject categories with the largest increase in book title output between 1969 and 1975—law, sociology, economics—also had the largest increase in average price.

Inflation in other major publishing countries combined with decline in the purchasing power of the American dollar naturally posed greater problems for research libraries than for other types of libraries. Estimates of foreign purchases as a percentage of total acquisitions in university libraries, as found in selected annual reports, ranged from approximately 25 percent to 60 percent during the early 1970s. As the American dollar dropped in value abroad in 1971 and was officially devalued twice in 1972–1973, the cost of foreign materials increased significantly. In addition, foreign prices rose in relation to the inflation of the economy in individual countries. Prices for British publications, which are a large part of foreign purchases for most libraries in the United States, increased even faster than did prices for U.S. publications in 1975.

B. Other Aspects of the Academic Environment

Aspects of the academic environment other than the economic situation have greatly affected the demand for library services, in most cases causing an increased demand. More students, larger faculties, new teaching methods, new areas of study, new research methods and interests have all required more library materials and more copies of many books.

According to a survey of trends published in the *Chronicle of Higher Education* (September 2, 1975) and based on figures from the National Center for Educational Statistics, enrollments in colleges and universities continued to increase in the early 1970s, although the increases were much smaller than those of the 1960s. Estimates of future enrollment show continued increases through 1981, with small decreases predicted for 1983 in undergraduate for-credit and graduate students. The number of nondegree students decreased in 1969 and 1971, but before 1969 and after 1971 there were larger increases in this category than in others; larger increases are predicted for future years, ending with a small increase for 1983.

Similarly, the number of degrees awarded (bachelor's, first professional, master's, and doctor's) increased sharply through the 1960s; increases were smaller in the early 1970s, and still smaller year-to-year increases are predicted for the later 1970s and early 1980s. The number of instructional staff increased somewhat more slowly than the number of graduate students during the 1960s; very small increases are predicted through the later 1970s and small decreases in the early 1980s.

Growth in student enrollments has required increased duplication of books used in advanced courses as well as in large undergraduate courses. Changes in teaching methods, such as a shift from lecture-textbook courses toward teaching by means of lectures and discussions based on large reading lists, have required a wider range of books for these courses and substantial provision of duplicate copies. The introduction of students to independent research at an earlier stage has increased demands for advanced materials. Separate libraries established to provide better service to undergraduate students acquire a very high percentage of books of which copies are needed elsewhere in the library system; few of their acquisitions are unique.

New studies and methods such as the development of area and interdisciplinary studies, new interest in previously neglected areas of study such as ethnic and women's studies, the application of social science techniques to new disciplines, and new methods of study in traditional fields, as, for example, enumerative history (which uses such things as census materials, army lists, genealogical records, and church and university lists of members to investigate and measure the effects of historical movements and events) have created demands for library materials in new fields and additional materials in areas of the collection previously considered strong. Scholarly interest in current events and recent movements has also increased greatly in recent years and has led to demands for increased provision of newspapers and for materials such as summaries of recent developments, estimates of trends, and similar materials which were formerly considered of little use to scholars and of no more than temporary value. Now needed for serious study, these materials are likely to be expensive.

Publishers have responded quickly to new scholarly and teaching interests and to new technological possibilities. During the 1960s, the increased availability of scholarly reprints became both an acquisitions benefit and a budget and selection problem. Again in recent years, although it has been possible to strengthen collections greatly through the availability in microform and computer printout of archival materials, research data, statistical reports, and reprints of publications and collections too extensive to warrant hardcover reprinting, the quantity of available and potentially useful material far exceeds most library budgets.

New teaching materials such as taped lectures and discussions, self-teaching programs, and video tapes and other audiovisual forms also present new opportunities and new costs. Most university libraries have been slow to assume responsibility for audiovisual teaching materials (Boss, 1972), leaving them to the teaching departments or to audiovisual centers which may or may not be closely connected to the library. Research materials, on the other hand, are likely to be acquired if they are needed and can be afforded, without regard to the form in which they are issued.

C. Administrative Adjustments to Changing Acquisitions Environment

1. INTRODUCTION

By 1972, most research libraries had found that their budgets had declined in purchasing power if not in amount, while demand for materials not only continued but increased. Action was directed toward contracting expenditures for materials with the least possible present and future damage to the collections. Although all university libraries have been affected, each situation has individual aspects, and a point of crisis has been reached at different times in different institutions. Administrative adjustments in many libraries began with formalization of collecting procedures, formulation of collection development policies, efforts toward formulas for budget allocation, explicit long-range planning, and increased coordination of collection development within the institution.

2. FORMALIZATION OF PROCEDURES

As larger numbers of staff members become involved in collection development, increased communication and explicit direction are required in order to avoid confusion and inconsistency. One of the most common administrative responses to this need has been the increasing formalization of collection development procedures: formal written statements of collection and acquisition policies and budget allocation formulas are examples of the trend toward more formal procedures.

a. Collection Development Policies. Even before the 1970s, a few university librarians were emphasizing the value of collection and acquisition policies (Henderson, 1960; Lane, 1968; Thompson, 1960) and discussing the construction of such policies (Danton, 1963; Hall, 1966). Until recently, however, strong advocates of written policies for large libraries were difficult to locate in the professional literature. By the early 1970s, more evidence of interest in policy statements began to appear (Ettlinger, 1973; Richter, 1970–1971; Rogers and Weber, 1971; Taggart, 1972, 1974; Ward, 1973; Wayne State University Libraries, 1974; Webster, 1972). The publication and wide distribution of policy statements by Stanford (1970), Cornell (1966), and Northwestern (1972) prompted increased activity in many libraries. A Systems and Procedures Exchange Center (SPEC) collection development survey (ARL, 1974b) conducted in 1974 found that 65 percent of the ARL libraries responding had a formal, written collection development policy. The SPEC kit on acquisition policies (ARL, 1974a) includes examples of policy statements from several of these libraries.

Reasons for undertaking such a major project as the writing of a collection development policy for a large library system are not often discussed in print (Osburn, 1977). Annual reports from ARL libraries indicate that policies are often produced in connection with other efforts undertaken to improve coordination and planning—as the final product of a collection evaluation, as the first responsibility of a new collection development officer or department, or as part of the university's long-range planning operation. Budgetary constraints sometimes coincide with or precede the development of written policies; sometimes participation in resource-sharing schemes forces the move.

Content and format of written policies vary from one library to another, although two or three patterns seem to have emerged as the most frequently followed. In some libraries the approach has been to state the arrangements which are presently in effect for the routine acquisition of various types of materials, list the individuals with responsibility for carrying out the arrangements, and note where in the library system such materials will be housed. Another pattern is to list, sometimes according to the Library of Congress (LC) Classification, all subject areas covered by the library's collections, and then to identify the level of collection (comprehensive, research, basic, etc.) to be developed in that subject. In other cases the decision is based primarily on departmental or divisional library responsibilities, with each separate unit developing its own policy.

Since one of the major arguments against the development of written collection policies is the amount of staff time and effort needed to keep such a document current, some libraries have turned to computer-based procedures for developing and revising policy statements. Yavarkovsky *et al.* (1973) reported on Columbia's attempt to create an on-line file which used descriptors associated with 1,300 classes from an abridged version of the LC Classification to record the current collecting goals of the principal libraries and collections in the system. Converse and Standers (1975) described the University of Calgary's project to gather on magnetic tape a great deal of information about collections desired for each academic department and about personnel who might assist with selection.

The recent activity of the Collection Development Committee of the Resources and Technical Services Division's (RTSD's) Resources Section is a final indication of the widespread acceptance of written policy statements. In 1974, this group appointed a task force to prepare guidelines for the formulation of collection development policies. According to the draft of the guidelines (ALA, 1977), one of the immediate objectives is to introduce some standardization of terms and forms into the writing of collection development policies so that they can be used more easily in resource-sharing projects. The draft statement includes a statement of assumptions underlying written policies, definitions of five levels of collecting, suggested language codes, and an outline of elements to include in a collection development policy statement.

b. Budget Allocation Formulas. Allocation of book funds is not a new development in academic libraries, but the need to rationalize the allocation of limited funds appears to have brought about a renewed interest in budget allocation formulas. The 1974 SPEC survey of collection development (ARL, 1974b) noted a "lively interest" in the topic, and the SPEC kit on collection development (ARL, 1974b) includes examples of budget allocation guides from several ARL libraries. Even before the budget cuts of the 1970s, the publication in 1965 of the Clapp-Jordan formula, which used quantitative criteria to estimate adequate collection size, and the increased reliance on formulas by funding agencies during the 1960s stimulated interest in formulas for the allocation of book budgets to academic departments.

Early efforts were directed toward finding the most appropriate combination of variables for a formula. McGrath and others (1969) selected nine groups of variables (43 variables in all) and attempted to determine which combination gave the best prediction of a department's need in relation to other departments. The groups of variables studied were number and cost of books published, strength of existing collection, faculty and faculty load, credit hours, enrollment, circulation, interlibrary loans, references in theses, and a group of other miscellaneous variables. Later McGrath (1975) suggested an allocation formula based on demand, the effect of which would be to add books in a given subject area in proportion to the number that were circulated in that area. The procedure requires describing an academic department in terms of Dewey or LC numbers and matching this against annual circulation figures of the library in order to obtain circulation estimates for each department. The average cost of books within each subject area must also be obtained and multiplied by the circulation of that area to produce a cost-use figure for each department. Each department's percentage of the library's total cost-use becomes its percentage of the book fund allocation.

The problem of adjusting for inflation rates has been considered by Burton (1975) and also by Kohut (1974), who proposed that allocations to departments be made in terms of "library-resource units" rather than dollar amounts. Such allocations might be made on the basis of any criteria thought appropriate—number of programs, weighted users, etc. After each department's "library-resource unit" allocation has been made, the proper monograph–serial ratio for each department would be determined, and the various inflation rates for each discipline and format would then be used to calculate the actual money to be spent by or for each department.

Some economists and operations researchers have offered suggestions for efficient ways to allocate the budget. Goyal (1973) used a linear programming model which provides for distribution of funds on the basis of "the importance of the department" (determined by estimating the importance which society and the university attach to the work of the department and the number of students in the department). Gold (1975), taking an economist's view of the problem, suggested that the budget should be allocated so as to equate marginal benefits and marginal costs for each department. For his approach, three pieces of information would be needed for each department: (1) credit hours taught; (2) use of library for the department's courses; (3) a value judgment about the importance of such use to the university's program. Kohut and Walker (1975), in a reply to Gold's article, noted the limitations of cost-benefit analysis in such institutions as academic libraries and argued that equity is the most important factor in budget allocation.

Recent interest in developing budget allocation formulas, although consistent with the general movement toward formalization and quantification of library operations, may appear to run counter to the trend toward librarian responsibility for selection. In 1964, Bach observed that academic librarians had made no significant changes in methods of handling book funds during the past twenty to thirty years. Bach emphasized the disadvantages of allocation and argued that those who favored allocation of funds suggested a belief that librarians should not have the responsibility for collection development. Hanes (1964) took exception to this view and responded that the amount of flexibility possible in method, degree, and control of allocation meant that allocation could be an effective administrative technique. Few large libraries rely entirely on formulas for their allocation decisions, but more frequently than in the past their decisions are checked by or expressed in a formula.

3. LONG-RANGE PLANNING

Explicit long-range planning in the form of statements of goals and objectives and estimates of the time and money needed to reach them are increasingly used to justify library requests to the university administration and to funding agencies; the process of developing these statements serves to develop and clarify objectives within the library. A 1970 study of university library management (Booz, Allen, and Hamilton, 1970) identified planning inadequacies—lack of comprehensive, long-range plans in many universities; little relation between university plans and library plans where they did exist; poorly defined university and library objectives which could not be applied to requirements for collections and services—as being among the major problem areas.

Planning activity in large university libraries has increased greatly since 1970. In some cases library plans have been developed as part of a university-wide planning effort or in response to a university's adjustment of its academic goals and priorities; in other cases, the university library has initiated planning efforts on its own, working independently and without the guidance of a university plan. Planning projects at Cornell (McGrath, 1973) and Columbia (Booz, Allen and Hamilton, 1973) have received wide publicity; the ARL's Office of Library Management Studies has published guides for planners (e.g., Webster, 1971); and a SPEC kit with descriptions of planning programs (ARL, 1974c) has been produced.

Some libraries have moved to long-range planning because of the necessity of budget planning. Without a clear plan of future priorities, a library's budgeting process is at the mercy of strong and probably conflicting pressures, both internal and external. Careful budgetary planning is long-range planning of a very important kind, as Martin (1977) demonstrates with his examples of the effects of certain kinds of allocation decisions on increasing, stable, or decreasing budgets. Without a plan, budget requests may be handled in an erratic or casual way, thereby leading to undesirable allocation decisions which cannot be easily reversed.

Long-range plans for libraries naturally devote attention to collection development, but some long-range plans, often those growing out of collection evaluation projects, are concerned primarily with collections. Published descriptions of collection evaluations which may form the basis for planning efforts, both at specific institutions (Cassata and Dewey, 1969; Golden, 1974; Webb, 1969) and in general terms (Bonn, 1974; McInnis, 1971, 1972; Ottersen, 1971; Stayer, 1971), have appeared frequently since the late 1960s. One example of the connection between collection evaluation and long-range planning is furnished by Schad (1970), who suggests basing budget allocation procedures on the needs of the collection by establishing goals for the collection, assessing specific needs, and determining the amount of money required to meet those needs. He emphasizes that following this approach could require librarian participation in university planning, since collection goals must be based on institutional programs and research objectives.

4. FORMAL COORDINATION OF COLLECTION DEVELOPMENT

Stable or declining materials budgets have increased the need for coordination of selection and acquisition between the different divisions of large libraries and for better communcation of selection decisions. In some libraries, the coordination of collection development activity is being formalized; in others, coordination is taking new forms. In 1974, the SPEC collection development survey (ARL, 1974b) verified this trend, which Sloan (1973) and others had noted through observation and analysis of publications from individual university libraries. Eighty-eight percent of the ARL libraries participating in the SPEC survey had either a collection development office and officer (23 libraries), a collection development committee (11 libraries), or both (23 libraries).

a. Collection Development Officers. In the 1960s many large university libraries added to the staff subject specialists with various kinds of collection development responsibilities, but in the 1970s the trend has been to add upper-level staff to coordinate the activities of all librarians involved in selection and to lead in the formulation of policies and procedures. Annual reports of ARL libraries since 1970 indicate the recency, in some libraries, of such titles as Assistant or Associate Director for Collection Development. In the SPEC survey previously mentioned (ARL, 1974b), 72 percent of the 46 collection development officers in the responding libraries report directly to the head of the library. Collection development officers in some libraries dominate the collection development process, while in other libraries they have more coordination responsibilities than policy-making power. The SPEC kit on collection development (ARL, 1974b) furnishes position descriptions for collection development officers and examples of how collection development offices are organized in selected ARL libraries.

  b. Collection Development Committees. The establishment of collection development committees appears to be a response to requests for increased staff involvement in library decisions as well as to a need for more formalized collection development procedures. The amount of authority exercised by such committees varies, but among the responsibilities which have been assigned to collection development committees are identifying areas where policies and procedures are lacking in the system, drafting policy and procedure statements, conducting surveys of the collections, producing budget allocation formulas, coordinating selection with academic departments, and approving requests costing more than a specified amount. In addition to general collection development committees, some libraries also have separate serials committees to review serial selection procedures and to coordinate and control serial requests. The variety of roles for collection development committees may be seen in the documents collected in the SPEC kit on collection development (ARL, 1974b).

One other clear trend in the organization of collection development is the increase in the number of staff members involved, particularly the increased involvement of public service librarians (ARL, 1974b; Reino, 1973; Sloan, 1973). From data collected in 1976, Metz (1977) found that collection development in large university research libraries is more likely to be professionalized than in smaller, less complex libraries. Increased staff participation in any activity brings the need for better communication among all those involved. To a certain extent, collection development committees serve as communication devices; the development of procedure manuals, policy statements, and adequate files also improves the communication which is needed for smooth functioning (Tuttle, 1969b). In addition, there has been an increasing tendency to publish policies, procedures, and discussion of current collection development problems in staff bulletins and other publications with unrestricted circulation.

5. IMPROVED PROCESSING PROCEDURES

Many libraries have also reviewed their acquisitions and technical services procedures and assumptions, either in the hope of reducing staff time and improving efficiency or as a response to personnel cuts made in order to maintain book budgets. In a study funded by the Council on Library Resources, Reid (1976) found that the ten ARL libraries visited had made organizational changes intended to improve work flow and minimize backlogs, had revised their procedures in the hope of reducing paper work and unnecessary record keeping, had reviewed their budget procedures, and had examined their relationships with dealers and the possibility of economies in operation, in order to free as large a portion as possible of the library budget for the acquisition of materials.

IV. ADJUSTMENTS IN SELECTION PRIORITIES

A. Review of Previous Commitments

As budgets have declined in purchasing power and as more desirable material has become available, many libraries have been forced to review their collecting assumptions and establish new selection priorities and criteria. Some of the changes in selection policy which became common during the early 1970s are reflected in the annual reports of many ARL libraries: cancellations of serial subscriptions, reduction of blanket orders, and restrictions on retrospective collection and on foreign purchases. A new interest developed in cooperative programs which might ease the strain of responsibility for comprehensive collections in many subjects, and competition for a larger share of the materials budget became keen among subject areas, between serial and monograph purchases, and between teaching and research needs. Edelman (1975) describes the process of accommodating budget reductions in one library: the budget problem, the adjustment of the selection and acquisitions program to new conditions, and the effect of the changes on the library staff, the faculty, and the relationship between them.

In most libraries attention was first directed to serial subscriptions as an area in which expenditures are heavy and in which substantial savings can be made by a few decisions (see Section V, A). Annual reports also record decisions to reduce the scope of blanket orders and approval plans, or to cancel them altogether and rely on title-by-title selection, which may bring in fewer titles but is more precisely suited to the needs of the library than blanket coverage can be. In some libraries where staffing reductions were necessary, blanket orders have been maintained in order to acquire books promptly with less cost for personnel.

Selection patterns and policies can be revised even more quickly than serials can be canceled or blanket orders reduced: the decision to pare or to eliminate retrospective buying, to select less comprehensively or to eliminate selection for marginal subjects, or to buy fewer or no foreign publications may be made after deliberation by library administrators or coordinators of selection activity or, almost unconsciously, by individual selectors responding to decreased allocations. Unless special provision is made for the consideration of expensive purchases, selectors experiencing budget restrictions may tend to postpone these decisions, while continuing to select or to accept less expensive materials routinely. This tendency may be damaging to the collections and may also explain a smaller decline in receipts than would be expected from a decline in purchasing power.

The risk of damage to individual research collections by year-to-year fluctuations in collection depth is well recognized, and most libraries have taken steps to minimize the danger by ensuring that, insofar as possible, decisions are deliberate and consistent. The risk of loss to the national research capability through similar decisions by research libraries—i.e., the risk that all libraries will buy only the most important materials in a given subject and none will acquire the marginal materials formerly supplied under the Farmington Plan, which was developed to avoid precisely this situation—has also been recognized. To this risk also, responses have been attempted. The Center for Research Libraries' "Expanded Journals Project" makes it possible for member libraries to have access to little-used serials which they cannot afford to maintain, and most cooperating library groups attempt to assign responsibility for strong collections in specific subjects to each of the member libraries (see Section VI).

B. Emphasis on Current Domestic Publications

The decision to reduce selection of foreign and retrospective publications and to emphasize current domestic publications has been justified on several grounds. Current domestic publications in English are accessible to all readers—undergraduates as well as advanced students and faculty, nonspecialists as well as specialists. They can be acquired more easily than foreign books, and because of the availability of LC and other sources of cataloging information they can be cataloged by less-skilled staff. Most books are in greatest demand while they are new; if they are not acquired then, their possible use is greatly reduced. If current publications are collected consistently, there will be less need to fill in gaps in the future. In many subject fields, faculty interest in foreign publications has decreased or vanished altogether; their only interest is in American research publication. Similarly, while historians are likely to want large quantities of retrospective publications even in fields in which the library collection is strong, and while students of the humanities request both antiquarian and reprinted books, in other subject fields faculty and students seldom request older publications and do not object if the library staff asserts that current domestic publications must be preferred.

These arguments are accepted more readily in colleges and smaller universities, however, than in the large research libraries. Scholarly books are often published in small editions, and much research publication is issued outside the book trade. These materials may never be obtained if they are not acquired immediately. Desirable retrospective publications which are not acquired when they are available may never be offered again, or may be obtainable only after long and expensive search.

C. Conflicts between Research and Teaching Needs.

In a budget situation in which it is impossible to maintain the level of previous collecting in all fields, it has been increasingly suggested that immediate needs, whether for teaching or for research, should be preferred to the building up of collections to support future research. The usual justification for this policy is that immediate needs are known, while future needs are to some extent speculative. (It is also true that immediate needs are made known by flesh-and-blood persons to present librarians; and that while future gaps will be a matter of regret, future staff members will not have to take the responsibility for them.)

Another argument for emphasizing immediate needs is based on the circulation studies by Trueswell (1968, 1969a,b, 1976) and others (e.g., Chen, 1976; Lazorick; 1970; Morse, 1968), which have regularly demonstrated that 70 percent *or less* of a library's collection satisfies 90 percent of the demand. Buckland (1975), Buckland and Hindle (1976), Gore (1976), and Saracevic *et al.* (1977) argue that reader satisfaction can best be improved by adding more duplicate copies of the most-used materials and reducing the purchase of titles less in demand. This argument is persuasive and has been acted on to some extent even in research libraries, but to accept it completely and to devote all available resources to satisfying present needs still seems wrong to most librarians responsible for research collections. While none of the use studies has attempted to identify the reasons for acquiring the books in the present collection which are now being used, it is improbable that they are the multiple copies bought to serve students of past generations.

D. Competition among Various Subject Fields and Forms of Publication

The inability of research libraries to supply all needs has increased the competition for available funds and sharpened the criticism of budget allocations and selection decisions. Although some libraries have chosen to maintain their serials collections at whatever expense to other parts of the collection, this option cannot be maintained indefinitely unless funds can be greatly increased (DeGennaro, 1977). In other institutions the tendency has been to maintain the percentage of the materials budget allocated to each main section of the library and to divide the allocation between monographs and serials as seems best for that subject. This option assumes that the proportionate allocations were satisfactory before the budget came under pressure and ignores any change in relative needs and costs. It has caused pressure, in turn, on the physical sciences, technology, medicine, and the natural sciences, as extreme price increases were experienced.

A number of rules of thumb and intuitive judgments have been expressed and acted upon: it is better to maintain serials, since desirable monographs can be acquired more easily later; serials are much more important than monographs in the sciences; scientific serials may be more important than scientific monographs, but they are not necessarily more important than monographs in the humanities or reserve books for undergraduate courses; current books should be obtained before they go out of print, while microform purchases may be postponed with little risk that they will be unavailable later; books and journals likely to be heavily used or used by many people should be acquired in preference to research materials of interest to one or a few people; hard-pressed libraries should try to maintain their strongest collections rather than cover the whole field of knowledge; the most essential publications in all fields of interest should be acquired even if no subject can be developed comprehensively; books in some fields are likely to be of long-term value and should be acquired rather than those in fields in which even good books will be superseded quickly. Few of these judgments have been or can be justified by factual data, and only necessity would prompt their proponents to assert them. They are merely efforts at making the best of a bad situation.

An attempt to provide factual data on some of the problems mentioned is being undertaken at the Research Center for Library and Information Science of the Indiana University Graduate Library School, which received (October 1976) a grant from the National Endowment for the Humanities to investigate the institutional decision-making process affecting the acquisition of humanities publications by libraries. This study is considered of major significance because the humanities, unlike the sciences and social sciences, lack predictive mechanisms that can be used to foretell the usefulness of newly published material and are also less responsive to obsolescence through aging.

V. SPECIAL PROBLEMS AND RESPONSES

A. Serials

The drastic price increases for serials in many subject fields, their importance, particularly in science, and the potential for damage to strong collections by indiscriminate or even by discriminating cancellation of subscriptions has probably attracted more attention in most research libraries than any other aspect of the budgetary pinch. A survey (White, 1976; Fry and White, 1977) covering purchases of serials by academic libraries between 1968 and 1973 noted that "the most significant and dramatic shift revealed... was the transfer of funds from the book to the serials budget." According to the same survey, large academic libraries were spending twice as much for books as for serials in 1969; but by 1973, the expenditures for books were only slightly higher. Annual reports of individual libraries indicate that the portion of the budget spent on serials has continued to increase and that, in some cases, almost 100 percent of a departmental allocation may be absorbed by serial subscriptions.

Serials specialists have been pointing out for years that it is more difficult to select serials than books, because serial subscriptions represent a continuing commitment against materials budgets and any mistake can have long-term effects (Osborn, 1973). An active search for simple and valid decisions rules for serial selection, particularly in scientific and technical fields, has developed during the 1970s (Abell, 1972; Duncan, 1971; Dym and Shirey, 1973; Glover and Klingman, 1972; Kraft, 1971; Kraft et al., 1976; Kraft and Hill, 1973; Robertson and Hensman, 1975; Subramanyam, 1975; Windsor, 1973). Closely related to selection decisions are the "copy-or-buy" decisions (Brookes, 1970; Pitt and Kraft, 1974; Van Toll, 1972; Williams et al., 1968). Among the variables which have been suggested as possible factors in determining the worth of a journal to a collection are volume of use in a library, volume of photocopy requests, volume of interlibrary loan requests, articles published in a journal in a specified period of time, frequency of citation of a journal in other primary journals, frequency of citation of a journal in abstracting journals or annual reviews, and cost.

The two most common responses to the problems of increasing serial costs and decreasing materials budgets are to cancel as many duplicate subscriptions and infrequently used titles as possible and to turn to cooperative schemes to provide those titles not held locally. Some libraries have imposed no-growth rules for serials holdings by requiring cancellation of one presently held title in a subject area for each new title added in that area or by requiring cancellation of subscriptions costing an amount equal to the cost of the new subscription. In other libraries the proportion of the budget devoted to serials is being reviewed frequently, and increases in serials at the expense of monographs are being resisted. Pressure to reduce subscriptions is so great that some cooperating institutions have established committees to ensure that no title is canceled by all members of the group without review. In most cases, decisions about which titles to cancel are painful and subjective. Attempts to identify categories of serials which are infrequently used, in order to make cancellation decisions more objective, have been reported by Rush *et al.* (1974), Bourne and Gregor (1975a,b), and Holland (1976).

It has long been recognized that not even the largest university library can supply from its own collection all of the currently published journals required by faculty and students, but shrinking budgets have exacerbated the problem and have focused renewed attention on the possibility of interlibrary cooperation in this field (Bourne and Gregor, 1975a,b; DeGennaro, 1975; Dobroski and Hendricks, 1975; Gregor, 1974; Hendricks, 1971). Because of the cost associated with their acquisition and storage, serials are often considered obvious first choices for cooperative projects (see Section VI).

B. Gifts and Gift Funds

University libraries vary considerably in the extent to which they devote staff attention to the fostering of gifts. A 1976 survey of 41 ARL libraries showed that the number of gifts received annually ranged from 930 in one library to 145,000 in another; 61 percent of the responding libraries reported receiving between 3,000 and 25,999 gifts annually (ARL, 1976). Some libraries limit themselves to accepting, acknowledging, and processing the gifts which are offered; others make considerable effort to encourage donors, publicize needs, and solicit desirable gifts and gifts of money.

Lane (1970) and McCree (1975) discuss some of the advantages and problems of gift programs; Rogers and Weber (1971) offer hints on the cultivation of donors. The positive effects of gifts of money and collections have often been discussed by those reviewing the history of individual university libraries, and such gifts are regularly acknowledged with gratitude in annual reports. In more general treatments of special collections, Vosper (1971) discussed the role of private collectors in the development of some research libraries, and Skelley (1975) included gift collections in his preliminary investigation to determine the effect of adding large collections to American research libraries.

As current monographs and serials have consumed larger percentages of materials budgets, some libraries have been forced to maintain special collections almost exclusively on gift funds. Although libraries are usually grateful for any money given them, restricted funds may affect the development of the collection. As recent annual reports from a few ARL libraries indicate, unusual imbalances may result when restricted gift funds easily exceed the amount needed to maintain the designated collections and general funds fail miserably to meet the needs of other collections with higher potential use.

Considerable attention has been given recently to library policies concerning gifts and the ethics of gift appraisal. Briggs discovered in 1968 that policies regarding appraisal varied widely. A panel discussion at a 1975 ALA Conference program meeting of the Rare Books and Manuscript Section of ACRL revealed that wide variations in policies continue to exist, in spite of the Section's publication in 1973 of a "Statement on Appraisal of Gifts" and a "Statement on Legal Title." The SPEC kit on gifts and exchange functions (ARL, 1976) offers examples of gift policies from selected ARL libraries.

C. Exchanges

During the early 1970s exchange agreements in a number of libraries were adjusted or curtailed. Some libraries analyzed the cost effectiveness of exchanges, determined that some materials were more expensive to acquire and process through exchange than through purchase, and reduced their agreements so as to receive only materials which could not be acquired by purchase. In some cases agreements expired because certain publications ceased to be available through gift or exchange; in other cases, libraries began receiving bills for local publications that formerly had been supplied free for exchange purposes. Some libraries still able to draw on generous receipts from the university press continue to rely on exchanges for substantial additions to their collections. In the previously mentioned survey on gifts and exchanges (ARL, 1976), 57 percent of the responding libraries maintained 1,000 or more exchange agreements.

Even libraries which must purchase U.S. publications in order to participate in exchanges frequently establish foreign exchange agreements. For more than 50 percent of the respondents in the survey of ARL libraries, exchange agreements with foreign organizations represented 75 to 100 percent of the total agreements. International exchange of publications—the advantages, effective procedures, etc.—has been a topic of steady interest in the professional literature through the 1960s and early 1970s (Ash, 1969; Collins, 1966; Kanevskij, 1972; Letheve, 1971; Moran, 1973; Pease, 1975; Schiltman, 1973; Shinn, 1972; UNESCO, 1964).

D. Replacement and Duplication

University librarians have become increasingly concerned in recent years about the quantity of lost and mutilated material which must be replaced. Few statistics are available, but most librarians are convinced that both kinds of damage have increased and that the most likely reason is the increased number of potential library users. The drain on already inadequate personnel and book budgets caused by the need for replacements and duplications has approached serious proportions in some places. One ARL library noted in its 1970–1971 annual report that over 20 percent of the next year's general book budget probably would be spent on replacements, and one of the largest university libraries in the country reported in 1972–1973 that 15 percent of all new books purchased for one campus library had been replacement copies. Loss is sometimes reported as a percentage of the total collection; a more realistic measurement would be as a percentage of books circulated, since only losses from the active collection are regularly noticed.

The problem of which titles to duplicate in order to ease the pressure from users is being studied with growing interest. The use of computerized circulation systems has supplied more data on past and present circulation patterns than were ever easily available before, and this has led to attempts to predict future use patterns (Arms and Walter, 1974; Buckland, 1975; Goyal, 1972; Grant, 1971; Saracevic *et al.*, 1977; Simmons, 1971). The trick, of course, is to duplicate where necessary but to avoid wasting money by overordering. The latter problem has been attacked in some libraries by modifying the formulas which had been used for determining the number of copies of reserve books to order.

E. Variations in Funding

Nearly all university libraries have experienced some decrease in the purchasing power of their book budgets during the 1970s. Additional problems in most libraries have been the timing of cuts, the alternation between low and high budget years, and the supplementing of appropriated funds by federal and other grants. All of these factors have made it more difficult to plan a consistent policy of collection development, and particularly to maintain serial subscriptions which must be continued from year to year. A quick survey of annual expenditures for library materials by ARL libraries between 1964–1965 and 1974–1975 shows that only three libraries experienced stable or increasing levels of expenditures through all those years; all other libraries suffered at least one decrease in annual expenditures and some had decreases in four or five years. Even these figures do not show the true extent of uncertainty about level of funding which faced collection development personnel, since many libraries maintained their apparently stable annual expenditure levels only because of end-of-the-year supplemental allocations. Annual reports offer numerous examples of midyear budget cuts, real and anticipated. Various techniques have been developed for making the best use of varying funds, but variation in funding remains a principal difficulty and requires time and attention from those responsible for collection development.

F. Weeding and Storage

Partly because of the expense of weeding by the traditional title-by-title approach and partly because of the conviction that anything in a research library may be useful eventually, many large university libraries have never had formal weeding programs. Among the few published descriptions of weeding programs in research libraries are those of Yale's "selective book retirement program" (Ash, 1963,) Columbia's weeding criteria for the Chemistry Library (Cooper, 1968), and Minnesota's worn-book weeding (Mattison, 1970). Space problems caused by the rapid growth rates of research libraries during the 1960s combined with the lack of funds for new buildings in the 1970s have led to a new interest in weeding and storage; and cooperative storage facilities, such as the New England Deposit Library, have encouraged the search for quick and accurate ways to choose little-used materials for storage (Harrar, 1962; 1964; Orne, 1960; Stuart-Stubbs, 1970).

Simple circulation counts have shown that a small proportion of any library collection accounts for a large percentage of the total circulation (Chen, 1976; Lazorick, 1970; Morse, 1968; Saracevic et al., 1977;

Trueswell, 1968, 1969a, 1976). This has led to suggestions that large parts of most research collections could successfully be sent to storage. Weeding for the purpose of storage means identifying those materials in less demand and making them less accessible than other parts of the collection. In order to divide collections into various levels of accessibility, future patterns of use must be predicted. Among the predictors of future use which have been tested in research libraries are language (Fussler and Simon, 1969), age of materials (Burns, 1970; Fussler and Simon, 1969; Lister, 1967), amount of past use (Fussler and Simon, 1969; Lister, 1967), and last circulation date (Trueswell, 1965, 1969b). Although no single criterion has proved successful for all subjects and all types of materials, Fussler and Simon (1969) concluded after collecting data in large university libraries that, in general, past use is the best predictor of how much use a work will receive in the future. The growing literature documenting the search for patterns of use and for easily applied weeding criteria has been reviewed by Seymour (1972), Thompson (1973), Line and Sandison (1974), and Slote (1975). Guidelines for weeding and transfer to storage are being prepared by the Resources Section of RTSD and are expected to be published in late 1977.

Besides taking note of predictions about the volume of future use of specified groups of materials, storage decisions must incorporate estimates of the costs involved—costs of storage facilities, costs of shifting and transporting books, costs of transferring and changing records, and costs to some users of the time lost while materials are retrieved from storage. Lister (1967), Simon (1967), and Ellsworth (1969) provide examples of economic analyses of the storage problem. Decisions made in connection with the establishment of a remote storage facility at Princeton have been outlined by Conger (1970). The complicated nature of the storage decision and the number of variables to be analyzed, as well as the special nature of a research collection as opposed to a teaching collection, probably explain why few large university libraries have found the staff time to undertake extensive weeding and storage programs, except under pressure.

G. Conservation

Librarians have been aware for some years that materials already in their collections, if they were to continue to be useful, required better protection and maintenance than it was possible for the library to provide and that since all published materials deteriorate, some very quickly, there is danger that some publications and some information may become unavailable because no readable copy exists. Behind all the effort to develop collections, to improve care of the individual collection, and to balance consideration for the books against the convenience and cost savings of mass methods of shelving and binding, use of book return receptacles, and other means of saving either personnel or money, there has been the knowledge that no effort in an individual library could be more than temporarily successful in preserving nineteenth- and twentieth-century publications from disintegration.

The problem has seemed so enormous that there has been a tendency in many university libraries to think about something else—to do what can be done about one's own collection, ignoring the overall situation in favor of problems where accomplishment seemed attainable. Most of the preservation effort in individual libraries has until recently been local and incoherent. Much effort has been directed toward caring for rare book collections, protecting fragile stack materials by restricting circulation, attempting to improve storage and stack conditions, improving handling standards, and deciding whether to microfilm an uncommon book in poor condition or to refuse to microfilm because the material would be unusable thereafter. Although improved methods of handling books are desirable, and microfilm preserves the content of a book (so long as the film remains in good condition), the amount that has been accomplished by these efforts is negligible when compared to what is needed.

W. J. Barrow's research, funded by the Council on Library Resources, first developed an estimate of the extent and urgency of the problem: 40 percent of the books published in the United States between 1900 and 1939 would be unusable within 25 years of the study (i.e., by 1983), and another 40 percent could be expected to last only 50 years (i.e., until about 2009) (ARL, 1964). Barrow's later work identified acidity as a principal cause of deterioration in modern paper, developed a deacidification process for preserving books, and produced specifications for an acid-free paper which would be both permanent and durable (Gwinn, 1977).

The Association of Research Libraries has been concerned with these problems. A study directed by Gordon R. Williams proposed a national center for storing publications at cold temperatures, which research had shown would greatly delay deterioration. Microfilm copies would be provided for ordinary use, while the original volumes would be available when necessary (ARL, 1964). No action was taken on this proposal, perhaps because it would have required large amounts of money and a high degree of cooperation between the participating institutions. A few years later, the annual conference of the University of Chicago Graduate Library School was devoted to the topic of deterioration and preservation of library materials, covering both technical and administrative aspects (Winger, 1970).

Preservation and conservation activities have continued; microfilming and hard-copy reprinting have preserved the content of many fragile books; improved techniques of restoration and improved storage conditions have slowed the deterioration of many actual copies. The Library of Congress has not only microfilmed large numbers of brittle books but has reported in the *National Register of Microform Masters* and in *Newspapers in Microform* similar filming done in other libraries. Some individual libraries have developed programs to conserve and repair original books by the most modern methods and under the direction of experts in conservation.

By 1976 awareness of the problem was widespread and approaches to concerted effort were being made. In a paper presented at a conference sponsored by the library schools of Columbia and Rutgers in April 1976, Darling (1976) described the necessary elements of a preservation program in an individual library. A proposal for the conservation of its collections was prepared at the University of California at Berkeley in the fall of 1976 (Brock, 1976). In an address presented at the American Library Association Conference, July 1976, Banks (1976) discussed cooperative approaches to the conservation of library books. The Office of the Assistant Director for Preservation, Library of Congress, held an invitational planning conference in December 1976, as a first step in the development of a National Preservation Program (Darling, 1977). These proposals and discussions provide some reason to hope that real progress in the conservation of library materials may be made before time runs out.

VI. COOPERATIVE PROGRAMS

While it is almost an axiom that no single library can provide all the materials of potential interest to its users, librarians (and the faculties of their universities) have not always been willing to acknowledge this in the operation of their own institutions. Of all the reasons offered for entering into cooperative programs—increased quantity and cost of current publications, increased demands by users for materials difficult and expensive to locate, lack of storage space for continuing collection growth at the present rate, and recognition of the fact that valuable materials already in libraries cannot be preserved without special efforts—the most convincing argument seems to be a limited budget. Cooperation had its adherents all through the 1950s and 1960s; but the interest in resource sharing, as reflected in comments of ARL library directors in their annual reports and other publications, has definitely risen as financial problems have become more pressing in the 1970s. Current interest in resource sharing may be partially judged by the amount of attention paid to two 1976 conferences on the subject, one at the University of Pittsburgh (summarized in *Library Journal,* November 15, 1976) and the other at the University of California at San Diego (summarized in *Library Journal,* December 1, 1976).

A. Increased Interest in Long-Standing Arrangements

Cooperation, involving the sharing of both bibliographic information and physical texts, is not a new idea for university librarians. Stuart-Stubbs (1975) reviewed a number of cooperative arrangements attempted in the United States prior to 1910, and Weber (1976) covered a century of such arrangements. Since World War II, most research libraries have participated in cooperative programs to some extent, although not always with enthusiasm and conviction. Two of the most publicized projects of the postwar period were the Farmington Plan and the Latin American Cooperative Acquisitions Project (LACAP), both formally terminated at the end of 1972. The history of the Farmington Plan, under which participating research libraries accepted responsibility for acquiring, cataloging, and lending foreign materials from specific subject fields and geographic areas, has been documented by Williams (1961), Vosper (1965), Skipper (1966), and in the *Farmington Plan Newsletter* (now the *Foreign Acquisitions Newsletter*). Reasons for the decline of the Farmington Plan were reviewed by Edelman (1973). LACAP's development has been recorded by Savary (1968) and Shepard (1969), as well as in the proceedings of the Seminar on the Acquisition of Latin American Library Materials.

In addition to these two projects, many local, state, and regional cooperative arrangements have been carried out for years, without fanfare. Several states funded projects to speed up communications and delivery within the state in order to improve interlibrary loan service, and in other states groups of university libraries have organized to share information on serials holding and cancellations. Most of these efforts are not well known except to the participants, but some local, state, and regional projects involving large academic libraries have been discussed in the professional literature. Among these are programs in the New York City area (Edelman, 1969; Simkin, 1970); upper New York State (Wilden-Hart, 1970a); Detroit (Sullivan, 1969); Chicago (Goderich, 1970); the Southeast (Orne, 1971); Louisiana (Heard, 1972); and Texas (Hendricks, 1971; Houze, 1968, 1971). General reviews of cooperation in U.S. libraries have been offered by Downs (1970), McDonald (1974a,b), and Quick (1975). Chang (1976) includes other items on the subject in an annotated bibliography of empirical literature, most of it published in the 1970s, on academic library cooperation.

The most prominent example of a postwar cooperative project which experienced a surge of growth and interest in the late 1960s and early 1970s is the Center for Research Libraries (CRL). This organization, founded in 1949 by ten Midwestern universities, was operated as the Midwest Inter-Library Center until 1964, when a survey recommended that the Center expand its organization and programs to a national base. Recommendations of the survey and the rationale behind them have been reviewed by Williams (1965) and by Kaplan (1975), and in CRL's (1965) report of the survey. Since the membership was opened to libraries outside the Midwest, the number of members has steadily increased. In March of 1966, there were 22 members; by July 1970, full members totaled 44; in January 1972, more than 50 libraries had full membership; and by the latter part of 1976, there were about 90 members. Clearly, CRL is offering something that research libraries find worth the cost of membership.

One of the most popular programs of CRL, according to the annual reports of selected member libraries, is the "Expanded Journals Project," begun in 1973 with a five-year grant from the Carnegie Corporation. This project provides access directly or through the British Library Lending Division to all journals published since 1970 in the sciences (except medicine) and the social sciences (except history). Originally, selection of titles for the project was based on cancellations by member libraries; since 1974, CRL has attempted to cover all titles in the subject fields included. Annual reports in which ARL library directors have announced new memberships in CRL stress the advantages of membership generally—relatively easy access to infrequently used materials without the cost of acquiring, processing, and storing them—in relation to the cost of membership, and usually mention the journals project specifically.

B. Development of Newer Arrangements

Discussions of resource-sharing activities in the 1970s have emphasized two areas of cooperation, one involving improved bibliographic access and the other concerned with physical access to materials through one or more central libraries. The sharing of cataloging information, made easier by the Ohio College Library Center (OCLC), the BALLOTS system developed at Stanford University, and the various regional networks affiliated with them, has been an important stimulus to projects involving acquisition agreements and active interlibrary loan operations, while the Center for Research Libraries and the British Library Lending Division have furnished models for national library centers designed to store and lend materials not available in member libraries.

By the mid-1970s, the need for some sort of national plan to provide for the acquisition and storage of materials not held, or not held in sufficient quantities, by the country's research libraries was being widely discussed as a solution to the problem of physical access (De-Gennaro, 1975). Among materials suggested as appropriate for collection in central libraries were foreign language materials, microform collections, and serials. The Center for Research Libraries was cited as a successful example of an operation which concentrates on infrequently used materials; the British Library Lending Division was offered as the most successful example of a central facility designed to provide quick and sure access to current and heavily used materials, primarily serials.

Serials are, of course, always among the materials most often suggested for inclusion in central storage facilities. Increased reliance on cooperative arrangements and intensified efforts to reach such agreements are frequently concentrated on serials, for the same reasons that an individual institution experiencing budget pressure may work first on its subscription lists: serial subscriptions are expensive and increasing in price, more money may be saved by a few decisions than with other kinds of materials, and the processing cost is comparatively small. In addition, the distinction between duplicate subscriptions received for reader convenience and unique titles which may contribute to the research collection is clear, although the choice between them is not always obvious. Studies have been made and proposals offered on the best approach to the problem of cooperative access to serials in the United States (DeGennaro, 1975; Palmour et al., 1974); but a decision has yet to be reached. The National Commission on Libraries and Information Science has formed a task force on a national periodicals system which is scheduled to issue a report and recommendations in late 1977 or 1978.

One of the most publicized cooperative arrangements of the 1970s has been that of the Research Libraries Group (RLG) formed by Harvard, Yale, and Columbia Universities and the New York Public Library. The planning study for this consortium (Rosenthal, 1973) recommended common procedures for interlibrary loan, photocopy, and access to special collections; wide involvement of staff members from the four libraries in planning and review of consortium programs; the establishment of a bibliographic center; assignment of responsibilities for intensive collection development; coordination of expensive purchases and new serials acquisition; and cooperation in conservation and preservation of holdings. By 1975, a serials task force and committees on collection development and preservation were operating in the area of collection coordination and planning (Bryant, 1975). Since serial publications always offer an attractive starting point for specialization agreements, early efforts have been made there by the RLG; but other categories of materials identified for possible future programs of cooperative acquisition include those in "exotic" languages; nontrade publications; materials in nonbook formats (e.g., maps, magnetic tapes); and those "requiring special acquisition procedures or arrangements to obtain" (Rosenthal, 1973).

On the west coast, Stanford University and the University of California at Berkeley have made plans, some of which were announced in early 1977, for a cooperative program involving coordinated acquisitions policies, reciprocal lending privileges, daily delivery service of books and people, and expansion of Stanford's BALLOTS system to Berkeley. According to one announcement (*College and Research Libraries News,* February 1977), the two libraries hope to be able, by avoiding unnecessary duplication, to reallocate at least 5 percent of their current acquisitions budget for additional titles.

Resource sharing by large research libraries has become a controversial issue, as publishers' reactions to the establishment of the RLG illustrate, although RLG library directors issued a statement in the fall of 1974 saying that the group would "operate within the fair use doctrine applicable to the Copyright Law." Any library cooperation projects which appeared to rely on extensive photocopying and interlibrary loan furnished fuel for the discussions surrounding the passage in 1976 of new copyright legislation. Librarians have been aware of the need to respect authors' and publishers' rights and many efforts have been made to improve library service without violating either the spirit or the letter of the copyright law. As the previously mentioned statement by the RLG directors noted, it is libraries' decreased buying power leading to increased selectivity, rather than attempts at coordination of collection development and sharing of resources, which may prove harmful to publishers of marginal-quality materials. Effects of the revised copyright law on large-scale projects for resource sharing remain to be seen.

VII. QUANTITATIVE APPROACHES TO CONTROL AND EVALUATION

Although librarians have not been noted for their wide use of quantitative methods, there have always been university librarians who recognized the possible values of quantification and who experimented with areas of collection development where sampling, formulas, and other quantitative approaches seemed natural. While budget allocation has been an area where the use of numbers was always necessary, complex budget allocation formulas designed to consider and weigh a variety of factors have recently become common (see Section III, B, 2, b). Standards for library collections have traditionally been expressed in quantitative terms, sometimes by a formula designed to predict adequate collection size or acquisition rates; Clapp and Jordan (1965) and Voigt (1975) illustrate this approach. In a related area, Drake

(1976) describes quantitative forecasting techniques which may be used in estimating collection size. Sampling techniques, long used in some libraries, are becoming of greater interest to all librarians as simple measurements grow more costly. Estimating lost volumes and determining the need for partial or complete collection inventories are examples of problems which may be handled efficiently by sampling (Bluh, 1969; Braden, 1968; Clark, 1974; Niland and Kurth, 1976).

Another example of a relatively simple quantitative approach to collection development is the cooperative shelflist measurement project using methods developed at the University of California at Berkeley, which offers promise of identifying large collections in various large libraries. The most recent compilation (Ortopan, 1976) contains data on the holdings of 26 large university libraries in 482 categories covering the entire LC classification scheme. Number of titles held according to shelflist count in 1975, percent of change between 1973 and 1975, and growth rate for each category for the two-year period have been reported. While the largest collections are not always the strongest, they are obviously likely to be stronger than smaller collections; and the project furnishes a basis for cooperative agreements and for local decisions about the relative importance and appropriate support of specific subject collections. The measurement technique is well developed for material arranged by LC classification, but comparable data are more difficult to obtain for materials in other classifications and for unprocessed collections.

In the 1970s, techniques of operations research have been applied increasingly to library matters, including collection development problems (Chen, 1976; Montgomery *et al.*, 1976; Morse, 1968; Swanson and Bookstein, 1972). As the use of computers has become more common in library record-keeping operations, those trained in such techniques as linear programming, decision theory, and queuing theory have used the data produced by the computerized systems to construct and test mathematical models of library processes. Models have been or are being developed for a variety of collection development decisions, such as predicting the need for multiple copies (Arms and Walter, 1974; Goyal, 1972; Grant, 1971); weeding decisions (Lister, 1967; Sinha, 1970; Trueswell, 1965); and serials selection and cancellation decisions (Bourne and Gregor, 1975a,b; Duncan, 1971; Dym and Shirey, 1973; Glover and Klingman, 1972; Kraft, 1971; Kraft *et al.*, 1976; Kraft and Hill, 1973; Pitt and Kraft, 1974; Rush *et al.*, 1974). In other applications of mathematical modeling, Rouse (1976) has presented an approach to the problem of evaluating library networks; Buckland and Hindle (1976) have suggested ways to look at trade-offs between acquisitions rate, weeding rate, decentralization, automation, and collection size; and DePew (1975) has attempted to model the entire acquisitions decision process by assigning weights to such factors as identity and power of requester, subject requested, and whether or not the requested title has been reviewed.

In spite of all the attempts to define problems and conditions affecting collection development in measurable and comparable terms, there are still areas where quantitative methods are not widely accepted. In some cases the literature presenting the methods is not intelligible to all librarians; in other cases, the proposed approaches are based on inadequate data or involve a very simplified analysis of the problem. In addition, there are those who distrust the seemingly precise results obtained from manipulation of basic figures subjectively assigned. In some of the operations research applications, models are based on assumptions which cannot be verified by librarians in their day-to-day experiences with library users. It seems apparent, though, that librarians and nonlibrarians alike will continue to propose and promote the use of quantitative approaches to the control and evaluation of collections; as an article by an economist (Machlup, 1976) illustrates, if those responsible for collection development cannot learn to gather information about their procedures and problems in quantitative form, others will try to do the job for them.

VIII. CONCLUSION

This review of collection development in large university libraries has briefly outlined the major trends of the late 1960s in order to contrast that period with the 1970s. The concerns of university librarians, as expressed through their annual reports and other published writings, have shifted dramatically as the purchasing power of their budgets has declined; and although few wish to emphasize the point, there seems to be a developing consensus that libraries will not see increased materials budgets in the near future (DeGennaro, 1975; Schmidt, 1975; Smith, 1975). This means that the actions and adjustments considered to be temporary at the time they were started may become permanent aspects of collection development in many university libraries.

From the emergency adjustments being made by librarians to meet budget cuts, three trends emerge as among the most significant: greater selectivity in new acquisitions, more emphasis on efficient procedures, and increased reliance on other libraries. Greater selectivity in new acquisitions is partly indicated by the favoring of current monographs over retrospective works and by the reduction of serial subscriptions, foreign acquisitions, and purchases of rare, expensive, or esoteric materials. There is strong pressure from some sources to spend the limited funds available for library materials in areas where they will benefit the most people and to rely on the Center for Research Libraries or arrangements with other libraries for the very expensive and infrequently used materials.

While budget decreases may appear to force the decisions leading to more selectivity and cooperation, the overall pressure for increased efficiency in libraries has surely had some effect on these developments. Studies of collection use, most of them based on scientific and technical collections (e.g., Saracevic *et al.,* 1977; Trueswell, 1976), have shown that a very small percentage of the collection accounts for most of the use, and that the library's failure to purchase a particular title is less likely to be a cause of user frustration than the library's failure to have enough copies of certain titles. Recently, much attention has been focused on the appropriateness of judging a library by its availability rate (or how well it can make quickly available what a user requests) rather than on its total size or holdings (e.g., Buckland, 1975; Gore, 1976). Perhaps the study of library acquisitions in the humanities to be done at Indiana University Graduate Library School will furnish a basis for distinguishing among types of materials in considering whether to emphasize reader satisfaction by means of generous duplication and assistance to readers or to provide the extensive collections which have previously seemed most desirable. Emphasis on the former approach clearly could lead to major adjustments in policies and procedures for collection development in large university libraries.

REFERENCES

Abell, D. F. (1972). Guidelines in recommending back numbers of scientific journals for purchase. *Illinois Libraries* 54, 231–233.

American Library Association, Association of College and Research Libraries, Rare Books and Manuscripts Section, Committee on Manuscript Collections (1973a). Statement on appraisal of gifts. *College and Research Libraries News* 34, 49.

American Library Association, Association of College and Research Libraries, Rare Books and Manuscripts Section, Committee on Manuscript Collections (1973b). Statement on legal title. *College and Research Libraries News* 34, 49–50.

American Library Association, Resources and Technical Services Division. Resources Section, Collection Development Committee (1977). Guidelines for the formulation of collection development policies. *Library Resources and Technical Services* 21, 40–47.

Archer, H. R. (1970). Special collections. *Library Trends* 18, 354–362.

Arms, W. Y., and Walter, T. P. (1974). A simulation model for purchasing duplicate copies in a library. *Journal of Library Automation* 7, 73–82.

Ash, J. (1969). The exchange of academic dissertations. *College and Research Libraries* 30, 237–241.

Ash, L. (1963). "Yale's Selective Book Retirement Program." Archon Books, Hamden, Connecticut.

Association of Research Libraries, Committee on the Preservation of Research Library Materials (1964). "The Preservation of Deteriorating Books: An Examination of the Problems with Recommendations for a Solution; Report." (Prepared for the Committee by G. R. Williams.) Washington, D.C.

Association of Research Libraries, Systems and Procedures Exchange Center (1974a). "Acquisition Policies in ARL Libraries." Association of Research Libraries, Office of University Library Management Studies, Washington, D.C.

Association of Research Libraries, Systems and Procedures Exchange Center (1974b). "Collection Development in ARL Libraries." Association of Research Libraries, Office of University Library Management Studies, Washington, D.C.

Association of Research Libraries, Systems and Procedures Exchange Center (1974c). "Planning Systems." Association of Research Libraries, Office of University Library Management Studies, Washington, D.C.

Association of Research Libraries, Systems and Procedures Exchange Center (1976). "Gifts and Exchange Functions in ARL Libraries." Association of Research Libraries, Office of University Library Management Studies, Washington, D.C.

Axford, H. W. (1971). The economics of a domestic approval plan. *College and Research Libraries* 32, 368–375.

Babb, J. T. (1966). The Yale University Library. *Library Trends* 15, 206–214.

Bach, H. (1964). Why allocate? *Library Resources and Technical Services* 8, 161–165.

Banks, P. N. (1976). Cooperative approaches to conservation. *Library Journal* 101, 2348–2351.

Baumol, W. J., and Marcus, M. (1973). "Economics of Academic Libraries." American Council on Education, Washington, D.C.

Blanchard, J. R. (1968). Planning the conversion of a college to a university library. *College and Research Libraries* 29, 297–302.

Bluh, P. (1969). A study of an inventory. *Library Resources and Technical Services* 13, 367–371.

Bonn, G. S. (1974). Evaluation of the collection. *Library Trends* 22, 265–304.
Booz, Allen and Hamilton, Inc. (1970). "Problems in University Library Management; A Study Conducted for the Association of Research Libraries and the American Council on Education." Association of Research Libraries, Washington, D.C.
Booz, Allen and Hamilton, Inc. (1973). "Organization and Staffing of the Libraries of Columbia University: A Case Study." Redgrave Information Resources, Westport, Connecticut.
Boss, R. W. (1972). Audio materials in academic research libraries. *College and Research Libraries* 33, 463–466.
Bourne, C. P., and Gregor, D. (1975a). "Methodology and Background Information to Assist the Planning of Serials Cancellations and Cooperative Serials Collection in the Health Sciences." Institute of Library Research, University of California, Berkeley, California. (ED 104 409.)
Bourne, C. P., and Gregor, D. (1975b). Planning serials cancellations and cooperative collection development in the health sciences: methodology and background information. *Medical Library Association Bulletin* 63, 366–377.
Braden, I. A. (1968). Pilot inventory of library holdings. *ALA Bulletin* 62, 1129–1131.
Briggs, D. R. (1968). Gift appraisal policy in large research libraries. *College and Research Libraries* 29, 505–507.
Brock, J. A. (1976). "A Program for the Conservation and Preservation of Library Materials in the General Library, University of California, Berkeley." University of California, Berkeley, California.
Brookes, B. C. (1970). Photocopies v. periodicals: cost-effectiveness in the special library. *Journal of Documentation* 26, 22–99.
Bryant, D. W. (1975). Strengthening the strong: the cooperative future of research libraries. *In* "The Sixth and Seventh Annual Alumnus-in-Residence Programs," pp. 37–46. School of Library Science, University of Michigan, Ann Arbor, Michigan.
Buckland, M. K. (1975). "Book Availability and the Library User." Pergamon Press, New York.
Buckland, M. K., and Hindle, A. (1976). Acquisitions, growth, and performance control through systems analysis. *In* "Farewell to Alexandria; Solutions to Space, Growth, and Performance Problems of Libraries" (D. Gore, ed.), pp. 72–104. Greenwood Press, Westport, Connecticut.
Burns, R. W., Jr. (1970). "An Investigation into the Significance of Age as a Factor in Selecting an Optimum Circulation Period(s) for Serials." Colorado State University, Fort Collins, Colorado. (ED 048 881.)
Burton, R. E. (1975). Formula budgeting: an example. *Special Libraries* 66, 61–67.
Byrd, C. K. (1966). Subject specialists in a university library. *College and Research Libraries* 27, 191–193.
Cassata, M. B., and Dewey, G. L. (1969). The evaluation of a university library collection: some guidelines. *Library Resources and Technical Services* 13, 450–457.
Center for Research Libraries (1965). "Report of a Survey, with an Outline of Programs and Policies." Center for Research Libraries, Chicago, Illinois.

Chang, D. M. (1976). Academic library cooperation: a selective annotated bibliography. *Library Resources and Technical Services* 20, 270–286.
Chapin, R. E., and McCoy, R. E. (1966). The emerging institutions: Michigan State University and Southern Illinois University. *Library Trends* 15, 266–285.
Chen, C. (1976). "Applications of Operations Research Models to Libraries." MIT Press, Cambridge, Massachusetts.
Clapp, V. W., and Jordan, R. T. (1965). Quantitative criteria for adequacy of academic library collections. *College and Research Libraries* 26, 371–380.
Clark, J. B. (1974). An approach to collection inventory. *College and Research Libraries* 35, 350–353.
Collins, J. A. (1966). The international exchange service. *Library Resources and Technical Services* 10, 337–341.
Coney, D., and Michel, J. G. (1966). The Berkeley Library of the University of California: some notes on its formation. *Library Trends* 15, 286–302.
Conger, L. (1970). The annex library of Princeton University: the development of a compact storage library. *College and Research Libraries* 31, 160–168.
Converse, W. R. M., and Standers, O. R. (1975). "Rationalizing the Collections Policy: A Computerized Approach." (Paper presented at the Canadian Conference on Information Science, Quebec, May 7–9.) (ED 105 861.)
Cooper, M. (1968). Criteria for weeding of collections. *Library Resources and Technical Services* 12, 339–351.
Coppin, A. (1974). The subject specialist on the academic library staff. *Libri* 24, 122–128.
Cornell University Libraries (1966). Acquisition policy statement. Unpublished draft, November. Cornell University Libraries, Ithaca, New York.
Crossley, C. A. (1974). The subject specialist librarian in an academic library: his role and place. *Aslib Proceedings* 26, 236–249.
Danton, J. P. (1963). "Book Selection and Collections: A comparison of German and American University Libraries." Columbia University Press, New York.
Danton, J. P. (1967). The subject specialist in national and university libraries, with special reference to book selection. *Libri* 17, 42–58.
Darling, P. W. (1976). A local preservation program: where to start. *Library Journal* 101, 2343–2347.
Darling, P. W. (1977). Preservation: a national plan at last? *Library Journal* 102, 447–449.
DeGennaro, R. (1975). Austerity, technology, and resource sharing: research libraries face the future. *Library Journal* 100, 917–923.
DeGennaro, R. (1977). Escalating journal prices: time to fight back. *American Libraries* 8, 69–74.
DePew, J. N. (1975). An acquisitions decision model for academic libraries. *Journal of the American Society for Information Science* 26, 237–246.
DeVilbiss, M. L. (1975). The approval-built collection in the medium-sized academic library. *College and Research Libraries* 36, 487–492.
DeVolder, A. L. (1972). Approval plans—bounty or bedlam. *Publishers' Weekly* 202, 18–20.
Dobbyn, M. (1972). Approval plan purchasing in perspective. *College and Research Libraries* 33, 480–484.

Dobroski, C. H., and Hendricks, D. D. (1975). Mobilization of duplicates in a regional medical library program. *Medical Library Association Bulletin* 63, 309–318.
Downs, R. B. (1966). The University of Illinois Library. *Library Trends* 15, 258–265.
Downs, R. B. (1970). Future prospects of library acquisitions. *Library Trends* 18, 412–421.
Downs, R. B. (1971). The significance of foreign materials for U.S. collections: problems of acquisition. *Foreign Acquisitions Newsletter* 34, 1–7.
Downs, R. B. (1974). Library resources in the United States. *College and Research Libraries* 35, 97–108.
Drake, M. A. (1976). Forecasting academic library growth. *College and Research Libraries* 37, 53–59.
Dudley, N. (1970). The blanket order. *Library Trends* 18, 318–327.
Duncan, E. E. (1971). "Development of a Decision Model for Acquisition of Current Periodical Titles Based on Usage of Periodical Literature by Chemical Personnel." Unpublished dissertation, University of Pittsburgh.
Dunn, O. C., Tolliver, D. L., and Drake, M. A. (1973). "The Past and Likely Future of 58 Research Libraries, 1951–1980: A Statistical Study of Growth and Change, 1971–72." Purdue University Libraries and Audiovisual Center, Lafayette, Indiana. (ED 082 780.)
Dym, E., and Shirey, D. L. (1973). A statistical decision model for periodical selection for a specialized information center. *Journal of the American Society for Information Science* 24, 110–119.
Edelman, H. (1969). "Shared Acquisitions and Retention Systems (SHARES) for the New York Metropolitan Area; A Proposal for Cooperation Among METRO Libraries." New York Metropolitan Reference and Research Library Agency, New York. (ED 039 906.)
Edelman, H. (1972). Subject specialists and job requirements: notes, comments and opinions from an administrative viewpoint. *In* "Final Report and Working Papers of the 17th Seminar on the Acquisition of Latin American Library Materials," pp. 209–218. Amherst, Massachusetts.
Edelman, H. (1973). The death of the Farmington Plan. *Library Journal* 98, 1251–1253.
Edelman, H. (1975). Reduction reduction reduction reduction. *Cornell University Library Bulletin* 195, 8–10.
Edelman, H., and Tatum, G. M., Jr. (1976). The development of collections in American university libraries. *College and Research Libraries* 37, 222–245.
El-Erian, T. S. (1972). "The Public Law 480 Program in American Libraries." Unpublished dissertation, Columbia University.
Ellsworth, R. E. (1969). "Economics of Book Storage in College and University Libraries." Association of Research Libraries and Scarecrow Press, Metuchen, New Jersey.
Ettlinger, J. R. T. (1973). "Nation-Wide Rationalization of Acquisition Policies in Canadian College and University Libraries: Are Total World Coverage and Nonduplication of Resources Part of an Impossible Dream?" (Paper presented at the Canadian Association of College and University Libraries Workshop on

Collection Development, Sackville, New Brunswick, Canada, June 16–17.) (ED 087 492.)
Evans, G. E. (1969). "The Influence of Book Selection Agents Upon Book Collection Usage in Academic Libraries." Unpublished dissertation, University of Illinois.
Evans, G. E. (1970). Book selection and book collection usage in academic libraries. *Library Quarterly* 40, 297–308.
Evans, G. E., and Argyres, C. W. (1974). Approval plans and collection development in academic libraries. *Library Resources and Technical Services* 18, 35–50.
Fry, B., and White, H. S. (1977). "Publishers and Libraries." Heath/Lexington Books, Lexington, Massachusetts.
Fussler, H. H., and Simon, J. L. (1969). "Patterns in the Use of Books in Large Research Libraries." University of Chicago Press, Chicago, Illinois.
Gamble, L. (1972). Blanket ordering and the University of Texas at Austin Library. *Texas Library Journal* 48, 230–232.
Glover, F., and Klingman, D. (1972). Mathematical programming models and methods for the journal selection problem. *Library Quarterly* 42, 43–58.
Goderich, M. (1970). Cooperative acquisitions: the experience of general libraries and prospects for law libraries. *Law Library Journal* 63, 57–61.
Gold, S. D. (1975). Allocating the book budget: an economic model. *College and Research Libraries* 36, 397–402.
Golden, B. (1974). A method for quantitatively evaluating a university library collection. *Library Resources and Technical Services* 18, 268–274.
Gore, D. (1976). Farewell to Alexandria: the theory of the no-growth high-performance library. *In* "Farewell to Alexandria; Solutions to Space, Growth, and Performance Problems of Libraries" (D. Gore, ed.), pp. 164–180. Greenwood Press, Westport, Connecticut.
Goyal, S. K. (1972). Systematic method for reducing overordering copies of books. *Library Resources and Technical Services* 16, 26–32.
Goyal, S. K. (1973). Allocation of library funds to different departments of a university—an operational research approach. *College and Research Libraries* 34, 219–222.
Grant, R. S. (1971). Predicting the need for multiple copies of books. *Journal of Library Automation* 4, 64–71.
Gration, S. U., and Young, A. P. (1974). Reference-bibliographers in the college library. *College and Research Libraries* 35, 28–34.
Gregor, D. (1974). "Feasibility of Cooperative Collecting of Exotic Foreign Language Serial Titles Among Health Sciences Libraries in California." Institute of Library Research, University of California, Berkeley, California. (ED 104 407.)
Gregory, R. S. (1970). Acquisition of microforms. *Library Trends* 18, 373–384.
Guttsman, W. L. (1965). "Learned" librarians and the structure of academic libraries. *Libri* 15, 159–167.
Guttsman, W. L. (1973). Subject specialisation in academic libraries: some preliminary observations on role conflict and organizational stress. *Journal of Librarianship* 5, 1–8.
Gwinn, N. E. (1977). The Council on Library Resources, a 20-year report. *Library Journal* 102, 330–334.

Hall, M. M. (1966). Theoretical considerations of selection policy for university libraries: their relevance to Canadian university libraries. *Canadian Library Journal* 23, 89–98.

Hanes, F. W. (1964). Another view on allocation. *Library Resources and Technical Services* 8, 408–410.

Haro, R. P. (1967). Book selection in academic libraries. *College and Research Libraries* 28, 104–106.

Haro, R. P. (1969a). The bibliographer in the academic library. *Library Resources and Technical Services* 13, 163–169.

Haro, R. P. (1969b). Some problems in the conversion of a college to a university library. *College and Research Libraries* 30, 260–264.

Harrar, H. J. (1962). "Cooperative Storage Warehouses." Unpublished dissertation, Rutgers University.

Harrar, H. J. (1964). Cooperative storage warehouses. *College and Research Libraries* 25, 37–43.

Harrer, G. A. (1969). "Book Selection and the Subject Specialist in the University Library." (Paper presented at the Institute on Acquisitions Procedures in Academic Libraries, University of California at San Diego, August 25–September 5). (ED 043 341.)

Heard, J. N. (1972). Suggested procedures for sharing acquisitions in academic libraries. *Louisiana Library Association Bulletin* 35, 17–21.

Henderson, W. T. (1960). "Acquisitions Policies of Academic and Research Libraries." Unpublished master's thesis, University of Chicago.

Hendricks, D. D. (1971). Interuniversity Council cooperative acquisitions of journals. *Texas Library Journal* 47, 269–270, 296.

Holbrook, A. (1972). The subject specialist in polytechnic libraries. *New Library World* 73, 393–396.

Holland, M. P. (1976). Serial cuts vs. public service: a formula. *College and Research Libraries* 37, 543–548.

Houze, R. A. (1968). CORAL: San Antonio's success story in library cooperation. *Texas Library Journal* 44, 151–152, 185–188.

Houze, R. A. (1971). The Council of Research and Academic libraries, San Antonio, Texas. *Texas Library Journal* 47, 263–268.

Huff, W. H. (1970). The acquisition of serial publications. *Library Trends* 18, 294–317.

Humphreys, K. (1967). The subject specialist in national and university libraries. *Libri* 17, 29–41.

Jay, D. F., and McGowan, F. M. (1969). The Library of Congress PL-480 Program. *DC Libraries* 40, 29–33.

Kanevskij, B. P. (1972). The international exchange of publications and the free flow of books. *Unesco Bulletin for Libraries* 26, 141–149.

Kaplan, L. (1975). Midwest Inter-Library Center, 1949–1964. *Journal of Library History* 10, 291–310.

Kohut, J. J. (1974). Allocating the book budget: a model. *College and Research Libraries* 35, 192–199.

Kohut, J. J., and Walker, J. F. (1975). Allocating the book budget: equity and economic efficiency. *College and Research Libraries* 36, 403–410.

Kosa, G. A. (1972a). Book selection trends in American academic libraries. *Australian Library Journal* 21, 416–424.

Kosa, G. A. (1972b). "Computer-Assisted Book Selection Using Machine Readable Cataloging (MARC II) Tapes." Unpublished dissertation, Indiana University.

Kosa, G. A. (1975). Book selection tools for subject specialists in a large research library: an analysis. *Library Resources and Technical Services* 19, 13–18.

Kraft, D. H. (1971). "The Journal Selection Problem in a University Library System." Unpublished dissertation, Purdue University.

Kraft, D. H., and Hill, T. W., Jr. (1973). A journal selection model and its implications for a library system. *Information Storage and Retrieval* 9, 1–11.

Kraft, D. H., Polacsek, R. A., Soergel, L., Burns, K., and Klair, A. (1976). Journal selection decisions: a biomedical library operations research model. *Medical Library Association Bulletin* 64, 255–264.

Kraft, M. (1967). An argument for selectivity in the acquisition of materials for research libraries. *Library Quarterly* 37, 284–295.

Lane, A. H. (1970). Gifts and exchanges: practicalities and problems. *Library Resources and Technical Services* 14, 92–97.

Lane, D. O. (1968). The selection of academic library materials; a literature survey. *College and Research Libraries* 29, 364–372.

Lane, D. O. (1969). "Approval and Blanket Order Acquisitions Plans." (Paper presented at the Institute on Acquisitions Procedures in Academic Libraries, University of California, San Diego, August 25—September 5.) (ED 043 342.)

Lazorick, G. J. (1970). "Demand Models for Books in Library Circulation Systems: Final Report." School of Library and Information Studies, State University of New York, Buffalo, New York. (ED 061 980.)

Leach, S. (1976). The growth rates of major academic libraries: Rider and Purdue revisited. *College and Research Libraries* 37, 531–542.

Letheve, J. (1971). Project for standard book-exchange request forms. *Unesco Bulletin for Libraries* 25, 282–284.

Line, M. B., and Sandison, A. (1974). "Obsolescence" and changes in the use of literature with time. *Journal of Documentation* 30, 283–350.

Lister, W. C. (1967). "Least Cost Decision Rules for the Selection of Library Materials for Compact Storage." Unpublished dissertation, Purdue University.

Lopez, M. D. (1969). A guide for beginning bibliographers. *Library Resources and Technical Services* 13, 462–470.

McCarthy, S. A. (1966). Felix Reichmann and the development of the Cornell Library. *Library Trends* 15, 215–221.

McCree, M. L. (1975). Good sense and good judgment: defining collections and collecting. *Drexel Library Quarterly* 11, 21–33.

McCullough, K. (1972). Approval plans: vendor responsibility and library research; a literature survey and discussion. *College and Research Libraries* 33, 368–381.

McCullough, K. (1975). "Approval Plans and Departmental Fair Share." Purdue University Libraries and Audiovisual Center, Lafayette, Indiana. (ED 111 340.)

McDonald, J. P. (1974a). Interlibrary cooperation in the U.S. *In* "Issues in Library Administration: (W. M. Tsuneushi, T. R. Buckman, and Y. Suzuki, eds.), pp. 125-137. Columbia University Press, New York.

McDonald, J. P. (1974b). "National Planning and Academic Libraries." (Paper presented at the General Council Meeting of the International Federation of Library Associations, Washington, D.C., November 17-23.) (ED 104 444.)

McGrath, W. E. (1973). "Development of a Long-Range Strategic Plan for a University Library." Cornell University Libraries, Ithaca, New York.

McGrath, W. E. (1975). A pragmatic book allocation formula for academic and public libraries with a test for its effectiveness. *Library Resources and Technical Services* 19, 356-369.

McGrath, W. E., Huntsinger, R. C., and Barber, G. R. (1969). An allocation formula derived from a factor analysis of academic departments. *College and Research Libraries* 30, 51-62.

Machlup, F. (1976). Our libraries: can we measure their holdings and acquisitions? *AAUP Bulletin* 62, 303-307.

McInnis, R. M. (1971). Research collections: an approach to the assessment of quality. *IPLO Quarterly* 13, 13-22.

McInnis, R. M. (1972). The formula approach to library size: an empirical study of its efficacy in evaluating research libraries. *College and Research Libraries* 33, 190-198.

McNiff, P. J. (1963). Foreign area studies and their effect on library development. *College and Research Libraries* 24, 291-296, 304-305.

Maher, K. E., Lane, D., Schmidt, M., and Townley, C. (1969). "How Good Is Your All Book Plan?" University of Oklahoma, Norman, Oklahoma.

Martin, M. (1977). Budgetary strategies: coping with a changing fiscal environment. *Journal of Academic Librarianship* 2, 297-302.

Mattison, L. (1970). Worn book checklist for academic libraries. *Library Resources and Technical Services* 14, 559-561.

Merritt, L. C. (1968). Are we selecting or collecting? *Library Resources and Technical Services* 12, 140-142.

Metz, P. D. (1977). "The Academic Library and Its Director in Their Institutional Environments." Unpublished dissertation, University of Michigan.

Meyer, B. J., and Demos, J. T. (1970). Acquisition policy for university libraries: selection or collection. *Library Resources and Technical Services* 14, 395-399.

Michalak, T. J. (1976). The role of the subject specialist librarian. *College and Research Libraries* 37, 257-265.

Miller, R. A., and Moriarty, J. H. (1966). University library development in Indiana, 1910 to 1966. *Library Trends* 15, 248-257.

Montgomery, K. L., Bulick, S., Fetterman, J., and Kent, A. (1976). Cost-benefit model of library acquisitions in terms of use. *Journal of the American Society for Information Science* 27, 73-74.

Moran, M. (1973). Foreign currency exchange problems relating to the book trade. *Library Resources and Technical Services* 17, 299-307.

Morrison, P. D. (1968). A symposium on approval order plans and the book selec-

tion responsibilities of librarians. *Library Resources and Technical Services* 12, 133–145.
Morse, P. M. (1968). "Library Effectiveness: A Systems Approach." MIT Press, Cambridge, Massachusetts.
Niland, P., and Kurth, W. H. (1976). Estimating lost volumes in a university library collection. *College and Research Libraries* 37, 128–136.
Northwestern University Library (1972). "An Acquisition Policy for the Northwestern University Library, Evanston Campus." Northwestern University Library, Evanston, Illinois.
O'Brien, R. (1966). Nine campuses—one university: the libraries of the University of California. *Library Trends* 15, 303–320.
Opello, O., and Murdock, L. (1976). Acquisitions overkill in science collections—and an alternative. *College and Research Libraries* 37, 452–456.
Orne, J. (1960). Storage and deposit libraries. *College and Research Libraries* 21, 446–452.
Orne, J. (1971). Newspaper resources of the southeastern region: experiment in coordinated resource development. *Southeastern Librarian* 21, 226–235.
Orne, J., and Powell, B. E. (1966). The libraries of the University of North Carolina and of Duke University. *Library Trends* 15, 222–247.
Ortopan, L. D. (1976). "Titles Classified by the Library of Congress Classification: National Shelflist Count." General Library, University of California, Berkeley, California.
Osborn, A. D. (1973). "Serial Publications; Their Place and Treatment in Libraries," 2d Ed., Rev. American Library Association, Chicago, Illinois.
Osburn, C. B. (1977). Planning for a university library policy on collection development. *International Library Review* 9, 209–224.
Ottersen, S. (1971). A bibliography on standards for evaluating libraries. *College and Research Libraries* 32, 127–144.
Palmour, V. E., Bellassai, M. C., and Gray, L. M. (1974). "Access to Periodical Resources: A National Plan." Westat, Rockville, Maryland.
Paulson, P. J. (1970). Government documents and other non-trade publications. *Library Trends* 18, 363–372.
Pease, M. (1975). A reason for being: a national government document agency and the exchange of official publications. *Government Publications Review* 2, 259–271.
Pitt, W. B., and Kraft, D. H. (1974). Buy or copy? A library operations research model. *Information Storage and Retrieval* 10, 331–341.
Quick, R. C. (1975). Coordination of collection building by academic libraries. *In* "New Dimensions for Academic Library Service" (E. J. Josey, ed.), pp. 100–120. Scarecrow Press, Metuchen, New Jersey.
Raney, L. (172). "An Investigation into the Adaptability of a Domestic Approval Program to the Existing Pattern of Book Selection in a Medium-Sized Academic Library." Unpublished dissertation, Indiana University.
Rebuldela, H. K. (1969). Some administrative aspects of blanket ordering: a response. *Library Resources and Technical Services* 13, 342–345.

Reichmann, F. (1970). Purchase of out-of-print material in American university libraries. *Library Trends* 18, 328–353.
Reid, M. T. (1976). Coping with budget adversity: the impact of the financial squeeze on acquisitions. *College and Research Libraries* 37, 266–272.
Reino, C. (1973). A conversation with Hendrik Edelman. *Cornell University Library Bulletin* 182, 4–7.
Richter, E. A. (1970–1971). Academic library acquisitions policy. *New Mexico Libraries* 2, 95–99.
Robertson, S. E., and Hensman, S. (1975). Journal acquisition by libraries: scatter and cost-effectiveness. *Journal of Documentation* 31, 273–282.
Rogers, R. D., and Weber, D. C. (1971). "University Library Administration." H. W. Wilson, New York.
Rosenthal, J. A. (1973). "The Research Libraries Group: Proposals for Cooperation among the Libraries of Columbia, Harvard and Yale Universities and the New York Public Library." (n.p.)
Rouse, R. (1970). Automation stops here: a case for man-made book collections. *College and Research Libraries* 31, 147–154.
Rouse, W. B. (1976). A library network model. *Journal of the American Society for Information Science* 27, 88–99.
Rush, B., Steinberg, S., and Kraft, D. H. (1974). Journal disposition decision policies. *Journal of the American Society for Information Science* 25, 213–217.
Samore, T. (1973). "Acquisition of Foreign Materials for U.S. Libraries." Scarecrow Press, Metuchen, New Jersey.
Saracevic, T., Shaw, W. M., Jr., and Kantor, P. B. (1977). Causes and dynamics of user frustration in an academic library. *College and Research Libraries* 38, 7–18.
Savary, M. J. (1968). "The Latin American Cooperative Acquisitions Program; An Imaginative Venture." Hafner, New York.
Schad, J. G. (1970). Allocating book funds: control or planning? *College and Research Libraries* 31, 155–159.
Schad, J. G., and Adams, R. L. (1969). Book selection in academic libraries: a new approach. *College and Research Libraries* 30, 437–442.
Schiltman, M. J. (1973). "International Exchange of Publications; Proceedings of the European Conference held in Vienna from 24–29 April 1972." Verlag Dokumentation, Munich.
Schmidt, C. J. (1975). Resource allocation in university libraries in the 1970's and beyond. *Library Trends* 23, 643–648.
Seymour, C. A. (1972). Weeding the collection: a review of research on identifying obsolete stock. *Libri* 22, 137–148, 183–189.
Shepard, M. D. (1962). "Seminars on the Acquisition of Latin American Library Materials: A Seven Year Report, 1956 to 1962." Pan American Union, Washington, D.C.
Shepard, M. D. (1969). Cooperative acquisitions of Latin American materials. *Library Resources and Technical Services* 13, 347–360.
Shinn, I. E. (1972). Toward uniformity in exchange communication. *Library Resources and Technical Services* 16, 502–510.
Simkin, F. (1970). "Cooperative Resources Development; A Report on a Shared

Acquisitions and Retention System for METRO Libraries." New York Metropolitan Reference and Research Library Agency, New York. (ED 039 903.)

Simmons, P. (1971). "Collection Development and the Computer; A Case Study in the Analysis of Machine Readable Loan Records and Their Application to Book Selection." University of British Columbia, Vancouver, British Columbia.

Simon, J. L. (1967). How many books should be stored where? An economic analysis. *College and Research Libraries* 28, 92–103.

Sinha, B. K. (1970). "Operations Research in Controlled Acquisition and Weeding of Library Collections." Unpublished dissertation, University of Pennsylvania.

Skelley, G. T. (1975). Characteristics of collections added to American research libraries, 1940–1970: a preliminary investigation. *College and Research Libraries* 36, 52–60.

Skipper, J. E. (1966). National planning for resource development. *Library Trends* 15, 321–334.

Sloan, E. C. (1973). "The Organization of Collection Development in Large University Research Libraries." Unpublished dissertation, University of Maryland.

Slote, S. J. (1975). "Weeding Library Collections." Libraries Unlimited, Littleton, Colorado.

Smith, E. R. (1972). The specialist librarian in the academic research library: the role of the area studies librarian. *In* "Final Report and Working Papers of the 17th Seminar on the Acquisition of Latin American Library Materials," pp. 101–122. Amherst, Massachusetts.

Smith, E. R. (1974). The impact of the subject specialist librarian on the organization and structure of the academic research library. *In* "The Academic Library: Essays in Honor of Guy R. Lyle" (E. I. Farber and R. Walling, eds.), pp. 78–81. Scarecrow Press, Metuchen, New Jersey.

Smith, E. R. (1975). Changes in higher education and the university library. *In* "New Dimensions for Academic Library Service" (E. J. Josey, ed.), pp. 34–49. Scarecrow Press, Metuchen, New Jersey.

Spyers-Duran, P. (1969). "Proceedings of the First International Seminar on Approval and Gathering Plans in Large and Medium Size Academic Libraries." Western Michigan University Libraries, Kalamazoo, Michigan.

Spyers-Duran, P., and Gore, D. (1970). "Advances in Understanding Approval and Gathering Plans in Academic Libraries; Second International Seminar on Approval and Gathering Plans in Large and Medium Size Academic Libraries." Western Michigan University Libraries, Kalamazoo, Michigan.

Spyers-Duran, P., and Gore, D. (1972). "Economics of Approval Plans; Third International Seminar on Approval and Gathering Plans in Large and Medium Size Academic Libraries." Greenwood Press, Westport, Connecticut.

Stanford University Libraries (1970). "Book Selection Policies of the Libraries of Stanford University." Stanford University Libraries, Stanford, California.

Stayer, M. S. (1971). A creative approach to collection evaluation. *IPLO Quarterly* 13, 23–28.

Steele, C. (1970). Blanket orders and the bibliographer in the large research library. *Journal of Librarianship* 2, 272–280.

Stevens, N. D. (1968). National Program for Acquisitions and Cataloging: a progress report on developments under the Title IIC of the Higher Education Act of 1965. *Library Resources and Technical Services* 12, 17-29.

Stevens, R. D. (1963). The Library of Congress Public Law 480 programs. *Library Resources and Technical Services* 7, 176-188.

Stevens, R. D. (1970). Acquisitions for area programs. *Library Trends* 18, 385-397.

Stevens, R. E. (1970). Introduction to problems of acquisition for research libraries. *Library Trends* 18, 275-279.

Stuart-Stubbs, B. (1970). "The New England Deposit Library and the Hampshire Inter-Library Center: A Survey of Two Storage Libraries Performed for the University Libraries of British Columbia." University of British Columbia, Vancouver, British Columbia. (ED 046 478.)

Stuart-Stubbs, B. (1975). An historical look at resource sharing. *Library Trends* 23, 649-664.

Stueart, R. D. (1971). "Area Specialist Bibliographer; An Inquiry into His Role." Unpublished dissertation, University of Pittsburgh.

Subramanyam, K. (1975). Criteria for journal selection. *Special Libraries* 66, 367-371.

Sullivan, H. A. (1969). Ten years after: the joint acquisition committee in Detroit. *Stechert-Hafner Book News* 23, 129-131.

Swanson, D. R., and Bookstein, A. (1972). "Operation Research: Implications for Libraries." (Proceedings of the 35th Annual Conference of the Graduate Library School.) University of Chicago Press, Chicago, Illinois. (Also published in *Library Quarterly* 42, 1-160.)

Taggart, W. R. (1970). Blanket approval ordering—a positive approach. *Canadian Library Journal* 27, 286-289.

Taggart, W. R. (1972). Preparing a collections policy for the academic library. *Canadian Association of College and University Libraries Newsletter* 4, 53-56.

Taggart, W. R. (1974). Book selection librarians in Canadian universities. *Canadian Library Journal* 31, 410-412.

Thom, I. W. (1969). Some administrative aspects of blanket ordering. *Library Resources and Technical Services* 13, 338-342.

Thompson, J. (1973). Revision of stock in academic libraries. *Library Association Record* 75, 41-44.

Thompson, L. S. (1960). Dogma of book selection in university libraries. *College and Research Libraries* 21, 441-445.

Thompson, L. S. (1970). Acquisition of books and pamphlets. *Library Trends* 18, 280-293.

Tolman, M. (1971). The book budget *is* "The Iron Maiden"—the plight of the research library. *Bookmark* 31, 34-37.

Trueswell, R. W. (1965). A quantitative measure of user circulation requirements and its possible effect on stack thinning and multiple copy determination. *American Documentation* 16, 20-25.

Trueswell, R. W. (1968). Some circulation data from a research library. *College and Research Libraries* 29, 493-495.

Trueswell, R. W. (1969a). Some behavioral patterns of library users: the 80/20 rule. *Wilson Library Bulletin* 43, 458-461.

Trueswell, R. W. (1969b). User circulation satisfaction vs. size of holdings at three academic libraries. *College and Research Libraries* 30, 204–213.
Trueswell, R. W. (1976). Growing libraries: who needs them? A statistical basis for the no-growth collection. In "Farewell to Alexandria; Solutions to Space, Growth, and Performance Problems of Libraries" (D. Gore, ed.), pp. 72–104. Greenwood Press, Westport, Connecticut.
Tsien, T. H., and Winger, H. W. (1966). "Area Studies and the Library." (Proceedings of the 30th Annual Conference of the Graduate Library School.) University of Chicago Press, Chicago, Illinois. (Also published in *Library Quarterly* 35, 203–386.)
Tuttle, H. W. (1969a). An acquisitionist looks at Mr. Haro's bibliographer. *Library Resources and Technical Services* 13, 170–174.
Tuttle, H. W. (169b). "Operating an Effective Acquisition Department." (Paper presented at the Institute on Acquisitions Procedures in Academic Libraries, University of California, San Diego, August 25—September 5.) (ED 043 344.)
Tuttle, H. W. (1970). Library-book trade relations. *Library Trends* 18, 398–411.
United Nations Educational, Scientific and Cultural Organization (1964). "Handbook on the International Exchange of Publications," 3d Ed. UNESCO, Paris.
Van Toll, F. (1972). "A Cost Analysis Comparison of University Funded Faculty Facsimile Service and Faculty Journal Circulation Privileges." Wayne State University, School of Medicine, Library and Biomedical Information Service Center, Detroit. (Report no. 60)
Voigt, M. J. (1969). "Case Study of the California Experience in Library Collection Building." (Paper presented at the Institute on Acquisitions Procedures in Academic Libraries, University of California, San Diego, August 25—September 5.) (ED 043 345.)
Voigt, M. J. (1975). Acquisition rates in university libraries. *College and Research Libraries* 36, 263–271.
Vosper, R. (1965). "Farmington Plan Survey; A Summary of the Separate Studies of 1957–1961." Graduate School of Library Science, University of Illinois, Urbana, Illinois. (Occasional Papers, No. 77.)
Vosper, R. (1967). International implications of the shared cataloging program: planning for resource development. *Libri* 17, 285–293.
Vosper, R. (1971). Collection building and rare books. In "Research Librarianship; Essays in Honor of Robert B. Downs" (J. Orne, ed.), pp. 91–111. R. R. Bowker, New York.
Ward, K. L. (1973). Collection policy in college and university libraries. *Music Library Association Notes* 29, 432–440.
Wayne State University Libraries (1974). "Structuring for a Collection Development Policy." Wayne State University Libraries, Detroit, Michigan. (Working Paper No. 10.) (ED 098 927.)
Webb, W. (1969). Project CoED: a university library collection evaluation and development program. *Library Resources and Technical Services* 13, 457–462.
Weber, D. C. (1976). A century of cooperative programs among academic libraries. *College and Research Libraries* 37, 205–221.
Webster, D. E. (1971). "Planning Aids for the University Library Director." As-

sociation of Research Libraries, Office of University Library Management Studies, Washington, D.C. (Occasional Papers No. 1.)

Webster, D. E. (1972). "Library Policies: Analysis, Formulation and Use in Academic Institutions." Association of Research Libraries, Office of University Library Management Studies, Washington, D.C.

Wedgeworth, R. (1970). Foreign blanket orders: precedent and practice. *Library Resources and Technical Services* **14**, 258–268.

White, C. M. (1969). "Duplicated Information Acquired by Libraries." (Paper presented at the Institute on Acquisitions Procedures in Academic Libraries, University of California, San Diego, August 25—September 5.) (ED 043 346.)

White, H. S. (1976). Publishers, libraries, and costs of journal subscriptions in times of funding retrenchment. *Library Quarterly* **46**, 359–377.

Wilden-Hart, M. (1970a). "Cooperative Resource Development in the Five Associated University Libraries; A Study with Recommendations." Five Associated University Libraries, Syracuse, New York. (ED 049 768.)

Wilden-Hart, M. (1970b). Long-term effects of approval plans. *Library Resources and Technical Services* **14**, 400–406.

Williams, E. E. (1961). "Farmington Plan Handbook." Association of Research Libraries, Ithaca, New York.

Williams, G. R. (1965). Center for Research Libraries: its new organizations and programs. *Library Journal* **90**, 2947–2951.

Williams, G. R., Bryant, E. C., Wiederkehr, R. R. V., Palmour, V. E., and Siehler, C. (1968). "Library Cost Models: Owning Versus Borrowing Serial Publications." National Science Foundation, Office of Science Information Services, Washington, D.C. (ED 026 106.)

Williamson, W. L. (1968). "Impact of the Public Law 480 Program on Overseas Acquisitions by American Libraries." (Proceedings of a Conference held May 12, 1967.) University of Wisconsin-Madison, Library School, Madison, Wisconsin.

Wilson, L. R. (1966). Introduction to current trends in collection development in academic libraries. *Library Trends* **15**, 197–205.

Windsor, D. A. (1973). Rational selection of primary journals for a biomedical research library: the use of secondary journal citations. *Special Libraries* **64**, 446–451.

Winger, H. W. (1970). "Deterioration and Preservation of Library Materials." (Proceedings of the 34th Annual Conference of the Graduate Library School.) University of Chicago Press, Chicago, Illinois. (Also published in *Library Quarterly* **40**, 1–200.)

Woodhead, P. (1974). Subject specialization in three British university libraries: a critical survey. *Libri* **24**, 30–60.

Yavarkovsky, J., Mount, E., and Kordish, H. (1973). Computer-based collection development statements. *American Society for Information Science Proceedings* **10**, 240–241.

The Library of Congress in American Life

JOHN Y. COLE
Library of Congress

    I. Introduction 55
   II. The Legislative and the National Roles 57
       A. Introduction 57
       B. Services to Congress 58
       C. Services to the Federal Government 59
       D. Services to the General Public 60
       E. Services to Authors and Publishers 61
       F. Services to Scholars and Researchers 61
       G. Services to Libraries and Librarians 62
  III. Disagreements Concerning the Library's Role 63
  IV. The Task Force on Goals, Organization, and Planning 68
   V. The Task Force Recommendations 71
       A. The Legislative and the National Roles 71
       B. Organizational Changes 73
       C. National Responsibilities 74
       D. Relationship to Previous Reviews and Recommendations 76
     References 78

I. INTRODUCTION

On November 12, 1975, in a ceremony held in the Great Hall of the Library of Congress and attended by President Gerald R. Ford and

Vice President Nelson A. Rockefeller, historian Daniel J. Boorstin took the oath of office as the twelfth Librarian of Congress (see Daniel J. Boorstin sworn in, 1975). The oath, taken on a Bible from the Library's Jefferson collection, was administered by Carl Albert of Oklahoma, the Speaker of the House of Representatives. Congressman Lucien N. Nedzi of Michigan, chairman of the Joint Committee on the Library, presided. In his remarks, Representative Nedzi reminded the audience that the Library of Congress was not only a legislative library but also "of equal importance, if not more so, it is a national library that serves all the people of the United States." President Ford, in his brief address, noted that it was "particularly appropriate on the eve of the Nation's Bicentennial for Dr. Boorstin to become the Librarian of Congress," since he "will bring to this post a love of learning and a scholar's appreciation of the importance of libraries and of the unique contribution of the Library of Congress to American life." (Text of remarks . . . , 1975).

The induction of a new Librarian of Congress truly is an event worthy of such ceremony. In the first place, it does not take place very often. The first Librarian was appointed in 1802 and since then only a dozen men have held the position. Second, the job is unique. The Library of Congress is part of the legislative branch of government, but the Librarian of Congress is nominated by the President of the United States. The Senate did not have the power to confirm the President's choice until 1897. Concurrently, the office of Librarian of Congress was granted unique powers: the authority and responsibility for making the Library's rules and regulations and for hiring the Library's employees was transferred from the Joint Committee on the Library to the office of the Librarian.

Finally, the Library of Congress itself occupies a unique place in American civilization. Established as a legislative library, it grew into a national institution that today is the largest library in the world, containing over 18 million volumes and 75 million pieces of research material, and employing more than 5,000 persons. In fiscal year 1978 the Congress appropriated over $150 million for its operations. The Library is an international as well as a national institution, collecting materials from all parts of the world which in turn are made available to librarians, scholars, government agencies, and citizens from around the world. The comprehensive scope of its collections is the foundation for a variety of cultural and educational programs that are offered nowhere else. In sum, each Librarian of Congress has a unique opportunity to shape and influence American librarianship, scholarship, and culture.

The purpose of this chapter is to examine the national role of the Library of Congress. Its focus is on a year-long study of the Library initiated by Librarian of Congress Daniel J. Boorstin in January 1976, but its starting point is a review of the Library's historical role as a legislative and a national library.

II. THE LEGISLATIVE AND THE NATIONAL ROLES

A. Introduction

The most remarkable feature of the Library of Congress is its dual nature as both a legislative library for the Congress and a national library for the country at large. In this sense, the Library of Congress brings together the common concerns of government, scholarship, and librarianship—an uncommon combination, perhaps, but one that has been of great benefit to American society and culture.

The dual nature of the Library of Congress stems from events in the early years of the nineteenth century, when the Library began its gradual expansion into an institution that served both the Congress and the rest of the nation. The extension of the services of the Library of Congress was a direct result of the expansion of the scope of the Library's collections; in other words, the functions of the Library have derived from its collections, not vice versa (Lacy, 1950).

There were two events of particular importance in shaping the future of the institution. The first was the purchase by Congress, in 1815, of the personal library of former President Thomas Jefferson, which provided the legislators with "a most admirable substratum for a National Library." Furthermore, in offering to sell his library to the government, Jefferson used a phrase that applies equally well today in justifying the comprehensive nature of the Library's collections: "There is . . . no subject to which a member of Congress may not have occasion to refer" (Mearns, 1947).

The second "event" was the thirty-two-year administration of an ardent collection builder, Ainsworth Rand Spofford, who served as

Librarian of Congress from 1865 to 1897 and applied Jefferson's rationale on a grand scale. Spofford was responsible for the centralization of all U.S. copyright activities at the Library, the construction of the monumental Library of Congress building, and above all, for permanently linking the legislative and national functions of the Library. Spofford's basic concept of the Library of Congress as both the legislative library for the American Congress and the national library for the American people has been wholeheartedly accepted by his successors as Librarian of Congress: John Russell Young (1897–1899), Herbert Putnam (1899–1939), Archibald MacLeish (1939–1944), Luther H. Evans (1945–1953), L. Quincy Mumford (1954–1974), and Daniel J. Boorstin (1975–   ) (see Cole, 1975).

In 1962 Douglas W. Bryant, associate librarian of Harvard University, accurately observed: "The major functions of the Library of Congress might have been assigned to three or four agencies... an explanation of why they have been combined would call for a study of history rather than of administrative logic" (Bryant, 1962). Today the Library of Congress serves six principal constituencies—the Congress, the federal government, the general public, authors and publishers, scholars and the research community, and the professional library community. The services to the Congress have priority; the other constituencies are listed roughly in the order in which they received access to the Library's collections and services. A brief outline of the development of services to each of these constituencies indicates not only the scope of the Library's services but also the pervasiveness of its influence in American cultural life.

B.   Services to Congress

The Library of Congress was founded in 1800 when Congress appropriated $5,000 "for the purchase of such books as may be necessary for the use of Congress" after it moved from Philadelphia to the new capital city of Washington. Until 1870, when the copyright law was passed, the Library served primarily as a legislative library—even though its use was not restricted to Congress. The new copyright law, like the Jefferson purchase half a century before, greatly expanded the Library's scope. It also gave the Library a new national role, a role enhanced and even enshrined when the monumental new Library of

Congress building across the east plaza from the Capitol opened in 1897.

A separate legislative reference unit was created within the Library in 1914. The Legislative Reorganization Act of 1946 expanded the responsibilities of the Legislative Reference Service in assisting Congress and its committees and gave the Service permanent statutory basis as a separate Library department. It also authorized increased appropriations so the Service could employ nationally recognized specialists in certain subject fields. The Legislative Reorganization Act of 1970 changed the name of the Service to the Congressional Research Service (CRS) and expanded its policy research responsibilities as well as its services to Congressional committees. It also gave the CRS maximum administrative and fiscal autonomy within the Library's organizational structure, stipulating that the Librarian of Congress shall "in every possible way, encourage, assist, and promote the Congressional Research Service," according the Service "complete research independence and the maximum practicable administrative independence" (Goodrum, 1974). In fiscal year 1976, the CRS answered nearly 300,000 Congressional requests, ranging from simple telephone inquiries to questions that required extensive study by highly qualified subject specialists.

C. Services to the Federal Government

The President and Vice President of the United States have been able to use the Library since 1802. The same law that granted them Library privileges provided for the creation of a Joint Committee on the Library to establish the Library's rules and regulations and for the appointment of a Librarian of Congress by the President. The Justices of the Supreme Court were authorized to use the Library's books in 1812, and in 1830 President Andrew Jackson approved a joint resolution of Congress that granted the use of the books to several executive agencies. In 1832 the chief justice of the Supreme Court was given the power to approve purchases for the Library's law collection. Six years later the Library of Congress became the official agency of the U.S. government for foreign exchanges, a role soon to be shared with the Smithsonian Institution (Johnston, 1904). In 1866 the Library of Congress acquired its first major transfer from a government-related agency, the deposit of the Smithsonian library. In 1870 the Library became the sole copyright agency for the government and, with the receipt of the private library of Joseph M. Toner twelve years later, it began accepting "gifts to the nation" from private citizens. In 1903 U.S. government agencies began transferring surplus materials to the Library of Congress. In the same year, President Theodore Roosevelt directed the transfer of many official records, including certain presidential collections, from the State Department to the Library. Shortly after World War II, the Library began a number of contract research projects for the government. Today several projects are carried out on a transferred funds basis; moreover, federal agencies and their libraries are among the heaviest users of the Library's collections.

D. Services to the General Public

As a government library, the Library of Congress is a tax-supported institution. The general public has been able to use books in the Library of Congress since about 1815, and, in the middle years of the century, members of the public could even borrow books if an appropriate sum were left on deposit. In 1892 college students from the District of Columbia were officially granted use privileges. The Main Building, opened in 1897, was intended as a public showplace. Its elaborate decorative scheme illustrates the best American art and sculpture of the period, and tourists have always been welcome to admire its architecture and decoration. A reading room for the blind was established in 1897, forming the nucleus for one of the Library's best-known public activities, the services of its Division for the Blind and Physically Handicapped. Primarily for the benefit of the public, the Library began evening hours in 1898; Sunday hours were started in 1902. In 1925 an endowment from Elizabeth Sprague Coolidge enabled the Library to begin sponsoring chamber music concerts which were open to the public. The Library of Congress Trust Fund Board, created in the same year, enabled the Library to accept money or bequests of personal property for the benefit of the Library, its collections, or its service. The Library began sponsoring public literary events in 1942. A Children's Book Section was established in 1962. Today the Library's chamber music concerts are broadcast throughout the United States on FM radio, its exhibits are shown in many parts of the country, and its publications program reaches a worldwide audience.

E. Services to Authors and Publishers

From 1846 until 1859 and again from 1865 until 1870, the Library of Congress was one of several government agencies that received copyright deposits. In 1870, however, all U.S. copyright deposit and registration activities were centralized at the Library of Congress, giving the Library a special responsibility for the legal protection of authors and artists and in promoting "the progress of science and the useful arts" (Cole, 1971). In 1897 the position of Register of Copyrights was established and the Copyright Office became a separate Library department. Special cooperative programs between the Library and the publishing community have included the All-the-Books program and, more recently, the Cataloging-in-Publication (CIP) program. As administrator of the nation's copyright law, the Library naturally has been deeply involved in copyright law revision. The new copyright law, approved by President Ford on October 19, 1976, greatly enlarged the responsibilities of the Library of Congress in all aspects of copyright protection (Copyright law revision, 1977).

F. Services to Scholars and Researchers

Scholars did not find the collections of the Library of Congress particularly useful until after the Civil War. The acquisition of the Smithsonian library in 1866 and the Peter Force library of Americana in 1867 provided scholars with unique research materials, but the development of the collections on a systematic basis did not begin until 1870, when the copyright law provided for the comprehensive development of book, map, music, and graphic arts collections. In 1901, Congress officially extended access to the Library's collections to "scientific investigators and duly qualified individuals." Interlibrary loan services were begun the same year. The Library became a leading center for historical research after the transfer in 1903 of many historical and Presidential papers from the Department of State. The Library's extensive program of preparing and publishing scholarly bibliographies started in the same decade. Special study facilities have been available for serious scholars throughout most of this century. Today many of the Library's Americana collections are unsurpassed and many of its foreign language collections are surprisingly strong.

G. Services to Libraries and Librarians

The Library of Congress has been the largest American library since 1867, but it did not begin offering "national library" services for the benefit of other libraries and librarians until 1901. In that year the first new classification schedule was offered for sale, the sale and distribution of printed catalog cards was begun, and the interlibrary loan service was inaugurated. In 1908 the Library assisted in the preparation of the Anglo-American cataloging rules, and it has been a leader in catalog code revision ever since. In 1930 the Library began putting Dewey decimal classification numbers on its printed cards. In more recent times, national library services undertaken by the Library of Congress have included the Public Law 480 acquisitions program in 1961, the National Program for Acquisitions and Cataloging in 1966, the MARC (Machine-Readable Cataloging) program in 1966, and the Cataloging-in-Publication program in 1971 (see Goodrum, 1974; The Library of Congress as the national library, 1969). Today the Library is recognized as the keystone of the nation's bibliographic system.

The legislative and the national functions of the Library of Congress are inherent parts of the Library's basic fabric, and their growth reflects the institution's deep roots in the political and cultural development of the nation. For the Library of Congress, primarily because of the unique circumstances of its origin and early development, is a product of American nationalism—and that nationalism is the unifying force between Congress, the Library, and the nation. Today the Library of Congress is a national cultural symbol that draws its support from all segments of American society.

The Library also has drawn criticism from the segments of society that it serves in both its legislative and its national roles. That criticism has come primarily from the two constituencies that the institution strives the hardest to serve—the Congress and the professional library community, illustrating the delicate balance that the Library must maintain in carrying out its diverse responsibilities. For example, whenever a President nominates a nonlibrarian to be Librarian of Congress, the nature of the Library itself is an important consideration in the ensuing controversy. Such controversies have created tensions, but in the long run those tensions probably have benefited the Library, especially when they result in assessments of its functions and activities. Furthermore, these disagreements are themselves good illustrations of the unique role of the Library of Congress among American institutions.

III. DISAGREEMENTS CONCERNING THE LIBRARY'S ROLE

In 1896, on the eve of the Library's move into its new building, Congress held hearings on the organization of the institution. These hearings marked a sharp turning point in the relationship between the Library of Congress and the American library movement—which was represented by the American Library Association (ALA). For the first time the ALA, albeit cautiously, offered its advice to Congress about the organization and functions of the Library of Congress. It is interesting to note that the ALA leaders who were advocating an expanded national role for the Library of Congress hoped that these changes would result at the very least in its formal designation as the National Library and perhaps even in its transfer to the executive branch of government (Cole, 1973). In 1896–1897, as in later years, Congress refused to consider seriously either a name change or giving up its jurisdiction over the Library.

By 1899 the ALA had lost all shyness regarding the Library. After the sudden death of Librarian Young, the Association began a concerted campaign in favor of the appointment of Herbert Putnam, head of the Boston Public Library, to be Librarian of Congress. President William McKinley eventually acceded, and the Senate approved. The appointment and forty-year administration of Librarian Putnam, an experienced librarian, firmly linked the policies of the Library of Congress with the broader interests of American librarianship. Furthermore, it encouraged the ALA to try and influence President Franklin D. Roosevelt's nomination of Putnam's successor.

In searching for a successor to Putnam, Roosevelt asked Supreme Court Justice Felix Frankfurter whether Archibald MacLeish would make a good Librarian of Congress. Frankfurter endorsed the idea, primarily because "only a scholarly man of letters can make a great national library a general place of habitation for scholars." Furthermore, according to the Justice, the Library of Congress "is not merely a library and in the immediate future even more so than in the past it will be concerned with problems quite outside the traditional tasks associated with collecting, housing, and circulating books." Roosevelt nominated MacLeish in June 1939 and the American Library Association responded with a resolution opposing the nomination because "the Congress and the American people should have as Librarian... one who is not only a gentleman and a scholar but who is also the ablest library administrator available." ALA representatives testified against MacLeish in the Senate hearings on the nomination, but the nominee was confirmed by the full Senate by a vote of 63 to 8 (Benco, 1976).

Librarian Putnam greatly expanded the Library's national services and enhanced its national role. During the Putnam administration, however, new functions and services simply had been appended to the Library's administrative structure. MacLeish's most significant contribution to the Library was a complete administrative reorganization. The catalyst was a two-month study undertaken by the "Librarian's Committee," which consisted of Professor Carleton B. Joeckel, University of Chicago Library School (chairman), Paul North Rice of the New York Public Library, and Andrew D. Osborn of the Harvard University Library. With the aid of additional outside advisors from the library community, and many staff committees, between 1939 and 1944 MacLeish divided the staff of over 1,000 persons into new, functional departments (MacLeish, 1944). Moreover, for the first time in the history of the institution explicit statements of objectives developed. The statements, termed "Canons of Selection" and "Canons of Service," incorporated earlier practices and did not present any new concepts. They did, however, clearly reaffirm the priority afforded to the Congress in the Library's services.

The ALA was unable to influence President Harry Truman's appointment of MacLeish's successor, even though the Association tried. In June 1945, political scientist Luther H. Evans, then the acting Librarian and formerly a top official in MacLeish's administration, was confirmed as the tenth Librarian of Congress.

Probably the strongest Congressional criticism ever directed at the Library occurred during the administration of Librarian Evans and centered on the question of legislative versus national functions. In

1946 Evans submitted a lengthy budget justification to Congress that called for an increase in the Library's appropriation from about $5 million to nearly $10 million and a considerable expansion of the Library's national activities. The Appropriations Committee balked, maintaining that "the kind of Library of Congress proposed by the estimates had not been endorsed in clear policy terms by Congress itself." The Library received approximately $6 million, but it was put on the defensive. As a result, considerable effort was spent during the Evans years in explaining and justifying the Library's many diverse activities. *The Story Up to Now,* David C. Mearns' brief but delightful history of the Library up to 1946, is one example.

A Library of Congress Planning Committee was created "to consider what should be the functions of the Library." Chaired by Keyes D. Metcalf, director of libraries at Harvard University, the committee reviewed the Library's policies, emphasizing its relationships with Congress and with its other users. The Planning Committee report, published in the Librarian's 1947 *Annual Report,* strongly urged the expansion of the Library's national role. It (1) stated the conviction "that the actual status of the Library as a National Library should be officially recognized in its name and that it should be designated 'The Library of Congress, the National Library of the United States of America'"; (2) advocated the creation of a National Library Advisory Council to aid the Librarian of Congress "in his relations with research libraries of the nation and to help in his efforts to avoid unnecessary duplication" of library services; and (3) recommended that its report, after the Joint Library Committee had made the revisions it deemed proper, serve "as a basis for a Charter for the Library of Congress, which will provide the legislative authorization required for present and proposed activities of the Library."

The relationship between Congress and Evans was uneasy, and the Librarian never was able to expand the Library in the style or at the pace he felt appropriate. When Evans resigned in 1953 to become director general of UNESCO, the Library's annual appropriation was approximately $9 million (Sittig, 1976).

The American Library Association heartily approved of President Eisenhower's nominee as Evans' successor, for he was L. Quincy Mumford, librarian of the Cleveland Public Library and ALA president-elect. Mumford was the first graduate of a professional library school to be nominated for the post. He took office in 1954 and proceeded to guide the Library of Congress through the greatest expansion period in its history (Powell, 1976). Mumford always moved cautiously in his relations with Congress, respecting a statement made by the House Committee on Appropriations in May 1954: "The new Librarian should be mindful that the Library is the instrument and creature of Congress." The first years of the Mumford administration were primarily years of consolidation. He deliberately concentrated on strengthening the Library's collections and services "because so central is the Library of Congress to the library economy and research efforts of the country, to the extent that the institution is weak, the whole fabric of library service is weak" (Mumford, 1962).

Debate about the Library's legislative and national functions continued into the Mumford administration. In 1959 the Brookings Institution sponsored a survey of federal departmental libraries, which was directed by former Librarian of Congress Luther H. Evans. A principal recommendation of the survey was that the Library of Congress be transferred into the executive branch of government, a conclusion strongly disputed by Librarian Mumford.

In 1962, at the request of Senator Claiborn Pell of the Joint Library Committee, Douglas W. Bryant of the Harvard University Library prepared a memorandum on "what the Library of Congress does and ought to do for the Government and the Nation generally." Bryant urged further expansion of the Library's national activities and services; many of his proposals, in fact paralleled those made by the Library of Congress Planning Committee in 1947. There were several differences, however. Bryant felt it would be "desirable" to transfer the Library to the executive branch of government, a subject not mentioned in the 1947 report. The Harvard librarian advocated a National Library Advisory Board, but one located in the executive branch and with much wider responsibilities than those held by the Library of Congress. Although he did not feel that the transfer of the Library to the executive branch was essential, he did feel it was essential "that legislation recognize officially what the Library is and what it ought to do" (Bryant, 1962).

A salutary effect of the Bryant memorandum was the reply it evoked from Librarian Mumford—probably the best statement of Mumford's view of the Library's national role and responsibilities. The reply came in the Librarian's 1962 annual report. The Librarian strongly defended the Library's position in the legislative branch and reiterated his opposition to changing or altering the Library's name to reflect its national role: "The Library of Congress is a venerable institution, with a proud history, and to change its name would do unspeakable violence to tradition." The Librarian asserted that "on the question of being the national library the substance is more important than the form," pointing out that, while fulfilling its legislative responsibilities, the Library of Congress also performed "more national library functions than any other national library in the world" (Mumford, 1962).

Both legislative and national services were strengthened during the Mumford years, but particularly the national services, which were expanded to include activities such as NPAC, MARC, and CIP. The Library's appropriation climbed from approximately $9 million in 1954 to more than $96 million in 1974, reinforcing an assumption that Mumford made in his 1962 annual report, that Congress could be depended on to recognize "the national responsibilities of the Library in a way that matters most—with understanding and consistent support."

L. Quincy Mumford retired at the end of 1974. In June 1975 President Gerald R. Ford nominated Pulitzer-prize winning historian Daniel J. Boorstin to be Librarian of Congress, and the ensuing controversy echoed many aspects of the 1939 dispute over the MacLeish nomination. Once again a cultural figure, rather than a professional librarian, had been nominated to head the largest American library. Professional librarians protested and, at the ninety-fourth annual conference of the American Library Association, the ALA adopted a resolution opposing Boorstin's nomination because "Dr. Boorstin's background, however distinguished it may be, does not include demonstrated leadership and administrative qualities which constitute basic and essential characteristics necessary in the Librarian of Congress." In September 1975 Boorstin's nomination was confirmed without debate in the U.S. Senate and on November 12 he took the oath of office as the twelfth Librarian of Congress.

The nomination and easy confirmation of Boorstin as Librarian of Congress reflected the general preference of both the President and the Congress for a cultural figure as Librarian of Congress. When one considers the national character of the Library's history and the diversity of its present functions and services, this preference is hardly surprising. If this pattern continues, it undoubtedly will disappoint many librarians. Their disappointment will result partly from reasons of professional pride, but also because librarians simply would like the Library of Congress to strengthen and expand many of the services it now offers to the nation's libraries. The basic question in their minds concerns the willingness and the capacity of the Library of Congress to exercise leadership in the library world while the U.S. Congress is its most important client. A second concern is whether a Librarian of Congress, who is not a professional librarian, can truly appreciate the importance of the Library's national role and fully understand the technical aspects of the problems faced by the library world. Librarians have grappled with both of these questions since the turn of the century. The first question also was faced by the Library of Congress itself when Librarian Boorstin, as one of his first major actions, appointed a staff Task Force on Goals, Organization, and Planning.

IV. THE TASK FORCE ON GOALS, ORGANIZATION, AND PLANNING

The Task Force was created on January 16, 1976, to carry out "a full-scale review of the Library and its activities." In explaining to the staff why the review was needed, Boorstin recalled the review initiated by Librarian Archibald MacLeish:

> A third of a century has passed since the Library last undertook a full-scale, comprehensive review. These decades have been full of momentous change. Our nation has suffered the pangs of adjustment after a World War and has been involved in two other wars. In vast territories of the world the free flow of information is obstructed.
>
> We have lived through a technological revolution more intimate and more pervasive than any before.... No part of the Library of Congress has been untouched by these transformations. Today hundreds of our staff are engaged in activities never imagined a half-century ago. The traditional activities of our Library—acquisitions, cataloging, helping the nation's libraries, and communicating information to the Congress—have also been reshaped.
>
> At the same time, the size of our Library has multiplied. When Librarian Archibald MacLeish initiated the last full-scale review 37 years ago, the Library had a book collection of some six million volumes, an annual budget of about $4 million, and a staff of 1,000. Today our book collection has at least trebled and we have added whole new types of materials. Our annual budget is $116 million and our staff numbers over 4,600.
>
> During these decades the Library of Congress has been given a vast range of new statutory responsibilities.... Plainly the time has come for a review. The

arrival of a new Librarian of Congress and the near completion of the Madison Building make such a study especially appropriate now.

Therefore I am now commencing a major review of the Library's goals, organization, and planning. This will require close consultation with the Congress, will draw on the suggestions of our staff, and will reach outside for the constructive criticism and imaginative suggestions of all our constituencies. After full study and careful reflection, our conclusions will, I hope, produce a more effective and efficient Library of Congress, better adapted to the needs of the Congress and the nation as we enter our third century.... The review will be wide-ranging, free and imaginative. It will start from our primary duty to serve the Congress. It will take account of those changes in technology, in the nation and the world, which affect our usefulness to the Congress and our effectiveness as a national library.
(Statement by the Librarian of Congress, 1976.)

The Librarian explained that he expected recommendations from the Task Force and the advisory groups by January 1977. He also outlined the major questions to be considered. These questions, listed below, called for nothing less than a redefinition of the role of the Library of Congress in American life:

1. How well are we serving Congress? How can we better serve the Congress?
2. How well are we serving other Government agencies? How should we be serving them?
3. How well are we serving the nation's libraries? How (within our legal mandate) can we better serve the nation's public libraries, special libraries, research libraries, and other educational institutions?
4. Are our collections as widely and as fully used as they ought to be, by scholars, scientists, historians, lawyers, social scientists, poets, composers, performers, and members of the business community? How can improved administration, the addition of private and foundation resources, and more widely diffused information about our resources increase our usefulness to creative persons? How can we more effectively encourage research and creativity in the interest of the Congress and the nation?
5. How have new technological resources increased our opportunities for service to traditional constituencies and opened avenues of service to new constituencies? What can we do that we are not now doing to serve the blind and physically handicapped, to improve the nation's capacity to read, and to help instill the habit of reading? How can we better serve the media?
6. How has new technology shaped our opportunities and our duty to preserve a full record of American civilization in our time?
7. As the quantity of informational and cultural materials increases, what can we do that we are not now doing to keep the citizen from being overwhelmed by quantity, and to guide the reader and the viewer through the thickening wilderness of printed and graphic matter?
8. In a period of change in technology and in the legal protection of authors and

artists, what can the Library of Congress and its Copyright Office do "to promote the progress of science and the useful arts"?
9. In the midst of rapidly changing technology, what can the Library do to preserve and enrich the tradition of the Book?
10. In a world where many governments censor and restrict publication and inhibit free expression, are we doing everything necessary and appropriate to keep knowledge and information freely flowing into our Library from everywhere? Are we doing well all that we can to provide the Congress and the nation with a fully stocked free marketplace of the nation's and the world's knowledge and ideas? What can we do to make our collections more speedily available?

Eleven Library of Congress staff members served on the Task Force. The author of this chapter was chairman; the other members were Alan Fern, Beverly Gray, Tao-Tai Hsia, Edward Knight, Lucia Rather, Lawrence Robinson, Norman J. Shaffer, Robert D. Stevens, Elizabeth Stroup, and Glen Zimmerman. More than 160 staff members served on the 14 subcommittees established by the Task Force. The subcommittees investigated selected topics and made recommendations for Task Force consideration. The topics were: area studies, automation and reference services, bibliographic access, the bibliographic role of the Library; collection development; the cultural role of the Library; documents; loan and photoduplication services; personnel and staff development; serials; services to Congress; services to libraries; the staff as users; and the user survey. A generous grant from several private foundations enabled the Library to establish eight outside advisory groups; about ten distinguished individuals were members of each group. Each panel met at least twice during the year at the Library, reviewing the activities of the institution and suggesting possible improvements. The advisory panels and their chairmen were: arts, Patrick Hayes, managing director, Washington Performing Arts Society; humanities, Jaroslav Pelikan, dean, Graduate School, Yale University; law, Phil Neal, professor, Law School, University of Chicago; libraries, Robert Wedgeworth, executive director, American Library Association; media, David Schoumacher, WMAL-TV, Washington, D.C.; publishers, Dan Lacy, senior vice-president, McGraw-Hill, Inc.; science and technology, Gerard Piel, publisher, *Scientific American*; and social sciences, W. Allen Wallis, chancellor, University of Rochester.

The purpose of the Task Force effort was twofold: (1) to review the present activities of the institution and make recommendations for their improvement; and (2) to obtain "the constructive criticism and imaginative suggestions" of the Library's staff and others outside the Library. The staff of the Library responded to the Task Force's request for suggestions with more than 500 separate memoranda. These suggestions, plus the subcommittee and advisory group recommendations, were incorporated into the final Task Force report, which was presented to Dr. Boorstin on January 28, 1977.

On the same day, Librarian Boorstin created a new Office of Planning and Development which was given the assignment of recommending a program of action based on the Task Force and advisory group reports. At the presentation ceremony the Librarian stated that the Task Force report would serve as "the raw material, the basis of a program for a renaissance of this Library, an improvement and enlargement of our services to the Congress and to the Nation," and emphasized that its presentation was only a stage in a continuing effort, "not the epilogue but the first scene in the first act of a drama of refreshment and revival for the Library of Congress" (Librarian receives Task Force report, 1977).

V. THE TASK FORCE RECOMMENDATIONS

A. The Legislative and the National Roles

In its recommendations, the Task Force dealt directly with the question of the Library's legislative and national responsibilities, along with many other questions raised by the Librarian of Congress, the staff, and the outside advisors. The recommendations were presented in seven chapters: For Congress and the Nation (Service to Congress, Basic Responsibilities of the Library, The National Role); Access (Collection and Information Services, The Researcher in the Library, The Researcher Outside the Library); Collection Development; Bibliographic Control (A National Bibliographic System, Control of the Library's Collections); The Cultural and Educational Program of the Library; Staff Development and Communication; and Planning and Management. The final chapter, titled Unique Opportunities for Services, summarized the organizational changes outlined in earlier chapters and outlined a program for national and international library leadership.

The Task Force report is a planning document that cannot be easily summarized. It was presented to Librarian Boorstin in four parts: recommendations, supplementary documents, subcommittee reports, and advisory group reports. The Task Force recommendations (Part I) were contained in a 73-page document that represented the Task Force's distillation and evaluation of the ideas presented by the Library's staff, the subcommittees, and the advisory groups, to which the Task Force added its own insights and opinions.

The Task Force recommendations emphasized two points: that the Library of Congress should develop a sense of wholeness and a greater sense of service to all its users. The Task Force urged a continuation and a strengthening of the Library's dual role as a legislative and a national library, pointing out that "the entire Library serves both the Congress and the Nation." It deplored the administrative fragmentation that it found in the Library, noting that "each administrative unit must view itself as an integral part of the Library of Congress, not solely as an individual department or division that serves a special clientele." In the letter of transmittal accompanying the report, the panel explained:

> The creation of a sense of wholeness and the strengthening of a sense of service will take time. We feel it will result from a sharper definition of the Library's functions and responsibilities, improved planning, the unabashed exercise of leadership, a more clearly defined decision-making process, sensitivity to the needs and demands of the staff, and a greater willingness to consult with individuals and organizations outside the Library.

The Task Force, in dealing with the question of the Library's legislative and national roles, asserted that the Library of Congress could indeed provide national and even international library leadership while serving primarily as the legislative library of the U.S. Congress. In fact the Task Force stated that "the Library can fulfill the high hopes we have expressed for it only if it remains in the legislative branch." The panel affirmed its full agreement with the view expressed by the eminent librarian S. R. Ranganathan in 1950 on the occasion of the Library's sesquicentennial: "The institution serving as the national library of the United States is perhaps more fortunate than its predecessors in other countries. It has the Congress as its godfather. This stroke of good fortune has made it perhaps the most influential of all the national libraries of the world." The Task Force pointed out that in recent years the Congress has shown, through generous appropriations, an increasing appreciation for the national library leadership exercised by the Library of Congress. National library services of course benefit libraries in every part of the country. In this sense, according to the Task Force, "Congress itself has a unique opportunity to serve the entire nation through the Library of Congress."

The Task Force asserted that the fundamental question before the Library of Congress at this stage in its history was one of organizational unity: how could the Library of Congress as a whole better serve both Congress and the Nation? It pointed out that the wide-ranging needs of Congress and its committees required a comprehensive library with worldwide coverage that used the most modern information technology. Because the resources of the Library of Congress were available to the public, the national and international roles of the Library were inseparable from its most important function—serving as the library of the United States Congress. The Task Force therefore recommended "that the Library of Congress as a whole focus its total energies and resources on providing Congress with the most effective and responsive service possible."

B. Organizational Changes

The Task Force felt that the adoption of a statement of purposes, privileges, and responsibilities would be the first step in developing a formal set of policy guidelines that could be used for evaluating the Library's present services. Not only did the Library's internal services need improved coordination, but several of its activities needed refocusing and perhaps consolidation. The organizational changes recommended by the Task Force included:

1. The improvement of book delivery services through a new, unified administrative structure.
2. The establishment of a new reader guidance system which would include a reader advisory office.
3. A new focus on making the Library an active center for advanced research and scholarship.
4. The creation of a new reference department.
5. Departmental status for the Division for the Blind and Physically Handicapped.
6. The creation of a collection development office.

7. The establishment of new cataloging and automation committees.
8. The centralization of overall responsibility for the Library's cultural and educational programs.
9. A new emphasis on Library-wide planning and program review.
10. The establishment of a research office.
11. The clarification of the Library's decision-making process, primarily through a reorganized committee structure.

C. National Responsibilities

In the opinion of the Task Force, improved internal organization and communication would enable the Library of Congress to fulfill its national responsibilities in a more effective manner. The panel emphasized that the Library "must do a better job in sharing—collections, information, and people," emphasizing its function as a national clearinghouse and referral center. To do so, the Library must pay closer attention to the needs of all its users, including Members of Congress, librarians, information specialists, researchers, scholars, and the general public. For this reason the Task Force recommended, "that the Librarian of Congress establish a Board of Advisors to assist the Library in articulating and fulfilling its national responsibilities. The Board should include as members the chairman and vice-chairman of the Joint Committee on the Library and distinguished representatives from the library and scholarly communities, as well as from the Library's other constituencies." The Task Force emphasized that the proposed Board of Advisors would in no way impinge on the oversight functions now performed by the Joint Committee on the Library, nor would it replace other ad hoc advisory boards created by the Library for assistance on specific projects or programs. In fact, the Task Force felt "that the Library should consult far more frequently with representative groups from its various constituencies."

The Task Force called for the Library of Congress to work more closely with all the nation's libraries, noting that what Melvil Dewey said before the Joint Committee on the Library in 1896 was still true: the Library of Congress must become "a center to which the libraries of the whole country turn for inspiration, guidance, and practical help which can be rendered so economically and efficiently in no other possible way." It pointed out the need for the Library to create new, formal channels of communication between itself and other libraries and to encourage suggestions or criticism. For this reason, the Task Force recommended the creation of a national library office "to coordinate the services offered by the Library of Congress to other libraries, receive comments from those libraries about national services, and act as a continuing liaison between the Library and the library community." Located in the Office of the Librarian, this national library office would coordinate the Library's activities with the National Library of Medicine, the National Agricultural Library, and, through the Federal Library Committee, with all federal libraries. It would serve as a continuing liaison with all major library associations and groups, including the National Commission on Libraries and Information Science.

The Task Force recommended a program of national and international library leadership in which it was incumbent upon the Library of Congress, as a national library to:

1. Provide strong leadership in the development of a comprehensive national bibliographic system.
2. Assume leadership in creating a national preservation program.
3. Enlarge its national telephone reference service and national referral center.
4. Assume leadership in creating a systematic loan network and a national referral center.
5. Continually seek ways of making the Library's products available at a price within the financial reach of all libraries.
6. Establish a systematic outreach program through workshops, internships, and consultant services.
7. Continue to provide leadership in the establishment of standards and guidelines.
8. Enlarge its role in the cooperative acquisition of foreign materials.

The review by the Task Force on Goals, Organization, and Planning was the most conprehensive review in the Library's history. The wide scope of the review was defined by Librarian Boorstin in his charge to the Task Force. Boorstin, like Librarian MacLeish before him, viewed the Library of Congress as much more than a library—it was and should remain a national cultural institution with special obligations to the American people. This view of the Library is a natural extension of Ainsworth Rand Spofford's basic concept of the Library of Congress as both the legislative library for the American Congress and the national library of the American people. The Task Force and advisory groups without exception accepted this basic premise.

D. Relationship to Previous Reviews and Recommendations

The Task Force recommendations naturally differed in both scope and content from the recommendations of the groups or individuals mentioned earlier—the Librarian's Committee established by MacLeish in 1940 (See MacLeish, 1944), Evans' Library of Congress Planning Committee (see Library of Congress, 1947), and the Bryant memorandum along with Librarian Mumford's reply (see Mumford, 1962). The 1940 study was concerned primarily with internal matters, in particular the organization and operation of the Library's processing activities. That report also presented, however, in a skeletal outline, an organization plan for the entire Library that was eventually adopted by the MacLeish administration. The Task Force report, especially the 14 subcommittee reports, contains detailed analyses of most aspects of the Library's internal operations, including many reorganization proposals. While many organizational changes are proposed in the Task Force recommendations, no overall organizational plan is put forward.

Perhaps the major concern of both the 1947 Planning Committee report and the 1962 Bryant memorandum was the role of the Library of Congress in exercising national library leadership. Both urged the Library to demonstrate greater leadership and to expand its national library services. The 1977 Task Force report (see Library of Congress, 1977) agreed with the need for an increased leadership role for the Library, but it defined that role rather carefully and placed it in a broader context than the earlier statements: "The Task Force does not believe that everything should be collected at the Library of Congress any more than it believes that everything should be done by the Library in the area of bibliographic control." The Task Force emphasized that "the role of a national library leader is a difficult one," since in fulfilling it the Library "must be simultaneously a leader and a partner," assuming the responsibility for seeing that essential tasks are performed but always remembering "that those tasks might be best performed elsewhere."

As mentioned earlier, the Task Force dealt directly with the question of transferring the Library of Congress to the executive branch: it strongly opposed the notion and in fact advocated even closer ties with its legislative function through strengthening the Library's services to Congress. The Task Force also opposed the idea of transferring any segments of the Library to the executive branch, particularly the oft-repeated proposals to transfer either the Copyright Office of the Division for the Blind and Physically Handicapped. The question of changing or altering the Library's name to reflect its national role was considered superfluous and not addressed in the report. The 1977 recommendation to create a Board of Advisors was, however, basically the same proposal made in the 1947 report of the Library of Congress Planning Committee. Furthermore, the Planning Committee report, the Bryant memorandum and Librarian Mumford's reply, and the Task Force report all agreed on the need for new legislation that would formally recognize the Library's national role and responsibilities. The Task Force recommended that the Library prepare for Congressional action on a codification of the laws relating to the Library of Congress. Furthermore, it recommended that a statement of purposes, privileges, and responsibilities be included in the codification. Adoption of a statement such as the one that follows would formally recognize, for the first time, the important role that the Library of Congress plays in American life:

> The purpose of the Library of Congress is to provide to the Congress and its staff any reference, research, advisory, and interpretative services necessary for the performance of its legislative and representative duties. To perform this function, the Library has been granted special privileges not available to other libraries, including the receipt of copyright deposits for addition to the collections, legal provision for the acquisition of federal documents, and special treaty arrangements for the acquisition of foreign documents. These privileges carry with them obligations to serve as a major repository of the record of American civilization and a significant repository of the record of world civilization, to serve as a cultural and educational resource, to make its collections readily available for the purpose of research and scholarship, and to provide reference and information services to all citizens. These privileges also impose upon the Library the responsibility of serving as a national bibliographic center and as a leader of cooperative activities in acquisitions, cataloging, preservation, and reference work. These privileges impose related international responsibilities as well, including keeping

knowledge and information flowing freely between the United States and other nations of the world.

REFERENCES

Benco, N. L. (1976). Archibald MacLeish: The poet librarian. *Quarterly Journal of the Library of Congress* 33, 233–249.
Bryant, D. W. (1962). Memorandum on the Library of Congress, *In* "Annual Report of the Librarian of Congress for the Fiscal Year Ending June 30, 1962," pp. 89–94. Library of Congress, Washington, D.C.
Cole, J. Y. (1971). Of copyright, men, and a national library. *Quarterly Journal of the Library of Congress* 28, 114–136.
Cole, J. Y. (1973). LC and ALA, 1876–1901. *Library Journal* 98, 2965–2970.
Cole, J. Y. (1975). For Congress and the nation: The dual nature of the Library of Congress. *Quarterly Journal of the Library of Congress* 32, 118–138.
Copyright law revision. (1977). *Library of Congress Information Bulletin* 36, 30–34.
Daniel J. Boorstin sworn in as 12th Librarian of Congress. (1975). *Library of Congress Information Bulletin* 34, 447–449.
Goodrum, C. A. (1974). "The Library of Congress." Praeger, New York.
Johnston, W. D. (1904). "History of the Library of Congress, 1800–1864." U.S. Government Printing Office, Washington, D.C.
Lacy, D. (1950). The Library of Congress: A sesquicentenary review. I. The development of the collections. *Library Quarterly* 20, 157–179.
Librarian receives Task Force report. (1977). *Library of Congress Information Bulletin* 36, 89–91.
Library of Congress Planning Committee (1947). Report. *In* "Annual Report of the Librarian of Congress for the Fiscal Year Ending June 30, 1947," pp. 101–108. U.S. Government Printing Office, Washington, D.C.
Library of Congress Task Force on Goals, Organization, and Planning (1977). "Report to the Librarian of Congress." Library of Congress, Washington, D.C.
MacLeish, A. (1944). The reorganization of the Library of Congress, 1939–1944. *Library Quarterly* 14, 277–315.
Mearns, D. C. (1947). The story up to now. *In* "Annual Report of the Librarian of Congress for the Fiscal Year ending June 30, 1946," pp. 13–227. U.S. Government Printing Office, Washington, D.C.
Mumford, L. Q. (1962). Report on the Bryant memorandum. *In* "Annual Report of the Librarian of Congress for the Fiscal Year Ending June 30, 1962," pp. 94–111. Library of Congress, Washington, D.C.
Powell, B. E. (1976). Lawrence Quincy Mumford: Twenty years of progress. *Quarterly Journal of the Library of Congress* 33, 269–287.
Sittig, W. J. (1976). Luther Evans: Man for a new age. *Quarterly Journal of the Library of Congress* 33, 251–267.
Statement by the Librarian of Congress. (1976). *Library of Congress Information Bulletin* 35, 233–234.

Text of remarks exchanged . . . at swearing-in, November 12, 1975. (1975). *Library of Congress Information Bulletin* **34**, 458–461.

The Library of Congress as the national library: Potentialities for service. (1969). A statement prepared by the staff of the Library for the National Advisory Commission on Libraries. *In* "Libraries at Large: Tradition, Innovation, and the National Interest" (D. M. Knight and E. S. Nourse, eds.), pp. 435–465. Bowker, New York.

Affirmative Action and American Librarianship

ELIZABETH DICKINSON

Broward County Division of Libraries,
Fort Lauderdale, Florida

and

MARGARET MYERS

American Library Association

I. Introduction	82
II. Affirmative Action and Librarianship	83
A. Legal Aspects	83
B. Socioeconomic Trends	86
C. Librarians' Commitment to the Concept	97
III. Prospects for the Future	121
A. Trend and Survey Data	121
B. Research Needs	122
C. Recruitment and Training Efforts	124
D. Employment Procedures and Practices	124
IV. Conclusion	127
References	128

I. INTRODUCTION

The principles of nondiscrimination and equal employment opportunity have evolved from Constitutional guarantees regarding basic human and civil rights which have been defined through various federal and state legislation and judicial decisions. Equal employment opportunity was part of the larger civil rights movement along with the other issues of voting rights, fair housing, public accommodation, and educational equality. In addition, the women's movement has added emphasis to educational and employment equality concerns.

Early efforts in preventing discrimination, beginning in the 1940s, were based on the assumption that open hiring practices would eliminate discrimination. Primarily, the attempts to eliminate discrimination focused on federal employment. By the 1960s, however, it was clear the discriminatory patterns still remained even if there was no conscious intent or overt discrimination on the part of employers. The patterns would persist until there was more deliberate action; therefore, a series of programs were initiated to effect positive or affirmative action. Perhaps the 1960s can best be viewed as an era of legislation, while the 1970s should be considered the era of enforcement, as regulations appear and more concerted efforts at monitoring institutions and organizations are taking place.

Affirmative action has become part of the national policy of the United States. Discrimination is not only a legal issue, but a moral and financial one as well. Affirmative action goes beyond neutral, nondiscriminatory policies. The concept of affirmative action implies that discrimination in employment will be eliminated only through systematically identifying and changing institutional structures that perpetuate inequality. As used by the federal government, affirmative action refers to an employer-initiated set of specific result-oriented policies, guidelines, and procedures designed to ensure that job applicants and employees are treated without regard to race, color, religion, sex, or national origin. Affirmative action requires that specific steps be taken to eliminate conditions which have resulted in limited participation by women and minorities. It commits an employer to apply "good faith" efforts to eliminate both the present effects of past discrimination as well as future discrimination. This involves developing and implementing a plan which identifies sources of discrimination and details steps for its alleviation as well as monitoring, evaluating, and modifying ongoing procedures.

Walton (1974) suggests a two-stage definition of affirmative action: (1) those activities the organization undertakes to ensure that no policy, procedure, or practice in its personnel system unfairly or adversely affects the interests of any group of applicants and/or employees; (2) those activities the organization undertakes to assist applicants and employees to overcome societal discrimination or biased organizational personnel policies, procedures, and practices, and achieve that maximum opportunity to fulfill their highest potential. He labels the first stage as *corrective* affirmative action, which involves a critical examination of the personnel system in order to determine if any practice is discriminatory. The second stage is seen as *positive* affirmative action which consists of a more sensitive application of personnel policies and creative ways to address recruitment, job development, selection, training, reassignments, and transfers.

Unfortunately, however, there is still much confusion and uncertainty over what affirmative action is intended to accomplish, how well it is working, what the effects have been, and what the future will hold. Many librarians are just beginning to learn of the implications of affirmative action in their own work settings. Meanwhile, the literature of affirmative action grows each year, and a large number of services, businesses, and organizations have been formed to provide assistance in affirmative action planning and implementation. "Affirmative action programs" is a phrase now beginning to find its way into the subject heading nomenclature (King, 1977).

This chapter attempts to give an overview of the legal and socioeconomic aspects of affirmative action in general, as well as the present commitment within librarianship to this concept, and its prospects for the future.

II. AFFIRMATIVE ACTION AND LIBRARIANSHIP

A. Legal Aspects

Equal employment opportunity is mandated by a variety of presidential executive orders, federal and state antidiscrimination laws, judicial decisions, and laws regulating collective bargaining agreements. In addition, individual institutional policies prohibit discrimination and, thus, support affirmative action in employment.

Equal employment legislation prohibits discrimination in many areas: access to employment (recruitment, advertising, application, and interviewing procedures); hiring and promotion (selection practices, tenure, demotion, layoff, or termination); compensation; job assignments; leaves of absence; fringe benefits; and labor organization contracts or professional agreements.

The various laws and executive orders are detailed in numerous publications and will only be briefly described in this review (Higgins, 1976; U.S. Equal Employment Opportunity Commission, 1974, 1975; U.S. Office for Civil Rights, 1972; U.S. Office of Education, 1975). Because libraries are affected by this general legislation, it is important to be aware of the various requirements.

The Equal Pay Act of 1963, an amendment to the Fair Labor Standards Act, prohibits discrimination on the basis of sex in payment of wages for equal work in jobs that require equal skill, effort, and responsibility, and are performed under similar working conditions, even when job titles and assignments are not identical. Amendments in 1972 and 1974 extended this act to all professionals, outside salespersons, and federal, state, and local government employees. The Department of Labor Wage and Hour Division enforces this act, along with the U. S. Civil Service Commission; the latter monitors most federal government employees (except Library of Congress, Postal Service, and TVA).

The Title VII of the Civil Rights Act, as amended by the Equal Employment Opportunity Act of 1972, prohibits discrimination by sex, race, color, religion, or national origin. This includes hiring, firing, wages, fringe benefits, classifying, assignment, promotion, training, retraining, apprenticeships, or any other terms, conditions, or privileges of employment. The 1972 amendments extended coverage to educational institutions, state and local governmental agencies, and political subdivisions with more than 15 employees; thus they cover all academic, school, and most public libraries. The Equal Opportunity Commission enforces this act, although, where state or local fair employment practices laws provide procedures for the handling of discrimination complaints, the complaint is referred to the state agency first. The Equal Employment Opportunity Commission (EEOC) guidelines provide specific policies and practices to follow, while judicial interpretations have further defined the nature of discrimination and the remedial actions necessary to alleviate it.

The Executive Order 11246 of 1965, as amended by 11375 in

1968, states that employers with federal contracts in excess of $10,000 must take affirmative action to ensure that applicants are employed (and their employment treated) without regard to race, religion, color, sex, or national origin. This mandate is implemented with Department of Labor regulations through the Office for Federal Contract Compliance (OFCC). Responsibilities for monitoring are assigned by OFCC to a number of executive departments or agencies. The OFCC has designated the Department of Health, Education, and Welfare as the compliance agency for all college and universities.

Revised Order 4 of 1970 assures that nonconstruction contractors with federal contracts of $50,000 or more, and with more than 50 employees, have written affirmative action programs within 120 days after commencing the contract. The plan must determine if minorities and women are underutilized and set forth specific goals and timetables for remedying any underutilization. This represents a process of self-analysis by the employer intended to determine what must be done to ensure the prompt and full utilization of minorities and women.

The Age Discrimination in Employment Act of 1967 prohibits employers, employment agencies, and labor unions from discrimination on the basis of age against any person between 40 and 65 in hiring, firing, promotion, or other aspects of employment. This applies to employers of 20 or more and is administered by the Department of Labor Wage & Hour Division.

The Vocational Rehabilitation Act of 1973 and the Rehabilitation Act Amendments of 1974 instruct every employer with more than $2,500 in contracts with the federal government to take affirmative action to employ and advance qualified handicapped people without discrimination based on their physical or mental handicap. Section 503 of the Act deals with this requirement and is enforced through the Department of Labor. Regulations of Section 504 will be monitored by the Department of Health, Education, and Welfare and will provide for nondiscrimination in any institution receiving federal financial assistance.

The Vietnam Era Veterans Readjustment Act of 1974, Section 402, amends the 1972 act and ensures that government contractors holding contracts of over $10,000 take affirmative action to employ and promote disabled veterans and veterans of the Vietnam War. The act is enforced by the Department of Labor.

Title IX of the 1972 Education Amendments prohibits discrimination on the basis of sex in employment (or recruitment) in any educational program or activity which receives federal financial assistance. The Office for Civil Rights in the Department of Health, Education, and Welfare monitors implementation of Title IX.

Judicial interpretations of Title VII, and related federal laws, have extended the principles of affirmative action. Precedents have been established for a number of key concepts. Action to eliminate employment discrimination must apply to all members of the "affected class" to which an individual complainant belongs. It is not the intent, but the consequences, of an employment practice which determines whether discrimination exists. Even if an employment practice is neutral in intent or is fairly administered, it might be considered discriminatory if it has a "disparate effect" on members of a "protected class" (those groups specified in the law). Unless the policy is shown to be a "business necessity" and is validated, it constitutes unlawful discrimination.

The burden of proof is on the employer to show that highly disproportionate representation of minorities or women in any job classification in relation to their availability in the population or work force are not the result of overt or institutional discrimination.

Additional judicial decisions will undoubtedly continue to specify the coverage, procedures, and requirements for corrective and affirmative action in the future. Enforcement agency interpretations are also subject to modification.

B. Socioeconomic Trends

1. GENERAL

According to Staines *et al.* (1976), discrimination indicators fall into objective and subjective categories. Subjective indicators measure the level of consciousness-raising among those discriminated against. Objective indicators trace the economic impact of discrimination upon women and minorities. Generally, changes in objective discrimination lag behind awareness-level, subjective trends.

Staines *et al.* analyzed national surveys taken under comparable conditions in 1969–1970 and 1972–1973 to determine trends in sex discrimination. The study indicates that the number of individuals surveyed who felt they had been discriminated against in their jobs on the basis of sex doubled, jumping from 8 percent in 1969 to 16 percent in 1973. In the same period, reported discrimination among minorities who were surveyed remained fairly constant, from 17 percent of the minority members polled in 1969 to 15 percent in 1973. To measure subjective discrimination respondents were asked "Do you feel in any way discriminated against on your job because you are a woman?" (or member of a minority group). The question measures only a limited aspect of subjective discrimination, but is one indicator of changes in levels of discrimination awareness.

The average annual salary discrimination, measuring the difference between actual pay of all women surveyed and what they should have been earning compared to men in analogous positions, with similar years of education and experience, remained virtually unchanged, from −$3,242 in 1969 to −$3,208 in 1973. (These figures illustrate the negative impact on women's salaries.) Women in professional and administrative positions found objective discrimination easing somewhat over the three-year period. Women in the top job category, however, still experienced high levels of disparity in salary (−$3,500 or more) in 49 percent of the cases, which was down from the 1969 level of 69 percent.

The Women's Bureau of the Department of Labor has reported that the earnings gap between male and female workers is increasing. The current differential is $3,433 a year for full-time women workers, while in 1955 the difference was half that amount (Affirmative (In) Action, 1977). Census statistics indicate that the salary gap between 1950 and 1970 changed very little. In 1950 the median earnings of experienced women professional workers was 60.7 percent that of male professionals, while in 1970 the percentage of the earnings of female professional workers was 61.7 percent that of their male counterparts (Reilly and Bouvier, 1976).

2. LIBRARIANSHIP

Few, if any, studies exist which measure the extent to which librarians are aware of discrimination within the profession (subjective indicators). On the other hand, we are beginning to collect good objective trend data on earning power and position between male and female librarians and, to a lesser degree, for minority versus nonminority librarians.

Despite the lack of statistical studies treating subjective indicators of discrimination in librarianship, there are numerous signs that our consciousness is being raised. Within this decade a number of women's and minority groups have formed, in part, to serve as forums on discrimination-based problems and to lobby for an end to inequities. Minority groups within librarianship include the Black Caucus, the Asian American Librarians Caucus, Library Services for American Indian People, and REFORMA: National Association of Spanish-Speaking Librarians. The American Library Association sponsors several women's units including the Task Force on Women, the Committee on the Status of Women in Librarianship, and discussion groups within some of the divisions. The American Association of Library Schools added an interest group on women in librarianship in 1976. Additionally, Women Library Workers and groups within the Canadian Library Association and other organizations are helping to raise the awareness level of the profession with regard to discrimination. The ALA Office for Library Personnel Resources (OLPR) compiles a list of minority and women's organizations within librarianship, which is available with ALA/OLPR's (1975a) *Affirmative Action Information Packet*.

Although there is some statistical evidence indicating improved status for women and minorities, most objective indicators show little or no change in their educational or economic stance. With few exceptions, Schiller's (1974) observation remains true: "a review of national surveys of librarians over the past twenty-five years reveals a consistent pattern: a continuing existence of significant salary and position level differentials between men and women. At no time during this period has the status of women librarians been equal to men's." A similar note may be echoed with regard to minority librarians. The relatively static conditions indicate the need for strengthened affirmative action programs and also cast some doubt on the effectiveness of current plans.

a. Educational Programs. The most comprehensive and current information available on the ethnic and sexual composition of library degree programs is gathered by the American Library Association annually. A recent survey of degree programs (published in 1977) contains data for the academic year 1974/1975. The ethnic composition of the graduates of all types of library degree programs in 1974/1975 was essentially unchanged over the previous year (Table I).

In 1974/1975 graduates from master's degree programs of all types were 89.8 percent white, 5.3 percent Black, 1.9 percent Asian–

TABLE I
Ethnicity of Graduates from All Types of Library
Education Programs 1973–1974 and 1974–1975[a]

Ethnic group	1973–1974	1974–1975
White	89.2%	90.2%
Black	5.7%	5.2%
Asian–American	2.0%	1.9%
Other	1.5%	1.5%
Spanish-surnamed	1.3%	1.1%
American Indian	0.1%	0.2%

[a] From American Library Association, Office for Library Personnel Resources (1975b, table 1; 1977, table 1).

American, 1.1 percent Spanish-surnamed, .2 percent American Indian, and 1.7 percent other. (ALA/OLPR, 1977, Table 1). When the 1973/1974 data were compared to *Racial and Ethnic Data from Institutions of Higher Education, Fall 1970* (U.S. Department of Health, Education, and Welfare) and other sources, the OLPR staff concluded that Black and Asian–American degree recipients occur in numbers equal to their availability in the pool of undergraduate degree holders, while American Indian and Spanish-surnamed library school graduates are not represented as well as their availability pools would indicate (ALA/OLPR, 1975b). Although the percentages of minority enrollment in library degree programs is approaching the number available, the figures are still quite small compared to the total minority population within the United States. More clearly needs to be done to attract qualified minorities into general undergraduate programs, and then into library school programs.

According to the latest ALA/OLPR library degree program survey, 78.9 percent of master's level graduates are women, while only 37.2 percent of the doctorate level graduates are women (ALA/OLPR, 1977, Table 1). The WEAL Education and Legal Defense Fund determined that between 1969 and 1972, 81.34 percent of the master's degrees in library science were earned by women, while 38.46 percent of the doctorates were conferred upon women (WEAL, 1975). The WEAL figures show a slow trend toward equalization. While the percent of total master's degrees in library science awarded to women decreased between 1969 and 1972 by 3.14 percent, the number of doctorates given to women librarians increased by 3.75 percent.

b. Employment Picture—Women. Schiller (1974) cites many salary and position trend surveys for female librarians to 1972. The following review is meant to update Schiller's analysis. The data show, for the most part, continuing and sizable differentials between male and female librarians.

Schiller (1971) reports that the percentage of female deans and directors of ALA-accredited library schools in the United States dropped steadily from 1950 to 1970: from 50 percent in 1950, to 27 percent in 1960, and 19 percent in 1970. Bidlack (1976, 1977) reports little improvement. During the 1975/1976 academic year, in the United States and Canada, only 20 percent of the deans and directors of accredited library school programs were women, and in 1976/1977 the percentage of women library school heads had dropped to 19 percent.

According to the salary figures Bidlack (1976) collected from 62 schools reporting for the academic year 1975/1976, the median salary for the female library school deans (on a fiscal year appointment) was $29,707, while the median for their male counterparts was $31,250—a 5 percent differential in salary. Of the 697 full-time faculty reported in the Bidlack survey the salary differentials work in favor of male faculty members by 5 percent for those on fiscal year appointments and by 14 percent for those appointed on an academic year basis (Bidlack, 1976, derived from table). Bidlack's 1976/1977 survey reveals no change in the pay differential for full-time fiscal year faculty, although the discrepancy had decreased to 10 percent for women faculty appointed on an academic year basis (Bidlack, 1977, derived from tables).

The Association of College and Research Libraries salary survey (ALA/ACRL, 1976) gives the latest and most comprehensive picture of the status of women in academic libraries as indicated by salary and position data. This survey reveals that, while women compose 61.5 percent of the academic librarians, they head only 35.8 percent of the libraries. There is a difference in salaries at every level, increasing with level of position, from 3.2 percent for beginning professionals to 23.3 percent for academic library directors.

Trend information cited by Tarr (1973) further illustrates the erosion of the position of women in academic libraries. In 1930, 19 of the heads of the 74 largest college and university libraries were women, while in 1969 there were only three women in the top posts in these same libraries.

Goldstein and Hill surveyed 140 health science libraries for data on the current librarian and the 1950 incumbent. Predictably, the survey reveals a decline in the position of women in these libraries. In these 140 libraries 77.4 percent of the total staff were women, and yet men headed 59.4 percent of the same libraries. In 1950 men directed only 17 percent of these libraries. When data for the 25 largest libraries is tallied, the figures indicate that larger institutions are even more likely to be headed by men. In the 25 largest health science libraries studied, 75.2 percent of all staff were women, while 75 percent of the directorships were held by men (Goldstein and Hill, 1975).

The Special Libraries Association salary survey conducted every three years illustrates the static nature of the salary differentials over a period of time. The median salary for women respondents was 77 percent of that for male special librarians surveyed in 1970, and 76 percent in 1973. In 1976 the median salary, however, had increased to 81 percent of that for males. This latest survey also documents a familiar pattern in that salary discrimination increases with the age of the respondents. A cross-correlation of age and sex shows that salary distribution is almost identical for males and females in the 20- to 29-year group but a difference in favor of the males appears in the 30- to 39-year age group and increases thereafter (SLA, 1970, 1973, 1976).

Shifts in power have also occurred in public libraries. Marley (1975) determined through the 1951 and 1974 editions of the *American Library Directory* that in the 25 largest communities in each of four states—Indiana, Kentucky, Michigan, and Ohio—there was a 27-percent decrease in the number of public libraries directed by women. The authors checked the same cities in the 1976/1977 edition of the *American Library Directory* and discovered another 2 percent decline in the percentage of women library directors in these libraries. The comparison of 1950 data with that of 1976 yields a 29-percent drop in the number of directorships that women fill.

The Carpenter and Shearer biennial surveys of public library support and salaries (Carpenter and Shearer, 1972, 1974; Shearer and Carpenter, 1976) provide useful trend information on the support provided to public libraries directed by women compared with those run by men. On the bright side, Carpenter and Shearer see a decrease in the difference between the per capita income commanded by male- and female-directed libraries. The male-directed libraries received 30 percent more in per capita income in 1971 than libraries headed by women, 23 percent more in 1973, but only 19 percent more in 1975 (Shearer and Carpenter, 1976).

Although the differential in pay between male and female directors is decreasing slightly (Table II) Shearer and Carpenter (1976) comment, "Sex continues to account for substantial variation in directors' salaries, nearly unchanged from our earlier surveys."

Since the 750,000+ category contained just two women in 1973 and three in 1975, these results may be largely ignored. The figures for both years, however, suggest that salary discrimination decreases as the size of the library (by population served) increases.

The Frarey and Learmont (1974, 1975) placement and salary studies, as updated by the Learmont and Darling (1976) survey, delineate salary differentials between beginning level male and female librarians (Tables III and IV). The figures in Tables III and IV imply, for the most part, static conditions with respect to the pay differential between male and female beginning librarians. The only notable change is the increase, from 4.8 percent to 15.1 percent between 1974 and 1975, in the median salary difference between male and female school librarians. No explanation of this phenomenon can be discerned

TABLE II
Differential in Directors' Median Salaries in 1973 and 1975 by Sex of Director and Size of Population Served[a]

	Differential male-to-female salaries	
Size of population	1973	1975
100,000–199,999	$3,850 (26%)	$3,520 (20%)
200,000–399,999	$2,360 (14%)	$2,860 (14%)
400,000–749,999	$1,940 (9%)	$1,900 (7%)
750,000+	−$ 120 (−0.4%)	−$2,360 (−7%)
All	$4,740 (30%)	$5,250 (28%)

[a]From Carpenter and Shearer (1974, table 4, p. 104) and Shearer and Carpenter (1976, table 5, p. 781).

TABLE III
Median Salaries for Beginning Professional Librarians in the United States and Canada, in All Types of Libraries, 1973–1975[a]

	1973	1974	1975
Male	$9,303	$10,184	$10,350
Female	$9,000	$9,600	$9,980
Percentage difference male–female	3.3%	5.7%	3.6%

[a] From Frarey and Learmont (1974, data from table 7, p. 1771), Frarey and Learmont (1975, data from table 7, p. 1772), and Learmont and Darling (1976, data from table 7, p. 1492).

TABLE IV
Median Salaries for Beginning Professional Librarians in the United States and Canada by Type of Library, 1973–1975[a]

Type of library and personnel	1973	1974	1975
Public libraries			
Male beginning librarians	$8,911	$9,890	$9,820
Female beginning librarians	$8,728	$9,500	$9,500
Percentage difference male–female	2.1%	3.9%	3.3%
Academic libraries			
Male beginning librarians	$9,325	$10,000	$10,545
Female beginning librarians	$9,000	$9,500	$10,000
Percentage difference male–female	3.5%	5.0%	5.2%
School libraries			
Male beginning librarians	$9,625	$10,500	$12,250
Female beginning librarians	$9,075	$10,000	$10,400
Percentage difference male–female	5.7%	4.8%	15.1%
Other types of libraries			
Male beginning librarians	$10,020	$10,469	$10,500
Female beginning librarians	$9,400	$9,600	$10,000
Percentage difference male–female	6.2%	8.3%	4.8%

[a] From Frarey and Learmont (1974, data from table 11, p. 1773), Frarey and Learmont (1975, data from table 11, p. 1773), and Learmont and Darling (1976, data from table 11, p. 1493).

from the data. Further research would also be required to explain the relatively low differences in pay between male and female beginning-level public librarians compared with those in other types of libraries. Perhaps the prevalence of civil service systems in public libraries, with well-developed pay structures, plays a role in keeping the salaries of beginning male and female public librarians relatively equal.

There are signs that the position and salary picture with regard to women librarians may be improving, although sizable discrepancies in the employment status of male and female librarians continue to exist even for those with equivalent levels of education and experience. Schiller (1974) concludes that the salaries of women librarians are, overall, 75 percent of that of men. The U.S. Bureau of Labor Statistics (BLS) (1975) *Library Manpower* study estimates that in 1969 this differential in the mean salaries of male and female librarians was 35 percent. While the pay situation of women librarians who have reached the highest levels remains highly disadvantaged, women with fewer years of experience and at lower classification levels do not fare as badly. Perhaps another five to ten years of salary surveys will tell whether the younger female librarians of today will fall victim to the unfortunate pattern of the past, or will be the recipients of genuine "equal pay for equal work."

c. Employment Picture—Minorities. Statistical data on the position and salaries of minority librarians are scarce and incomplete. Minority work-force and salary information remains one of the areas in which further research is most needed. The ALA Library Administration Division conducted a survey in 1969 which concluded that only 8 percent of the professionals in public libraries and 4 percent in academic libraries were minority members (Frame and Anderson, 1969). The Bureau of Labor Statistics (BLS) conducted a survey in 1973 which indicates that 26 percent of the professionals in school libraries are minorities, with the corresponding figures of 13 percent in public and 9 percent in academic libraries (US BLS, 1975).

A limited survey by the Black Caucus in 1974 of 10 public and 13 academic libraries revealed that Black librarians represented 8 percent of the staffs in the public libraries surveyed and 2 percent in the academic libraries (Josey, 1975). Rayford (1972) conducted a study on the status of Black librarians in law school libraries and discovered few Blacks in the libraries surveyed. The lack of credentials or the resources necessary to obtain advanced degrees were cited as major barriers for Blacks in qualifying for employment as law librarians.

In a 1976 Special Libraries Association (SLA) salary survey an attempt was made to determine the relative representation of minority groups among SLA members. Of 4,233 respondents, 192 or 4.5 percent indicated minority status (1.5 percent Black; 2.3 percent Asian, and 0.7 percent American Indian, Spanish-speaking, and other). The means and medians of salaries for all minority groups were below the overall averages.

Table V gives the race or ethnic background of male and female library workers as represented in the 1970 census. This tabulation of old data is the most comprehensive information available on the numbers of minority librarians in the work force.

Trejo (1976) identified 245 individuals of Hispanic heritage for his directory of Spanish-speaking/Spanish-surnamed librarians, *Quien es quien*. There is only one Hispanic-heritage librarian per 43,171 Spanish-speaking or Spanish-surnamed individuals in the United States, whereas there is one librarian in the aggregate for every 1,800 Americans in the total population. Most of the Spanish-speaking librarians are concentrated in California (50), Puerto Rico (34), Florida (27), New York (25), and Texas (23). Trejo concludes, "while there is a margin for error in our figures they obviously reveal the paucity of Spanish-speaking librarians available to serve this ever-increasing segment of the population of the U.S."

One of the most recent and revealing surveys of minority librarians is contained within the Association of College and Research Libraries (ACRL) salary survey (ALA/ACRL, 1976). Minority men and women account for 9.6 percent of all librarians in the 1,208 academic libraries that responded to the survey. The largest percentage of these minority librarians work at the lowest professional level (11 percent), or in subject specialties (10.6 percent), while fewer are represented in the highest category (6.8 percent at the director level). The ACRL survey concludes that, while minority male librarians are paid more than female minority professionals, the average salaries for all minority librarians "are at every level less than for all staff combined."

The "best guess," based on the scanty aggregate data, is that approximately 10–12 percent of the librarians with master's-level training are members of a minority group. They are recruited into library schools, according to the ALA/OLPR data, in numbers which begin to

TABLE V

Race and Spanish Origin of the Experienced Civilian Labor Force by Detailed Occupation and Sex: 1970[a,b]

Position	Total[c]	White	Black	Ethnic groups				
				American Indian	Japanese	Chinese	Filipino	Persons of Spanish origin[d]
Male librarians	22,819	21,052	1,298	51	88	215	45	524
Female librarians	100,325	92,102	6,670	147	527	561	183	1,430
Male library attendants and assistants	27,081	23,948	2,586	—	178	252	22	910
Female library attendants and assistants	100,926	91,717	7,563	266	624	529	70	1,835

[a] From *Census of Population: 1970, Occupational Characteristics*, Subject Reports, Final Report PC (2)-7A, Bureau of the Census, 1973, pp. 12 and 17. In American Library Association, Office for Library Personnel Resources (1975a).
[b] Data based on 5 percent sample.
[c] Total includes other races not shown separately.
[d] Persons of Spanish origin may be of any race. Thus, all persons included here are also included in the race categories.

match their availability among undergraduate degree holders, particularly if they are Blacks or Asian–Americans. Libraries employ minority librarians at the lower professional levels in numbers which approach the availability of the minority individuals who hold master's degree credentials (ALA/ACRL, 1976; Frame and Anderson, 1969; Josey, 1975; US BLS, 1975). The promotional opportunities for minority librarians need further study. The ALA/ACRL survey (1976) and comments from respondents to the 1974 Black Caucus questionnaire (Josey, 1975) indicate that minorities are not represented in decision-making positions within libraries in numbers comparable to their availability.

C. The Librarian's Commitment to the Concept

Elizabeth Martinez-Smith (1971) wrote, "What this profession needs is commitment to the recruitment of minorities. Until we have this commitment—backed up by money—we only play the game of 'institutional racism'". Equal opportunity laws and library affirmative action plans are never effective without the determined effort and cooperation of professional associations, library school recruiters, and library employers.

1. ASSOCIATION ACTIVITIES

To enhance the commitment within librarianship, library associations must take a leadership role in interpreting affirmative action requirements and statistical data, in lobbying for clearer regulations and more effective enforcement, and in monitoring the results of affirmative action plan development.

The American Library Association has made a number of significant contributions. The ALA Council passed a policy statement regarding equal employment opportunity in January 1974. It resolved to review Association policies and procedures, provide investigation of discrimination-based complaints that are brought to the Association's attention, lobby for antidiscrimination legislation, provide guidelines on prevention of discrimination, and conduct a review of library and library school plans. The policy assures "equality of opportunity for all library employees, or applicants for employment, regardless of race, color, creed, sex, age, physical or mental handicap, individual life style (viz., manner and mode of attire, sexual preference, political persuasion) or national origin" (ALA, 1976a). The protection of library workers on the basis of life style goes beyond federal requirements. The other categories are all mandated by federal regulations.

Under the direction of Barbara Slanker and Marilyn Salazar, the American Library Association sponsored an Affirmative Action Institute in December 1974 to provide academic and public library directors and personnel officers with an introduction to personnel policies and practices that would aid them in the development of affirmative action programs. Participants were to begin to develop plans during the week-long institute. The program was also to serve as a model for additional workshops (Slanker, 1975). The efforts of the University of Wisconsin in this regard are described in an article by Jane E. Marshall (1975).

The 1971 American Library Association preconference on the recruitment of minorities recommended that the Association fund a minority recruiter (Childers and Adams, 1972). In 1972 the American Library Association created this position, now within the Office for Library Personnel Resources. Major duties of the Minority Recruitment Specialist have included referral of qualified minorities to library schools, consultation with minority educational associations and representation at their conferences, compiling the annual *Survey of Graduates and Faculty of U. S. Library Education Programs Awarding Degrees and Certificates,* and managing the Illinois Minorities Manpower Project (May 1972–August 1974).

The Office for Library Personnel Resources distributes an *Affirmative Action Information Packet* (ALA/OLPR, 1975a), which contains guidelines for affirmative action plan development, the American Library Association's policy statement, a list of federal and state laws and major court cases, reprints of articles on library affirmative action, and statistical data. This packet is of value to any library in the process of writing or revising an affirmative action plan.

The Equal Employment Opportunity Subcommittee of ALA's OLPR Advisory Committee is charged with carrying out the Association's mandate to review the affirmative action plans of all those libraries and library schools voluntarily submitting them, and to offer guidance on improvements that might be made within these plans. The Subcommittee, in operation since 1975, has developed guidelines for library affirmative action plans, and is in the process of reviewing the documents that have been received (ALA, EEO Subcommittee,

1976). The EEO Subcommittee's role is educational, while investigations of discrimination-based "requests for action" received by ALA are assigned to the Staff Committee on Mediation, Arbitration, and Inquiry (SCMAI).

Many other ALA and related units have contributed to an understanding of, and commitment to, affirmative action within the profession. Various minority caucuses provide resource lists or directories. The caucuses and the Task Force on Women have generated many of the affirmative action-oriented resolutions brought before the ALA membership and Council, and have helped to raise the level of consciousness within the profession through programs on affirmative action. The Public Library Association (PLA) sponsored as part of its Idea Exchange Program at the 1976 annual ALA conference a workshop offering basic information on affirmative action. The Library Administration Division (LAD) is developing a list of permissible and inadmissible interview questions. The Health and Rehabilitation Services Division (HRSD) offered a program at the 1977 ALA conference in Detroit on affirmative action for the handicapped.

The Committee on Accreditation (COA) is obligated to take into account the commitment to affirmative action at each library school it visits and to report annually to Council on its findings. In 1975–1976 it concluded that "it is apparent from COA's experience during the past two years that considerable progress has been made throughout institutions of higher education to correct salary and other inequities in relationship to women and minority faculty members" (ALA, Committee on Accreditation, 1976). The Legislation Committee and the ALA Washington Office testified before Congress in 1975 in support of increased funding for the affirmative action enforcement programs of the U. S. Department of Health, Education, and Welfare (ALA, Legislation Committee, 1976).

ALA Council's affirmative action-oriented activities during 1976–1977 include approval for a checkoff on ALA membership renewal forms for the minority scholarship and passage of a resolution calling on various ALA units to "combat racism and sexism in the library profession and in library service" through revision of biased cataloging terminology and development of racism/sexism awareness training programs (ALA, 1976d; Jones, 1977). In addition, a resolution was adopted to encourage graduate library schools to enrich their curricula to ensure the inclusion of course content which reflects the cultural heritage and needs of the Spanish-speaking and to add bilingual/bicultural individuals to their faculties (ALA, 1976c).

Other library groups have sponsored affirmative action programs. The Michigan Library Association held two workshops on affirmative action at its 1976 annual conference. The California Library Association (CLA) has been particularly active in this regard. It adopted a policy statement on affirmative action in 1975 (Garland, 1975). The 1977 CLA annual conference posted no less than 11 sessions devoted to minority or women's concerns or discrimination issues (Berry, 1977). The Mountain-Plains Library Association created a slide-tape show on affirmative action, and in 1976 the Pennsylvania State Library conducted a three-day institute on affirmative action. The 1975 WICHE/USOE Institute on Training for Staff Development also included sections on affirmative action.

Both the Special Libraries Association (SLA) and the Medical Library Association (MLA) have passed policy statements on equal employment opportunity. In June 1974 SLA adopted a resolution calling for "equal pay for equal work, equal opportunity for professional growth and promotions to a higher administrative echelon in special libraries" (SLA, Special Committee, 1976). The Special Committee on the Pilot Education Project of SLA was charged with launching an educational program to alert librarians and others to the need for equal pay and opportunity. The MLA affirmative action policy includes a plan for the Association itself, and a resolution urging MLA members to employ and train qualified minority members and to combat prejudicial attitudes among medical library staff through awareness programs (MLA, 1973a). One result of this resolution was the development of a human rights bibliography (MLA, 1973b).

2. RECRUITMENT AND TRAINING

The Illinois Minorities Manpower Project (Salazar, 1976), a cooperative effort between the Illinois State Library, ALA, Rosary College School of Library Science, several library systems, and minority community representatives, successfully recruited and trained several minority members to librarianship. Especially noteworthy was its attempt to follow through the whole process in one program, from initial recruitment, scholarship award, master's-level training, internship program at Chicago-area library systems, counseling, and job placement. Eight of the original ten applicants finished the program and were successfully placed in professional positions. Several have received promotions since that time. Although the project experienced some problems, most notably in the areas of attracting qualified candidates from all minority groups and in obtaining full cooperation from all of the groups originally involved in the planning, it remains a model for other recruitment efforts (Salazar, 1976).

A number of other library organizations and educational institutions have undertaken minority recruitment projects. These include the University of Texas, Austin, the states of California, Massachusetts, and Illinois, the New England Library Association and the California Library Association (Salazar, 1976). Other recruitment programs were launched in the early 1970s by the University of Michigan School of Library Science and Columbia University. The Columbia minority intern program funded seven minority members during a three-year period. The program was discontinued in 1975–1976, according to documentation returned with the authors' survey, because Columbia University Libraries "were not able to attract applicants who were interested in academic librarianship or who were able to meet the requirements for admission to the School of Library Service." The Tucson Public Library and the California State Library also have instituted minority scholarship programs.

In a survey of American accredited library schools, Salazar (1977) found that financial assistance was considered essential if library schools were to recruit minorities. Funds from the U. S. Office of Education through the Higher Education Act (HEA) Title II-B Fellowship and Institute program played the largest role, followed by individual institutional funding. Recruitment of minority students was also accomplished through contacts with academic librarians employed in undergraduate institutions where there were high concentrations of minorities enrolled. Special brochures were distributed and contacts were made through alumni or faculty–student committees. Advertising and career days were used less frequently.

In testimony to the House Labor-HEW Appropriations Committee regarding funding for library training programs under HEA II-B, Bidlack (1975) pointed out that during the past four or five years, the emphasis of the Title II-B training program has been to attract minorities to careers in librarianship. For example, the University of Michigan library school minority enrollment had increased from about 4 percent in 1968 to 10 percent in 1975; this would have been impossible without federal support.

Likewise, in 1974, a cooperative doctoral program in library science was offered by a number of midwestern universities (Wisconsin, Minnesota, Michigan, Illinois, Chicago, and Indiana), where an HEA II-B grant enabled 18 minority librarians to receive fellowships to study at the doctoral level. It is interesting to note that more than 100 minority librarians applied for these 18 fellowships.

In addition to HEA II-B institutes on services to, and materials for, ethnic and handicapped populations, institutes have been federally funded during 1974–1977 for training American Indian library technical assistants (Fort Wright College, Spokane); library aide training for American Indians (University of New Mexico); design of affirmative action plans (American Library Association); multicultural librarianship (University of Michigan); introducing handicapped persons as paraprofessionals in libraries (California Community College, Sacramento); intercultural communication processes (University of Texas, Austin); women in library management (State University of New York–Buffalo); and paraprofessional training for American Indian Information Centers (Oklahoma City University).

HEA II-B also provided funding for 15 Spanish-speaking librarians to complete graduate degrees at the University of Arizona in 1975/1976. Cabello-Argandoña (1976) describes funding over a three-year period from 1972 to 1975 for recruiting and training Chicano librarians at California State University, Fullerton.

In 1976, Norman Higgins, Professor of Education at Arizona State University, received a U. S. Office of Education research and demonstration grant to study ways of improving the recruitment of American Indians and Spanish-surnamed students into the profession. His study focuses on the Library Training Institute programs developed during the past five years to train minorities under HEA II-B. An effort will be made to identify program-planning practices which have been effective.

Besides the federally funded institutes, it is encouraging to note that library schools are including some affirmative action-related programs in their continuing education efforts. For example, Emory staged a workshop on affirmative action in 1975, while Pratt Institute held a workshop on federal regulations and the handicapped in 1977. Women in librarianship was the topic of the Rutgers annual alumni symposium in 1973 (Myers and Scarborough, 1975).

A few seminar courses in the M.L.S. program have focused on women in librarianship and sexism in children's and young adult's literature. As a result of the ALA Council resolution on racism and sexism, a survey is being undertaken by the ALA Library Education Division (LED) to determine what library schools are doing in the area of racism and sexism awareness training.

3. AFFIRMATIVE ACTION PLAN DEVELOPMENT

a. Plan Format. The ALA EEO (Equal Employment Opportunity) Subcommittee has developed a checklist of information that should be included in a good affirmative action plan (ALA EEO Subcommittee, 1976). The basic outline should follow a pattern similar to the following:

I. Affirmative Action Authority
   A. Policy Statement
      Written and endorsed by the highest policy-making level within the institution or government body.
   B. Implementation Method Delineated
      1. A high-level administrator reporting directly to the chief officer of the institution should be charged with the implementation of affirmative action. The responsibilities and authority of this individual must be spelled out, and it should be clear that this individual has been allocated sufficient time to carry out these functions.
      2. An affirmative action committee can be used to carry out some of the duties that might otherwise be assigned to an individual officer. The committee may be helpful, for example, in disseminating information on affirmative action to the staff and soliciting their input. Staff contribution to the development and implementation of an affirmative action plan is a particularly important—and often overlooked—element of a sound affirmative action program.
      3. The plan should be widely disseminated to staff and the outside community.
      4. A schedule for review of the plan on at least an annual basis should be stated.

II. Identification of Problem Areas
   A. Utilization Analysis
      1. Data on employees should delineate numbers and percentages by race, ethnic, and sex categories: White, Black, Hispanic, Asian and Pacific Islanders, American Indian and Alaskan native, male, female; and by occupational category: Officials/Administrators, Professional, Technician, Paraprofessional, Office/Clerical, Skilled Craft, Service/Maintenance, and others where appropriate. Vacancies and other factors affecting the long-term employment picture of the institution should be projected.
      2. National and local work-force data should be listed.
   B. Personnel Procedures and Practices
      Analyze all procedures that have impact on the selection, hiring, promotion, training, grievances, layoff, demotion, or firing of staff. Validate testing and other selection procedures wherever necessary.
III. Goals and Timetables
   Numerical goals and timetables for hiring and promoting women and minorities should be set based on the analysis of the pool of potential qualified women and minority candidates against the analysis of current staff. The Project on the Status and Education of Women (Association of American Colleges, 1972) notes that: "That obligation to meet the goal is not absolute; if the best qualified person is white and male, he can be hired, but the institution must be able to document what effort was made to recruit women and minorities, that such candidates were treated fairly, and that the white male was indeed 'better qualified.'" Generally, goals at the professional and administrative levels should be set with national availability statistics in mind, while lower classification levels should be matched against local data. Objectives for personnel procedure review and other problem areas should also be set with realistic dates for their completion.
IV. Internal Audit and Reporting System
   A complete audit should be done annually, with reports evaluated by the EEO Officer, administration, the affirmative action committee, and others. The staff and public should be

V. Action Program

Specific action should be outlined for each problem area. A number of other sources are available to aid in developing and formulating plans. The most comprehensive general guide is the U.S. Equal Employment Opportunity Commission's (1974) two-volume work, *Affirmative Action and Equal Employment: A Guidebook for Employers*. All educational institutions should obtain for purposes of plan development the U.S. Office for Civil Rights' (1972) *Higher Education Guidelines: Executive Order 11246,* which contains copies of HEW guidelines, Executive Order 11246, Revised Order No. 4, and other executive orders, laws, and agency interpretations related to plan development for educational institutions. The ALA/OLPR (1975a) *Affirmative Action Information Packet* also contains a number of resources for plan development, including an *Outline of a Strategy for Affirmative Action Planning in Educational Institutions* developed by the William Karp Consulting Co., Inc. (1972). Higgins (1975, 1976) provides a good analysis of the process of establishing goals and timetables and an outline of the various laws.

b. Institutional Programs. As of early 1977, six months after the call for affirmative action plans was issued, the EEO Subcommittee had received about a dozen plans to review. The majority of these were from public and state agency libraries. One can only speculate on the reason for the submission of so few academic library plans. One plausible explanation is the existence of institutional plans on many campuses which provide general, but not specific, coverage of libraries. In January 1974 all Association of Research Libraries (ARL) were covered by affirmative action plans, but only 10 of 61 ARL libraries responding to a survey had developed individual plans (ARL, 1974).

The authors sent questionnaires to a list of academic library personnel directors, directors of libraries that have submitted affirmative action plans to the ALA EEO Subcommittee, and others involved in plan development to gain a greater understanding of the commitment to affirmative action within librarianship. Of 80 questionnaires sent, 34 were returned, 20 from academic libraries, 11 by public libraries, and 3 from state library agencies. Most of the public library plans were developed independently, while the academic libraries generally must follow affirmative action guidelines established by a larger unit. The comments on each question display a wide range of experiences and results among plan developers.

Several of the academic librarians who responded to the questionnaire expressed difficulty in achieving affirmative action goals because of communication problems with a larger unit. Umbrella plans developed without the active participation of library representatives are not as apt to reflect the specific needs of the library, as indicated by responses from two academic librarians:

> The Library's plan was only part of the University plan. . . . We were merely asked to fill out a form which collected data on the utilization of women, minorities, and others. . . . There were no unique features to our plan because of the format.
>
> The library must depend most heavily upon the University Personnel Office for recruitment of applicants for open positions. Therefore, the availability of minorities having requisite skills is for the most a reflection of operating standards within the Personnel Department.

More research is needed on the participation level of libraries in the development of their institutions' affirmative action plans, and the applicability of the resulting goals, timetables, and action programs to these libraries. Close cooperation between the library and its parent institution is vital if affirmative action programming is going to receive adequate commitment and support within the library.

The EEO Subcommittee does not restrict its review of plans to independently developed programs. It feels that its affirmative action checklist is applicable to both umbrella and library-developed plans.

A number of positive or unique features and accomplishments of affirmative action plan development are mentioned on questionnaires returned for the authors' survey. The positive results include:

1. Better management, staff, and library board commitment to affirmative action.
2. More open recruitment, and better search and screening procedures; in general a help in resolving everyday personnel matters.
3. Library salary structures and job descriptions have been reviewed, which benefits all.

4. A successful scholarship was instituted.
5. Better utilization of women and minorities.
6. In general, achievement of goals for more equal participation among all groups would have taken longer without a plan.

Some respondents (all academic libraries) either noted that no or "very few" positive achievements have come from plan development or did not respond to the question.

Among the unique features or accomplishments of the affirmative action plans developed by questionnaire respondents' institutions are:

1. A skills bank to be used in conjunction with a staff development program (District of Columbia Library).
2. Restructuring of jobs that previously required professional knowledge of librarianship (D.C. Library).
3. A minority intern program (Columbia University).
4. Announcement of all openings, even for half-time positions (Univ. of North Carolina).
5. Active staff and community input at all phases of plan development (Dayton and Montgomery County Public Library).
6. A monitoring system (Rutgers University).
7. Ability of the Library's affirmative action committee to recruit and refer candidates directly to individual libraries that have vacancies (Rutgers).
8. Emphasis on recruitment of minority men at professional and nonprofessional levels (Los Angeles County Public Library), or on men in general at the entry level (Duke University).
9. Encouragement of local colleges and universities to enroll minorities in library science programs (Los Angeles County).
10. Using a Citizen's Advisory Committee (Tacoma Public Library).
11. Participatory plan development with entire staff (Montclair Public Library).
12. Use of Staff Trust Fund and local philanthropies for minority scholarships (Montclair).
13. Sponsorship of management and other training programs for women employees (Montclair).
14. Development of a full-scale career ladder (Orange County Library).

Many questionnaires were returned, however, with no innovative programs listed.

Many of the plans reviewed by the EEO Subcommittee contain positive and innovative features. Some of the most creative elements within the plans involve the use of a Citizen's Committee representative from minority communities to advise on the library plan development, show particularly strong programs to involve the staff in plan development and review, or offer particularly creative training programs. One state agency is funding a job analysis at certain classification levels that will benefit not only its library but also libraries throughout the state. The same state agency hired a minority specialist to develop services to disadvantaged sectors of the public and pledged also to cooperate with library schools to improve recruitment efforts for minority library training.

The Association of Research Libraries' (1974) study of academic library plans revealed that "the plans frequently call for increased and/or mandatory efforts at minority recruitment, the upgrading of training and career development programs, and the increased utilization of intern programs for minority employees."

The U.S. President's Committee on Employment of the Handicapped (1975) conducted a survey of 5,000 public and academic libraries to determine the level of commitment exhibited by these institutions to equal employment opportunity for the handicapped. Of the 1,399 institutions that replied, 627 libraries indicated that they hired qualified handicapped persons. A total of 907 full-time and 358 part-time handicapped workers were employed by these libraries. Some of the libraries noted that modifications were required to accommodate the handicapped, including work reassignment, phone amplification, rearrangement of furniture and shelving, and designated handicapped parking spaces. Generally, the library systems which employed the handicapped responded positively on the experience. Unfortunately, a large number of libraries either did not return the questionnaire (3,601 libraries), or responded that they do not employ the handicapped (771 institutions). Of the latter 771 institutions, 572 libraries did not choose to respond to the question of why none were employed, and a number of the 199 who answered gave negative reasons. The questionnaire results clearly indicate a need for a program to educate librarians to the job potentials of handicapped employees and the legal requirements regarding their employment.

Because of its size and impact on the library profession, the Library of Congress (LC) serves as a good case study of institutional commitment to affirmative action and equal employment opportunity. LC has reported on its equal employment practices since 1962, when its first Fair Employment Practices Officer was named (LC, 1962). It has published semiannual reports on affirmative action progress at the Library since the early 1970s, providing trend data and innovative programming ideas.

Statistics indicate slow progress toward better racial and sexual balance at various LC classification levels. Women scored some successes in the top grade, GS-16-18, but decreased in numbers between 1973 and 1976 in GS-12-13 and GS-14-15 categories (Table VI). Clearly, more needs to be done at the Library of Congress to hire, train, and promote women into middle management positions.

Although minorities gained considerably in upper clerical and lower professional categories and showed moderate gains in upper levels between 1971 and 1976 (Table VII), over all classification levels there was little change for any minority group (Table VIII). Note that only the Other (Caucasian) and Asian-American groups gained over time. Black and Spanish-surnamed categories dropped in percentage, perhaps because of the decline in percentage of minorities in the GS-1-4 level delineated in Table VIII.

In 1973 LC conducted a survey of the staff to determine their preferences on programs that could be developed under the Library's affirmative action plan (LC, 1973). The staff recommended top priority for training and educational programs, promotional and reassignment programs, and analyses of staff potential. The Library's recent efforts have focused upon these areas through training courses to upgrade employee skills, cooperative efforts with educational institutions to prepare employees with less than twelve years of school for the General Equivalency Diploma, tuition reimbursement, analyses of mobility patterns within various classifications, and career counseling. The Training, Appraisal, and Promotion Program (TAP), although not limited to minorities and women, places primary emphasis on preparing for advancement individuals in classification levels heavily represented by protected class groups. The slow, but steady, shift of minorities out of the lowest classification level into higher ones may be one indication that LC training and promotion programs are working.

Other LC affirmative action programs include test and selection

TABLE VI
Percentage of Women Employed at the Library of Congress by
Classification Level, GS-1–18, 1973–1976, with Percentage Change of
Women in Each Classification Over Reporting Period[a]

Classification level	July 1973	June 1975	Nov. 1976	Percentage change from 1973 to 1976
GS-1–4	60.2%	59.7%	58.5%	−1.7%
GS-5–8	58.9%	59.4%	60.5%	+1.6%
GS-9–11	50.9%	50.4%	51.9%	+1.0%
GS-12–13	42.0%	42.0%	41.5%	−0.5%
GS-14–15	19.7%	17.7%	19.1%	−0.6%
GS-16–18	6.1%	13.0%	11.1%	+5.0%

[a] From Library of Congress (1973, p. 265; 1975, p. 254; 1976, p. 804).

procedure analysis, an LC Federal Women's Committee study on the status of women at the Library, the establishment of a Women's Program Office in 1976 with a full-time coordinator, a 1975 Job Opportunity Day for the Washington Latino community, and other programs designed to meet the special needs of Spanish-surnamed library employees.

  c. *Problems in Plan Development.* The authors' questionnaire respondents note a number of problem areas related to plan development

TABLE VII
Percentage of Minorities Employed at the Library of Congress by
Classification Level, 1971–1976, with Percentage Change of Minorities
in Each Classification Over Reporting Period[a]

Classification level	May 1971	May 1973	June 1975	Nov. 1976	Percentage change from 1971 to 1976
GS-1–4	76.7%	70.5%	66.7%	61.4%	−15.3%
GS-5–8	48.1%	51.1%	54.6%	54.3%	+6.2%
GS-9–11	19.1%	25.4%	27.3%	27.8%	+8.7%
GS-12–13	12.3%	13.7%	15.0%	14.9%	+2.6%
GS-14–15	6.0%	6.6%	6.8%	8.3%	+2.3%
GS-16–18	1.6%	7.6%	5.2%	4.4%	+2.8%

[a] From Library of Congress (1973, p. 265, 1975, p. 254, 1976, p. 804).

TABLE VIII
Percentage of Minorities Employed at the Library of Congress by Minority Groups, 1972–1976, with Percentage Change within Each Minority Group Over Reporting Period[a]

Minority group	Nov. 1972	June 1973	Nov. 1974	May 1975	Nov. 1976	Percentage change 1972–1976
American Indian	0.1%	0.1%	0.1%	0.1%	0.1%	0 %
Black	37.7%	38.5%	38.4%	37.9%	36.6%	−1.1%
Asian–American	2.7%	2.9%	3.0%	3.0%	2.8%	+0.1%
Spanish-surnamed	1.1%	0.8%	0.8%	0.8%	0.7%	−0.4%
Other	58.4%	57.8%	57.7%	58.2%	59.8%	+1.4%

[a] From Library of Congress (1973, p. 265, 1975, p. 254, 1976, p. 804).

and implementation. Some find it difficult to recruit qualified minorities. Several reasons were cited including the small number of qualified minorities in the availability pool, lack of resources to recruit effectively, lack of commitment from the parent organization, poor information on minority recruitment sources, or lack of interest. A low level of expertise on the part of affirmative action committees, supervisory staff, and others presents a problem for many of the responding libraries. Furthermore, affirmative action guidelines are confusing and laced with jargon that is incomprehensible to many administrators. Finding statistical work-force data and setting up internal utilization analyses are the most frequently mentioned plan-related difficulties. Two or three respondents experienced some negative reactions to their affirmative action programs on the part of staff or community members who felt that the plans contained elements of reverse bias.

A working group in affirmative action at the 1974 ALA Social Responsibilities Round Table Task Force on Women Preconference identified a number of shortcomings in the development of plans (J. K. Marshall, 1975). Frequently, library staffs get little opportunity to contribute to plan development. Even the appointment of an affirmative action committee can be ineffective as a means of soliciting broad-based input if the committee is hampered by limited expertise, time, administrative support, or authority. All in all, participation in affirmative action programming is an important, but frustration-filled, activity for library staff according to Preconference participants.

Cunningham (1976) believes that the most common reasons for failure of affirmative action plans include these pitfalls: (1) no visible commitment on the part of the employer to the program, (2) inadequate resources available to support the programs, (3) an inadequate program for training and motivating supervisory and management staff, (4) personnel procedures that fail to meet equal employment opportunity standards.

Libraries and other educational institutions face an uphill battle in achieving positive action toward equal opportunity. Edwards and Zaretsky (1975) cite an HEW report that concludes that as of 1974 only 29 of approximately 1,300 colleges and universities required to write affirmative action plans had submitted acceptable plans.

The fact that some libraries have faced charges of discrimination in the past several years is yet another indication of the weaknesses of current plans and the need to develop more effective programs. Libraries that have been under fire within the courts or before state or federal enforcement agencies include the Library of Congress, the Louisiana State University, the Los Angeles Public Library, and more recently Stanford University and the San Diego Public Library.

The development of an affirmative action plan is an important task for any employer, even when not required by law. Voluntary development of a plan can demonstrate commitment to equal employment opportunity and clarifies the institution's policies for employees and the community. An employer's voluntary development of a plan may be an important consideration if charges of discrimination are brought at a later date.

4. OTHER CONCERNS AND PROBLEMS

a. Economic Conditions. Just as laws were upgraded to protect minorities and women, the bottom fell out of the job market. The general economic picture affected the library scene immediately; budget cuts, job freezes, and other setbacks have been well documented in the library press. Coupled with the increase in graduates coming from library schools, the reduced budgets combined with the tight job market resulted in little turnover or expansion. Also, federal support for minority fellowships was shrinking. Some money through the Comprehensive Employment and Training Act (CETA) has been of assistance in hiring minorities, particularly at the support staff level, but often these jobs are discontinued when federal money is no longer available.

Within many organizations and industries, the recession forced employers to lay off large numbers of employees. Where union contracts were in force, workers were let go on the basis of seniority (length of service). "Last hired, first fired" became a catchword to pinpoint the fact that minorities and women were the most recently hired, in many cases in response to the push in affirmative action hiring, and were also the first to be let go. Gains in affirmative action hiring have been halted or set back, as many of these new employees have been laid off because of labor union seniority protection. A fair resolution of this dilemma has yet to be worked out. Alternative solutions to layoffs, however, have been attempted in some companies, such as voluntary reduction of work time, corporate reduction of work hours, voluntary reduction of fringe benefits, reduction or elimination of miscellaneous benefits, and various methods of work sharing. Pogrebin (1975) discusses some of these issues and possible solutions.

b. Legal and Enforcement Uncertainties. Because there is no central government unit which regulates the overall EEO programs or provides information related to total requirements, information is often inconsistent and confusing. The complexities result from the variety of laws in force and the numerous agencies enforcing the laws. There are also weaknesses in enforcement, administration, and coordination. The laws and orders are often stated so vaguely that several years are required to translate them into specific requirements by the enforcement agencies. In turn, these requirements often have to be ruled on by the courts before much attention is given. Employers often find that they are subject to as many as four separate compliance investigations at a time. Furthermore, the agencies involved frequently utilize widely varying standards, evaluation criteria, or definitions. Administrators complain that considerable time and money is needed to make the increasingly sophisticated utilization analyses that are required. According to various reports and government hearings, the enforcement agencies frequently suffer from backlogs in investigations, lack of records, inadequate means of evaluating progress in job gains, and a reluctance to take action. It is especially difficult to acquire data on those hired as a result of affirmative action programs.

The Carter administration appears to be determined to achieve a better record than its predecessors. In his first speech, Secretary of Labor Ray Marshall stated the administration would press for simplification of rules for handling EEO cases. Joseph A. Califano, Jr., Secretary of HEW, has pledged stepped-up enforcement of EEO statutes and stated that the way to ensure compliance is to make it clear that funds will be denied to contractors who are not in compliance.

Confusion still reigns in the area of legislation relating to the handicapped. Former HEW Secretary David Mathews declined to sign the regulations on discrimination against handicapped students and workers before leaving office in January 1977, because he said further guidance from Congress was needed regarding its intent. Mathews also felt the regulations' application to drug addicts and alcoholics was in doubt. He wondered if any steps would be taken to help institutions and businesses bear the costs of altering facilities to accommodate handicapped individuals. Califano set up a task force to go over the regulations. Final regulations of Section 504 of the Rehabilitation Amendments were then published in the May 4, 1977 *Federal Register*. Section 504 will have a particular impact on libraries since the section provides for a nondiscrimination provision in any federal grant given to such institutions as schools, hospitals, and libraries (U.S. Department of Health, Education, and Welfare, 1977).

Another area of uncertainty relates to a Supreme Court decision in December 1976, which ruled in *General Electric vs. Gilbert* that within the meaning of the 1964 Civil Rights Act it is not sex discrimination to exclude pregnancy and related disabilities from health or disability insurance or sick-leave plans. The ruling was a setback to women's rights. However, a bipartisan group of senators and congressmen quickly proposed legislation designed to override the ruling, and confirm their belief that the 1964 act does forbid discrimination based on pregnancy, childbirth, and related medical conditions.

c. Reverse Discrimination. Early in 1977 the Supreme Court agreed to hear the appeal of the University of California at Davis Medical School, which had been found guilty by the California Supreme Court in a case which ruled the University practiced reverse discrimination by admitting minority students over white applicants with better credentials. To this point the high court has refused to deal directly with the question of preferential treatment. The DeFunis case came before the Supreme Court in 1972, but it ruled the issue moot in light of the fact that the plaintiff, DeFunis, had been admitted and graduated from law school before the case reached the Supreme Court. Justice Douglas, however, noted in a separate opinion that color-conscious employment decisions are not to be tolerated unless the courts have specifically mandated such a solution. The Civil Rights Act of 1964 requires equal employment opportunity for all, and thus forbids discrimination against any segment of the population. Douglas, however, states that "Nothing in [the EEOC Guideline] shall be interpreted as diminishing a person's obligation under both Title VII and EO 11246 as amended by EO 11375 to undertake affirmative action to ensure that applicants or employees are treated without regard to race, color, religion, sex, or national origin. Specifically, the use of tests which have been validated pursuant to these guidelines does not relieve employers, unions, or employment agencies of their obligations to take positive action in affording employment and training to members of classes protected by Title VII" (see Garland, 1975). Clearly, the courts and regulatory agencies must provide clearer guidelines to aid employers in determining the legal limits of programs designed to train and employ "protected class" individuals.

The Los Angeles County Public Library has been caught between opposite rulings on discrimination. In 1972 the California Fair Employment Practices Commission ruled that the Library failed to hire and promote minorities, since of 222 professionals only 17 were members of minority groups. As a result, the Library embarked on a program to increase minority employment within the library system. It used a procedure of "selective certification" to promote a Black woman and a Mexican–American woman to Principal Librarian posts ahead of seven applicants scoring higher on the examination (California court, 1975). In the resulting litigation the California Supreme Court ruled that LACPL had indeed practiced "reverse discrimination" in selectively certifying and hiring the minority candidates. This ruling is being appealed.

Unfortunately, there is a danger that "reverse discrimination" will be used as an excuse for affirmative inaction. Certainly most activities surrounding affirmative action programming are designed to assure equal employment opportunity for all, and will never bring about a charge of "reverse bias." A large part of affirmative action planning revolves around the analysis and validation of personnel practices and procedures to assure that they do not adversely affect *anyone*. As Justice

Douglas pointed out, the establishment of goals (as opposed to quotas), which guide an employer toward a more representative work force, and the establishment of training programs and other procedures designed to eliminate employment barriers for "protected class" people, are all legitimate pursuits of affirmative action plans. Nyren (1976) concluded his survey of librarian opinions on this subject by saying "that cry of 'reverse discrimination' . . . should never be raised against an affirmative action policy that is properly nurtured and brought to maturity in a community or institution that has given it birth."

  d. *Civil Service Requirements.* Civil service systems can work both for and against library affirmative action. On the positive side, merit systems frequently provide well-structured, written, job-related personnel procedures. Classification and clearly delineated salary structures typically found in civil service systems mitigate against "equal pay for equal work" complaints. Job descriptions, written grievance procedures, and unbiased oral examination requirements for professional positions are also common within merit systems. Because a large part of affirmative action is fulfilled through the provision of sound personnel policies and procedures, merit systems typically help to assure equal employment opportunity.

  The same system that espouses impartial selection procedures, ironically, sometimes serves to discriminate against certain groups. For example, merit systems assume that there is a "best" candidate who can be discovered through careful testing procedures. Most advanced positions, however, are so complex in nature that the test process is by its very nature subjective (Affirmative (In) Action, 1977). Most civil service systems, until recently at least, used standard tests of general knowledge or intelligence to screen candidates for positions at various levels; tests which have often been found to discriminate against minority groups. An American Library Association Library Administration Division survey of state and public libraries serving over 100,000 population discovered that of 43 libraries testing clerical and nonprofessional personnel, all but four used general knowledge or intelligence tests. Only two had validated testing procedures (Simon, 1972). Affirmative action regulations require that testing procedures be validated to show that they do not adversely affect any particular group of people.

In assuming that only the "best" person can be selected for a job many civil service systems adopt rules of three, which require that the interviewing and selection be limited to the candidates at the top of the list. Unless a number of minority candidates are among the group to be ranked, the chances are small that a minority group member will place high on the list. Expanding the selection pool to five or ten, making the selection criteria as liberal as possible, and vigorously recruiting for a large group of "protected class" individuals for high level posts would help to alleviate the affirmative action problems that exist in Civil Service systems.

Many states emphasize veterans' preference, and assign additional points to the scores of qualified veterans on civil service examinations, and sometimes require absolute selection of a veteran if an individual claiming veterans' preference appears on a certification list. Veterans' preference laws have been specifically exempted from equal employment opportunity controls even though they have been shown to adversely affect the hiring and promotion of qualified women and minorities. Veterans' preference may, on the other hand, aid in the affirmative hiring of disabled and Vietnam era veterans, who are now also protected under federal law. Generally speaking, however, absolute preference laws should be removed from state law codes because of their negative effect on affirmative action for nonveteran groups.

3. Collective Bargaining Impact. Laws regarding collective bargaining agreements are primarily covered by the National Labor Relations Act. Public employees are not covered by this act, although numerous state laws provide for public employees' collective bargaining. Since librarians are becoming more involved with unionization, there will undoubtedly be more concern with the relationship of collective bargaining to affirmative action. Since the primary responsibility of any labor organization is equal representation of all its members, a collective bargaining agreement may be ruled invalid if it is demonstrated that classes of members are not being represented. Negotiated agreements cannot violate federal antidiscrimination laws. Every collective bargaining agreement should include a nondiscrimination clause, and contracts should specify that arbitration of discrimination grievances will follow Title VII principles. In many situations, a union can file a class action suit under Title VII on behalf of its members or refer an employee to the appropriate compliance agency.

One method of instituting an affirmative action plan is to require the development of a plan to be included in the collective bargaining package of employer groups. Since under the law, both the employer and labor organization may be liable for damages resulting from discriminatory contract provisions or practices, it is essential that both be involved in the development and monitoring of affirmative action plans.

Some unions have joined women's rights groups in protesting the Supreme Court ruling that company disability pay plans which exclude payments during pregnancy do not violate the Civil Rights Act. Where women outnumber men, the unions will be pressed to push this point in collective bargaining agreements. However, there may be resistance in unions where males predominate.

The issue of "last hired, first fired" discussed above, has brought the question of affirmative action versus collective bargaining into sharp relief. Discriminatory clauses have been found in some seniority provisions. Although a *bona fide* seniority system is legal, its operation can prove to be discriminatory. Up to now, the courts have not provided a clear-cut answer to the question of layoffs, although the May 31, 1977 Supreme Court decision upholding the legality of job-seniority systems which perpetuate discrimination that began before the enactment of the 1964 Civil Rights Act, points the direction in which seniority cases will be handled. The 1977 case, involving a nationwide trucking firm (T.IM.E.–D.C. Inc.), dealt with the right of employees to bid into higher paying jobs based on seniority. The high court stated that the use of existing seniority lists should not be outlawed, although the trial court was ordered to determine whether unsuccessful minority applicants for long-haul jobs were discriminated against after passage of the 1964 law and are thus entitled to retroactive seniority. Frakin (1975) outlines the issues, particularly as they relate to higher education, and states that the objectives of collective bargaining may be subverted unless all parties recognize the importance of complying with the federal mandates regarding equality. Frakin warns that otherwise unionization may merely serve to institutionalize many aspects of present-day discrimination.

A report by the U.S. Commission on Civil Rights (1977) states that the long and extensive use of the policy of "last hired, first fired" by employers, particularly during periodic economic recessions, is one reason why income remains consistently lower (and unemployment rates higher) for minorities and women than for the labor force as a whole. This study addresses the seniority, layoff, work-sharing, and civil rights aspects of national economic policy.

f. Selection Procedures. The Equal Employment Opportunity Commission has stated that the selection process is responsible for more charges of discrimination than any other employment practice. In most cases, it appears that employers do not consciously intend to be discriminatory (Higgins, 1976). In order to alleviate this situation the "Federal Executive Agency Guidelines on Employee Selection Procedures" were adopted in November 1976 by the Departments of Justice and Labor, the Civil Service Commission, and the Civil Rights Commission. Along with the Equal Employment Opportunity Commission, these groups are members of the Equal Employment Opportunity Coordinating Council (EEOCC), charged by law to eliminate inconsistencies among federal agencies and departments responsible for enforcement of laws (US EEOCC, 1976). However, the EEOC is still operating under its 1970 guidelines (US EEOC, 1976). Both sets of guidelines provide a framework for determining proper use of tests and other selection procedures in any employment decision such as hiring, promotion, or selection for training.

If an employment practice discriminates against members of the "protected classes," it is considered illegal. Preferential treatment is, however, forbidden; job qualifications are to control employment. The courts are now reviewing questions involving testing, primarily because the laws stipulate that the personnel selection criteria be job related. If a selection procedure has an adverse impact on minorities and women, it must be validated in accordance with the federal guidelines, or an employer must find alternative procedures which have as little adverse impact as possible.

Prior to setting any selection criteria, it is necessary to determine exactly what on-the-job performance is required of each employee. This requires a task analysis which identifies the skills and knowledge needed for successful completion of the tasks. Once the requirements are identified, the employer must establish some means of measuring the skills and knowledge of the applicants.

Some are now asking whether or not the MLS from an ALA-accredited library school can be used as the sole minimum criteria for entry into the profession. It has been reported that Tucson, Cleveland,

and Sacramento (California) have recently changed their selection criteria to allow experienced paraprofessionals to be considered for professional positions. Considerable controversy has been generated by this decision, particularly in response to the announcement of an examination by the Sacramento City–County Library, which allows paraprofessionals with five years of experience (or three years experience and two years of college) to be considered for professional status. This move has been supported by the Council on Library Technical Assistants (COLT). The Cleveland Public Library alternative plan for certification has been described by Johnson (1976).

To date, little has been done to determine the validity of the M.L.S. degree. If it is demonstrated to be the most valid hiring criterion and that alternative measures are unavailable, the degree may be required. Garland (1975) analyzes these issues in relation to the California scene. The Selection Consulting Center in cooperation with the California State Library is now attempting to determine what constitutes a professional library classification and is reviewing minimum qualifications for entry-level employment.

In addition to the questions regarding the validation of the M.L.S. degree, libraries are finding that affirmative action procedures are affecting the mechanics of recruitment and selection. Christofferson (1977) and Caruthers and Demos (1976) describe the effect of affirmative action on academic library hiring. Disadvantages cited are delays in hiring due to time-consuming advertising and interview procedures, the flood of applications for entry-level positions, and the high cost of selection due to increased paperwork and advertising costs. Advantages cited are that candidates have a greater awareness of employment opportunities and the library has a larger pool of candidates, which usually improves the chances of finding a highly qualified candidate for the job.

Affirmative action procedures have also raised questions as to the legality of certain interviewing questions. Many questions are commonly asked of applicants quite innocently but may establish a basis for discrimination because of race, color, religion, sex, or national origin. Some questions are permissible if asked of all applicants and if the responses are treated alike. However, many states prohibit certain questions; some states with Fair Employment Practice laws have prepared lists of what they consider proper or improper preemployment inquiries. Questions regarding arrest and conviction records, marital status, child-care situations, physical characteristics, and other personal questions are suspect, because generally they are not central to the applicant's suitability for a particular job.

III. PROSPECTS FOR THE FUTURE

A. Trend and Survey Data

When the authors asked library personnel directors and others, "What do you see as the prognosis for the future of affirmative action in librarianship?" the answers ranged from cynical to relatively optimistic. For some, affirmative action represents only "game playing" at the expense of women and minorities. Some expressed frustration that libraries frequently develop little more than paper plans with no real commitment on the part of libraries, government agencies, or professional associations to back them up. Others placed blame for affirmative action's lack of effectiveness on our inability to recruit qualified minorities to library schools or the library job market, and the abuses which have sometimes taken place in promoting "protected class" individuals who do not have the necessary qualifications.

On the other hand, some respondents expect to see "a steady and constant movement toward more adequate reflection in library staffs of the composition of the population, i.e., the communities served." One librarian responded, "the library community realizes, more fully than others perhaps, that there are many people to serve in many different ways. Outreach efforts in our service patterns are conducive to affirmative action. If we practice what we preach, equal access to knowledge for all should be our goal and equal opportunity for all is a natural corollary." Most respondents agree that until "protected class" individuals are reflected more equitably in the library employment picture, affirmative action programming must continue.

Trend data leave a similarly ambivalent picture of affirmative action's future. The scanty information on the utilization of minorities in libraries seems to indicate a slow, but steady, increase in the numbers of minorities trained and employed at the professional level. The progress, however, neither matches the service needs of minority communities, nor, in most cases, does it match the availability of minorities qualified to choose librarianship as a career. The future with regard to minority employment depends very much upon vigorous recruitment efforts at both the undergraduate and graduate levels, plus active in-service training programs designed to prepare minorities for professional library careers.

The picture does not look as bright, based upon trend data, for the improved status of women in librarianship, nor for higher level promotional opportunities for minorities. Research on the aggregate statistics is needed in order to determine the causes for the static situation with regard to the attainment of higher level positions by women and minorities.

The sluggishness of objective economic trends may be due to the fact that objective indicators generally lag behind the subjective change factors (Staines et al., 1976). The blossoming of minority and women's groups within professional associations, greater activity in the area of women and ethnic studies, and the burgeoning of affirmative action literature are all indicators of a higher level of awareness concerning the problem of discrimination. Consciousness-raising is the first step toward the elimination of employment barriers. Individuals who are aware of their rights are less likely to accept employment discrimination, and are more likely to engage in career planning and educational efforts that will enhance their opportunities. Employers who are aware of past discrimination practices are less likely to engage in biased practices in the future. It takes longer, however, before positive gains begin to register as economic benefits. The process is also subject to temporary setbacks when recession or backlash against affirmative action sets in. It is unlikely, however, that the raised level of consciousness with regard to the employment rights of women and minorities can ever be totally reversed, and thus, it is only a matter of time before more positive gains are seen in objective trend data.

B. Research Needs

Until a pattern of positive change is established, surveys on the salaries and positions of male/female librarians must continue to display data specified according to sex. More reliable and regular analysis should be made of the economic indicators for minority librarians. Without such trend data on salaries and position level we will never be able to trace the impact of affirmative action on librarianship. Studies need to be conducted, if it is not already too late, on the effect of the recession of the mid-seventies on affirmative action programs.

The Staines et al. (1976) concept of subjective and objective indicators of discrimination should be extended to librarianship. What are the subjective indicators of discrimination within librarianship and how precisely do they interrelate with salary and position-level trend data? How are these factors changing over time?

A profile of library affirmative action plans is needed which will accurately portray their nature and effectiveness. One interesting offshoot of such a survey might be an investigation of the commitment to affirmative action in those libraries that function under umbrella plans. Does coverage under the plan of a parent organization limit the relevance of the program to specific library affirmative action problems? Do umbrella plans tend to limit the participation/commitment on the part of the library administration and staff in plan development?

When the authors asked librarians in their survey what areas needed further research and clarification, many of the responses reflected the general confusion over affirmative action procedures. Respondents wanted further clarification on setting goals and timetables, on the debate on "reverse discrimination," on how to judge the "best" qualified, and on the inclusion of handicapped and veterans in affirmative action plans. They expressed a desire to reduce paper work and expense and wondered what the real costs of implementing affirmative action were. They asked about the effect of affirmative action on staff morale and requested guidelines for pursuing affirmative action goals in times of little staff turnover. Some requested help in recruiting male applicants for traditionally female jobs (clerical) and in identifying minority group librarians. The need for data on the composition of the library work force was stressed; statistics on minorities and women organized by type of library, geographical region, level of employment, and rate of advancement were desired. Others emphasized the need to develop valid and reliable professional qualification tests.

The ALA Office for Library Personnel Resources has been attempting to obtain funding for data collection on the ethnic and sexual composition of a sampling of the library work force. While the Library General Information Survey (LIBGIS) data provide some information on breakdown of male/female staff, this data is inadequate for our purposes. Collection of data on the four minority groups identified for affirmative action purposes (Asians or Pacific Islanders, Blacks, American Indians or Alaskan Natives, and Hispanic people) requires separate data cells and has made it difficult for the National Center for

Educational Statistics to incorporate these data into their LIBGIS forms.

C. Recruitment and Training Efforts

The library schools recognize a commitment to recruit minorities, but some are clearly more active than others in this area. If the HEA Title II-B fellowship application requests continue to exceed the funds available, it will be difficult to attract qualified minorities unless other sources of funding are found. To this end, the ALA Office for Library Personnel Resources is urging library school administrators to explore the possibility of acquiring funds for the training of bilingual school media specialists under the Elementary and Secondary Education Act Title VII. One of the objectives of the newly formed ALA Minority Recruitment Subcommittee is to find new ways of supporting training costs.

Career development for the "protected classes" will continue to be pushed by the women's groups and minority caucuses, particularly in the area of management training. Increased activity in management training is apparent as a result of stepped-up continuing education and staff development efforts in librarianship. Women and minorities may benefit from these programs as well as specialized training development efforts for "protected classes." There is no consensus as to whether management training for women or minorities should be separated from that of regular courses in this area. Specialized intern programs, such as the Association of College and Research Libraries' management intern program for Black librarians, do provide opportunities which minorities and women might not otherwise be able to afford.

D. Employment Procedures and Practices

Although in many quarters, the overall feeling might be that affirmative action is not working or that interest is waning, there is evidence that changes in employment practices have come about because of affirmative action implementation.

Salary adjustments have been made, and procedures regarding antinepotism, maternity leave, part-time employment, and training opportunities have been reexamined and changed in many instances.

Documentation of existing bias has forced recognition of real problems and some attitudinal changes have occurred as a result. Opening the system to all qualified candidates has produced more and better candidates, according to some employers. Probably the most important development has been the standardization of personnel procedures, which benefits all staff members, not just women and minorities. Affirmative action programs can be effectively utilized in attempts to clarify institutional personnel policies, and in efforts to remove discriminatory procedures.

There are still many unanswered questions, however. What is needed are effective techniques for translating federal law into meaningful practices and policies. It is still uncertain as to what effect the economy will have on affirmative action implementation. Will reduced budgets mean a reduced framework for affirmative action implementation? The job shortage should not be used, however, as an excuse to slow down affirmative action efforts. The question of layoffs and preferential treatment will continue to be debated in the courts.

There may be more discrimination complaints filed as staff become increasingly aware of age discrimination laws and those regulations affecting the handicapped. Questions are being raised regarding the rising job requirements especially for entry-level positions. At the same time, the flood of applicants for each advertised position can discourage even the most dedicated advocate of affirmative action.

To date, it appears that academic libraries and large public libraries have been the most heavily involved with affirmative action programs. This is probably due to the steady pressure exerted by centralized university and municipal affirmative action officers. Because special librarians and school media specialists often operate one-person libraries, they are not as likely to be involved with affirmative action planning as are their colleagues in larger library operations. It is likely that smaller public libraries will become more aware of the need for affirmative action procedures, however, in the near future. Increased participation by staff in library decision making will also increase the number of staff members involved with either affirmative action committees, or search and screening committees.

Prospects for the future in librarianship include increased activity in the validation of selection procedures, particularly in the debate over job-related degree requirements. As expressed by one survey respondent in the authors' survey, the "career ladder issue will continue until it is determined one way or another that the graduate degree is the only valid test of professional training." The ALA Library Education Division sponsored a program at the 1977 Annual Conference on the issue of examinations in lieu of formal training as a means of qualifying for professional appointment or promotion. The ALA policy on "Library Education and Personnel Utilization" states that "until such examinations are identified that are valid and reliable tests of equivalent qualifications, the academic degree... is recommended as the single best means for determining that an applicant has the background recommended for each category" (ALA, 1970). This would appear to encourage the development of examinations. However, it is unlikely that many will advance from the ranks of the paraprofessional levels that way. It may also be difficult for these persons to achieve mobility from one library to another. It seems likely, however, that many employers will add "or its equivalent" to job descriptions requiring an M.L.S. degree from an accredited school.

Another change in employment practices in the future may be the upgrading of the status of part-time work and an increase in the number of job-sharing opportunities. Job sharing has been advocated by many groups as one way of promoting affirmative action goals—it provides for hiring more women and minorities, and also allows time for continuing education activities. Acceptance of part-time work will rest largely on economic arguments, such as evidence of proof that employers benefit through the creation of part-time options at all levels of employment.

Legislation is pending before the 95th Congress in both the Senate and House to establish permanent part-time work opportunities in each executive agency in the federal government so that within five years, part-time staff will constitute 10 percent of the work force. A House bill designed to stimulate this type of employment in the private sector is also pending. Some states (Massachusetts and Maryland) have enacted similar legislation (Levine, 1977; National Conference on Alternative Work Schedules, 1977; Olmsted, 1977).

The ALA Council passed a resoltuion in 1976 urging ALA to encourage libraries to recognize the right to part-time employment on a par with full employment with prorated pay and fringe benefits and opportunity for advancement (ALA, 1976d).

If subjective and objective indicators of discrimination against women and minorities appear to show that a long remedial process will be required, then the indicators with regard to affirmative action for the handicapped suggest an even longer process. Awareness of the needs and capabilities of the handicapped lags far behind that for women and minorities. A letter to the editor of *Library Journal* (Velleman, 1977) illustrates the point: "It was with some sense of disappointment . . . that I read the article reviewing and picturing some of the Public and Academic Library buildings of 1976. Nowhere was any mention made of efforts to make these buildings accessible to the handicapped." The survey conducted by the U.S. President's Committee on Employment of the Handicapped (1975) illustrates the lack of awareness on the part of library employers relative to the employment capabilities of the handicapped.

In 1967 the American Library Association's Library Administration Division passed a policy statement on the employment of the handicapped in libraries (Dalton, 1968). While recognizing the need for equal opportunity for the handicapped, the policy delineates an extremely limited set of circumstances under which the handicapped should be employed in libraries (e.g., only when individuals have the freedom of movement to reach and tote heavy library materials, have the manual dexterity to file, are sighted, have clear speech and accute enough hearing to communicate well with the public and staff). This policy statment clearly needs review and revision.

Some general materials on the employment of the handicapped include the U.S. President's Committee on Employment of the Handicapped (1976), DeLury (1975), and Dyer and Ford (1976). Until librarians are aware of the barriers to the employment of the handicapped and the legal obligations to eliminate these hurdles, few positive economic changes will occur with regard to handicapped library workers.

IV. CONCLUSION

Despite the many uncertainties and problems surrounding affirmative action, the idea is here to stay. Setbacks have occurred as a result of the recession, conflicting regulations and legal decisions, poorly supported enforcement programs, and, in many cases, inadequate institutional affirmative action plan development. Because of the pressures for social change and an increasing awareness of the importance of equal employment opportunity, however, these delays should not permanently hinder progress in affirmative action programming.

It is, in fact, the subjective indicators of social change—the raised consciousness levels and increased activity among women's and minority groups within librarianship—that point most positively toward the success of affirmative action. As the social climate within the profession becomes more hospitable, more women and minorities will take advantage of career development programs and opportunities for advancement. More will file grievances when they recognize instances of discrimination. These social changes should also bring about an increased sensitivity on the part of employers to the waste of human resources that occurs when patterns of discrimination persist. Programs designed to extend library services to the disadvantaged should also enhance affirmative action employment possibilities within libraries. In time, these new social patterns will reinforce themselves, leading to permanent employment gains for women and minorities.

The objective economic indicators of social change for affirmative action within librarianship are lagging behind the subjective trend data. The only statistics to register steady, if somewhat measured, increases throughout the decade are those for the training and hiring of members of certain minority groups for beginning-level professional positions. It is hoped, however, as the social climate becomes more supportive of female and minority employment, that the objective indicators will also show more positive signs of progress.

Social change generally takes place in evolutionary fashion. It is therefore likely that affirmative action programs will continue to register moderate gains over an extended period of time. We are only beginning to see the subjective and objective effects of change. Further periodic reviews of affirmative action and librarianship will be needed if we are to chart our progress toward affirmative action goals.

REFERENCES

Affirmative (In) Action (1977). *Equal Rights Monitor* 3, 8–9.
American Library Association (1970). "Library Education and Personnel Utilization." American Library Association, Chicago, Illinois.
American Library Association (1976a). Equal employment opportunity: a statement of policy of the American Library Association. *American Libraries* 7, 450–451.

American Library Association (1976b). "Resolution on Racism and Sexism Awareness." American Library Association, Chicago, Illinois. (Council Document No. 83.)

American Library Association (1976c). "Resolution on Library Education to Meet the Needs of Spanish-Speaking People." American Library Association, Chicago, Illinois. (Council Document No. 23.)

American Library Association (1976d). "Resolution on Permanent Part-Time Employment." American Library Association, Chicago, Illinois. (Council Document No. 7.)

American Library Association, Association of College and Research Libraries (1976). "Salary Structures of Libraries in Higher Education for the Academic Year 1975-76." Association of Research Libraries, Chicago, Illinois.

American Library Association, Committee on Accreditation (1976). "Report of Committee on Accreditation to ALA Council." American Library Association, Chicago, Illinois. (Council Document No. 22.)

American Library Association, Equal Employment Opportunity Subcommittee (1976). ALA Equal Employment Subcommittee Guidelines for library affirmative action plans. *American Libraries* 7, 451–455, 475.

American Library Association, Legislation Committee (1976). "Affirmative Action: Background Information and Progress Report." American Library Association, Chicago, Illinois. (Council Document No. 45.2.)

American Library Association, Office for Library Personnel Resources (1975a). "Affirmative Action Information Packet." American Library Association, Chicago, Illinois.

American Library Association, Office for Library Personnel Resources (1975b). "Survey of Graduates and Faculty of U.S. Library Education Programs Awarding Degrees and Certificates, 1973-74." American Library Association, Chicago, Illinois. (Mimeograph copy.)

American Library Association, Office for Library Personnel Resources (1977). "Degrees and Certificates Awarded by U.S. Library Education Programs 1974-1975." American Library Association, Chicago, Illinois. (Mimeograph copy.)

American Library Association, SRRT Task Force on Women (1970). "Women in Librarianship: A Bibliography." American Library Association, Chicago, Illinois. (Updated annually.)

Association of American Colleges, The Project on the Status and Education of Women (1972). "Summary of Federal Policy Concerning Twenty-five Affirmative Action Issues in Employment." Association of American Colleges, Washington, D.C.

Association of Research Libraries (1974). Affirmative action in the ARL libraries. *Spec Flyer* 4(January).

Berry, J. (1977). The California input. *Library Journal* 102, 335–341.

Bidlack, R. E. (1975). "Letter to the Honorable Daniel J. Flood, October 29, 1975." American Library Association Washington Office, Washington, D.C. (Mimeograph copy.)

Bidlack, R. E. (1976). Faculty salaries of 62 library schools, 1975-76. *Journal of Education for Librarianship* 16, 258-267.

Bidlack, R. E. (1977). "Memo to Deans and Directors Who Shared 1976–77 Salary Data." University of Michigan, Ann Arbor, Michigan. (Mimeograph copy.)
Cabello-Argandoña, R. (1976). Recruiting Spanish-speaking library students. *Library Journal* 101, 1177–1179.
California court to rule on reverse bias case. (1975). *Library Journal* 100, 1051–1052.
Carpenter, R. L., and Shearer, K. D. (1972). Sex and salary survey. *Library Journal* 97, 3682–3685.
Carpenter, R. L., and Shearer, K. D. (1974). Sex and salary update. *Library Journal* 99, 101–107.
Caruthers, R. L., and Demos, J. T. (1976). Affirmative action and the hiring of professional librarians. *Kentucky Library Association Bulletin* 40, 5–9.
Childers, T., and Adams, K. (1972). Recruitment of minorities. *American Libraries* 3, 612–621.
Christofferson, R. (1977). The high cost of hiring. *Library Journal* 102, 677–681.
Cunningham, J. (1976). Avoiding common pitfalls in affirmative action programs. *Personnel Journal* 55, 125–127, 136.
Dalton, J. (1968). The handicapped as librarians: facing the problem. *Wilson Library Bulletin* 43, 318–321.
De Fichy, W. (1973). Affirmative action: equal opportunity for women in library management. *College and Research Libraries* 34, 195–201.
DeLury, B. E. (1975). Equal job opportunity for the handicapped means positive thinking and positive action. *Labor Law Journal* 26, 679–685.
Dickinson, E. (1976). Personnel and employment: affirmative action. *In* "The ALA Yearbook: A Review of Library Events 1975" (R. W. Wedgeworth, ed.), pp. 257–260. American Library Association, Chicago, Illinois.
Dickinson, E. (1977). Personnel and employment: affirmative action. *In* "The ALA Yearbook: A Review of Library Events 1976" (R. W. Wedgeworth, ed.), pp. 237–239. American Library Association, Chicago, Illinois.
Dyer, F. C., and Ford, C. W. (1976). Training the handicapped: now it's their turn for affirmative action. *Personnel Journal* 55, 181–183.
Edwards, H. T., and Zaretsky, B. L. (1975). Preferential remedies for employment discrimination. *Michigan Law Review* 74, 1–47.
Frakin, S. (1975). Collective bargaining and affirmative action. *Journal of College and University Personnel Association* 26, 53–62.
Frame, R. P., and Anderson, J. F. (1969). Library employment of minority group personnel. *ALA Bulletin* 63, 985–987.
Frarey, C. J., and Learmont, C. L. (1974). Placements and salaries 1973: not much change. *Library Journal* 99, 1767–1774.
Frarey, C. J., and Learmont, C. L. (1975). Placements and salaries 1974: promise or illusion? *Library Journal* 100, 1767–1774.
Garland, H. W. (1975). The M.L.S., affirmative action, equal employment opportunity, and equivalency. *California Librarian* 36, 40–44, 46–49, 51–59.
Goldstein, R. K., and Hill, D. R. (1975). The status of women in the administration of health sciences libraries. *Medical Library Association Bulletin* 63, 356–395.

Higgins, J. M. (1975). The complicated process of establishing goals for equal employment. *Personnel Journal* 54, 631-637.
Higgins, J. M. (1976). A manager's guide to the equal employment opportunity laws. *Personnel Journal* 55, 406-418.
Johnson, D. T. (1976). The alternative plan for certification at the Cleveland Public Library. *COLT Newsletter* 9, 1-4.
Jones, C. S. (1977). ALA president views the racism/sexism resolution. *American Libraries* 8, 244-245.
Jongeward, D., and Scott, D. (1973). "Affirmative Action for Women: A Practical Guide." Addison-Wesley, Reading, Massachusetts.
Josey, E. J. (1975). Can library affirmative action succeed? *Library Journal* 100, 28-31.
King, J. (1977). Pathfinder on affirmative action. *News of Women in Michigan Libraries* No. 6, 4.
Learmont, C. L., and Darling, R. L. (1976). Placements and salaries, 1975: a difficult year. *Library Journal* 101, 1487-1493.
Levine, J. A. (1977). Part-time work... Full-time parents. *Working Woman* 2 (March), 74-76.
Library of Congress (1962). Fair employment practices. *Library of Congress Information Bulletin* 21, 15-16.
Library of Congress (1973). L. C.'s affirmative action plan: a survey of progress. *Library of Congress Information Bulletin* 32 261, 264-266, A115-120.
Library of Congress (1975). L.C. minority employment, June 1975. *Library of Congress Information Bulletin* 34, 254.
Library of Congress (1976). L.C. minority employment, November 1976. *Library of Congress Information Bulletin* 35, 804.
Marley, S. (1975). A comparative analysis of library directorships in four midwestern states. *Focus on Indiana Libraries* 29(Fall/Winter), 4-6.
Marshall, J. E. (1975). Implementation of institute concepts: the U. Wisconsin Library experience. *American Libraries* 6, 572-573.
Marshall, J. K. (1975). Affirmation action workshop. *In* "Women in a Woman's Profession: Strategies" (B. C. Sellen and J. K. Marshall, eds.), pp. 23-25. American Library Association Task Force on Women, New York.
Martinez-Smith, E. (1971). The hold-back advocacy. *American Libraries* 2, 784.
Medical Library Association (1973a). Plan of affirmative action. *Medical Library Association Bulletin* 61, 356-357.
Medical Library Association (1973b). "Developing a Plan for Affirmative Action—Human Rights Bibliography." Medical Library Association, Chicago, Illinois. (Working Paper No. 3.)
Myers, M., and Lynch, B. (1975). Affirmative action and academic libraries. *Directions: A Journal for Academic Libraries* 1, 12-15.
Myers, M., and Scarborough, M. (1975). "Women in Librarianship: Melvil's Rib Symposium." Rutgers University School of Library Service, New Brunswick, New Jersey.
National Conference on Alternative Work Schedules (1977). "Resource Packet."

(Prepared for Conference, Chicago, March 21-22). National Council for Alternative Work Patterns, Inc., Washington, D.C.

Nyren, K. E. (1976). Affirmative action and charges of "reverse bias." *Library Journal* 101, 985-987.

Olmsted, B. (1977). Job sharing—a new way to work. *Personnel Journal* 56, 78-81.

Pogrebin, B. B. (1975). Who shall work? *Ms.* 4 (Dec.) 67, 70-72, 114-115.

Rayford, V. A. (1972). A Black librarian takes a look at discrimination: by a law school library survey. *Law Library Journal* 65, 183-189.

Reilly, M. E., and Bouvier, L. F. (1976). "Women in American Society: A Historical and Demographic Profile." Center for Information on America, Washington, Connecticut. (Population Profiles, No. 15.)

Roberts, R. A. (1975). "The Job Classification Plan as an Instrument for Affirmative Action." Master's thesis, California State University, Fullerton. (ERIC ED 115894.)

Salazar, M. (1976). "Illinois Minorities Manpower Project, May 1972-August 1974: Final Report." American Library Association, Chicago, Illinois. (Mimeograph copy.)

Salazar, M. (1977). "Summary Report: U.S. ALA Accredited Library Education Minority Recruitment Programs." American Library Association, Chicago, Illinois. (Mimeograph copy.)

Schiller, A. R. (1971). Aware. *American Libraries* 2, 1215-1216.

Schiller, A. R. (1974). Women in librarianship. *In* "Advances in Librarianship" (M. J. Voight, ed.), Vol. 4, pp. 103-147. Academic Press, New York.

Shearer, K. D., and Carpenter, R. L. (1976). Public Library support and salaries in the seventies. *Library Journal* 101, 777-783.

Simon, B. (1972). EEOC Guidelines for preventing discriminatory employment practices. *American Libraries* 3, 1207-1209.

Slanker, B. O. (1975). "ALA Affirmative Action Institute, December 2-6, 1974, Chicago: Final Report." American Library Association, Chicago, Illinois. (Mimeograph copy.)

Special Libraries Association (1970). SLA Salary Survey 1970. *Special Libraries* 61, 333-348.

Special Libraries Association (1973). SLA Salary Survey 1973. *Special Libraries* 64, 594-628.

Special Libraries Association (1976). SLA Salary Survey 1976. *Special Libraries* 67, 597-624.

Special Libraries Association, Special Committee on the Pilot Education Project (1976). "Equal Pay for Equal Work: Women in Special Libraries." Special Libraries Association, New York.

Staines, G. L., Quinn, R. P., and Shepard, L. J. (1976). Trends in occupational sex discrimination: 1969-1973. *Industrial Relations* 15, 88, 98.

Tarr, S. A. (1973). The status of women in academic libraries. *North Carolina Libraries* 31, 22-32.

Trejo, A., ed. (1976). "Quien Es Quien: A Who's Who of Spanish-heritage Librarians in the United States." University of Arizona, Tucson, Arizona. (Graduate Library School Monograph No. 5.)

University of California, Library Affirmative Action Program for Women Committee (1971). "Report on the Status of Women Employed in the Library of the University of California, Berkeley, with Recommendations for Affirmative Action." Berkeley, California. (ERIC ED 066-163.)

U.S. Bureau of Labor Statistics (1975). "Library Manpower: A Study of Demand and Supply." Department of Labor, Washington, D.C. (Bulletin No. 1852.)

U.S. Commission on Civil Rights (1977). "Last Hired, First Fired: Layoffs and Civil Rights." Commission on Civil Rights, Washington, D.C.

U.S. Department of Health, Education, and Welfare (1977). Nondiscrimination on the basis of handicap. *Federal Register* 42, 22676-22702.

U.S. Equal Employment Opportunity Commission (1974). "Affirmative Action and Equal Employment: A Guidebook for Employers," 2 vols. Equal Employment Opportunity Commission, Washington, D.C.

U.S. Equal Employment Opportunity Commission (1975). "Laws and Rules You Should Know." Equal Employment Opportunity Commission, Washington, D.C.

U.S. Equal Employment Opportunity Commission (1976). Employee selection procedures. *Federal Register* 41, 51984-51751.

U.S. Equal Employment Opportunity Coordinating Council (1976). Employee selection procedures. *Federal Register* 41, 29016-29022.

U.S. Office for Civil Rights (1972). "Higher Education Guidelines: Executive Order 11246." Department of Health, Education, and Welfare, Washington, D.C.

U.S. Office of Education (1975). "Programs for Educational Equity: Schools and Affirmative Action." Department of Health, Education, and Welfare, Washington, D.C. (DHEW Publication No. (OE) 75-03301.)

U.S. President's Committee on Employment of the Handicapped (1975). "Analysis of Library Employment Questionnaire." President's Committee on Employment of the Handicapped, Washington, D.C. (Mimeograph copy.)

U.S. President's Committee on Employment of the Handicapped (1976). "Affirmative Action to Employ Handicapped People: A Pocket Guide." U.S. Government Printing Office, Washington, D.C.

Velleman, R. A. (1977). Barriers for the handicapped. *Library Journal* 102, 523-524.

Walton, E. (1974). Accentuating the positive in affirmative action. *Wilson Library Bulletin* 49, 135-136.

Women's Equity Action League, Educational and Legal Defense Fund (1975). "Women Graduates." WEAL, Washington, D.C. (Mimeograph copy.)

William Karp Consulting Co., Inc. (1972). "Outline of a strategy for Affirmative Action Planning in Educational Institutions." William Karp Consulting Co., Chicago, Illinois. (Mimeographed copy.)

American Indian Library Service

CHARLES T. TOWNLEY
School of Library Science
University of Michigan

I.	Introduction	136
II.	Indian America in the 1970s	137
	A. Demographic Data	137
	B. Self-Determination	140
III.	American Indian Library Service to 1973: Defining the Domain	142
	A. Community Libraries	143
	B. School Libraries	144
	C. Postsecondary and Research Libraries	145
	D. Continuing Education and Professional Activities	147
	E. Goals for Indian Library and Information Service	148
IV.	American Indian Library Service since 1973: Demonstration and Testing	149
	A. National Indian Education Association Library Project	149
	B. Rough Rock Community School Library	152
	C. Standing Rock Tribal Library	154
	D. Akwesasne Library–Culture Center	157
	E. Sioux City Public Library Indian Library Project	159
	F. Shoshone–Bannock Library and Media Center	160
	G. Arizona	161
	H. New Mexico	162
	I. Wisconsin	164
	J. Newberry Library Center for the History of the American Indian	166

K.	Professional Education	166
L.	Professional Associations	167
V.	Findings: The Knowledge Base of American Indian Library Service	168
A.	Indian Communities Possess Specific Information Needs	169
B.	Demand for Information Is Increasing	169
C.	Indian Control Is Necessary	169
D.	Services Strategies	170
E.	Materials, Equipment, and Facilities	170
F.	Funding	171
G.	Personnel Utilization and Training	171
VI.	Implementing American Indian Library Service: The Next Five Years	172
A.	Policy Development	172
B.	Development of a Continuing Funding Base	174
	References	174

I. INTRODUCTION

The winds of change have blown strongly in both the American Indian and library communities during recent years.* American Indian and other native peoples have worked diligently to achieve the goal of self-determination. As a result of this effort, Indian people have come to realize that access to, and the use of, information is the first requirement for successful decision making. Librarians, seeking to reach new publics, have come to understand that native Americans possess a unique set of information needs and service requirements. In some communities these perceptions have come together to create American Indian library service—library and information services which meet the information needs of American Indian people in a manner compatible with the social and cultural milieu of the Indian community served.

*One of the many changes is the growing number of terms used to describe the first residents of the Americas; native Americans, first Americans, native peoples, Indians, American Indians, and many others. Since no consensus exists on the preference for any one term, this chapter will use all of them interchangeably. For the purposes of this review all of these terms may be defined as including those individuals who: (1) are members of a tribe, band, or other organized group, including those tribes, bands, or groups terminated since 1940 and those recognized now or in the future by the state in which they reside, or who are descendants, in the first or second degree, of any such member; or (2) are considered by the Secretary of the Interior to be Indians for any purpose; or (3) are Eskimo or Aleut or other Alaska natives (United States, 1972).

This chapter examines the state of the art in American Indian library service. To provide the reader with a basic understanding of the environment of Indian communities, the first section presents a statistical summary and policy analysis of Indian America. Following this, the origins of American Indian library service will be traced. The third section is devoted to case studies describing the current state of American Indian library service as it has developed in selected Native American communities. Findings of research and experience are presented in the fourth section. The last section addresses two major national issues that are central to the future development of American Indian library service.

This review is limited in its scope and objectives. It avoids extended discussion of the role of libraries as transmitters of American Indian culture to the non-Indian world. This is a topic that is as large as or larger than American Indian library service and deserves serious treatment of its own. Second, materials about Indian people are discussed only as they directly relate to American Indian library service. A comprehensive work on American Indian bibliography is still badly needed. Finally, this work is based on the perceptions of one writer. There are, undoubtedly, other interpretations.

II. INDIAN AMERICA IN THE 1970s

To begin to understand the information needs of American Indian people, librarians must have a clear perception of native Americans and the communities in which they live. In this section two approaches, a statistical summary of demographic data and an analysis of the Indian policy environment, will be used to create a composite picture of Indian America in the 1970s.

A. Demographic Data

Indian America is young and growing rapidly. In the ten years between 1960 and 1970, the number of native Americans living in the United States has grown from 527,591 to 792,730. The median age, 20.4 years, is some eight years below the national average. The birthrate is 37.4 per thousand compared with 17.8 per thousand in the total population. American Indian people constitute one of the most rapidly growing racial groups in the United States (U.S. Bureau of the Census, 1973b, pp. 4–7). The geographic distribution of American Indian people is also changing. Significant Indian communities are now located in every state. Table I provides a breakdown of the 1970 Indian population by state.

Indian population is growing most rapidly in cities where a growing number of native Americans are moving in search of employment. In 1960 less than a third of the Indian population resided in urban areas. By 1970, the figure had climbed to almost one half. Table II identifies eighteen Standard Metropolitan Statistical Areas with American Indian populations exceeding 4,000 individuals.

According to census figures 40 percent of Indian families have income below the poverty level, in contrast to 10.7 percent for the

TABLE I
Indian Population by State, 1970[a]

Alabama	2,443	Montana	27,130
Alaska	16,276	Nebraska	6,624
Arizona	95,812	Nevada	7,933
Arkansas	2,014	New Hampshire	361
California	91,018	New Jersey	4,706
Colorado	8,836	New Mexico	72,788
Connecticut	2,222	New York	28,355
Delaware	656	North Carolina	44,406
District of Columbia	956	North Dakota	14,369
Florida	6,677	Ohio	6,654
Georgia	2,347	Oklahoma	98,468
Hawaii	1,126	Oregon	13,510
Idaho	6,687	Pennsylvania	5,533
Illinois	11,413	Rhode Island	1,390
Indiana	3,887	South Carolina	2,241
Iowa	2,992	South Dakota	32,365
Kansas	8,672	Tennessee	2,276
Kentucky	1,531	Texas	17,957
Louisiana	5,294	Utah	11,273
Maine	2,195	Vermont	229
Maryland	4,239	Virginia	4,853
Massachusetts	4,475	Washington	33,386
Michigan	16,854	West Virginia	751
Minnesota	23,128	Wisconsin	18,924
Mississippi	4,113	Wyoming	4,980
Missouri	5,405		

[a]Source: U.S. Bureau of the Census (1973b).

TABLE II
Urban Indian Communities Exceeding 4,000 Population[a]

Los Angeles–Long Beach	23,908
Tulsa	15,183
Oklahoma City	12,951
San Francisco–Oakland	12,041
Phoenix	10,127
New York	9,984
Minneapolis–St. Paul	9,911
Seattle–Everett	8,814
Chicago	8,203
San Diego	6,007
San Bernardino–Ontario–Riverside	5,941
Albuquerque	5,822
Buffalo	5,606
Dallas	5,500
Detroit	5,203
San Jose	4,407
Denver	4,104
Portland	4,059

[a]Source: U.S. Bureau of the Census (1973b).

entire population. The median Indian family income is $5,832. The national median family income is $9,590. Only 10 percent of Indian workers hold professional and technical jobs. The unemployment rate is three times the national average and 25 percent of Indian people live in overcrowded housing compared with 8.5 percent of the rest of the country (U.S. Bureau of the Census, 1973b, pp. 10, 13, 17). Alcoholism and mental health problems constitute major health hazards (U.S. Congress, Senate, 1969, pp. 17–18). Life expectancy is seven years below the national norm (Fuchs and Havighurst, 1972, p. 32).

Indian education is improving, but remains inadequate. In 1960, only 20 percent of American Indian people over 25 years of age possessed a high school diploma. By 1970, this figure had increased to 33 percent. But it remains significantly lower than the national average of 52.3 percent. The median of years of education for Indian people over 25 years of age is 9.8 compared with the national median of 12.1 years (U.S. Bureau of the Census, 1973b, pp. 14–15). Adult functional illiteracy is reported to exceed 33 percent in some reservation communities (U.S. Congress, Senate, 1969, p. xii).

No consensus exists on the total number of Indian children of school age. The Bureau of Indian Affairs reports that 187,613 Indian children between the ages of 5 and 18 residing on or near reservations attended school in 1973. Another 17,159 did not attend school or the place of attendance was unknown. Of the group attending school, about 70 percent went to public school, 25 percent attended Bureau of Indian Affairs (BIA) schools, and 5 percent attended Indian-controlled or private schools (U.S. Bureau of Indian Affairs, 1973, p. 6). These figures are representative for that half of the Indian population living on or near reservations. Statistics for Indian children attending schools in urban areas are much less certain. The best conservative estimate suggests that urban enrollments exceed 125,000 (U.S. Office of Education, 1975, p. 67). The force out rate for Indian students is high. Only half the currently enrolled students can expect to complete high school (Fuchs and Havighurst, 1972).

American Indian involvement in postsecondary education has increased greatly in recent years. Bureau of Indian Affairs postsecondary fellowships rose from 623 in 1961 to 13,558 in 1973. Of this number approximately two-thirds enroll in technical and vocational programs. Of the third enrolled in academic programs, 770 were granted bachelors and 168 were awarded postgraduate degrees in 1973 (U.S. Bureau of Indian Affairs, 1973, p. 38).

American Indian demographic data have several implications for librarians. The rapid rate of population growth suggests that Indian people can no longer be ignored. The vanishing Indian is no more. The changing geographic distribution implies that the development of American Indian library service is a concern for urban librarians as well as their colleagues in rural areas. Age distributions indicate the need for programs directed to young people. Economic and living conditions suggest that the provision of practical, life-coping information should be a major concern of American Indian library service. Educational statistics imply a strong need for culturally supportive, school-based programs and adult independent learning. The high rate of functional English illiteracy suggests the use of bilingual materials in all media formats.

B. Self-Determination

The policy environment of Indian America consists of the contractual and behavioral relationships between native Americans and the

European peoples. Contractual relations have evolved through treaties between Indian tribes and the federal government. In these treaties the tribes gave up much of their land in return for status as domestic dependent nations retaining certain types of sovereignty and the promise of various social, economic, and educational benefits (Cohen, 1940). While more often honored in the breach, treaties remain the law of the land. Behavioral relationships have no standing in law, but have a powerful impact on the policy environment at any given time. If the American public, acting through Congress and the Executive, decides that Indians are unimportant, then treaty obligations are no longer valued and Indian people are open to exploitation. If, on the other hand, the American public is concerned with Indian people, then Indians have an opportunity to prosper. The key is achieving and maintaining public recognition of the law.

Self-determination is the sixth policy environment established to guide Indian–white relations over the past two hundred years (U.S. Congress, Senate, 1969, pp. 139–207). Unlike its predecessors self-determination has emerged from the Indian community and has been accepted over time by the federal establishment and the American public. The scope and objectives of self-determination are best illustrated in the documents central to its development:

> We, the Indian People must be governed by principles in a democratic manner with a right to choose our own way of life. . . . The basic principle involves the desire on the part of Indians to participate in developing their own programs. . . . The Indians as responsible individual citizens, as responsible tribal representatives, and as responsible Tribal Councils want to participate, want to contribute to their own personal and tribal improvements and want to cooperate with their Government on how best to solve the many problems in a business-like, efficient and economical manner as rapidly as possible (American Indian Chicago Conference, 1961, p. 4).

> No program imposed from the outside can serve as a substitute for one willed by Indians themselves. Nor should their ostensible consent to a plan be deemed sufficient. Such "consent" may be wholly passive, indicating only a surrender to what seems unavoidable; or their consent may be obtained without their full understanding or before they are either able or desire to shoulder additional obligations. What is essential is to elicit their own initiative and intelligent cooperation (Commission on the Rights, Liberties and Responsibilities of the American Indian, 1966, p. 4).

It is long past time that the Indian policies of the Federal government began to recognize and build upon the capacities and insights of the Indian people. Both as a matter of justice and as a matter of enlightened social policy, we must begin to act on the basis of what the Indians themselves have long been telling us. The time has come to break decisively with the past and create the conditions for a new era in which the Indian future is determined by Indian acts and Indian decisions (Nixon, 1970, p. 565).

The Congress hereby recognizes the obligation of the United States to respond to the strong expression of the Indian people for self-determination by assuring maximum Indian participation in the direction of educational as well as other Federal services to Indian communities so as to render such services more responsive to the needs and desires of those communities (United States, 1975, p. 1).

Self-determination is the first policy environment to reflect Indian values as the proper locus and process of decision making. In the Indian world view policy decisions can not be made by the individual, they must be made by the community. As Lurie says:

... there is a preference and relaxed patience for reaching decisions by consensus. While often baffling to the white observer, the process is patterned, and Indian people of widely varying tribal backgrounds are able to conduct business together according to mutually understood "rules" (Lurie, 1971, p. 444).

Self-determination has two clear implications for librarians. First, as Indian people are actively involved in making decisions regarding their future, the demand for information in Indian communities will greatly increase. Informed decision making, whether it be personal or corporate, demands rapid access to and the use of accurate information (U.S. Congress, American Indian Policy Review Commission, 1976). Second, the ultimate fate of American Indian library service must reside where it should—with the people. Librarians will be accountable to Indian people for the success or failure of American Indian library service.

III. AMERICAN INDIAN LIBRARY SERVICE TO 1973: DEFINING THE DOMAIN

Historically the role of libraries in Indian America has been inconsequential. While colonial colleges were not above making appeals for books to educate Indians, little evidence exists that resources, once received, were ever used for their stated purpose. In the nineteenth century missionaries used a few books to introduce Indian people to the rites of Christianity (Jacobs, 1972). More recently those few Indian schools that possessed the semblance of a library used them, if at all, to support the accepted educational goal of assimilation (Szasz, 1974). Public libraries did not exist. In short, most Indian people had no access to information other than by word of mouth. The few who did found little that addressed Indian information needs.

As Indian people evolved the goal of self-determination and librarians became concerned with serving a wider public, a community of interest was generated dedicated to finding ways to meet the information needs of Indian people. The years between 1957 and 1973 represent a period when American Indians and librarians sought to identify the domain and major dimensions of American Indian library service. Events of the period have been described in detail by Smith (1971) and Naumer (1974). This discussion is intended only to summarize the major events and innovations of the period.

A. Community Libraries

The Colorado River Tribes Public Library was the first library in the country developed specifically to meet Indian information needs. Established in 1957 by the Tribal Council, in 1969 it provided the community with research on local Indian history, a collection exceeding 10,000 volumes, story hours for children, and access to nonprint media. Support for the Library came from the Tribes' community development funds, Save the Children Foundation, and the Arizona Department of Libraries and Archives (Welsh, 1969).

In the period prior to 1973, basic library and information services were developed in several Indian communities. Urban Indian organizations, such as the American Indian Center in Chicago, the Cleveland Indian Center, and the Seattle Indian Center, worked with local public libraries to develop small collections of Indian-related materials. A few large reservations made efforts to establish tribal libraries (Cunningham, 1969, 1971; Smith, 1971). With the advent of the Library Services and Construction Act (LSCA) and other Great Society programs, state library agencies initiated bookmobile services in Indian communities (Dolejsi, 1974; Farrington, 1969; Gordon, 1969; Groulx, 1972, 1973).

Naumer (1974) discusses lessons learned in the early efforts to develop American Indian library service at the community level. First, community involvement in planning and operating libraries is essential. More than one program originating in libraries learned this lesson the hard way. After planning and developing a program which they thought would be of use to Indian people, librarians were amazed to encounter indifference or hostility on the part of the community. Second, successful programs employ community residents. Libraries are new to Indian people. They must be introduced by someone the community trusts. Three, easy-to-read materials on practical or culturally supportive topics are preferred by adults. Childrens books of all varieties are in great demand. Finally, having demonstrated a need, librarians and Indian leaders are under an obligation to continue to fill it.

B. School Libraries

Among the first to recognize the need for library services addressing perceived Indian information needs were school librarians. In 1966, the Red Cloud Indian School on the Pine Ridge Reservation in South Dakota began to adapt its library services to meet the needs of the Lakota people. Collection development emphasized student interests. A paperback reading room was opened to meet student social requirements for an informal study atmosphere. Community as well as school use was encouraged (Rigel, 1970). Six other private and public schools reported the development of innovative programs during this period. Two school libraries developed outreach programs working with students on reading and study improvement. Three schools greatly increased their collections of materials on Indians. One school system provided its librarians with an orientation to the information needs and social characteristics of Indian students (Naumer, 1974; Smith, 1971; Vaughan, 1971). Most of these efforts were funded under the Elementary and Secondary Education Act, Title II (ESEA-II).

As the Bureau of Indian Affairs (BIA) schools began to adopt the policy of self-determination, BIA librarians initiated programs relating to the information needs of Indian students. ESEA-II funds were used extensively to improve library collections. An outstanding regional library was established to serve 34 villages in southwest Alaska, where deposit collections were rotated every 2 weeks by plane. Reference and interlibrary loan were provided using radio and bush plane

(Mudd, 1972). In the Dakotas two mobile media centers brought media services and arts classes to isolated community schools. A Research and Cultural Studies Section was established at the Institute of American Indian Arts and has provided a number of tribes with culturally supportive materials. A film library and professional collection was developed at Brigham City, Utah, to improve access to media materials and educational research Bureau-wide. Teachers and librarians were encouraged to borrow materials for professional and classroom use (Naumer, 1974).

Using knowledge gained from these experiments and the results of five research studies done by library school students, school librarians began to identify some of the necessary components of American Indian library service in school media centers. Administrative commitment was essential. In some locales, particularly public schools, racial prejudice still had to be overcome. Improved training, collections, and facilities were needed in most schools. Programs needed to relate more closely with student information needs (Ecrolin, 1971; Ford, 1968; Pipe, 1971; Ralph and Sheppard, 1969; Sargent, 1970).

Bromberg's (1972) study of BIA school media centers is the most perceptive needs analysis for school-based American Indian library service developed during this period. He found that BIA educational administrators were unaware of the appropriate role and potential contributions of a media center; that, with few exceptions, libraries in BIA schools were inadequate or nonexistent; and that available materials and services did not address the information needs of the students. Bromberg's 19 recommendations outline a vigorous program of administrative and budgetary action designed to provide effective American Indian library service for students and communities directly served by BIA schools. Unfortunately, the Bureau of Indian Affairs has not been able fully to implement these suggestions.

C. Postsecondary and Research Libraries

As American Indian people began to enter institutions of postsecondary education in increasing numbers, libraries in colleges with large Indian enrollments began to respond to Indian information needs. Townley (1971), reporting on 18 institutions with Indian studies or recruitment programs, found that in most cases efforts were limited to expanded acquisitions programs for materials about Indians and the provision of limited reference services such as supplying bibliographies. Some colleges did develop additional forms of service directly related to Indian information needs. Four institutions established reading rooms providing special materials or services. Two schools established bibliographic instruction programs for Indian students. The University of New Mexico Law Library began publication of the *American Indian Law Newsletter*.

Libraries in institutions serving only Indian students were established or upgraded during this period. Libraries at three postsecondary institutions operated by the BIA (Haskell Institute, Institute of American Indian Arts, Southwestern Indian Polytechnic Institute) were improved and efforts were made to provide services meaningful to the students (Blank, 1971). Four Indian-controlled colleges were established during this period. At Navajo Community College, the Library received several foundation grants to develop a comprehensive collection of Navajo materials, offered a course in bibliographic instruction and attempted to make the Library relevant to Navajo information needs and cultural attitudes (Richardson, 1970). Sinte Gleska College and the Lakota Higher Education Center libraries used Ford Foundation grants to develop programs of library service to meet Lakota information needs. Deganawidah–Quetzalcoatl University established strong ties with the neighboring University of California at Davis, Library to help it through its formative period.

A number of factors contributed to the gains made in library services for American Indians in academic institutions. Indian people administering academic programs recognized the existence of information needs unique to Indian students and pressed libraries to implement programs which met them. Foundations were willing to support library development in Indian-controlled colleges. Libraries felt a social responsibility to respond to the requests of minorities, and Indian materials were increasingly called for by many disciplines and students. The small relative cost of establishing and maintaining acceptable programs were not prohibitive in the larger academic libraries.

Research libraries began to make their collections more available to the Indian community. The libraries of the Museum of the American Indian and the Southwest Museum encouraged tribal historians and librarians to use their collections. The Smithsonian reproduced its photographic collections and inaugurated a museum training program for American Indians, and the National Archives produced a number of finding tools for those interested in American Indian research (Hill, 1965; Kelsay, 1954; Thomas, 1972). The National Indian Law Library (1972) printed its *Catalog* for use by lawyers and libraries.

D. Continuing Education and Professional Activities

As librarians and Indian people worked at defining the domain of American Indian library service, the need for continuing education and professional activities became apparent. Six Higher Education Act, Title II-B (HEA-IIB) institutes were held during the late 1960s and early 1970s. The purpose of these institutes was to introduce librarians to the information needs of Indian people and to build the skills required to meet those needs. Four of the institutes emphasized programs and materials for school and public libraries (ERIC, 1971; J. S. Smith, 1969; L. P. Smith, 1970). The University of Minnesota (1970) institute emphasized children's materials and produced a highly regarded bibliography. The evaluations of these institutes indicate that the participants returned to their work with an increased awareness of Indian information needs as well as many of the skills necessary to meet them. A one-year-long master's institute was held at the University of South Dakota. Its graduates have added much to the development of American Indian library service in South Dakota and elsewhere (Smith, 1971).

The American Indian Historical Society established criteria for the evaluation of materials used by Indian young people (Costo, 1970) and a guide for organizing reference collections (Henry, 1970). It has since been very active in reviewing and indexing Indian materials through *Wassaja* and the Indian Historian Press. The National Indian Education Association (NIEA) initiated a library discussion section beginning with its 1972 Annual Conference. The American Library Association (ALA) has had a number of committees active in the area. The Adult Services Division approved evaluation criteria for adult level material in 1971 (Smith, 1971), and the Office of Library Service for the Disadvantaged, Subcommittee on Library Service for American Indian People, has served as an information exchange for the development of American Indian library service. The Office for Library Personnel Resources initiated efforts to recruit American Indian people to the field of librarianship (American Library Association, Office for Library Personnel Resources, 1973).

E. Goals for Indian Library and Information Service

The first phase of Indian library development was complete by 1973. Exploratory Programs provided a set of operational concepts. There appeared to be a relevant domain for American Indian library and information service. In 1973, the National Indian Education Association and the American Library Association codified this experience in a joint policy statement.

> *Goals for Indian Library and Information Service*
> A Joint Policy Statement of
> National Indian Education Association
> and
> American Library Association
>
> In order to meet informational needs of American Indians and to purvey and promote the rich cultural heritage of American Indians, the following goals are presented as guidelines for programs of library and information service serving American Indians:
>
> Goal: *All library and information service must show sensitivity to cultural and social components existent in individual Indian communities.* All forms of library service will require the application of bi-lingual and bi-cultural principles to insure success.
>
> Goal: *Indian representation, through appointment to local boards and creation of local advisory committees concerning service to and about American Indians, is essential for healthy, viable programs.* Programs should have input from those persons they attempt to serve.
>
> Goal: *Materials which meet informational and educational needs and which present a bi-cultural view of history and culture must be provided in appropriate formats, quality and quantity to meet current and future needs.* The library should produce its own materials if they are not available in a language or format used by most of the community.
>
> Goal: *Library programs, outreach and delivery systems must be created which will insure rapid access to information in a manner compatible with the community's cultural milieu.* Library programs in Indian communities must take into account the local community's cultural life style.
>
> Goal: *American Indian personnel trained for positions of responsibility are essential to the success of any program.* Recruitment and training programs must be devised and implemented.
>
> Goal: *Continuing funding sources for library and information service must be developed.* Library service, as a function of education, is a treaty right of American Indians.

IV. AMERICAN LIBRARY SERVICE SINCE 1973: DEMONSTRATION AND TESTING

With 1973, Indian America began to achieve its goal of self-determination. For the first time Indian parents, operating under the provisions of the Indian Education Act (United States, 1972), achieved some control over the education of their children in public schools. More schools came under Indian control through the process of contracting. The BIA implemented new budget and personnel procedures designed to increase Indian input in decision making, and the advent of Federal Revenue Sharing gave most tribal councils their first source of discretionary funds for community development. The funding of the Navajo Community College Act and the formation of the American Indian Higher Education Consortium demonstrated a growing commitment to postsecondary education. What would become the Indian Self-Determination Act (United States, 1975) was introduced to a favorable Congress. Perhaps most important, Wounded Knee convinced the American public that the time had come for American Indians to shape their own destiny (Deloria, 1974).

The year 1973 also marked a major change in the development of American Indian library service. With a domain identified, American Indians and librarians could now concentrate on demonstrating good library and information service. Also, the growing national awareness of Indian America resulted in an increasing availability of funds for demonstration. Promising exploratory programs could now be replicated in many different Indian communities throughout the country, and new programs could be tested for effectiveness.

A. National Indian Education Association Library Project

The National Indian Education Association (NIEA) Library Project was a national research and demonstration effort in American Indian library service. The purpose of the NIEA Library Project was "to plan, develop and demonstrate library programs that meet informational needs in Indian communities" (Antell, 1974). The Library Project had four major objectives: (1) identification of information needs; (2) implementation of demonstration programs; (3) operation of demonstration programs; and (4) evaluation. Funded in large part by HEA-IIB, the Library Project began in late 1971, initiated demonstration operations in 1973, and completed its activities in 1975 (Townley, 1975a).

The first months of the NIEA Library Project were devoted to selecting three Indian communities to serve as research and demonstration sites, measuring information needs in these communities, and developing implementation plans for programs of American Indian library service. The NIEA Executive Board selected sites on the basis of criteria emphasizing community interest, the presence of educational facilities in the community, and social and geographic diversity among the sites. The Rough Rock community was selected on the basis of its strong traditional culture and its Indian-controlled school. The Standing Rock Sioux Reservation in North and South Dakota was chosen as a representative large reservation with a strong emphasis on tribal planning. The Saint Regis Akwesasne Reservation was selected as a bilingual/bicultural community with a relatively strong economic base and a clear commitment to library service.

To measure information needs, the University of Minnesota's Bureau of Field Studies conducted a survey at the three sites. The survey measured the strength of information needs in eleven categories: (1) American Indian culture; (2) family life; (3) American Indians in urban society; (4) service agencies; (5) legal and civil rights; (6) occupations and vocations; (7) consumer information; (8) academic disciplines; (9) health and safety; (10) recreation; and (11) contemporary events. Three subpopulations—elementary pupils, secondary pupils, and adults—were randomly sampled at each site. Survey items were developed by Indian graduate students using a modified jury technique. All survey instruments were reviewed and approved by the community prior to administration. Students were surveyed in school by Project personnel. Adult questionnaires were administered by bilingual community residents, and all adults were compensated for their time (University of Minnesota, 1972e).

The findings support the argument that Indian people recognize the importance of information. The forced choice scaling used in the survey indicates a high priority for information in the minds of most Indian people. Adult respondents indicated a strong interest in information on the history, culture, and language of their own tribes. Survival and quality of life issues also ranked quite high. High school students were interested in vocational information, while elementary students wanted cultural and curriculum-related information. Subsequent administrations of revised forms of this survey supported the validity of these broad areas of information need (Metoyer, 1976; Smith, 1974b; University of Minnesota, 1972a,b,c).

Using the survey data and information on existing library facilities, Library Project and community personnel developed models and operational plans for each site. Akwesasne would continue its efforts to develop a library and cultural center. Standing Rock would develop a tribal library system. Rough Rock would become a community school library.

Project staff spent most of the second year of the Project assisting the three sites in implementing services: local boards were organized and trained, space for library facilities was located, supplementary funds were obtained, local personnel were hired and basic training was provided, materials and equipment were selected and ordered, collections were organized, and program components were developed and implemented. By March 1973, each site was operating out of one or more facilities (Townley, 1975a).

In the third year site operations were emphasized. Site autonomy was established by means of formal contracts. Local facilities and collections were improved. Outreach and communication efforts, such as radio programming, newsletters, community workers, and bookmobiles, were inaugurated. Technically complex program components, such as video production centers and museums, were developed. All program components were reviewed, and several were dropped as a result of operational problems or lack of community response. An active public relations program was undertaken in the national library and Indian press. Each site was evaluated by an independent consultant (Antell, 1974).

As originally conceived the last year of the NIEA Library Project was to be devoted entirely to evaluation. This, however, proved to be undesirable. The three sites had not fully reached their operational goals and did not have sufficient funding for continuing operations. Also, NIEA staff were committed to improving state level planning and developing technical materials on American Indian library service. Thus it was decided to address all these objectives in the last year of the Project. Operational plans and contracts for the sites were developed by local staff and approved by their boards, while Library Project personnel remained available for technical assistance. Significant effort went into acquiring continuing funding for the sites. The Rough Rock Library was included in the normal operating budget of the school. At Standing Rock the Tribal Library received support from Revenue Sharing, the schools, and the state library agency. In New York the state government provided direct funding for the Akwesasne Library–Culture Center. State level planning was conducted in Wisconsin and Wyoming, and a filmstrip and a series of Indian Library Guides were prepared and made available to librarians and Indian people (Mathews, 1975a; Townley, 1975a,b).

The NIEA Library Project successfully demonstrated that programs of American Indian library service can meet the information needs of Indian people. Circulation statistics from all three sites revealed the use of printed material at rates exceeding the national average. High attendance and reference queries suggest the incorporation of information and referral services into community life. Most special programming efforts received a positive response (Townley, 1975a, pp. 109–111). Perhaps most important, all three communities saw fit to continue their libraries after completion of the Project, often at a considerable sacrifice. The project evaluation (Genia *et al.*, 1975) provides a valuable critique of the strengths and weaknesses of the Library Project, and it concludes by suggesting the replication of the Project in other locales.

B. Rough Rock Community School Library

The Rough Rock Community School Library serves a community of 1,500 Navajo people living in a 900-square-mile area of northeast Arizona. The community is among the most traditional in the Navajo Nation. Rough Rock is an isolated community with only one improved dirt road, electricity in less than 20 percent of the homes, and running water and telephone service available only at the school. Annual per capita income is less than $500. About one third of the adult population is functionally illiterate in English (University of Minnesota, 1972b).

The Library operates out of the Rough Rock School, the first Indian controlled school in the country. Both the School and the Library are committed to community-based decision making. For the Library this has meant creating a perceptible level of library awareness in the community. The Rough Rock Library worked at this task for the better part of three years. Several factors impeded rapid progress, not the least of which were: lack of attention on the part of NIEA Library Project personnel; continuing personnel turnovers in the library and the school; language and cultural barriers; and justified community reluctance to accept yet another program designed to "help" Indians. Nor was this a problem only for the Library. Even the School suffers to a degree because it is foreign to the Navajo way of life. Keys to the solution of the acceptability problem have been the employment of a Navajo librarian who can interact more fully with the community and support from the School's Director and Board (Townley, 1975a).

Four program components were emphasized in the Rough Rock Library. The print collection was organized and enlarged in areas where the youth indicated strong information need. Second, significant progress was made in incorporating the Library into the educational program. Teachers were trained in the use of the Library and media equipment, and story hours were regularly given. Independent and group use of the Library was encouraged, and films and other materials were ordered for classroom use. Curriculum materials were prepared in conjunction with the Navajo Curriculum Center.

The most successful program of the Library was the video production center. Video had a number of advantages for Rough Rock. It immediately overcame the language limitations of commercially available print or film, and content was adaptable to the unique information needs of the community. During the tenure of the NIEA Library Project, several hundred hours of tape were produced and 100 hours were retained for permanent use. Some of the more interesting productions included a secular adaptation of Changing Woman, a bilingual series on Navajo and European natural history, and demonstrations of home machines.

Community library and information service for adults remains in its infancy. Community residents are encouraged to use the library, but they do not feel entirely comfortable in the school building. It is still foreign. There is also the literacy limitation and the added costs involved in having to produce one's own materials. Two programs that have succeeded are Sunday evening films and the media van. Parents of boarding students bring their children to school on Sunday evenings. Many stay and watch a feature film and several educational shorts provided by the Library. The media van has been used to mount several programs. One program on sewing which used a video demonstration, simple bilingual instruction handouts, sewing books, and patterns has been well received. Limited staff and funds have made it impossible for the Library to use the media van to full advantage. But it does seem to offer the best potential for reaching and meeting adult information needs at Rough Rock (Townley, 1975a).

C. Standing Rock Tribal Library

The Standing Rock Sioux Reservation occupies about 3,700 square miles in North and South Dakota. The Reservation is allotted and less than 40 percent of the land remains in Indian control. About 4,700 Indian persons live in seven communities scattered around the Reservation. Educational and social characteristics are similar to the census data presented earlier. The community is bilingual with 80 percent of the adults fluent in either Lakota or Dakota and 95 percent literate in English (University of Minnesota, 1972c).

The Standing Rock Tribal Library was initiated by the Tribal Council in 1972 as the information and communication component of the *Developmental Plan* (Standing Rock Sioux Tribe, 1972). It served as a demonstration site for the NIEA Library Project from late 1972 through 1975. Since that time the Tribal Library has been sponsored in large part by revenue sharing. The Standing Rock Tribal Library is housed in four facilities located in different communities on the Reservation. The largest library is located at Fort Yates, the Tribal headquarters. Housed in a new community and skills center, it directly serves the community of Fort Yates, the Tribal government, and Standing Rock Community College. The Cannonball Community School Library is situated in the center of a new classroom facility at Cannonball. The Little Eagle and Bullhead Community School Libraries operate out of remodeled space in existing school facilities. These libraries work with the schools to meet the information and curricular needs of the students and with the Ft. Yates Library to meet the information needs of adults.

Initial development of facilities and collections was carried out between 1973 and 1974. Some difficulties in opening the facilities were encountered owing to missed construction deadlines and the remoteness of the community from sources of supply. Materials were initially selected by consultants and later by the staff using a collection development policy based on needs expressed in the survey. Additional funds for materials were provided by ESEA-II, LSCA, and the Johnson-O'Malley Act. Collections were organized using eight color codes. Each color represented a specific area of information need identified in the survey. Brief entry author and title cards were prepared, but this innovation proved to be a mixed success. It facilitated opening the facilities and was well received by the users, and yet the schools desired a cataloged collection, and reference work was made difficult. As a result some of the libraries have since converted to more traditional cataloging techniques. After some experimentation it was found that peer pressure, such as posting lists of delinquent borrowers, was the most effective means of encouraging the return of overdue materials.

The Standing Rock Tribal Library has made a number of efforts to take information to the community. During the first years of the Library's operation, a deposit collection of paperbacks and magazines established at the Public Health Service proved to be an effective means of introducing library services to the community. The Library also produces a weekly radio program and a fortnightly newsletter, *The Standing Rock Tribal Library Newsletter,* distributed free to the residents of the seven communities. Both productions emphasize Tribal information that can not be obtained from other media sources. The radio program is often bilingual.

The Library maintains an active selective dissemination of information program. *Hou Kola* (Standing Rock Tribal Library, 1974) provides each family on the Reservation with a comprehensive guide to educational, social, health, and recreational services available to Tribal members. Each entry provides a brief description of the service, eligibility requirements, and contact information. Organizational data, acquired for the publication of the guide, are now used by the library staff as a means for distributing information and publications, such as Federal grant guidelines, to the participating organizations.

Standing Rock Tribal Library works closely with Standing Rock Community College. The Fort Yates Library serves as the college library. The community school libraries serve as satellite learning centers for the College—offering classroom space, materials, and academic guidance for the students. This satellite learning center model has been adopted by the American Indian Higher Education

Consortium as the basis for proposals to develop libraries in its nine member institutions.*

The Cannonball and Little Eagle Community School Libraries emphasize children's programming. In the summer Cannonball works with the summer school on reading programs. A summer film festival has also been popular. During the winter, the Library sponsors adult arts and crafts classes and puppet shows for the children. At Little Eagle, the community takes great pride in the Library's video production center. It is used to record school activities for playback to parents and also important tribal business and community oral history for use in the cultural education program.

The Standing Rock Tribal Library has had to deal with two major areas of administrative concern during its development: personnel utilization and community input. From the beginning the Library has employed community people. This has been the most essential factor in creating community awareness and acceptance of library service. However, problems have developed in the areas of job expectancy, training, and retention. Several of the staff came to the job expecting to catalog and check out books for the rest of their lives. This was not surprising, since these were the only things they had seen librarians doing. It took some of the staff some time to abandon their limited views of the librarian's responsibilities. Second, it was very difficult to train the staff miles from the closest library of any size. During the tenure of the Library Project, several alternatives were tried, but none was ever completely satisfactory. The key to success appears to be in community-based training programs similar to those of the University of New Mexico and the Great Lakes Intertribal Council described later. Third, personnel turnover was high in many of the Indian libraries. Standing Rock Tribal Library slowly alleviated this problem as staff members became committed to the Library as an essential component in the Tribe's quality of life (Teachout, 1974).

During the initial development of the Standing Rock Tribal Library, one major concern was a suitable means of community input

---

*American Indian Higher Education Consortium members include; Cheyenne River Community College, Deganawidah–Quetzalcoatl University, Lakota Higher Education Center, Navajo Community College, Satellite Community College, Sinte Gleska College Center, Sisseton–Wahpeton Community College, Standing Rock Community College, and Turtle Mountain Community College.

and control. After considerable experimentation, the Planning Office and the Tribal Council placed overall policy control with the Board of Standing Rock Community College and operational control under the local schools. This proved to be a satisfactory, if complex, means of assuring local input and consensus (Genia *et al.*, 1975; Townley, 1975a).

D. Akwesasne Library–Culture Center

The Saint Regis Akwesasne Mohawk Reservation includes an area of 14,600 acres bordering the Saint Lawrence River in New York, Ontario, and Quebec. About 5,000 people live on the Reservation and are distributed rather evenly in several villages and along five main roads. Educational characteristics for adults are similar to census data presented earlier. Educational trends for children are higher. Because of their skill as ironworkers, the Mohawks of Akwesasne have a somewhat higher standard of living than most Indian people. The community is bilingual with 80 percent of the adults fluent in Mohawk and 90 percent claiming literacy in English (University of Minnesota, 1972a).

The Akwesasne Library–Culture Center enjoys great community support. The Center was established in the late 1960s when a number of people in the community decided to start a library-centered program to meet their cultural, educational, and informational needs. By 1971, they had raised enough money, mostly through community dinners and other grass roots projects, to construct a facility. Four community people received paraprofessional in-service training in nearby school and public libraries. A nonprofit educational corporation was established, and with the help of Saint Lawrence University, a carefully selected collection of 6,000 books was organized for use. The Akwesasne Library–Culture Center opened in September 1971 (Wells, 1974).

The library collection at Akwesasne has been built around the information needs of the people as expressed in the NIEA Library Project's information needs survey (University of Minnesota, 1972a). Unlike some other Indian communities at Akwesasne there is a comparatively high interest in recreational reading. Consequently there is a substantial fiction collection, supported with paperbacks and by the McNaughton Plan. The adult nonfiction collection emphasizes practical information, such as consumer information, how-to-do-it materials, vocational information, easy to read materials, and books used by students in the Center's college classes. Children's materials have been emphasized in the library and the bookmobile. One major collection goal is to obtain one copy of everything, print and nonprint, related to the Mohawks. Using a bibliography prepared by local college students, the Center has nearly achieved that goal (Garrow et al., 1974b). To encourage use, an edited version of this bibliography has been made available to every household on the Reservation (Garrow et al., 1974a).

The strength of the Akwesasne Library–Culture Center is found in the comprehensiveness and interrelatedness of its programs. The Center operates the library, a museum, and a Right to Read program. In conjunction with the education and health programs, it supports GED tutoring, college courses, and health care. The Center offers the normal circulation and reference services of a public library. In addition, it operates a bookmobile providing school library service to three community schools. Story hours and film showings are regular features, and nonprint media and equipment are circulated to individuals and community organizations. The Center produces a weekly radio show and the *Ka Ri Wen Ha Wi Newsletter* monthly. The Center sponsors periodic community art shows and purchases some material for its circulating and museum collections. As the central facility in the Center, the library is the place of first resort for information and referral service. Because of the strength of its programming, the Akwesasne Library–Culture Center won the New York Library Association's Asa Wynkoop Award for outstanding service in 1974 (Akwesasne Library–Culture Center, 1975).

The Akwesasne Library–Culture Center, like other libraries, has not been successful in all its program efforts. At the suggestion of the NIEA Library Project, the Center initiated a program to test the value of slide-tape presentations. Unfortunately, staff interest was low and insufficient preparation time was allowed. It was an excellent object lesson for the NIEA staff on the importance of not imposing programs from outside the community. Second, the concept of deposit collections proved successful only at the Saint Regis Old Age Home where staff was available to assist in use. Except for introductory purposes the use of deposit collections without the provision of personnel assistance does not appear to warrant the investment in time and money (Townley, 1975a). Third, access, particularly for those without a car, remains a problem. Metoyer (1976) concludes that access is the key to use in a community like Akwesasne. She suggests that the Center programs pool their resources to provide regular bus service for community residents, especially children.

The Akwesasne Library–Culture Center has been particularly successful in raising funds and serves as a model for those seeking to develop American Indian library service. During the three years that the Center participated in the NIEA Library Project, it raised more than $200,000. The sources of the funds included: LSCA, HEA-IIB, the National Endowment for the Arts, Revenue Sharing, Indian Education Act, Right to Read, the Canadian and New York State governments, and the Alcoa Foundation. The Center received gifts of materials and equipment from corporations, such as the Library Bureau, and churches and individuals. When all else failed the Board sponsored community dinners and bake sales to raise funds for special purposes. Successful funding appears to be the result of the Board's commitment to American Indian library service and the ability of the Board and staff to: (1) demonstrate to others the positive contributions of the Center to the community's quality of life; (2) develop sound long-range plans based on the information needs of the Mohawk people; (3) spend long hours preparing successful proposals; and (4) establish close working relationships with funding agency personnel in both the public and the private sectors.

E. Sioux City Public Library Indian Library Project

The Indian Library Project of the Sioux City Public Library is an excellent example of an urban library working jointly with an Indian community to improve Indian information access. The Project serves Indian people living in Sioux City and the nearby Winnebago Reservation. It operates an Information Center in the Sioux City Public Library, two small deposit collections in the urban Indian centers, and the Leona Johnson Memorial Library at Winnebago. Funding for the Project has been provided through LSCA grants from the Iowa and Nebraska Library Commissions. The operating philosophy is based on the principle of self-determination. Services are planned jointly with the community and delivered "by one of their own at a time and place and in a manner of their choosing" (Jones, 1975, p. 495).

Success is due in large part to the Indian library aides who operate the Project. Recruited from the community and trained in the Library, the aides are well equipped to identify community information needs. As links between the Library and the community, they are able to effectively focus the Library's professional skills and material resources on community information needs. As members of the Indian community, the programs they sponsor are more readily accepted by the community. These linkage roles are especially critical where services originate in a library facility that is not distinctly Indian.

Programs mirror the interests of a changing community. Classes in Indian culture and language, writing contests, and oral history projects reflect the desire to retain Indian culture while living in the city. The desire for children's programming, GED tutoring, and college counseling underline a growing commitment to formal education. As the community has grown more familiar with library service, the program focus has shifted from the group to the individual. Specific needs of individuals are addressed by the Information Center and *The Iowa Indian,* a monthly newsletter sent to Indian homes.

F. Shoshone–Bannock Library and Media Center

The 3,000 Shoshone and Bannock people living on the Fort Hall Reservation have worked to develop American Indian library service since the early 1960s. In 1964, the Tribal Education Committee opened a small collection in a corner of the recreation building. At about this time a bookmobile began making a monthly stop at the Reservation headquarters. Yet, as late as 1968, Senator Robert Kennedy was appalled to find only one Indian-related book, *The Captive of the Delawares* (complete with a scalping on the cover), in a local school library (U.S. Congress, Senate Committee, 1969). Shields and Sheppard (1970) found strong tribal interest in library services, but conditions had improved little.

Meaningful change began to occur in 1971. The Tribal Education Committee established a library in a temporary education facility where it would be readily accessible to Headstart and adult education programs. The Tribes also made some funds available out of its own budget for materials and personnel. The Idaho State Library provided a bookmobile to go from house to house throughout the Reservation. In 1974, the library moved to a new $882,000 facility housing all administrative, social, and educational programs of the Tribes. Occupying a central location, accessible to classrooms and offices, the new library facility was designed from the first to produce as well as use media of all types (Service on the reservation, 1974).

The Shoshone–Bannock Library and Media Center is governed by the Tribal Education Committee and funded primarily by Part B, Special Programs and Projects, of the Indian Education Act.

The Center has three general goals: (1) to acquire materials to meet the educational and recreational needs of the members of the Shoshone–Bannock Tribes; (2) to develop programs using the material for the educational benefit of the tribal members; and (3) to inform tribal members of available materials and services (Sayre, 1976, p. 64).

Multimedia collections are being developed using a recently approved collection policy. This policy treats four major areas of need: (1) curriculum-related materials for school children; (2) easy to read and practical materials for adults; (3) materials for adult continuing and college education; (4) culturally supportive materials on the Shoshone–Bannock and other Indian peoples.

Library and Media Center programming focuses on integration with other social and educational programs of the tribes. It provides media materials for the Alcoholism and Drug Rehabilitation Program; serves as a school library for the Alternate School; obtains research materials for curriculum development; prepares consumer survival kits for the Adult Learning Center; and shows films for the senior citizens. The Center operates the bookmobile in remote areas of the Reservation, and it is undertaking development of a museum. It operates the tribal communications system. Printing, duplication, and publication of the monthly newsletter and production of a radio program are all functions of the Center. Open 69 hours a week, the Center circulates over 2.5 books per capita. Walk-in use exceeds 30 people a day.

G. Arizona

American Indian library service is growing in many Indian communities in Arizona. The Bureau of Indian Affairs, the Arizona Department of Library, Archives and Public Records, and many public libraries and schools are cooperating to provide improved school and community library services (Mathews, 1975a). The Window Rock Public Schools have used Indian Education Act funds to equip and operate a large video and media center. Academic and special libraries are maintained at Navajo Community College, College of Ganado, Navajo Tribal Museum, and the Navajo Health Authority (Richardson, 1974; Wood, 1973). The Hopi Villages operate study centers for their children to use in the evening. A small collection of recreational reading and children's books at Supai receives periodic shipments of new materials. This is no mean feat when one considers that the Havasupai people live at the bottom of the Grand Canyon and books must be delivered by mule train. The Tucson Public Library works closely with the Papago Tribe in the operation of four media centers. County libraries are encouraged to provide bookmobile services to Indian communities in their areas of responsibility, and the state supports the operation of a bookmobile in Navajo communities. The Arizona Department of Library, Archives and Public Records has granted $87,000 in LSCA funds to 30 reservation libraries in the last two years.

H. New Mexico

American Indian library service in New Mexico has developed significantly since 1973. Three factors appear to be responsible for the increase in programming: (1) a growing library interest among tribal leaders and educators; (2) the development of training and demonstration programs operating from the University of New Mexico; (3) continuing support from the New Mexico State Library. Most of the tribes and pueblos in New Mexico are in the process of developing education and social service agencies. These agencies are responsible for providing social services, adult education, curriculum development, and support services to tribal members. In some cases they are planning to assume control of local public or BIA schools. The staffs and boards of these agencies want libraries that will meet community information needs and provide a place in the community where the young can study and grow in a culturally supportive environment.

The College of Education at the University of New Mexico has received four HEA-IIB grants to improve libraries in Indian communities throughout the state. The first two grants provided on-site training for 23 Indian people selected by their schools and communities. Participants were enrolled in University library and media courses, but class meetings usually took place in the community or school facilities the students were charged to develop. Participants developed competencies in the following areas: (1) acquisition and processing of materials; (2) selection of materials and equipment; (3) production of materials; (4) equipment operation and repair; and (5) programming.

The on-site, competency-based model proved to be an effective means of recruiting, training, and placing Indian people in libraries. More than 70 percent of the participants have gone on to jobs in school and community libraries they helped to create, and several are continuing their education at the bachelor's level. The model has now been adopted by several other programs across the United States. The major weakness of the model is the lack of continuing support, since paraprofessionals are forced to operate alone without professional guidance (McCrossen, 1974; Smith, 1974a,b, 1975a,b).

The last two years have been devoted to demonstrating American Indian library service in eight pueblos: Acoma, Cochiti, Jemez, Laguna, Santa Clara, Santo Domingo, Zia, and Zuni. Results to date have been impressive. The Sky City Community Library at Acoma emphasizes children's work with materials on pueblo history, story hours, movies, and games. The library aide is committed to using library services as a vehicle for promoting the welfare and social adjustment of the Acoma youth. The Cochiti library is opening a facility adjacent to social and health services for the Pueblo. Jemez Community Library offers its users an excellent collection and regular programs for Headstart children, while the Laguna Public Library works closely with the adjacent Social Services Center. The agencies work jointly to provide information services in the community. The Library also operates a most successful lunch and crafts program for elders, a summer reading program for youth, and a highly successful Library Fair for the community.

The Santa Clara Community Library emphasizes pueblo history and services for school children, and works closely with the recreation program sponsoring media events and a summer reading program. Santo Domingo and Zia are just developing their libraries. The Zuni Public Library occupies a former apartment house adjacent to major education facilities, its primary target audience is the school children who use the facility for learning and recreational activities (Scott, 1976). A major concern of the pueblo libraries is the acquisition of religious material. The religious leaders in some communities will not permit the Library to acquire materials on their religions. Two arguments are used: (1) the material is inaccurate; (2) it should not be recorded in any case. Several communities feel strongly enough about this issue to review all new materials before they go on the shelf. As a result, selecting cultural materials requires great sensitivity on the part of the community librarians.

The New Mexico State Library continues to support American Indian library service. It provides substantial grants to support the public libraries at Laguna and Zuni, and smaller grants for materials are made to nine Indian community libraries. Limited consultant time is made available for support and in-service training. Most important, the regional libraries provide monthly bookmobile service to Indian communities, especially those which have been unable to develop community libraries as yet. The ability of the bookmobiles to serve Indian people has been strengthened by the addition of Indian personnel and materials more directly related to Indian information needs (Blei, 1975).

I. Wisconsin

During the dark days of the termination policy, Wisconsin along with nine other states assumed responsibility for all Indian social and educational services through the provisions of Public Law 280.* By and large this action resulted in serious problems. Indian children were forced out of white-controlled schools, social services were ignored, and legal and civil rights violated. The story for library services in Wisconsin has been more positive. After the Menominee Reservation was terminated, the Wisconsin Division for Library Services supported the establishment of a county library and had the wisdom to hire and train a Menominee person to operate it. At the request of the Oneida Tribe, the Brown and Outagamie County Public Libraries have sponsored a small branch library at the Oneida Tribal Center. The Northwest Wisconsin Library System and the Wisconsin Valley Library Service have used some of their LSCA funds to serve Indian people.

In 1974, the Great Lakes Intertribal Council and the Wisconsin Division for Library Services agreed on the need for a statewide long-range plan. With technical assistance from the NIEA Library Project,

---

*States which have adopted the provisions of PL-280 include: California, Idaho, Michigan, Minnesota (except Red Lake), Nebraska, Oregon (except Warm Springs), Texas, Washington, and Wisconsin.

a joint committee worked for 6 months to establish the scope and priorities for future development of American Indian library service in the state. The resulting "Statewide Plan for the Development of Indian Library Service in Wisconsin" (Great Lakes Intertribal Council and Wisconsin Division for Library Services, 1975) identifies areas of need, establishes joint goals, and sets priorities. The plan stresses local autonomy for the thirteen Indian communities in Wisconsin and encourages the provision of support services from Great Lakes Intertribal Council, public library systems, and the Division for Library Services.

As a result of the plan, services in many of the communities have significantly improved. Mole Lake has used some of its Indian Education Act funds to develop a study center for its school children. The Northwest Wisconsin Library System provides bookmobile service and an Indian specialist to work in the six Indian communities in its area of service. The Division of Library Services works with Indian education personnel and school librarians to improve access to culturally supportive materials and services in school libraries. The Wisconsin Valley Library Service employs an Indian professional as children's and young adults' consultant with special responsibility for the development of services in the Chippewa, Potawatomi, and Winnebago communities (Beaudin, 1976). The Menominee County Library is improving its ability to serve the Menominee people as they restore their Reservation, and the Oneida Tribal Library has obtained Indian Education Act and tribal support to expand its services to children.

On the statewide level, the Great Lakes Intertribal Council's Indian Library Training Program provides community-based technical training. Funded by the Department of Labor's Indian Technical Assistance Center, the Program is training Indian people throughout the state to meet requirements as community librarians. The Program uses the University of Wisconsin's Educational Telephone Network for two courses; Basic Library Management and Indian Library Service. The advantage of the Educational Telephone Network lies in the fact that each community participant can attend classes in the nearest county seat. There the student interacts fully with the lecturer and other class members on a party line hookup. An Indian professional, who directs the program, also provides technical assistance and on-the-job training in each community on a rotation basis. LSCA funds are used for tuition and basic collections in each community (Tsosie, 1976).

J. Newberry Library Center for the History of the American Indian

The Newberry Library in Chicago opened its Center for the History of the American Indian in 1973 under the auspices of the National Endowment of the Humanities and several private foundations. Drawing its strength from the 100,000-volume Ayer and Graff Collections of American Indian history, the Center offers a number of programs of direct interest to Indian communities. The Chairman's Fellowships afford tribal librarians and archivists the opportunity to come to the Newberry for research on their own tribes. The Summer Institute is designed to give educators of Indian children the opportunity to develop new courses in Indian history. Several Indian scholars have participated in the Center's Academic Fellowship Programs for postgraduate research. The Center's American Indian Bibliography series is making available 30 critical bibliographies in American Indian history. The Newberry's efforts in these areas represent a major advance in opening research library collections to Indian people.

K. Professional Education

Two institutes to train Indian people as professional library personnel have been completed with HEA-IIB support since 1973. Arizona State University graduated twelve school library media specialists in 1974 and 1975, and the University of Arizona institute enrolled ten people in the MLS program in 1973–1974. Both programs were based on the normal curriculum with supplemental counseling, internships, and courses relating directly to Indian information needs. The programs experienced some difficulty in recruitment, retention, and replacement. At Arizona State these problems centered on recruiting students directly from high school. Career goals and coping skills were not highly enough developed to ensure retention during a four-year program. Retention problems were largely solved by recruiting at the junior level to replace dropouts, by holding regular meetings of the participants to encourage peer support, and by increased counseling. At the University of Arizona recruitment difficulties centered on finding, within two months, ten American Indians with bachelor's degrees and an interest in library science. An initial lack of sensitivity on the part of faculty created some retention difficulties. Problems were overcome by administrative reassignments and the development of a counseling program. Both programs experienced some difficulty in placing the graduates in libraries serving Indian people. In some cases students were limited by their spouses' place of employment, and in others, there were no library positions in the communities where they wanted to live (Higgins, 1975). Nevertheless, both programs have made a very positive impact on American Indian library service. Due to their efforts, the number of native Americans with professional degrees has doubled (American Library Association, Office for Library Personnel Resources, 1976).

L. Professional Associations

Professional associations continue to be a source of leadership in American Indian library service. The National Indian Education Association operates two projects designed to facilitate the development of Indian libraries. Project ILSTAC (Indian Library Services Technical Assistance Center), funded by HEA-IIB, had three major goals in 1977: (1) developing statewide plans for American Indian library service in Minnesota, North Carolina, New Mexico, and Washington; (2) publishing materials of use to Indian librarians and users; (3) providing on-demand technical assistance to libraries, tribes, and other organizations (Indian libraries, 1975). Libraries planning to expand their services to include Indian people are encouraged to contact Project ILSTAC for guidance and planning materials.

NIEA's Project MEDIA (Media Evaluation and Development by Indian Americans) addresses the difficult area of materials and evaluation. Its scope includes all materials that treat the information needs of Indian people. As a first step Project Media is focusing on materials about American Indians, and with assistance from the Indian Education Act, it is publishing a continuing guide, *Native American Evaluations of Media Materials* (National Indian Education Association, 1976), which provides evaluations of 2,000 items prepared by Indian people. Project MEDIA's index to bibliographies is the best source for reference materials known to this writer (National Indian Education Association, 1975).

The American Library Association has recently initiated publication of the *American Indian Libraries Newsletter* (Mathews, 1976). Sponsored by the Office for Library Service to the Disadvantaged's Library Service for American Indian People Subcommittee, this quarterly publication represents the first dependable communications system for American Indian library service. The Office for Library Personnel Resources maintains a directory of Indian professionals, monitors native American enrollments in library schools, and recruits Indian people for librarianship (American Library Association, Office for Library Personnel Resources, 1976). The Reference and Adult Services Division's American Indian Materials and Services Committee has produced a bibliography of selected Indian books (American Library Association, Reference and Adult Services Division, 1973), a listing on nontrade publishers specializing in Indian publications (Indian materials, 1976), and a pamphlet on Indian library users (American Library Association, Reference and Adult Services Division, 1976).

V. FINDINGS: THE KNOWLEDGE BASE OF AMERICAN INDIAN LIBRARY SERVICE

Experience since 1973 has confirmed the domain of American Indian library service stated in the *Goals for Indian Library and Information Service* (National Indian Education Association and American Library Association, 1973). Recent experience has also contributed to the development of a practical knowledge base for American Indian library service. Practitioners can now identify, with some degree of assurance, specific factors that are critical to any attempt to meet the information needs of a given Indian community.

A. Indian Communities Possess Specific Information Needs

The University of Minnesota (1972a,b,c,d,e) survey and subsequent replications (Metoyer, 1976; Smith, 1974b) confirm the supposition that native Americans perceive a need for information. Specific areas of need vary from community to community, among age groups, and over time, but some commonalities can be identified. Reservation communities, for example, are likely to be most interested in information on their own tribe. Urban communities are likely to want information on many tribes (Jones and Casaday, 1975). Elementary pupils most often seek cultural- and curriculum-related information, while adolescents usually want vocational information, and adults desire practical and cultural information that will improve their quality of life. The identification of specific local information needs is a necessary precondition for the development of successful American Indian library service in any community. Whiteman Runs Him (1975) suggests several alternatives for identifying information needs in Indian communities.

B. Demand for Information Is Increasing

Self-determination requires an informed public (U.S. Congress, American Indian Policy Review Commission, 1976). Indian people are increasingly making their needs known to responsible officials in both Indian and library hierarchies. Sahmaunt (1974) discusses six facets of this effort, and Teachout (1974) describes the role of libraries in meeting the information needs of the Sioux people. LaPointe identifies the inadequacies of existing information services, while Ellis (U.S. Congress, House Committee, 1976, pp. 151–182) makes a number of suggestions on the need for improved access to information. The Indian Education Task Force of the American Indian Policy Review Commission has received testimony on information needs and the role of libraries at several of its hearings.

Another index of the growing demand for information is to be found in the increasing number of library and information centers in Indian communities. NIEA's Project ILSTAC reports receiving an average of 25 inquiries a week from Indian communities and organizations interested in starting libraries. Arizona and New Mexico report that there are more than forty Indian libraries in their states. Parent committees are urging school libraries to be more responsive to the needs of Indian students.

C. Indian Control Is Necessary

Successful American Indian library service depends on community input and control. Native Americans believe they are the only ones capable of determining Indian information needs. Only Indian people can realistically evaluate the potential and actual effectiveness of alternative delivery systems, and the community is the only source of information on the opportunities and limitations imposed by its culture. Library services established without community input and approval will be rightly regarded as an insult.

A corollary of this rule is that library expertise is necessary in designing and operating effective programs. Christensen (1975b) and Smith (1975) provide the reader with useful suggestions on how to best establish productive relationships between Indian communities and libraries.

D. Service Strategies

American Indian library service is based on active interaction between Indian communities and libraries. Many services are bilingual and all support bicultural principles. The range of services is much broader than that provided by library service to more traditional publics. The case studies presented earlier indicate that successful programs take materials to the community, work closely with school and other community organizations, develop specialized programming, operate communications systems, and create as well as use media. Persons just beginning to develop programs of American Indian library service will be interested in the concepts presented in Jones and Casaday (1975), Mathews (1975b), Twonley (1975c,d), and Wittstock and Wolthausen (1975).

E. Materials, Equipment, and Facilities

Materials which meet the information needs of the community served should be provided in adequate formats, language, quantity, and quality. Christensen (1975a) summarizes existing criteria for selection of print and nonprint materials, and Project MEDIA (National Indian Education Association, 1976) will ultimately provide a comprehensive set of evaluations on materials meeting Indian information needs. Gotsick et al. (1976) provide access to useful survival materials. Even with this help the fact remains that the range of commercially available materials is inadequate to meet Indian information needs. Consequently, Indian libraries must be able to create as well as use materials. Experience suggests that visual media are especially valuable in Indian libraries because of their creative and bilingual potential. All facilities should be designed and equipped for the production of multimedia materials. Joint use facilities, where the library serves a number of education and social agencies as well as individuals, appear to be quite effective, particularly in small communities.

F. Funding

Current programs of American Indian library service are supported by a mix of soft monies from federal library programs, the Indian Education Act, Bureau of Indian Affairs, and some tribal resources. These agencies are to be commended for their willingness to make money available for demonstration programs. Reservations in the thirteen original states and PL-280 states should have access to state funds for library services in their communities. But, so far as this writer is able to determine, only New York and Washington have made legislative provision for the use of state funds for library services on reservations (Dolejsi, 1974; Service to Indians to be state backed in Washington, 1975; State $$ for Indian libraries, 1974). Some school libraries receive budget funds targeted for improving their services to Indian students. In urban areas Indian people share the problems of other minority groups who contribute tax support to libraries, but receive few services designed to meet their specific needs. Urban problems are aggravated by library reluctance to use limited funds to serve new publics. Until hard funds are designated to meet Indian information needs, librarians and Indian people will need to be consummate funding artists. Two primers are available to assist aspiring fund raisers (Brodsky, 1975; Cawley, 1974).

G. Personnel Utilization and Training

The key person in any program of American Indian library service is the man or woman who works directly with the Indian community. In order to be effective this person must have the trust of the community, and with very few exceptions this means the person must be an American Indian. Because of the small populations of some Indian communities, it may not always be possible to fund a professional to fill the position. In such a case it is preferable to recruit a mature adult who is committed to remaining in the community. The community paraprofessional requires on-site training and continuing professional guidance. Training programs developed by Smith (1974a,b, 1975a,b) and

Tsosie (1976) appear to meet this need in rural areas. Jones (1975) reports that in-library training is effective in urban areas. Both state library agencies and the Bureau of Indian Affairs should make commitments to provide continuing professional guidance.

A pressing need exists for Indian professionals. These people will determine the future direction and success of American Indian library service. To date, America's library schools have been unable to recruit and train Indian people, even at levels proportionate to the Indian population with bachelor's degrees. HEA-IIB-sponsored institutes appear to be a critical factor in motivating library schools to recruit and educate Indian librarians.

Finally, American Indian library service must pay close attention to personnel utilization. A single paraprofessional working alone in an isolated community must have periodic in-service training. A professional requires access to continuing education, particularly in a developing field. Both groups require a career ladder that will protect them against being locked into dead-end jobs. Wood (1975) has made a beginning in the study of personnel utilization, and research in progress at Arizona State University should provide additional insights on this problem.

VI. IMPLEMENTING AMERICAN INDIAN LIBRARY SERVICE: THE NEXT FIVE YEARS

American Indian library service is able and ready to meet the growing information needs of Indian America. Over the past few years Indian people and librarians have worked together to establish linkages, identify information needs, demonstrate services, and initiate training. The goal of American Indian library service for the next five years is nationwide implementation. Two factors will determine whether this goal is attained: (1) the establishment of a national policy commitment; and (2) the development of a continuing and adequate funding base for American Indian library service.

A. Policy Development

Policy development is underway. During 1974, the National Commission on Libraries and Information Science sought and received testimony from individuals and organizations regarding current access to library and information services in Indian communities. Mathews (1975c) summarized this input for the Commission and found that the policy picture was uniformly negative. Libraries in urban areas were ignoring the needs of potential Indian users, and the federal government had no policy on reservation library service. School libraries, where they existed, were not encouraged to meet Indian information needs. Only where demonstration programs of American Indian library services existed were the information needs of Indian people being met. These efforts were constantly threatened by the absence of a supportive policy.

The Commission has used these data in its first draft of a national plan, *Toward a National Program for Library and Information Services* (National Commission on Libraries and Information Science, 1975). It suggests that urban libraries take steps to meet the information needs of Indian and other minority people, and makes a very strong statement regarding federal responsibility for the provision of library and information services to Indian people living on reservations:

> The Commission is aware and very much concerned about the unique library and information needs of the American Indian and the responsibility of the Federal Government towards meeting these needs. In its treaties with Indian tribes, the Federal Government undertook an obligation to provide adequate education to Indians on their reservations, which includes a concomitant obligation to provide complementary library materials and services.... The new national program must provide a workable base for assistance and insure that Indian reservations are tied into the proposed national network (National Commission on Libraries and Information Science, 1975, pp. 41-42).

Not content with words, the Commission has established an Indian Subcommittee to work with concerned federal agencies and develop policies and programs for American Indian library service.

The Bureau of Indian Affairs (BIA) and the Department of the Interior's Office of Library and Information Services are working jointly to develop library policy and programs for Indian reservations. In July of 1976, BIA administrators, librarians, and tribal representatives met to outline the necessary steps in library policy development and to identify potential components of library programs (Bauman, 1976). Since that time a planning group has been working to develop a policy and program document for American Indian library service on reservations served by the BIA. When the document is endorsed by the Commission and the Bureau, implementation will begin.

B. Development of a Continuing Funding Base

American Indian library service on reservations must be supported by means of a continuing funding base provided by the federal government as a treaty obligation, dedicated to library programs and under the control of local Indian communities. Guidelines should be similar to Indian library funding in Canada (Canada, Department of Indian Affairs, 1968) where matching with other funds and contracting for service are permitted. Funding should be at a compensatory level to facilitate rapid development and allow for the added costs involved in local materials production.

In urban communities the task is somewhat different. Here, Indian people contribute to the local tax base. As taxpayers they have a right to library service that meets their information needs. Local libraries must be convinced that they have an obligation to meet Indian information needs. Success will be determined by the commitment of urban Indian people to meeting their information needs, the ability of library officials to perceive these needs, and the development of communication linkages between Indian people and local libraries.

Prospects for achieving nationwide implementation are good. American Indian library service has demonstrated its ability to provide information needed by the Indian community. It now enjoys growing support in libraries and Indian communities. With sustained support from native Americans, librarians, the National Commission, and other policy-making groups, the next five years should see American Indian library services become an integral and productive part of America Indian life.

REFERENCES

Akwesasne Library-Culture Center (1975). "Akwesasne." Akwesasne Library-Culture Center, Hogansburg, New York.

American Indian Chicago Conference (1961). "Declaration of Indian Purpose." University of Chicago, Chicago, Illinois.

American Library Association, Office for Library Personnel Resources (1973). "Indian Librarian, Why?" American Library Association, Chicago, Illinois.

American Library Association, Office for Library Personnel Resources (1976). "Survey of Graduates and Faculty of U.S. Library Education Programs Awarding Degrees and Certificates." American Library Association, Chicago, Illinois. (Mimeograph copy.)

American Library Association, Reference and Adult Services Division (1973). "Good Words: Notable Books on the American Indian." American Library Association, Chicago, Illinois. (ED 092 953.)

American Library Association, Reference and Adult Services Division (1976). "Factors in Serving American Indian Patrons." American Library Association, Chicago, Illinois.

Antell, L. (1974). "Identification of Information Needs of the American Indian Community That Can Be Met by Library Services: Phase III, Annual Report." National Indian Education Association, Minneapolis, Minnesota. (ED 105 855.)

Bauman, B. (1976). Bureau of Indian Affairs library workshop. *American Indian Libraries Newsletter* 1, 4–5.

Beaudin, J. L. (1976). Indian people need libraries. *Wisconsin Library Bulletin* 72, 117–119.

Blank, R. (1971). "The Development of an Instructional Materials Center at the Institute of American Indian Arts, Santa Fe, New Mexico." Unpublished thesis, San Jose State University. (ED 057 799.)

Blei, N. (1975). Three-day run on a Navajo, New Mexican spirit trail. *American Libraries* 6, 96–104.

Brodsky, J. (1975). "Directory of American Indian Private Funding Sources." American Indian Higher Education Consortium, Denver, Colorado.

Bromberg, E. (1972). "Media Services in the Bureau of Indian Affairs Schools: A Report and Recommendations." Southwestern Indian Polytechnic Institute, Albuquerque, New Mexico. (Also published in Townley, 1975a.)

Canada, Department of Indian Affairs and Northern Development, Indian Affairs Branch (1968). "Public Library Service to Indian Bands." Department of Indian Affairs and Northern Development, Ottawa, Ontario. (Circular No. 8.)

Cawley, R. (1974). "Guide to Funding Sources for American Indian Library and Information Services." U.S. Department of the Interior, Washington, D.C.

Christensen, R. A. (1975a). "Materials Selection for Indian Libraries." National Indian Education Association, Minneapolis, Minnesota.

Christensen, R. A. (1975b). "Working With Indian Communities and Agencies to Establish Indian Library Services." National Indian Education Association, Minneapolis, Minnesota.

Cohen, F. (1940). "Handbook of Federal Indian Law." U.S. Government Printing Office, Washington, D.C.

Commission on the Rights, Liberties and Responsibilities of the American Indian (1966). "The Indian: America's Unfinished Business." University of Oklahoma Press, Norman, Oklahoma.

Costo, R. (1970). "Textbooks and the American Indian." Indian Historian Press, San Francisco, California.

Cunningham, W. (1969). Anto Wicharti. *Library Journal* 94, 4496–4499.

Cunningham, W. (1971). The changing environment and changing institution: Indian project of the Northeast Kansas Library System. *Library Trends* 20, 376–381.

Deloria, V. (1974). "Behind the Trail of Broken Treaties." Delacorte Press, New York.

Dolejsi, M. (1974). Library service to Indians in Washington State. *Pacific Northwest Library Association Quarterly* 39, 4–5.
Ecrolin, P. R. (1971). "The Past, Present, and Recommended Role of Instructional Materials Centers in the Bureau of Indian Affairs." Unpublished thesis, Utah State University.
ERIC, Clearinghouse on Rural Education and Small Schools (1971). "Manual for Providing Library Services to Indians and Mexican Americans." New Mexico State University, Las Cruces, New Mexico. (ED 047 872.)
Farrington, W. H. (1969). Statewide outreach: Desert booktrails to the Indians. *Wilson Library Bulletin* 43, 864–871.
Ford, M. E. (1968). "A Study Concerning Library Services Accessible to Students in Selected Indian Schools in the United States in 1967." Unpublished thesis, San Jose State University. (ED 053 851.)
Fuchs, E., and Havighurst, R. J. (1972). "To Live on This Earth: American Indian Education." Doubleday, Garden City, New York.
Garrow, L., Jock, R., and Cooke, R. (1974a). "Mohawk People: Past and Present." Akwesasne Library-Culture Center, Hogansburg, New York. (ED 093 513.)
Garrow, L., Jock, R., and Cooke, R. (1974b). "A Selective Bibliography of the Mohawk People." National Indian Education Association, Minneapolis, Minnesota. (ED 093 514.)
Genia, A. L., Metoyer, C. A., and Smith, L. P. (1975). "Identification of Information Needs of the American Indian Community That Can Be Met by Library Services: Evaluation Report." National Indian Education Association, Minneapolis, Minnesota. (ED 125 670.)
Gordon, W. (1969). Service to Indian reservations. *Minnesota Libraries* 22, 348–349.
Gotsick, P., Moore, S., Cotner, S., and Flanery, J. (1976). "Information for Everyday Survival." American Library Association, Chicago, Illinois.
Great Lakes Intertribal Council and Wisconsin Division for Library Services (1975). Statewide plan for the development of Indian library services in Wisconsin. *Wisconsin Library Bulletin* 71, 293–304.
Groulx, J. (1972). "Final Report to the Four Corners Regional Commission on Mobile Library Services to Navajo, Apache, and Coconino Counties." Arizona Division of Library Archives and Public Records, Phoenix, Arizona. (ED 107 401.)
Groulx, J. (1973). "Final Report to the Four Corners Regional Commission on Mobile Library Services to Navajo, Apache, and Coconino Counties." Arizona Division of Library, Archives and Public Records, Phoenix, Arizona. (ED 107 402.)
Henry, J. (1970). "Organizing and Maintaining a Native American Reference Library." American Indian Historical Society, San Francisco, California. (ED 058 982.)
Higgins, N. C. (1975). "Narrative Evaluation Report: Library Training Institute for American Indians." Arizona State University, Tempe, Arizona. (mimeograph copy.)
Hill, E. E. (1965). "Records of the Bureau of Indian Affairs." U.S. National Archives, Washington, D.C.

Indian libraries: organization seeks improved services. (1975). *American Indian Journal of the Institute for the Development of Indian Law* 1,(October), 12–17.

Indian materials: an annotated list of nontrade book publishers. (1976). *RQ* 15, 215.

Jacobs, W. (1972). "Dispossessing the American Indian." Scribner's, New York.

Jones, M. C. (1975). To watch them stand tall; the Sioux City Public Library Indian Project. *American Libraries* 6, 494–496.

Jones, M. C., and Casaday, E. (1975). "Urban Indian Library Services." National Indian Education Association, Minneapolis, Minnesota.

Kelsay, L. E. (1954). "List of Cartographic Records of the Bureau of Indian Affairs." U.S. National Archives, Washington, D.C.

Lurie, N. (1971). "North American Indians in Historical Perspective." Random House, New York.

McCrossen, E. (1974). Emphasis on action—Lotsee Smith. *American Libraries* 5, 544.

Mathews, V. H. (1975a). "American Indian People and Library Learning Centers." National Indian Education Association, Minneapolis, Minnesota. (Sound filmstrip.)

Mathews, V. H. (1975b). "Continuing Adult Education and Indian Libraries." National Indian Education Association, Minneapolis, Minnesota.

Mathews, V. H. (1975c). "Report and Recommendations to the National Commission on Libraries and Information Science Relating to the Improvement of Opportunities for American Indians." National Commission on Libraries and Information Science, Washington, D.C. (Also published in Townley, 1975a.)

Mathews, V. H. (1976). American Indians and Libraries. *ALA Yearbook* 1, 76–78.

Metoyer, C. A. (1976). "Perceptions of the Mohawk Elementary Students of Library Services Provided by the National Indian Education Association Library Project As Conducted on the Akwesasne (St. Regis) Mohawk Reservation." Unpublished dissertation, Indiana University.

Mudd, I. (1972). Media by mail—library service to the unserved. *Native News and B.I.A. Bulletin* 9(March), 9–11.

National Commission on Libraries and Information Science (1975). "Toward a National Program for Library and Information Services: Goals for Action." U.S. Government Printing Office, Washington, D.C.

National Indian Education Association and American Library Association (1973). "Goals for Indian Library and Information Service." American Library Association, Chicago, Illinois.

National Indian Education Association, Project MEDIA (1975). "Index to Bibliographies and Resource Materials." National Indian Education Association, Minneapolis, Minnesota.

National Indian Education Association, Project MEDIA (1976). "Native American Evaluations of Media Materials." National Indian Education Association, Minneapolis, Minnesota.

National Indian Law Library (1972). "Catalog." National Indian Law Library, Boulder, Colorado.

Naumer, J. N. (1974). Library services to American Indians. *In* "Library and Information Services for Special Groups" (J. I. Smith, ed.), pp. 1–74. Science

Associates International, New York.
Nixon, R. M. (1970). Special message to Congress on Indian affairs. *In* "Public Papers of the Presidents of the United States: Richard Nixon, 1970," pp. 564–570. U.S. Government Printing Office, Washington, D.C.
Pipe, E. A. (1971). "Library Services Available in Bureau of Indian Affairs Schools." Unpublished thesis, Glassboro State College.
Ralph, M., and Sheppard, G. (1969). "A Survey of the Library in Indian Schools." Idaho State University, Pocatello, Idaho. (Mimeograph copy.)
Richardson, B. E. (1970). A wind is rising. *Library Journal* 95, 463–467.
Richardson, B. E. (1974). By red rocks. *Road Runner* 17, 1–17.
Rigel, T. (1970). Library services to the Sioux. *Catholic Library World* 42(December), 235–237.
Sahmaunt, J. (1974). "American Indian Information and Library Needs." (Presented at National Commission on Libraries and Information Science, Southwest Regional Hearing, San Antonio, March.)
Sargent, N. (1970). "Library Service to the American Indians in the Southwest." Unpublished thesis, University of Missouri.
Sayre, S. R. (1976). The Shoshone-Bannock Library and Media Center. *Idaho Librarian* 28, 64–65.
Scott, S. (1976). Just learning things day by day. *American Libraries* 7, 378–379.
Service on the reservation. (1974). *American Libraries* 5, 17.
Service to Indians to be state backed in Washington. (1975). *LJ/SLJ Hotline* 4,(April 28), 1.
Shields, G. R., and Sheppard, G. (1970). American Indians: search for Ft. Hall's library service. *American Libraries* 1, 856–860.
Smith, H. (1975). "Working With Library Agencies to Estblish Indian Library Services." National Indian Education Association, Minneapolis, Minnesota.
Smith, J. S. (1969). Serving Disadvantaged Adults: An Institute for Public Librarians held at the College of St. Catherine, S. Paul, Minnesota, June 2–13: Proceedings. *Minnesota Libraries* 22, 275–303.
Smith, J. S. (1971). Library service to American Indians. *Library Trends* 20, 223–238.
Smith, L. P. (1970). "Resources and Procedures for Improving the Indian American Use of Libraries." University of Oklahoma, Norman, Oklahoma. (ED 043 442.)
Smith, L. P. (1974a). Designing library education programs to meet community information needs. *In* "Progress in Urban Librarianship" (T. Samore, ed.), pp. 34–36. University of Wisconsin, Milwaukee, Wisconsin. (ED 104 422.)
Smith, L. P. (1974b). "Narrative Evaluation Report on the Institute for Training Library Aides in Pueblo Indian Schools." University of New Mexico, Albuquerque, New Mexico.
Smith, L. P. (1975a). "In-Service Training in Indian Libraries." National Indian Education Association, Minneapolis, Minnesota.
Smith, L. P. (1975b). "Library Aide Training Institue for American Indians." University of New Mexico, Albuquerque, New Mexico. (ED 122 865.)
Standing Rock Sioux Tribe (1972). "Developmental Plan: Phase III." Standing Rock Sioux Tribe. Fort Yates, North Dakota.

Standing Rock Tribal Library (1974). "Hou Kola! Directory of Services on the Standing Rock Sioux Reservation." Standing Rock Sioux Tribal Library, Fort Yates, North Dakota. (ED 101 901.)

State $$ for Indian libraries: bill may set precedent. (1974). *Library Journal* **98**, 1506.

Szasz, M. (1974). "Education and the American Indian: The Road to Self-Determination, 1928–1973." University of New Mexico Press, Albuquerque, New Mexico.

Teachout, M. (1974). "Statement." (Presented at the National Commission on Libraries and Information Science Mountain Plains Regional Hearing, Denver, September 18.) (ED 101 568.)

Thomas, J. D. (1972). Audiovisual records related to Indians in the National Archives, preliminary draft." U.S. National Archives, Washington, D.C. (ED 018 244.)

Townley, C. T. (1971). "A Preliminary Study of Library Programs Related to American Indian Studies Programs in Colleges and Universities." University of California, Santa Barbara, California. (ED 060 982.)

Townley, C. T. (1975a). "Identification of Information Needs of the American Indian Community That Can Be Met by Library Services: Final Report." National Indian Education Association, Minneapolis, Minnesota. (ED 125 835.)

Townley, C. T., ed. (1975b). "Indian Library Service Guides." National Indian Education Association, Minneapolis, Minnesota. (Each Guide is also listed under author.)

Townley, C. T. (1975c). "Locally Generated Information and Referral Services in Indian Libraries." National Indian Education Association, Minneapolis, Minnesota.

Townley, C. T. (1975d). "Promoting Indian Library Use." National Indian Education Association, Minneapolis, Minnesota.

Tsosie, M. A. (1976). Indian library training program. *American Indian Libraries Newsletter* **1**(Fall), 1–3.

United States (1972). "Indian Education Act." U.S. Government Printing Office, Washington, D.C.

United States (1975). "Public Law 93-638." U.S. Government Printing Office, Washington, D.C.

U.S. Bureau of Indian Affairs (1973). "Statistics Concerning Indian Education—1973." Haskell Institute, Lawrence, Kansas.

U.S. Bureau of the Census (1973a). "1970 Census of the Population. Subject Reports: American Indians." U.S. Government Printing Office, Washington, D.C.

U.S. Bureau of the Census (1973b). "We, the First Americans." U.S. Government Printing Office, Washington, D.C.

U.S. Congress, American Indian Policy Review Commission (1976). "Bureau of Indian Affairs Management Study." Warren King and Associates, Chicago, Illinois.

U.S. Congress, House Committee on Education and Labor (1976). "Oversight Hearings on Laws Affecting Indian Education." 94th Congress, 1st Session, U.S. Government Printing Office, Washington, D.C.

U.S. Congress, Senate Committee on Labor and Public Welfare, Special Subcommittee on Indian Education (1969). "Indian Education: A National Tragedy—A National Challenge." 91st Congress, 1st Session, U.S. Government Printing Office, Washington, D.C.

U.S. Office of Education, Office of Indian Education (1975). "Summary of Funded Districts." U.S. Department of Health, Education, and Welfare, Washington, D.C.

University of Minnesota (1970). "American Indians, An Annotated Bibliography of Selected Library Resources." University of Minnesota, St. Paul, Minnesota. (ED 040 004.)

University of Minnesota, Bureau of Field Studies (1972a). "A Design for an Akwesasne Mohawk Cultural Center." University of Minnesota, St. Paul, Minnesota. (ED 066 192.)

University of Minnesota, Bureau of Field Studies (1972b). "A Design for Library Services for the Rough Rock Community." University of Minnesota, St. Paul, Minnesota. (ED 066 193.)

University of Minnesota, Bureau of Field Studies (1972c). "A Design for Library Services for the Standing Rock Sioux Tribe." University of Minnesota, St. Paul, Minnesota. (ED 066 191.)

University of Minnesota, Bureau of Field Studies (1972d). "National Indian Education Association Library Project: Appendices." University of Minnesota, St. Paul, Minnesota. (ED 066 195.)

University of Minnesota, Bureau of Field Studies (1972e). "A Summary of the National Indian Education Association Library Project." University of Minnesota, St. Paul, Minnesota. (ED 066 194.)

Vaughan, J. E. (1971). "Some Suggestions for Librarians in High Schools with Native American Students." Minneapolis Public Schools, Minneapolis, Minnesota. (ED 051 917.)

Wells, R. N. (1974). "Community Mobilization and Leadership Development on the St. Regis (Akwesasne) Mohawk Reservation." (Presented at the Southwestern Sociological Association, Annual Meeting, Phoenix, March 29.) (ED 088 625.)

Welsh, D. C. (1969). Colorado River tribes public library first in the Nation. *Indian Historian* 2, 8–9.

Whiteman Runs Him, E. (1975). "Assessing Information Needs in Indian Communities." National Indian Education Association, Minneapolis, Minnesota.

Wittstock, L. W., and Wolthausen, J. H. (1975). "Alternatives to Standard Classification and Cataloging." National Indian Education Association, Minneapolis, Minnesota.

Wood, M. (1973). "A Survey of Library Services Available to Navajo People on the Navajo Reservation." University of Denver, Denver, Colorado. (Studies in Librarianship, No. 9.) (ED 102 934.)

Wood, M. (1975). "Initial Organization and Staffing Patterns for Indian Library Services." National Indian Education Association, Minneapolis, Minnesota.

Advances in American Library History

DAVID KASER

Graduate Library School
Indiana University

I.	Recent Attention to American Library History	181
	A. Dissertations Written	182
	B. Relevance of History Challenged	183
II.	Survey of Recent Research	184
	A. Academic Libraries	184
	B. Public Libraries	187
	C. Organization of Materials	190
	D. Library Associations	190
	E. Library Education	191
III.	Some General Observations	193
	A. Recent Gains and Future Opportunities	193
	B. The Utility of History to the Library Profession	194
	References	196

I. RECENT ATTENTION TO AMERICAN LIBRARY HISTORY

In 1959 Professor David Mead of the Department of English in Michigan State University observed in a general review (Mead, 1961) of research opportunities in American library history that "among the many major American libraries that need the historian's attention are the Detroit Public Library, the Cleveland Public Library, the Enoch Pratt Free Library, and the Peabody Institute Library." Today, seventeen years later, serviceable histories of three of the four exist (Cramer, 1972; Kalisch, 1969; Woodford, 1965). In addition to institutional histories Mead also noted a need for work on Poole, Cutter, and Dewey. Biographies of Poole and Cutter (Miksa, 1974; Williamson, 1963) are now complete and a thorough study of Dewey is underway. Mead went on to lament the absence of extended scholarly examinations of mechanics and mercantile libraries and of athenaeums. Today, mercantile libraries have received scholarly attention (Boyd, 1975), and several essays have enhanced considerably our understanding of mechanics' libraries and athenaeums.

And the litany could be continued. In virtually every aspect of American library history we are vastly better equipped today with sound, rigorous, scholarly understanding than we were a few years ago. In fact, we are now so blessed with good research it is hard to fathom the difficulty of earlier attempts to survey American library history when the number of serious monographs in the field numbered fewer than ten. In those days we could cite Shera (1949) and Ditzion (1947) and a half dozen other worthies, but thereafter our only recourse was to refer to memoirs, which are notoriously poor as history, or struggle with unorganized, undigested, and uninterpreted primary sources, an enlightening but time-consuming way of gaining a balanced historical perspective.

Harris (1970) called attention to the improvement in research on American library history:

> It appears from an examination of the increased rate of publication in the field, that there is a growing interest in American library history. It seems that after a brief lag during the fifties, research and publication in the field are again on the upswing. Books and periodical articles are appearing in ever greater numbers. It also looks as if the curve will continue to climb over the next few years.

A. Dissertations Written

1. NUMBER

Harris' augury proved correct; the amount of historical research in the library field continued to increase substantially, both in terms of quantity and in terms of the percentage of total research in all of librarianship. From 1965 through 1970, seventeen library school doctoral dissertations concerned history. From 1971 through 1976, however, the number jumped to forty-seven—a 276 percent increase. Historical studies comprised only 8 percent of the doctoral dissertations submitted during the earlier period, but by the later period they constituted 11.3 percent.

2. QUALITY

Citing an increase in quality of scholarship is never easy. Perhaps one can take some comfort in the wider spread historical competence among the directors of dissertations; some rising emphasis upon rigor and exactness among all scholars, including library historians; and some greater accessibility of exemplary work accomplished in the field. Certainly the "Golden Age" phenomenon is likely to function as readily here as elsewhere in society's perceptions of the past, shading contemporary events always downward. Countering this tendency, of course, will be the homely wisdom of the apothegm, adapted from Will Rogers, that "library history is not as good as it used to be, and it probably never was." In the final analysis, any shift in the quality of historical research will be determined by the retrospective aggregate judgment of the library history profession.

B. Relevance of History Challenged

The sustained popularity of history is less subject to argument, despite a "Revolution of 1969/70" which pitted it against the severest challenge perhaps since the seventeenth-century *Battle of the Books*. As university buildings burned, "relevance" became the rallying cry of the revolution. Many beleaguered library and other historians found themselves confronted by doubters who demanded to know of history, "What good is it?" In the face of the challenge, many universities in general and library schools in particular modified their curricula, reducing the profile of history offerings. No fewer than eight American library schools eliminated their history requirements during the first half of the 1970s; a number of others scrapped their history courses altogether. Despite the willingness of some library school faculties to diminish the historical component in their curricula, however, and the resulting falloff in enrollment in history courses in those particular schools, nationwide enrollment in library school history courses held remarkably firm. In fact, it edged up slightly. During the six-year period from 1965 through 1970 total enrollment in history courses in ALA-accredited schools was 13,173. In the subsequent six-year period it rose to 13,597, showing no significant decline in any one year. That is refreshing; perhaps students are less to be gulled by the fickle caprices of popular conceit than some had been wont to presume.

But the more strident baiting of library historians so prevalent only three or four years back seems largely to have abated. The almost apologetic, diffident tone in which many library historians often felt constrained to announce themselves a short time ago is gone, and they once again pursue their craft with impunity, if not yet with full confidence. Perhaps they are stronger for the interlude, having reexamined the fundamental tenets of their vocation. They had *felt* themselves to be under siege, albeit latter-day data have belied that perception, and they used the occasion to rethink and reaffirm the significance of historical research.

II. SURVEY OF RECENT RESEARCH

Yet it is not unreasonable for us to ask of history: "What good is it?" The data cited in the preceding section suggest the substantial expenditure of time and effort designed to provide an improved understanding of library history. What indeed has librarianship as a profession gained from all of this attention to its history in recent years? Wherein has our self-knowledge been enhanced, and what if any meaning does this enhancement presage? If self-knowledge is the beginning of wisdom, can we assume that as a profession we will proceed more wisely in the future than we have in the past? Perhaps a brief review of recent advances in library history will help us to answer these questions.

A. Academic Libraries

1. STUDIES OF INDIVIDUAL LIBRARIES AND LIBRARIANS

Coming into the 1960s the major preoccupation of American library historians had been with academic libraries or, more specifically, with university libraries. During the previous decade a substantial number of doctoral dissertations analyzed the history of some of the nation's large university libraries. McMullen (1949) scrutinized the first eighty years of the library at the University of Chicago. Bidlack (1954) studied the beginnings of the library at the University of Michigan. Yenawine (1955) examined the University of Illinois. Lowell (1957) looked at Indiana. Skipper (1960) investigated Ohio State, Rouse (1962) reviewed Baylor, and Munn (1962) studied West Virginia. Another group of related dissertations concentrated on the personalities of individuals closely associated with university libraries. Boromé (1950) wrote of Winsor at Harvard; Branscomb (1954) traced the life of Richardson at Princeton; Abbott (1957) described the work of Davis at Michigan. The 1950s also saw more library school master's theses written than has any other decade, and many of these papers concerned individual academic libraries or librarians (Harris, 1974).

Curiously, however, work on academic libraries and librarians has dropped off phenomenally in the past fifteen years. Sparks (1967) wrote of Bishop at Michigan, Peterson (1970) reported on the University of California Library, Moloney (1970) on the University of Texas, and Bentinck-Smith (1976) on Harvard, but the earlier interest in examining specific institutions appears for the time being to have abated. One can only speculate as to the reasons. It may have been simply that the community curiosity had been sated. It is easy to understand how, as the profession came in the 1950s to realize what vast new bibliothecal leviathans the academic research world had spawned, it was galvanized into describing them. But after a number had been described, the edge had been taken off the professional curiosity. The fact that no dissertations were written about individual college libraries, wherein change had been less startling, might tend to support this speculation. Or perhaps it was felt, after a number of cases had been handled, that almost all academic libraries were really special libraries organically inseparable from the specific teaching and research environments in which they found their being and were therefore too predictably deterministic in their outworking to continue to challenge. Or it may have been sensed that there were now enough studies of individual institutions to permit the profession to go on to a higher order of historical scholarship, namely the distillation of general truths about university libraries as a genre.

It strikes this writer as most notable that so very much of the library historical work in the 1950s was in this way "unidimensional" in its concern—that is, in its study of single institutions or individual librarians. Yet this reflects a pattern common to the origins of virtually all branches of scholarly study. Syntheses and generalizations generally cannot be made until the basic facts are determined. We cannot know what happens in libraries (*plural*) until we know what happened in Library A, Library B, Library C, etc., and this kind of descriptive, factual data is usually generated through unidimensional investigations. After analyses of individual cases, we can move on to more encompassing kinds of research.

One can analogize here with biological research, wherein scholarly investigation begins with the anatomy of individual specimens. Proceeding by comparison upward from a range of individual specimens, a taxonomy can eventually be developed, as specimens become grouped and described as species, which in turn are grouped as classes, and so forth on up to phyla. Conversely biological researchers can proceed downward within specimens to their very tissue structure itself, gaining understanding histologically of their healthy growth and pathologically of their unhealthy characteristics. So also with libraries. Given anatomical descriptions of many libraries, their rigorous classification can be accomplished on the one hand, or the microbiological scrutiny of their subordinate parts can be made on the other. Such research, in adequate quantity, can serve just as useful diagnostic and prognostic functions in librarianship as it does in medicine.

2. RISING EMPHASIS ON "HORIZONTAL" STUDIES

Have subsequent scholars proceeded beyond unidimensional studies to a higher level of generalization? The bibliographic record indicates that work has progressed but at a less rapid rate than might have been expected. Generalizing about academic libraries had begun prior to mid-century; it did not have to await these studies before it could begin. After all, we did know *something* about American academic library history prior to the compilation of these studies, although clearly less than we know at present. Drawing upon such primary sources as could then be identified, and building from contemporary scholarly perceptions, Shores (1934) was able to make some generalizations about colonial college libraries almost a half century ago that are still very useful. But historical perspectives have evolved considerably since then and the subject would seem to merit fresh analysis. Indeed the more recent work by Kraus (1960) improved upon Shores' account of the book collections available to colonial college students. Likewise Powell (1946) made some perceptive generalizations about the development of university libraries in the South, but it is likely that as more studies of individual southern libraries become available, it will be increasingly possible to test and sharpen his general perceptions. Similarly, Brough's (1953) generalizations—drawn from case studies at Yale, Chicago, Harvard, and Columbia—should be reassessed in the light of new knowledge of the four constituent institutions and also of the many other research libraries recently studied.

If we think of studies of individual institutions as being "vertical" in their thrust, then it can be reported that the number of "horizontal" studies—studies of particular aspects of academic library work—has also risen throughout the period although somewhat slowly. Rothstein's (1955) study of reference work is a good early example of horizontal research into a specific activity in a range of academic libraries. Erickson's (1961) review of academic library surveys is another. More recent studies of this kind include Boll's (1961) analysis of early college library buildings, Smith's (1965) study of libraries in land-grant universities, Miller's (1971) investigation of circulation work, and Johnson's (1974) accounting of the subject-divisional concept in university libraries. Most recently, a comprehensive collection of papers on academic library history was published in 1976 in *College and Research Libraries*. It seems reasonable to expect that the amount of historical scholarship devoted to studies of this genre will increase in the years ahead, with each new vertical study tending to sharpen the accuracy of subsequent horizontal studies, just as each new horizontal study tends to challenge or confirm the vertical studies.

B. Public Libraries

In the last decade the rise of the public library has fired the curiosity of American library historians. Perhaps because it is more uniquely American, perhaps because its once-vaunted social significance gives it greater romantic appeal, perhaps because the inscrutable vagaries of its motivation are more subject to interpretation—whatever the cause, the subject has proved very attractive to historians, and many have dedicated themselves to determining where, when, how, and most importantly *why* the American public library evolved the way that it did.

1. STUDIES OF INDIVIDUAL LIBRARIES AND LIBRARIANS

Studies of public library history are less susceptible to easy categorization than those of academic libraries. To be sure, studies of single public libraries and of individual public librarians are fewer in number than exist for the academic library field. Of the large libraries perhaps the first solid institutional history by modern standards was Spencer's (1943) *Chicago Public Library*. Volumes observing the centennials of the Boston Public Library (Whitehill, 1956) and the Cleveland Public Library (Cramer, 1972) appeared respectively in 1956 and 1972, and Woodford (1965) prepared an informative volume on the Detroit Public Library in 1965. Two important dissertations in this group were Dain's (1972) study of the beginnings of the New York Public Library, and Kalisch's (1969) history of the Enoch Pratt Free Library. Meanwhile Williamson (1963) had produced a sound professional biography of Poole in 1963, and Holley's (1963) life of Evans was published in the same year. Little else has been done on individual libraries and librarians save some master's theses, a few brief papers, some uncritical sketches, and a number of local history accounts.

2. STUDIES OF CERTAIN GEOGRAPHICAL AREAS

Recent writers have addressed other aspects of public library work, and our understanding of the nature of the institution has been much broadened and deepened as a result. Such studies as Anders' (1958) report on public libraries in the Southeast, Held's (1973) comprehensive work on public library development in California, and Colson's (1973) perceptive analysis of how public libraries came to Wisconsin have observed that the pattern identified for the northeastern part of the nation by Shera and Ditzion in the 1940s was not necessarily followed elsewhere. Few, of course, had ever claimed that it had been, but the temptation to generalize from the experience of the East had been tempting. Once burned, twice shy—hopefully we will be less hasty in making unwarranted generalizations in the future.

3. MICROCOSM

To return to the biological analogy used earlier, not only has recent scholarship permitted sharper taxonomic work to be accomplished through understanding of public library development outside of New England, but it has proceeded also to the microanalytical level within New England itself. Thus McCauley's (1971) detailed scrutiny of public library origins in selected mill towns of the area has enabled us to modify somewhat our previous perceptions of the movement as a whole. Likewise Garrison's (1973) work, Du Mont's (1975) analysis, and several papers by Harris (1973, 1974 [with Spiegler], 1975a,b, 1976a,b) have highlighted certain authoritarian and elitist motives behind the establishment of the public library within the region.

4. REVISIONISM

Some of the conclusions drawn by the scholars just mentioned have proven troubling to the profession. Yet it should not surprise the profession to find that the power brokers of the library world strove, as did the Almighty, to create others in their own image. Nor should it surprise us to find that they, as do other mortals, sometimes rationalized their desires or cloaked them in a rhetoric and appearance of social magnanimity. However, coming after generations of unquestioned acceptance that the fathers of the public library had been motivated solely by beneficent and selfless altruism, these new interpretations were not wholly welcomed.

Some of this recent scholarship has been, a bit self-consciously perhaps, designated as "revisionism," which of course it certainly is. It should be noted, however, that *all* of historical research might be called "revisionist," for if a historical study does not revise previous understanding, it has no purpose in being. All historical study, moreover, is destined to be itself "revised" by future historical study. Harris (1976a) captured this truth in the title of his essay, "The Priest Who Slew the Slayer and Shall Himself be Slain." Such is the fate of the historian that his work is ever to be superseded. The scholar's truism that "there is no such thing as a definitive study" is implied poetically in the title of Holley's (1967) volume, *Raking the Historic Coals;* the embers (for "embers" read "sources") contain the potential for renewed fire long after the flames have apparently died down. Recognition of this fact can keep us humble.

Other recent studies of American public library history have augmented valuably our understanding of the field. Guyton's (1975) timely study of unionization among public librarians helped us to understand the contemporary third "wave" of the movement. Long (1969) clarified the beginnings of library work with children. Carrier (1965) reported the agony of trying to get fiction a place on public library shelves. Oehlerts (1975) pieced together the story of the development of adequate public library buildings. Kramp's (1975) work on the public library in the Great Depression is among the very few studies of the institution at or after its zenith. All of these studies have increased the profession's ability better to understand itself.

C. Organization of Materials

Several studies of the past decade or so have also aided importantly in understanding that aspect of the librarian's work which is uniquely his own—namely, the rational organization of literature for storage and retrieval. Beginning with Ranz's (1964) report on the early, printed book catalog, this group has more recently included Scott's (1970) account of the organizing genius of J.C.M. Hanson, Comaromi's (1976) "biography" of the Dewey Decimal Classification itself, and Hanson's (1974) work on the role of the ALA in the development of American cataloging practice. Especially notable is Lehnus' (1974) citation analysis of writings on cataloging between 1835 and 1969, one of the few historical studies in American librarianship to apply the quantitative method. Several recent biographical accounts have also broadened knowledge in this field (e.g., Harris, 1975a; Miksa, 1974).

D. Library Associations

Library associations were "discovered" early in the 1970s as rewarding topics for study, and within five years seven dissertations and numerous articles focused on their rise. Thomison (1973) provided a chronological account of the ALA's first fourscore years which will long be useful as a framework for interrelating the professional events of the period. Mehl (1973) reported the first quarter-century of the American Theological Library Association, McGowan (1972) traced the first three decades of the Association of Research Libraries, Davis

(1974) related the experience of the Association of American Library Schools, and Hale (1976) recorded the existence of the Association of College and Research Libraries from 1889 to 1960. Also among this group must be counted Sullivan's (1976) excellent work on Milam and Young's (1976) study of the ALA in the first World War.

It would be interesting to know exactly what sparked this sudden curiosity about the profession's associational past. To a degree, the pervasive societal unease about the role and utility of its institutions generally that typified the "Revolution of 1969/70" probably whetted scholarly interest in their history. And, of course, the approach of the American Library Association Centennial stimulated a good deal of interest in the ALA's origins and concomitant growth. For the most part (except for Davis, who compared the experience of the Association of American Library Schools [AALS] with that of similar organizations), these studies tended to be unidimensional, and it may be that they will be followed soon by some horizontal analyses of specific commonalities within them. It certainly appears upon first reading, for example, that professional library organizations proceed by fits and starts through certain predictable stages of maturation. If this is the case, the profession might benefit from recognition of these stages, anticipating them, planning for them, and thereby minimize the periodic anguish. Perhaps analysis of other significant common characteristics would be helpful to the profession. A comparison of the behavior of library associations and the experience of other kinds of associations, is badly needed.

E. Library Education

Perhaps our most complete knowledge of any one aspect of librarianship is to be claimed relative to the history of education for librarianship in the United States. Vann (1961) brought the story from the beginning to 1923, Churchwell (1975) continued it to 1940, and Carroll (1970) extended it to 1960. Supplemented by Davis' aforementioned work on the AALS, White's (1976) interpretation of relevant events, and several accounts of individuals important in the movement—primarily Grotzinger's (1966) work on Sharp and Winckler's (1968) study of Williamson—these general histories constitute a good foundation for further and more intensive studies of specific topics within the broad subject. Some such studies have already been done, such as Evraiff's (1969) review of the training of school librarians and Webb's (1963) account of library education in Texas. Others can be expected.

Taken as a whole these works document long-term trends and developments in library education. The steady shift, for example, in library training emphasis from technique to principle may be the most important perception emerging from these historical works. Increasing training in the principles of librarianship has enabled growing numbers of librarians to see the significance of their labors beyond the simple accomplishment of the task at hand, to articulate their workaday accomplishments more readily with the overarching social mission of the library as a whole.

A number of other historical treatises have recently been written in American librarianship which are less easy to categorize than the preceding ones but which appear certain to be of significance nevertheless. The mosaicist will recognize the experience. Some pieces of the mosaic—properly shaped, balanced, and tinted—articulate easily among others so that the component of which they are parts begins to reveal its ultimate form; other pieces, however, although of obviously equal relevance, manifest less readily their relationship to others in the overall design. Such for the time being might be claimed for Brewster's (1976) recounting of the high adventure involved in the profession's overseas technical assistance activities between 1940 and 1970, or more importantly of its world significance. Likewise Baumann's (1972) analysis of the work of stack-manufacturer Angus Snead McDonald in making possible the kind of library building required by modern service concepts appears slated for prominence in the developing mosaic. Skallerup's (1974) thorough and exciting account of libraries and books for American seamen seems not to fit these categories. So also does Cole's (1971) study of Spofford's role in bringing about a "national library" in the United States still stand a bit apart, ironically, moreover, since the study succeeds in revealing Spofford's actions to be more fully integrated into the main currents of American library development than had previously been generally believed. These studies and several others like them seem clearly to be destined for positions of importance in our continuing effort to know ourselves as a profession. It must remain for some reviewer a decade hence, however, to place them in perspective.

III. SOME GENERAL OBSERVATIONS

A number of caveats must be observed concerning this survey of recent historical study in librarianship. First is that it has been generally limited to discussion of primary research only; reviews, attempts at broad synthesis, commentary, discussions of historiography or of method, and colloquies solely among historians, have been omitted in favor of works which provide new facts or interpretations of our professional past. This constraint is not intended to imply that the kinds of work omitted are unimportant. The intent has been rather to concentrate in these brief pages on the studies which provide opportunity for the profession to better understand its social function. Less justifiable perhaps has been the general omission herefrom of writings of less than monographic length. Patently a great many articles have appeared in recent years which have opened up previously unknown or imperfectly understood aspects of our past. Again their omission does not imply a value judgment as to their utility. It supposes instead that the monographs which have appeared constitute a relatively valid and vastly more manageable sample of the total work accomplished.

A. Recent Gains and Future Opportunities

A few general observations may be made about the historical work reviewed in this chapter. One is that recent studies in American library history—in general, although not in all cases—show a marked improvement over earlier work. They manifest greater scholarly rigor and acknowledge the importance of structure in research and writing, and the finer points of historical method. They are more likely to view library history in relevant social, political, cultural, and economic contexts rather than as an isolated phenomenon. In spite of these advances, however, there are areas where improvement would be especially welcome. The paucity of historical studies which employ quantitative methods, for example, is both puzzling and disappointing. Library history archives are replete with large corpuses of raw statistical data related to circulation, cataloging, acquisitions, and user registration, and would seem to lend themselves to study by the Cliometrician, but they have thus far attracted only very limited scholarly attention. It is also unfortunate that few library historians publish any scholarly monographs beyond their dissertations. It is clearly dysfunctional to have to train *de novo* the author of each new historical study. Somehow the psychic (and perhaps also the financial) rewards of the profession must be redressed so as to keep library historians, once trained, actively investigating their respective topics.

B. The Utility of History to the Library Profession

Right or wrong, good or bad, has the profession at large benefited from this increase in historical research? That is a tough question. This observer believes that the profession *could* benefit considerably, but whether it actually *has* benefited is another matter. For the profession to benefit, these research findings must be assimilated; left to languish they have no impact. If historians are heard only by other historians, their activities are precious and expensive antiquarianism, a kind of exercise in mutual congratulation. Historians themselves cannot be reformers, lest they forsake their detachment in support of a cause. Yet they are engaged constantly in providing the bases for reform by others. We must look critically at our past before we can intelligently plan for the future.

1. CHANNELS FOR GAINING ITS ASSIMILATION

There appear to be three primary channels by which the findings of historians might find their way into the consciousness of the profession. Potentially most influential would be the widespread dissemination of historical studies to large numbers of librarians. Since librarians are busy people this kind of direct assimilation seems unlikely. A second channel into the profession's psyche is through popularizations or concise syntheses in the library press. But, given the pragmatism of the library press and the space restrictions, it is very difficult to get such papers into periodicals which are widely read by practicing librarians. During the past year, however, by virtue of the fortuitous conjunction of the nation's bicentennial and the *annus mirabilis* of American librarianship, a great deal of space was dedicated to secondary accounts of library history, *Library Trends, College & Research Libraries, American Libraries,* and other journals dedicated space to historical pieces. Festschriften of historical essays were published, anthologies were prepared, and historians were welcomed for the occasion as speakers at professional gatherings. It is hoped that some assimilation of historical findings occurred. But clearly 1976 was an atypical year, and the conditions which then prevailed seem unlikely to recur soon.

The third channel by which historical understanding can gain assimilation into the profession is through the history courses taught in library schools. If enrollment in library history courses remains firm or increases, the benefits from recent historical research will probably infiltrate the library community.

3. POTENTIAL BENEFITS

What are the kinds of potential benefits? One key benefit that historical understanding can bring to the profession is a new awareness of the difference between transient and perpetual issues. Our responses to the former should differ from our responses to the latter. Too often the profession dissipates its energies and resources attempting to react to every meaningless blip that turns up on its radar screen. Often it appears to carom aimlessly from one rediscovered enthusiasm to another, oblivious to the facts that the profession has lived through these same enthusiasms in the past and that the record is replete with lessons once learned but now forgotten. A greater sensitivity to these earlier experiences might improve the profession's efficiency in current problem solving. Too often we feel compelled to discover the wheel anew instead of improving upon and adjusting our inherited wheels in the light of changing environmental conditions.

Another benefit that the profession could gain is an increase in its aggregate humility and self-respect. More often than necessary we have castigated our forefathers for their failure to recognize and solve the profession's big problems. The record indicates, however, that few, if any, significant problems existed of which our predecessors were unaware or against which they did not exercise intellect and strength. Greater awareness of these efforts should increase our professional self-esteem and alert us to our most severe shortcomings. The big problems of the profession remain *big* problems. It would be helpful to remember that fact.

Finally, it might inhibit our inclination to label everything "new." Perhaps there are *no* new phenomena under the library sun, perhaps all that ever change are the conditions and circumstances under which librarians must perform their immutable functions. Our efficiency in the service of society might be somewhat greater if we were to approach our tasks with this possible perspective *in pectore*.

REFERENCES

Abbott, J. C. (1957). "Raymond Cazallis Davis and the University of Michigan General Library, 1877–1905." Unpublished dissertation, University of Michigan.
Anders, M. E. (1958). "The Development of Public Library Services in the Southeastern States, 1895–1950." Unpublished dissertation, Columbia University.
Baumann, C. H. (1972). "The Influence of Angus Snead MacDonald and the Snead Bookstack on Library Architecture." Scarecrow Press, Metuchen, New Jersey.
Bentinck-Smith, W. (1976). "Building a Great Library: The Coolidge Years at Harvard." Harvard University Library, Cambridge, Massachusetts.
Bidlack, R. E. (1954). "The University of Michigan General Library: A History of Its Beginnings, 1837–1852." Unpublished dissertation, University of Michigan.
Boll, J. J. (1961). "Library Architecture 1800–1875: A Comparison of Theory and Buildings with Emphasis on New England College Libraries." Unpublished dissertation, University of Illinois.
Boromé, J. A. (1950). "The Life and Letters of Justin Winsor." Unpublished dissertation, Columbia University.
Boyd, W. D. (1975). "Books for Young Businessmen: Mercantile Libraries in the United States, 1820–1865." Unpublished dissertation, Indiana University.
Branscomb, L. C. (1954). "A Bio-Bibliographic Study of Ernest Cushing Richardson, 1860–1939." Unpublished dissertation, University of Chicago.
Brewster, B. J. (1976). "American Overseas Library Technical Assistance, 1940–1970." Scarecrow Press, Metuchen, New Jersey.
Brough, K. J. (1953). "Scholars Workshop: Evolving Conceptions of Library Service." University of Illinois Press, Urbana, Illinois.
Carrier, E. J. (1965). "Fiction in Public Libraries, 1876–1900." Scarecrow Press, Metuchen, New Jersey.
Carroll, C. E. (1970). "The Professionalization of Education for Librarianship, with Special Reference to the Years 1940–1960." Scarecrow Press, Metuchen, New Jersey.
Churchwell, C. D. (1975). "The Shaping of American Library Education." American Library Association, Chicago, Illinois.
Cole, J. Y. (1971). "Ainsworth Spofford and the 'National Library.'" Unpublished dissertation, George Washington University.
Colson, J. (1973). "The Public Library Movement in Wisconsin, 1836–1900." Unpublished dissertation, University of Chicago.
Comaromi, J. P. (1976). "The Eighteen Editions of the Dewey Decimal Classification." Forest Press, Albany, New York.
Cramer, C. H. (1972). "Open Shelves and Open Minds: A History of the Cleveland Public Library." Case Western Reserve University Press, Cleveland, Ohio.
Dain, P. (1972). "The New York Public Library: A History of Its Founding and Early Years." New York Public Library, New York.
Davis, D. G. (1974). "The Association of American Library Schools, 1915–1968: An Analytical History." Scarecrow Press, Metuchen, New Jersey.

Ditzion, S. H. (1947). "Arsenals of a Democratic Culture: A Social History of the American Public Library Movement in New England and the Middle States from 1850 to 1900." American Library Association, Chicago, Illinois.
Du Mont, R. R. (1975). "The Large Urban Public Library as an Agency of Social Reform, 1890–1951." Unpublished dissertation, University of Pittsburgh.
Erickson, E. W. (1961). "College and University Library Surveys, 1938–1952." American Library Association, Chicago, Illinois.
Evraiff, L. A. K. (1969). "A Survey of the Development and Emerging Patterns in the Preparation of School Librarians." Unpublished dissertation, Wayne State University.
Garrison, D. (1973). "Cultural Missionaries: A Study of American Public Library Leaders, 1876–1910." Unpublished dissertation, University of California.
Grotzinger, L. A. (1966). "The Power and the Dignity: Librarianship and Katherine Sharp." Scarecrow Press, Metuchen, New Jersey.
Guyton, T. L. (1975). "Unionization of Public Librarians; a Theoretical Interpretation." American Library Association, Chicago, Illinois.
Hale, C. E. (1976). "The Origin and Development of the Association of College and Research Libraries." Unpublished dissertation, Indiana University.
Hanson, E. R. (1974). "Cataloging and the American Library Association, 1876–1956." Unpublished dissertation, University of Pittsburgh.
Harris, M. H. (1970). The year's work in American library history—1968. *Journal of Library History* 5, 133–145.
Harris, M. H. (1973). The purpose of the American public library: a revisionist interpretation of history. *Library Journal* 98, 2509–2514.
Harris, M. H. (1974). "A Guide to Research in American Library History." 2nd ed. Scarecrow Press, Metuchen, New Jersey.
Harris, M. H. (1975a). "The Age of Jewett." Libraries Unlimited, Littleton, Colorado.
Harris, M. H. (1975b). "The Role of the Public Library in American Life: a Speculative Essay." University of Illinois Graduate School of Library Science. (Occasional Paper No. 117.)
Harris, M. H. (1976a). The priest who slew the slayer and shall himself be slain. *Journal of Education for Librarianship* 16, 229–231.
Harris, M. H. (1976b). Public libraries and the democratic dogma. *Library Journal* 101, 2225–2230.
Harris, M. H., and Spiegler, G. (1974). Everett, Ticknor and the common man: The fear of social instability as the motivation for the founding of the Boston Public Library. *Libri* 24, 249–276.
Held, R. E. (1973). "The Rise of the Public Library in California." American Library Association, Chicago, Illinois.
Holley, E. G. (1963). "Charles Evans, American Bibliographer." University of Illinois Press, Urbana, Illinois.
Holley, E. G. (1967). "Raking the Historic Coals." Beta Phi Mu, Urbana, Illinois.
Johnson, E. R. (1974). "The Development of the Subject-Divisional Plan in American University Libraries." Unpublished dissertation, University of Wisconsin.
Kalisch, P. A. (1969). "The Enoch Pratt Free Library: A Social History." Scarecrow Press, Metuchen, New Jersey.

Kramp, R. S. (1975). "The Great Depression: Its Impact on Forty-Six Large Public Libraries." Unpublished dissertation, University of Michigan.

Kraus, J. W. (1960). "Book Collections of Five Colonial College Libraries: A Subject Analysis." Unpublished dissertation, University of Illinois.

Lehnus, D. J. (1974). "Milestones in Cataloging: Famous Catalogers and Their Writings, 1835–1969." Libraries Unlimited, Littleton, Colorado.

Long, H. G. (1969). "Public Library Service to Children: Foundation and Development." Scarecrow Press, Metuchen, New Jersey.

Lowell, M. H. (1957). "Indiana University Libraries, 1829–1942." Unpublished dissertation, University of Chicago.

McCauley, E. F. (1971). "The New England Mill Girls: Feminine Influence in the Development of Public Libraries in New England." Unpublished dissertation, Columbia University.

McGowan, F. M. (1972). "The Association of Research Libraries, 1932–1962." Unpublished dissertation, University of Pittsburgh.

McMullen, C. H. (1949). "The Administration of the University of Chicago Libraries, 1892–1928." Unpublished dissertation, University of Chicago.

Mead, D. (1961). Popular education and cultural agencies. *In* "Research Opportunities in American Cultural History" (J. F. McDermott, ed.), p. 157. University of Kentucky Press, Lexington, Kentucky.

Mehl, W. R. (1973). "The Role of the American Theological Library Association in Protestant Theological Libraries and Librarianship, 1947–1970." Unpublished dissertation, Indiana University.

Miksa, F. L. (1974). "Charles Ammi Cutter." Unpublished dissertation, University of Chicago.

Miller, L. A. (1971). "Changing Patterns of Circulation Services in University Libraries." Unpublished dissertation, Florida State University.

Moloney, L. C. (1970). "A History of the University Library at the University of Texas, 1883–1934." Unpublished dissertation, Columbia University.

Munn, R. F. (1962). "West Virginia University Library, 1867–1917." Unpublished dissertation, University of Michigan.

Oehlerts, D. E. (1975). "The Development of American Public Library Architecture from 1850 to 1940." Unpublished dissertation, Indiana University.

Peterson, K. G. (1970). "The History of the University of California Library at Berkeley, 1900–1945." University of California Press, Berkeley, California.

Powell, B. E. (1946). "The Development of Libraries in Southern State Universities to 1920." Unpublished dissertation, University of Chicago.

Ranz, J. (1964). "The Printed Book Catalogue in American Libraries, 1723–1900." American Library Association, Chicago, Illinois.

Rothstein, S. (1955). "The Development of Reference Services through Academic Traditions, Public Library Practice and Special Librarianship." American Library Association, Chicago, Illinois.

Rouse, R. (1962). "A History of the Baylor University Library, 1845–1919." Unpublished dissertation, University of Michigan.

Scott, E. (1970). "J. C. M. Hanson and His Contribution to Twentieth Century Cataloging." Unpublished dissertation, University of Chicago.

Shera, J. H. (1949). "Foundations of the Public Library: The Origins of the Public Library Movement in New England, 1629–1855." University of Chicago Press, Chicago, Illinois.
Shores, L. (1934). "Origins of the American College Library, 1638–1800." Barnes & Noble, New York, New York.
Skallerup, H. R. (1974). "Books Afloat and Ashore." Archon Books, Hamden, Connecticut.
Skipper, J. E. (1960). "The Ohio State University Library, 1873–1913." Unpublished dissertation, University of Michigan.
Smith, J. C. (1965). "Patterns of Growth in Library Resources in Certain Land-Grant Universities." Unpublished dissertation, University of Illinois.
Sparks, C. G. (1967). "William Warner Bishop." Unpublished dissertation, University of Michigan.
Spencer, G. S. (1943). "The Chicago Public Library: Origins and Backgrounds." University of Chicago Press, Chicago, Illinois.
Sullivan, P. (1976). "Carl H. Milam and the American Library Association." Wilson, New York.
Thomison, D. V. (1973). "The History and Development of the American Library Association, 1876–1957." Unpublished dissertation, University of Southern California.
Vann, S. K. (1961). "Training for Librarianship before 1923: Education for Librarianship Prior to the Publication of Williamson's Report on 'Training for Library Service.'" American Library Association, Chicago, Illinois.
Webb, D. A. (1963). "Local Efforts to Prepare Library Assistants and Librarians in Texas from 1900 to 1942." Unpublished dissertation, University of Chicago.
White, C. L. (1976). "A Historical Introduction to Library Education: Problems and Progress to 1951." Scarecrow Press, Metuchen, New Jersey.
Whitehill, W. M. (1956). "Boston Public Library: a Centennial History." Harvard University Press, Cambridge, Massachusetts.
Williamson, W. L. (1963). "William Frederick Poole and the Modern Library Movement." Columbia University Press, New York.
Winckler, P. A. (1968). "Charles Clarence Williamson (1877–1965): His Professional Life and Work in Librarianship and Library Education in the United States." Unpublished dissertation, New York University.
Woodford, F. B. (1965). "Parnassus on Main Street: a History of the Detroit Public Library." Wayne State University Press, Detroit, Michigan.
Yenawine, W. S. (1955). "The Influence of Scholars on Research Library Development at the University of Illinois." Unpublished dissertation, University of Illinois.
Young, A. D. (1976). "The American Library Association and World War I." Unpublished dissertation, University of Illinois.

Trends in Library Education—Canada

JOHN P. WILKINSON

Faculty of Library Science
University of Toronto

```
    I. Introduction: The Canadian Milieu ...................  201
   II. Perspective: A Comparison with Education for Librarianship
       in Britain and Canada ...............................  204
  III. Regional and National Needs .........................  206
   IV. Curricular Responses ................................  209
    V. Stratification .....................................  216
   VI. Librarianship as an Academic Discipline .............  219
  VII. Practice Work in Libraries .........................  222
 VIII. Continuing Education ...............................  224
   IX. Harmonization of Qualifications ....................  226
    X. The Research Component ............................  229
   XI. Canadian Library Associations and Education for
       Librarianship ......................................  231
  XII. Extrapolation .....................................  233
       References .........................................  236
       Appendix ...........................................  238
```

I. INTRODUCTION: THE CANADIAN MILIEU

Someone once wrote that Canadian culture is a striated gruel of British conservatism and American "know-how," with a dash of

French *joie de vivre* floating on top. The aphorism has about as much truth as any other; but it does serve to introduce this study of advances in Canadian library education—a study which has been preceded by two others in the series: one (for the United States) by Lester Asheim in the 1975 *Advances,* and one (for Europe) by Donald Davinson in the 1976 volume.

Certainly Canadian library education, like much else in Canada, has borrowed freely from both Britain and the United States, if only because most of our texts, and many of our teachers, are produced in one country or the other; yet there is a distinctively Canadian milieu and library education in this country has made some response to it.

This is not the place to engage in the traditional Canadian pursuit of explaining ourselves to others. However, a few brief notes may be of interest. By 1986, 25.4 million Canadians may expent to find themselves spread across 3,851,809 square miles of frequently inhospitable territory. Omitting the Yukon and Northwest Territories, the population density of the country in 1971 amounted to approximately ten persons per square mile, and there is no permanent settlement in approximately 89% of Canada. However, such statistics obscure the high urban densities in the country which can reach close to 20,000 persons a square mile for such cities as Toronto and Montreal, and which presently account for more than three quarters of the population (the degree of urbanization on a provincial basis ranges from 38.3% in Prince Edward Island to 82.4% in Ontario). Moreover, this population is getting older, and can be expected to continue to do so. The proportion of Canadians of working age (generally regarded as those between fifteen and sixty-four) comprised 62.3% of the total population in 1971, compared with 59.4% in 1966 and 58.4% in 1961. The population is also increasingly English speaking, with the proportion reporting English as the mother tongue increasing from 58.5% in 1961 to 60.2% in 1971, while the population reporting French declined from 28.1% to 26.9% over the same period. Because of patterns of immigration, the Italian, Greek, Chinese, and Portugese languages, for example, all showed significant increases in use over the same ten years; while Ukrainian, German, and Yiddish declined. Eskimos (Inuit) and Indians, the native peoples of Canada, now represent only 2% of the population. For a variety of reasons, the needs of all such groups speaking languages other than English have become a matter of special concern in the country in recent years.

To serve this widespread and heterogeneous population, there existed in Canada in 1972 (the latest year for which accurate figures are available in all categories) a National Library of more than 500,000 volumes and 100,000 microcopied titles; some 746 public library systems serving approximately 22,000,000 people from a book stock of 29,450,861 volumes and full-time staff in excess of 5,181; 114 university and 154 college libraries reporting holdings totaling 31,126,615 volumes and 8,001 full-time staff members; some 18,124 elementary and secondary schools offering varying degrees of library service; and uncounted (and perhaps uncountable) numbers of "special" libraries.

It is within this demographic and library context, therefore, that library education must operate. Clearly the context incorporates problems of widely disparate urban and rural information needs, and of multilingualism (although the issues of French–English bilingualism and biculturalism are paramount). There are, moreover, issues concerning native peoples, regional disparities, types of libraries, and the overall coordination of library services under the umbrella of a National Library—this last in a country where most libraries are by constitutional fiat a provincial responsibility. The Canadian library school courses designed to meet these problems fall roughly into two broad categories, core courses which deal with those issues regarded as central to librarianship and which are therefore held to be essential to a grasp of library practice, and elective courses which deal with more specific topics of interest to the specialist but not essential to a basic understanding of (Canadian) librarianship. To accommodate these two types of courses, all of the six accredited library postgraduate schools in Canada offer a basic master's degree. Five of the schools have a two-year program, and the sixth school, The School of Library and Information Science of the University of Western Ontario (SLIS) with its three-semester program, is closer to the pattern in the United States.

The six accredited postgraduate schools are, from east to west, The School of Library Service, Dalhousie University, Halifax, Nova Scotia; The Graduate School of Library Science, McGill Univerisy, Montreal, Quebec; L'Ecole de Bibliothéconomie, Université de Montréal, Québec; The Faculty of Library Science, University of Toronto, Ontario; The School of Library and Information Science, University of Western Ontario, London, Ontario; and the School of Librarianship, University of British Columbia, in Vancouver. A seventh school, The

Faculty of Library Science of the University of Alberta, has not as yet had its new M.L.S. program accredited; but, for purposes of convenience, the Faculty will be treated along with the six accredited schools throughout this paper.

In addition there are in Canada twenty-four two-year library technician training programs in community colleges (Colleges of Applied Arts and Technology and Collèges d'Enseignement Général et Professionel) across the country: ten in Quebec, nine in Ontario, one in Manitoba, one in Saskatchewan, two in Alberta, and one in British Columbia (Angel and Brown, 1977). The college programs accept students who have completed grade twelve, but also receive applications from many baccalaureates and even the occasional holder of a doctoral degree.

Finally, there are, for school librarians only, courses offered in most Faculties of Education in Canada. Such courses will be discussed in more detail later in this study.

II. PERSPECTIVE: A COMPARISON WITH EDUCATION FOR LIBRARIANSHIP IN BRITAIN AND CANADA

Since this is the third stopover in what may appear to be a Cook's tour of education for librarianship, it seems desirable to place Canadian developments into perspective vis-à-vis the two earlier studies in the *Advances* series. Lester Asheim, in the 1975 volume, took 1965 and the announcement of the H.W. Wilson $75,000 grant for library education as the start of his survey. He centered the early part of his discussion around the theme of "constitutional" developments in the overall professional arena, with special reference to The Office for Library Education, The American Library Association's official *Library Education and Manpower* statement of 1970, and the functions of the ALA Committee on Accreditation together with the development of the 1972 standards for accreditation. His initial emphasis is perhaps representative of the American penchant for codification, a penchant which finds only a limited counterpart in Donald Davinson's "Trends in Library Education—Europe" in the 1976 *Advances,* and almost no equivalent on the Canadian scene.

As Davinson suggests, the patterns or lack of them, in library education "tend to arise out of differing cultural traditions rather than out of rationality." Thus in the United States a tradition of centralized federal concern for library education and library-related activities developed between 1956 and 1972, while in Britain "the prime influence on the pattern of development of education for librarianship has been that of the Library Association rather than of any individual academic institution or group of such institutions." In Canada, however, neither federal nor association influence as such has had much impact on the library schools. Rather, each school has largely shaped its own policy, although certainly under the influence of its parent institution, of interested alumni, of occasional joint action by all the library schools, and of accreditation criteria in the United States.

Moreover, Canadian education for librarianship would seem largely divorced from any "tradition of theoretical education for librarianship" such as Davinson claims for the United Kingdom. Indeed, the problem identified for Canada by Harlow (1965) over a decade ago still persists in its pristine primacy. "Problem one in the education of librarians [still remains] that no general theory of professional behaviour has been widely accepted . . . no theoretical base, no prototype upon which to pattern education and practice." Similarly, no effective codified approach such as that portrayed by Asheim has been offered to Canadian library educators. One recent effort, for example, to provide such an approach—the attempt by the Canadian Association of University Libraries to develop a 1970s update of its Guide to Canadian University Library Standards—initially failed acrimoniously (Beckman, 1972; Wilkinson, 1972) and the Institute of Professional Librarians of Ontario which made several attempts to codify professional criteria has died virtually unlamented.

On the other hand, unlike Britain, Canada has long possessed a tradition of professional education in its universities, and a considerable proportion of its secondary school graduates have attended university so that education for librarianship has been seen in Canada as appropriate to a formal postbaccalaureate degree. Thus, largely untrammelled by external codification and without prescriptive federal or association intervention, Canadian library schools have been, and still are, generally free to develop their own programs, subject, of course, to the broad constraints of ALA accreditation, under the specific aegis of each university, and within the informal limits of professional (and lay) acceptability. For better or for worse, therefore, American and

British concepts have blended in Canada to produce a response which is uniquely Canadian and which finds no close counterpart in either of the major traditions previously described in this series.

III. REGIONAL AND NATIONAL NEEDS

It has been said, facetiously (Whitteker, 1970, p. 2), "It is axiomatic in [Canada] . . . that we are divided into two parts—not necessarily equal—the West, where the scenery is; and the East, where the work is done." Others argue that there are at least twelve divisions in this country: the ten provinces and the Yukon and Northwest territories. A compromise between these two descriptions is to treat the Canadian library and sociocultural scene in six different contexts: the Atlantic Provinces, for which the library school focus is Dalhousie University, Halifax; the Province of Quebec, for which the Francophone focus is L'Ecole de Bibliothéconomie and the Anglophone focus is the McGill Graduate School of Library Science; Ontario, with library schools at the universities of Toronto and Western Ontario; the Prairie Provinces, served by the library school at the University of Alberta; British Columbia, with its school at the University of British Columbia; and the Territories, sparsely populated and with no library school located within their 1,458,784 square miles of land area.

In terms of library education, indeed, there may be some truth to Whitteker's aphorism. The West *was* long dependent upon the work done in library schools in the East (but then so were the Atlantic Provinces). Apart from in-service training, such as that provided by McGill University and the Toronto Public Library before the turn of the century, the first general training for librarians in Canada took the form of a 3-week McGill University Library Summer School, begun in 1904 by the Director of the McGill University Library, Charles Henry Gould, after consultation with Melvil Dewey in Albany. Ontario followed seven years later with a 4-week program under the Ontario Department of Education, and expanded the program to 4 months, under the Ontario Library School, in 1919. Eight years later the first full-year professional library school program in Canada was established at McGill; and a year later, in 1928, a second program was opened at the University of Toronto, replacing the Ontario Library School (Shera and Anderson, 1975). With the opening of classes at the University of

Toronto, the Toronto Public Library discontinued its in-service training program, and expected its new professional staff to have graduated from one of the two library schools in Canada or from one of those in the United States.

In the late 1930s two additional university library school programs were opened in central Canada, one in 1937 at L'Ecole de Bibliothécaires, (affiliated with l'Université de Montéal and renamed L'Ecole de Bibliothéconomie when it became a Department of the University in 1962), offering instruction in French only; and one in 1938 at the University of Ottawa, accepting both French- and English-speaking candidates. Of these four schools, only those at Toronto and McGill were accredited by the American Library Association; but course content at all the schools tended heavily toward the practical, requiring mastery of such routines as catalog filing, typing ability, and "library hand."

Ontario and Quebec continued to dominate education for librarianship in Canada for the next two decades. Not until 1961 did another Canadian library school open its doors, at which time the School of Librarianship at the University of British Columbia was founded under the direction of Dr. Samuel Rothstein who had completed his doctorate at the University of Illinois. Indeed, it is interesting to note that during this period not only was education for librarianship the responsibility of two (later four) schools, but also such responsibility was wielded essentially by a handful of long-term educators. Thus at Toronto, for example, the two full-time members of the staff in 1928, Winnifred Barnstead and Bertha Bassam, remained largely alone in that capacity (with other staff drawn as needed from the field or university) until 1938, when they were joined by Assistant Professor Mary Silverthorn. Miss Barnstead retired (as Director) in 1950; Professor Bassam retired (as Director) in 1964; and Professor Silverthorn retired only eight years ago.

Not, let it be stressed, that any fault was, or should have been found with the domination by a few schools and a handful of educators. The emphasis of Canadian librarianship during the first half of the twentieth century was upon preservation rather than upon dissemination. Books (and later microforms) rather than the sociology of the user were the librarian's primary concern; and normally this concern had a national or international rather than a regional focus. Thus it was that the famous (and unique) 1933 national Commission of Enquiry into library conditions and needs in Canada found no fault with the fact that there were only two library schools in the country, although the Commission *was* concerned over the lack of correspondence courses which would enable candidates to improve their qualifications without the need for extended leaves of absence. Indeed, even some thirty years later when the Canadian Library Association (1961) solicited responses on a national scale for a program of inquiry into *The Present State of Library Service in Canada,* there was no strong criticism of the lack of regional library schools although again attention was drawn to the need for basic courses to be offered outside of the regular winter sessions. It was not until the postwar period—with its increasing university affluence, its growing regional identities, and with, perhaps coincidentally, a recognition in at least some quarters that, as Bergen (1963) put it, "librarianship... should abandon its historical-bibliographic emphasis for a base in the social sciences,"—that Canada witnessed a burgeoning of library schools in all but one of its six regions.

If we do carry Bergen's adjuration into the field of regional need, we can certainly find regional differences in Canada which presumably have implications for library education and service. Apart from the obvious French language needs being met (at least in part) by L'Ecole de Bibliothéconomie in Montreal, there are different economic needs. The Atlantic Provinces, Manitoba, Saskatchewan, Quebec (excluding the Montreal-Hull corridor) and most of northern Ontario are, for example, officially designated as (economically) deprived areas; unable, presumably, to support the level of library service they would wish. Moreover, there are demographic differences: with Ontario, British Columbia, Alberta, and the Northwest Territories having growth rates higher than the national average between 1951 and 1971; Quebec and the Atlantic Provinces showing among the lowest growth rates; and Saskatchewan registering an actual decline between 1966 and 1971. In terms of children's library services, Quebec, British Columbia, and Ontario, in that order, had the lowest gross reproduction rates in 1973 (all below the replacement level). With respect to service to senior citizens and shut-ins, Saskatchewan had the highest life-expectancy rate while Quebec (although improving) had the lowest.

If library service to immigrants is to be considered, it is interesting to note that Ontario absorbed by far the highest proportion (56%) of immigrants to Canada, British Columbia came second, and the Atlantic Provinces (3%) were the lowest. If the ability of the population to support library service (or to buy their own books) were the issue, it may be noted that Canadian family incomes in 1973 averaged $12,716, Prince Edward Island's (P.E.I.) families were lowest with an $8,572 average, and British Columbia's were highest with $13,942. Only 31.3% of P.E.I. families earned over $10,000 in 1973. In Newfoundland the figure was 37.1%. In Ontario 61.9%, and in British Columbia 67.7%, earned above that figure (*Canada Yearbook,* 1974).

Of course, it is easy to parody the socioeconomic approach to regional library needs (what, for example, is one to make of the statistic that in 1973 roughly one in four of all births in the Territories were considered as illegitimate?); but, as opposed to the essentially bibiographic view that a book is a book is a book anywhere in Canada, the development of library schools in the regions of Canada since 1960 might be seen as an opportunity for each school to educate for the unique needs of its region.

IV. CURRICULAR RESPONSES

The difficulty with the theory of a growing sociobibliothecal recognition of regional need, however, is that it finds little support in the current calendar offerings of Canadian library schools. Unquestionably there is a strong *national* bias. At Toronto, for example, F. D. Donnelly has reported, in an internal memorandum, that all the F.L.S. core courses "have a significant component of Canadian content in specific units which lend themselves to study by means of the Canadian environment"; that eight of the elective courses are explicitly concerned with Canadian content; that many other electives are conducted in a Canadian context. The same is true of all the Canadian library schools, and there can be no question as to their distinctive efforts to meet the national need. However, within the Canadian context, there seems to be little evidence of overtly regional emphasis. Thus a rundown of the impressive number of electives offered by the various schools (sixty-seven at Toronto, twenty-eight at Dalhousie, fifty-three at Alberta, thirty-nine at McGill, forty-six at British Columbia, fifty-two at L'Ecole de Bibliothéconomie, and so on) appear to

TABLE
Present and Future Ph.D.

Region	Public		School		Research	
	Now	1971–1976	Now	1971–1976	Now	1971–1976
Atlantic	0	0	0	0	0	0
Quebec	0	0	0	0	2	2
Ontario	1	4	1	1	7	4
Prairie	2	0	1	2	1	1
British Columbia	0	0	1	—	4	5
Total	3	4	3	3	14	12

Type of library

[a] From Denis and Houser (1972).

reveal, with two exceptions, little *specific* regional emphasis. The two exceptions are the course, "Archives du Québec et du Canada" at L'Ecole de Bibliothéconomie, and the course on "Community Services: Local, Regional, National" given at SLIS.

If the stated curricular responses of Canadian schools are generally to a national rather than a regional need as such, how then *do* the schools respond to Canadian needs and how do their responses differ? The answer here would seem to be fourfold. First, there is the obvious distinction that two of the schools—Toronto and SLIS—offer the Ph.D. The Faculty of Library Science at Toronto began its doctoral program six years ago, has graduated one student, and has seven students currently enrolled. The School of Library and Information Science at the University of Western Ontario also initiated its Ph.D. program in 1971, has not yet graduated any students from the program, and has eight currently enrolled. Both programs stress theoretical research. Both focus on Canadian issues. SLIS has been formally charged (by the Advisory Committee on Academic Planning of the Council of Ontario Universities, which in 1972–1973 assessed the need for doctoral programs in library science in Ontario) with responsibility for the area of "bibliographic control." Toronto has been charged with responsibility for the areas of "social environment and libraries," "information resources and library collections," and "library administration." Both programs appear to represent a successful in-

I
Positions in Canada as of 1970[a]

Library schools		Unidentified		Total		
Now	1971–1976	Now	1971–1976	Now	1971–1976	Combined
0	0	0	0	0	0	0
2	3	0	0	4	5	9
18	10	0	1	27	20	47
1	1	0	0	5	4	9
0	0	0	0	5	5	10
21	14	0	1	41	34	75

tellectual achievement; yet neither has flourished as their initiators expected.

It seemed in 1972, and still in many ways seems today, that there are pressing needs for a Canadian Ph.D. in Library Science. Canadian nationalism, if nothing else, is putting strong pressure on the universities of this country to increase the number of their faculty who are Canadians with a Canadian orientation to their discipline. Moreover, there is an obvious lack of Canadian research on problems peculiar to Canadian librarianship, and a consequent dependence upon perhaps less appropriate research from the United States and Great Britain. Nor were the needs themselves unresearched. A series of attempts to estimate the placement opportunities for Ph.D. graduates in library science in Canada culminated in a report by Denis and Houser (1972) of the Toronto Faculty of Library Science, incorporating responses to a questionnaire sent to the heads of most major Canadian libraries. Eighty questionnaires were distributed, and sixty-three (79 percent) were returned. On the basis of the responses received, Denis and Houser compiled several tables, of which three are of particular interest for the present study (see Tables I—III).

Denis and Houser (1972, p. 27) concluded, "It would seem that if and when a Ph.D. program in library science is established in Canada, it will receive support from the profession. This questionnaire furnishes some evidence that there are an abundance of positions now and in the future which could be filled by a librarian holding a doctorate in library science." Of course, the two investigators could not have fore-

TABLE II
Number of Librarians To Be Released for Doctoral Studies by Region, 1971–1976[a]

Region	Year						Total
	1971	1972	1973	1974	1975	1976	
Atlantic	—	—	—	—	—	2	2
Quebec	2	2	2	2	—	1	9
Ontario	8	10	10	9	12	11	60
Prairie	—	3	2	2	2	2	11
British Columbia	1	—	1	—	1	—	3
Total	11	15	15	13	15	16	85

[a] From Denis and Houser (1972).

seen the deterioration of the Canadian economy in the years immediately following their report—a deterioration which adversely affected library personnel budgets and left many librarians fearful for their jobs (for one who did, see Land, 1970), but, in retrospect, they laid perhaps insufficient stress upon reactions they received *against* Ph.D. programs in library science, such as preferences for other subject specialization, skepticism as to the value of the Ph.D. in library sci-

TABLE III
Provision for Present Staff To Enrol in a Program in Library Science[a]

Length of leave	Frequency of mention		
	With full pay	With half pay	Without pay
One year	7	7	8
Two years	0	3	5
Other	2[b]	0	4[c]
Total (N = 36)	9	10	17

[a] From Denis and Houser (1972).
[b] Leaves less than one year.
[c] Leaves less than one year, with or without financial assistance not related to salary.

ence, and a general uncertainty as to whether "such a program is necessary to the development of Canadian librarianship." If Denis and Houser were in the event overly optimistic (and it can be argued that they were concerned with assessing need not predicting supply), their optimism was shared by many educators at the time; but the actual response to the two doctoral programs in the five years since their report has so far sadly failed to meet expectations.

In large part that failure results from the generally uncertain, even adverse economic conditions facing Canadians today; and it reflects a decline in enrollments which is affecting almost all doctoral programs in the country. To some extent, however, the problem also lies in the failure of the two schools, despite continuing program revision and considerable publicity, to convince the field of the need for and relevance of research. Such conviction may well develop if the impact of completed dissertations upon practical decision making becomes apparent.

A second way in which the Canadian library schools are offering curricular responses is through their master's programs; and here the Canadian schools were somewhat slower than their American counterparts to accept the M.L.S. as the basic professional degree. Traditionally, the universities of Toronto and McGill required a minimum of two years of study beyond the baccalaureate in order to earn a master's degree in fields in which there was no undergraduate preparation. Consequently, those completing the one-year postgraduate program in library science received a bachelor's degree. By 1950, both Toronto and Ottawa had instituted a master's degree awarded upon successful completion of one year of studies beyond the bachelor's in library science. McGill initiated a similar program in 1956 (Land, 1970).

However, in 1964 the McGill University Graduate School of Library Science decided to phase out its one-academic-year B.L.S. program and to institute a two-year academic program with the M.L.S. as the first professional degree. In the Fall of 1967, SLIS was established at the University of Western Ontario, also with the M.L.S. as the first professional degree, although awarded upon completion of a three-semester program of eleven months. On April 22–23, 1968, representatives of the seven existing library schools met in Toronto at the invitation of the Toronto school for a conference on the Structure of Degree Programs in Canadian Library Schools; and six of the seven schools supported the following resolution:

Resolved that this meeting endorse the principle of a four-term graduate program leading to a Master's degree in library science as the basic preparation for the professional practice of librarianship in Canada; and that Canadian library schools attempt to implement the new basic Master's program within five years, i.e., by 1973 (Land, 1970, p. 36).

The new School of Library Science at the University of Alberta abstained from supporting the resolution because it had only just finished developing its B.L.S. program and did not feel ready to change it immediately for an M.L.S. By 1971, however, Alberta too was offering the M.L.S., and in 1976 discontinued its B.L.S. program. The Ottawa Library School, on the other hand, after launching a new basic M.L.S. program in 1972, lost its recently appointed Dean, asked to be excluded from forthcoming planning assessments, decided not to admit any more students, and eventually over the next few years wound up its program and closed its doors. All seven remaining Canadian schools now, therefore, share a common degree base. Moreover, the curricular approach to the content of that degree is remarkably similar. As was noted earlier, every Canadian M.L.S. program contributes to the concept of required or "core" courses, and there is very considerable agreement as to what constitutes these core areas. Six of the seven schools teach some variation of "information resources and library collections" as a core. Six teach administration as a core. Six teach an introductory core course in data processing. Five teach "research methods"; five teach "reference sources" as cores; and three teach "the library in society" as a core. The "odd man out" in many cases is the School of Library and Information Science at Western Ontario, which according to its 1976–1978 calendar organizes its required courses "from the point of view of the user of libraries, and not from the point of view of the librarian. Therefore, [at SLIS] professional theory and methodology is not taught by traditionally dividing the subject into courses devoted to book selection, cataloguing, classification, and reference. . . . Fundamental aspects of the acquisition, organization, and use of resources in each subject are treated simultaneously while considering the needs of the users." The core courses at SLIS are, therefore, in addition to some standard nomenclatures, entitled "Professional Theory and Methodology" (in the Humanities, Social Sciences, and Sciences); "Language, Logic, and Mathematics"; and "Master's Seminar," which is required of all students in their final term and "is intended to encourage students to develop a philosophy of librarianship that will provide a broad base for professional life after graduation."

With respect to the "elective" (second-term or second-year) offerings in the Canadian library schools, these courses again show little difference in emphasis, although as we have seen specificity of Canadian content becomes more apparent. Indeed, the generally shared concern with universal or national rather than regional perimeters again leads to an impression of "sameness" in the curricular responses of all the schools considered. Even SLIS, tends to fall into line when it comes to elective courses, for its course titles, in, for example, Special Libraries, School Libraries, Academic Libraries, Canadiana, and Historical Development of Children's Literature have much more of the traditional ring.

There is, of course, nothing wrong with a certain sameness in the curricular responses of library schools if such uniformity reflects agreement on a common philosophy of library education and an overall appreciation of regional and national needs. To the extent, therefore, that such a philosophical consensus truly accounts for common curricular characteristics, it represents a major contribution by Canadian library educators. To the extent, however, that the sameness may derive from a certain lack of imagination, it becomes a matter for concern and further investigation.

A third curricular response involves practice work. Every school offers some degree of "field work" or "practicum" and, to this extent at least, does expose its students to the environment of its region and imbues them with the library lore and responses of its own locale. Moreover, insofar as each school involves librarians from its geographic area as instructors or special lecturers, regional emphases are likely to occur and these do constitute an important though perhaps unpredictable response to regional need.

In the same vein, another response involving field work also centers on provincial rather than national concerns. Under the immediate auspices of Geoffrey Chapman, the U.B.C. School of Librarianship has initiated a joint two-year program in librarianship *and* education, which was described in a preliminary statement as follows:

> This program is designed for graduates possessing an appropriate bachelor's degree, who wish to practice as fully qualified librarians *in British Columbia secondary schools* [my emphasis]. It enables students to complete, in two years (including a summer session), the requirements for the M.L.S. degree in the School of Librarianship and teacher certification in the Faculty of Education. Candidates must meet the normal admission and course requirements of both bodies. In the first year, students take the regular 8 required courses (15 units) of the First Year in

the School of Librarianship, and one course (1 1/2 units) in the Faculty of Education. In the second year, students take 6 School of Librarianship courses (9 units), and 7 1/2 units of Education courses. During the intervening summer, students take 2 Education courses (6 units). . . .

Prospective candidates should apply separately to both the Faculty of Education and the School of Librarianship, indicating to each they wish to take the joint program.

The fourth Canadian library curricular response to be mentioned here lies at the opposite pole to regionalism. It consists of the contribution made by individual educators to librarianship *outside* Canada. Normally, this contribution has been made on a personal rather than an institutional level (although SLIS, for example, with its links to Bangalore, the West Indies, and the Caribbean, refutes this generalization); and the response at present can be found more in the input it provides to Canadian library education than in any documented and far-reaching output to library education in other countries. Without choosing specific, and probably by omission invidious, examples, it can be said in this respect that Canadian library educators from every school in the country have learned much from such activities as serving as presidents or chairmen of American library education associations and committees, from editing foreign library education journals, from participation in international graduate summer schools, from participating as active members in the International Federation of Library Associations, from serving as consultants with foreign library agencies, from external examiner appointments, and from decision-making roles in groups producing international standards for librarianship. Such professional input, and the experience gained from it, is already having a noticeable effect upon curricular responses in education for librarianship in Canada. It can be expected to have even more important and broader consequences over the next two decades.

V. STRATIFICATION

We have not thus far more than mentioned the increasingly important role played by library technician programs in Canada, yet the very success of these programs presents a challenge to traditional concepts of education for librarianship. In many instances the library technicians now receive instruction in areas formerly covered by the one-year B.L.S. programs in the university schools of library science; and the onus is therefore on the graduate schools to now delineate more clearly than ever before between the more routine support functions in a library and the judgmental functions requiring a postbaccalaureate degree.

The first Canadian library technicians' program was started in 1962 by Gertrude Perrin in Winnipeg at the Manitoba Institute of Technology. Weihs (1977), whose excellent study of "The Library Technician" provides much of the data for the following section, remarks that those whose memories she evoked "recalled that there was opposition from librarians to the program," and that the second library technician's program, begun in the Vancouver City College in 1966, also "had little support from the library community." Indeed, what initial interest librarians did express in the new college programs frequently took the form of defensive reactions designed to protect the status of existing library personnel. However, with the decision of the Ontario government in 1967 to initiate five two-year library technician programs in the newly formed Colleges of Applied Arts and Technology in that province, it became clear that librarianship was going to have to accept technicians as part of the work force and the question then became what impact such technicians should have.

Most educational programs for library technicians are now two years in length. All but two of the programs outside Quebec are given in English. The exceptions are those at Algonquin College in Ottawa and Cambrian College in Sudbury, Ontario, in which instruction is offered in both French and English. Apart from the Quebec programs, all programs follow the *Guidelines for the Training of Library Technicians,* endorsed by the Canadian Library Association, as closely as the policies of the individual colleges permit (Marshall, 1973).

The *Guidelines* advocates the following mix of courses:

50% general academic studies "directed towards broadening the student's academic experience, education, and enhancing his career development." These optional subjects can include language, literature, environmental studies, history and/or philosophy of science, languages, life sciences, music, Canadian studies, philosophy, physical sciences, and social sciences.

25–30% library technical studies in which students learn the tools of their trade. These courses are practical and job-oriented for the most part.

20–25% related technical subjects which include a knowledge of the production of simple media and the routine maintenance of audiovisual equipment, an introduction to data processing, and office procedures with stress on a "reasonable competency" in typing.

The focus of technician courses is the job, the stress is on the needs of libraries today. The emphasis is more practical than theoretical, and the keynote is flexibility. Programs do not prepare graduates for particular types of libraries, and the procedures taught are those generally in use. Only two of the programs—those at Lakehead University in Thunder Bay, Ontario, and Concordia University in Montreal—are university based; and only at the latter institution can library science courses constitute a major subject area in the granting of a B.A. Nevertheless, because of the nature of much that goes on in libraries, intelligent technicians, given the same length of education as an M.L.S. student, can learn enough basic library techniques to enable them, after experience, to perform duties still regarded in some quarters as the prerogatives of the professional librarian. For instance, it is suggested that "an experienced and competent technician may be placed in charge of a small branch library, or of a department or section of a department supervising other technicians and clerical staff" (Weihs, 1977, p. 430).

The difficulty, therefore, appears to lie less in the definition of the legitimate responsibilities of the library technician than in a clarification of the responsibilities of the librarian; and the field has tended to be somewhat defensive in responding to this challenge. As Weihs notes, "Every profession has its quota of members who resist change and the library profession is no exception." However, graduate library school educators have also been tardy in grasping the full implication of recent developments in the colleges. If Weihs is correct in saying that "librarians should perform tasks which require a specialized subject background, an ability to analyse facts, and depth and perspective in their understanding of library science and management expertise," then "librarians must define the extent and nature of responsibility to be assumed by technicians and supervise their performance"; and we must recognize that the baccalaureate, whether of three or four years' duration, does not necessarily provide such specialized competencies. Nor does it ensure analytical ability or supervisory competence. M.L.S. programs can perhaps be developed to ensure that these competencies are taught. However, the present prevalence of electives, although providing flexibility, means that many students can "spread themselves" to meet what they assume to be the current eclectic nature of the job market. Apart from a somewhat rudimentary overview in the core, such students may even avoid management practices entirely.

Nor, despite the widespread use of entrance interviews, have the Canadian library schools been able to devise other than academic criteria for objective screening of applicants, and the competencies assumed by Jean Weihs are usually regarded as largely untestable.

VI. LIBRARIANSHIP AS AN ACADEMIC DISCIPLINE

The decision to make the M.L.S. the basic professional library degree in Canada placed the library schools and their programs firmly within the aegis of the graduate faculties of the universities. The scholastic criteria of graduate studies thus became totally applicable. These criteria, although they vary in detail from university to university, have generally been conceded as benefiting the library schools by introducing an insistence upon high and widely accepted standards. They have, however, represented at times a difficult transition from the less regulated B.L.S. programs of the past. Nowhere has this been more true than in the research requirement of graduate studies. This requirement has two facets: courses at the master's level are expected to develop a mastery of the theoretical research in a discipline; and graduate faculty themselves are expected to contribute to such research. Neither requirement was easily met by Canadian library schools in the early 1970s, for no strong tradition of research existed in the field or in the schools. Much of the literature of Canadian librarianship was either bibliographic or descriptive, and educational thinking tended to reflect these emphases.

The graduate library schools have, however, made continuous and impressive progress in adjusting to their new academic climate. The development of curricular research emphases at both the doctoral and the master's levels will be discussed later in this study. Equally important have been the changes in the responses of faculty themselves. Doctoral qualifications are no longer the exception for teaching staff, and at least some of the Canadian schools now regard possession of the advanced degree (or at the very least the A.B.D.) as necessary for appointment. At the same time faculty without the doctorate are responding with strenuous efforts to upgrade their qualifications. At Toronto, for example, which listed twenty-four full-time teaching staff in 1975–1976, there are currently twelve Ph.D.s, one LL.D. and three A.B.D.s on the faculty, and the school has made generous study-leave provision for the pursuit of doctoral studies. Similarly, SLIS listed seven out of nineteen full-time faculty with the Ph.D. in its 1976–1978 calendar; and Dalhousie listed six doctorates, one LL.D., and one A.B.D. in its latest report.

Faculty research and publication too have shown impressive growth. It would be invidious to select specific examples; but almost every school can point to the proliferation of scholarly monographs by its faculty over the past five years. Dalhousie and McGill have their own Occasional Papers series. Toronto has its new Centre for Research in Librarianship, about which more will be said later in this chapter, and the Centre has already generated two major monographs.

We have noted that it would be invidious to identify the publication efforts of only a few Canadian library educators. It would probably also be misleading. The responses of Canadian Library school faculty to the academic pressures of their respective graduate schools have, not unexpectedly, been less than uniform. However, as the following cursory analysis may indicate, the twin graduate school criteria of research and publication are indeed being met by many library educators; although there will probably be more faults found with the analysis than there are individuals encompassed by it. Be that as it may, a rough overview of writings in librarianship by Canadian library educators was obtained by checking relevant author entries in *Library Literature* from 1970 to 1975 inclusive; and the results appear in Table IV, tabulated by school and by professorial rank.

Clearly, Table IV covers only items published in library-oriented journals. On the other hand it might be expected that library school faculty would publish primarily in this area. Certainly not all the faculty on staff in 1975 have been so for any length of time, and this is particularly true of assistant professors. On the other hand it may not be unreasonable to suppose that recently appointed faculty were chosen, at least in some small part, because of their previous publication record. Admittedly, it is unfair to equate monographs and articles, and major and minor articles. On the other hand, length cannot be correlated to significance in writing and (having removed book reviews from our aegis) it can be argued that, lacking within the constraints of this study any objective qualitative criterion, we obtain at least a quantitative expression of an individual's need to give public expression to his or her ideas (and hence perhaps of the existence of such ideas?). Without question no one should make too much of a mere numerical expression of published creativity. On the other hand, although we can say little on the significance of five publications compared to seven or three, we can perhaps speculate on the meaning of an absence of any publication over a five-year span. Even allowing for the probability that many junior faculty may have been concentrating on their dissertations, one may be surprised that the median for listed items by assistant professors was zero; or that six (17.7%) of the associate professors had nothing listed between 1970 and 1975 (inclusive). There are those disciplines (although librarianship is apparently not one) in which publication is essential to academic promotion and where assistant and even associate professors are under heavy pressure to publish (or perish). Among library educators, however, production apparently increases with rank. Moreover, one tenth (9.20%) of library school educators in Canada produced over a third (36.07%) of the

TABLE IV

Publications of Canadian Full-Time Library Educators Listed in *Library Literature* 1970–1975

School	No. of full-time faculty 1975	No. of items listed in *Lib. Lit.*	Faculty mean	Faculty median	Faculty range
Univ. of Alberta	9	18.5[a]	2.06	1	0–8.5
Univ. of British Columbia	11	38	3.45	3	0–10
Dalhousie Univ.	8	35.5[a]	4.44	0.5	0–15
McGill Univ.	7	9	1.29	0	0–8
Univ. de Montréal	9	20.5[a]	2.28	2	0–5
Univ. of Toronto	23	65.5[a]	2.85	2	0–8
Univ. of Western Ontario	17	39.5[a]	2.32	1	0–11
Total	84	226.5[b]	—	—	—
Mean	12	—	2.67	—	0–9.36
Median	9	—	—	1	0–8.5

[a] Joint authorship = 0.5 of an item. Reviews by and items about are excluded.
[b] Number of items by (28) Assistant Professors: 30. Mean: 1.07. Median: 0. Range: 0–5.5.
Number of items by (34) Associate Professors: 87. Mean: 2.56. Median: 2. Range: 0–15.
Number of items by (22) Full Professors: 109.5. Mean: 4.98. Median: 4. Range: 0–15.

relevant material listed in *Library Literature* for the half-decade, 1970 to 1975.

VII. PRACTICE WORK IN LIBRARIES

The ambivalence with which many Canadian library educators face the issue of academic theory versus vocational practice is perhaps nowhere better illustrated than in the attitude of their schools toward the long-standing question of practice work. In the past, the schools involved have varied in their approach to such work from an earlier emphasis upon practical experience prior to and during the program, to a later virtual elimination of practice as a component of the degree. Three statements from calendars of the Toronto school 1950–1951; 1965–1966; 1975–1976, respectively, may serve to illustrate the shift in points of view.

> Arrangements have been made with the Board of the Toronto Public Library for practice work in the libraries of the city during a part of each week of the second term. In addition, each student will devote two continuous weeks to such practice work. . . . Applicants with a certificate of graduation from an approved University are required to submit before registration evidence of at least two weeks' practice under supervision in an approved library.
>
> Applicants who have not had library experience are strongly advised to work in a library under professional supervision before registration.
>
> The ultimate goal of education for librarianship should be to educate students who are able to think and act upon the issues presented to them as administrators, planners or practitioners. The emphasis of the education should be intellectual and theoretical so that librarians can think creatively about whatever area of librarianship they may be concerned with.

Unquestionably there is an advance in the level of flexibility and intellectualization represented by these three statements. Whether the practical needs of library school students relevant to the present state of the art are progressively better served is perhaps more open to question. The truth would seem to be that, in too many Canadian library hierarchies, management concepts and the appreciation of the subordinate's role are such that beginning librarians are not frequently presented with issues which call for initiative and an intellectual response to theoretical problems. As a result, library technician educators such as Jean Weihs can and do claim that their graduates are better prepared to meet the initial demands of library employment than are the graduates of the university library schools; and a demand for the reestablishment of (more relevant) practicums continues to be heard in the universities.

The answer for many of the library schools appears to lie in problem-centered field work. Thus Toronto offers a two-credit course entitled "Practicum in Community Services," and incorporates supervised field work into several of its courses. SLIS offers a group of four "practicum courses" which "emphasize simulation of technical functions in library and information systems by actually carrying out such professional and technical tasks under laboratory conditions." Dalhousie requires "100 hours of carefully planned and supervised work, if possible in a library of the student's choice and in the area of the student's interest," plus "field trips for the purpose of visiting various types of libraries. . . . and an Annual Field Trip to a city of major importance for the world of libraries"; and British Columbia specifies that "field trips and field work, as may be called for, are considered integral parts of the M.L.S. program." Such practice work and field trips are not intended to equal the emphasis placed by the library technicians' programs upon this aspect of library education; yet, even so, there are those among the graduate library schools' faculty who would maintain that already the resurgence of field work is sacrificing theory for practice at the graduate level.

The evidence suggests then that, as Davinson (1976, p. 238) remarked of education for librarianship in Europe, "Many librarians . . . find themselves in a real quandary when they attempt to teach librarianship. Are they to provide an education *for* librarianship or a training *in* librarianship?" The instructors in the colleges have apparently resolved the dilemma, and their programs clearly provide the practice for work *in* libraries. In Quebec the CEGEP program includes a full term of practice work; and in the Anglophone colleges all programs make substantial provision for either an extended period of part-time work in libraries or for "block placement"—full time for a shorter period. The graduate faculties of librarianship in the universities, however, remain torn between the desire to teach widely applicable principles (which they have not in many cases yet found) as the basis for a full professional career, and the need to place their students in a specific first job. Their quandary is increased by the evidence that in Canada, as in the United States, many employers are not concerned with the courses or academic grades achieved by library school students; let alone with the mastery of a theoretical body of knowledge. The students for their part generally and understandably seek out those courses which offer practical instruction and would welcome practice work as preparation for the initial and unyielding demands of the job they hope above all to receive.

VIII. CONTINUING EDUCATION

Both Asheim and Davinson pay considerable attention to the issue of continuing education, defined by Davinson (1976, p. 243) as "educational jargon which restates in brief the old adage that education ought to be a lifelong process"; and Asheim (1975, p. 170) notes that "as the demand increases for specialists, and as new knowledge is constantly added to the requirements for acceptable professional performance, there is every likelihood that the schools will be expected to offer more of these [i.e., post-master's] kinds of learning experiences."

In Canada, as elsewhere, the demand for opportunities to update knowledge in librarianship is, as we have already seen, almost as old as library education itself. Part of the demand stems from the desire to upgrade formal qualifications (e.g., to move from the B.L.S. to the M.L.S. degree), and such demand can only be met through credit courses; but this requirement is lessening as the B.L.S. becomes more distant, and the increasing emphasis is upon the type of need described by Asheim. There remains, however, a wish in the field for extension courses which will permit the obtaining of an M.L.S. "on the job"; and this wish still conflicts with the residence requirements of graduate studies in Canadian universities.

Again to turn to the published calendars of the seven Canadian library schools, the School of Library Service at Dalhousie has one of only two full descriptions of a continuing education program, and its 1977-1978 Calendar may be quoted in full as a basis for discussion.

> The School of Library Service has always recognized its responsibility to provide programmes for the professional development of both its own graduates and the practising librarians in the Atlantic Provinces. It has three specific programs. . . .

The first is a lecture series open to all interested persons. During the course of each Year, the School brings to the Campus fifteen to twenty guest lecturers from different parts of Canada, the United States, and occasional visitors to Canada from overseas. Drawn from many aspects of library work, information handling, and the book trade, these lecturers are involved with an open discussion following their contribution. Those who attend come from many parts of Nova Scotia and other Atlantic Provinces.

The second program in continuing education relates to workshops held at the School. Recent workshops have been on Government Documents, Libraries and the Law, Selecting and Evaluating Non-print Materials, and the services of The National Library of Canada. Highly qualified speakers and resource persons are secured from Canada and the United States for these workshops, with participants coming from all four Atlantic Provinces and many other geographical areas.

Librarians in the Halifax-Dartmouth area also have opportunities to participate in the School's regular academic program. Since its beginning the School has admitted non-degree students as auditors to its courses.

For the rest, only Toronto devotes a substantial section in its 1975–1976 calendar to a description of its continuing education program, noting that "this program was inaugurated in the 1972–73 regular session. In it are offered institutes and workshops lasting for several concentrated days or running weekly over part of a term. . . . In 1975–76 institutes were offered in Data Processing: Canadian MARC; Government Publications: the U.S. and the U.K.; Computer-based Reference Services [and] Letters in Canada: Contemporary Collections." The Toronto program is, for the most part, offered by members of F.L.S., but is administered by the University's School of Continuing Studies which handles registration and publicity and collects fees.

The absence of emphasis upon continuing education in most of the Canadian library school calendars does not, of course, necessarily signify the absence of such education in those schools which do not report. It does suggest, however, that, as was noted in one response to the general letter of inquiry which was sent in preparation for this chapter, "probably Continuing Education is not yet the bandwagon business it is in the States." It is likely that the concept of continuing education will remain just that as far as the schools are concerned: a noncredit continuation of professional education beyond the master's degree. As such it is apparently extremely popular and the Toronto offerings, for example, are well attended.

Clearly, however, at both Dalhousie and Toronto, the substance of the continuing education lectures or courses tends to represent specialized and advanced treatment of areas of change rather than *Gestalt* treatments of core concern. Whether such specialized treatment can be used, as Davinson (1976) suggests, deliberately to avoid overfilling basic courses with esoteric data, remains to be seen. Certainly, for example, international programs of education for librarianship could play a role in this respect, for comparative librarianship is still an area of relative weakness in many Canadian M.L.S. programs; but at present the formal relationship between courses at the master's and continuing education level in our library schools does not appear to be sufficiently developed to permit predictable integration.

IX. HARMONIZATION OF QUALIFICATIONS

The willingness of the American Library Association to accredit Canadian library schools on the same basis as those in the United States, and the willingness of the Canadian schools to be so accredited, has resulted in a high degree of harmony between the qualifications expected of the graduates of the accredited schools. This was true even before the Canadian schools moved to establish the M.L.S. as their basic degree, for "The ALA Committee on Accreditation respected the [B.L.S. degree] traditions of McGill and Toronto and both were subsequently re-accredited under the 1951 *Standards for Accreditation*" (Land, 1970, p. 37). Similarly, the School of Librarianship of the University of British Columbia also had its one-year B.L.S. program accredited in 1962. The decision of the American and Canadian agencies concerned to accept (albeit not always without question on the part of the Canadian) such a modus vivendi has resulted in a relatively free academic interchange of postgraduate students between the libraries and library schools of both countries.

Such harmony has not, however, always marked the relationship between Canada and other countries offering education for librarianship. Because the Canadian concept of professional librarianship has, like that in the United States, included the requirement of a postbaccalaureate university degree, it has run headlong into the "persistent unwillingness of [for example] British librarianship to accept the requirement that the top echelons of the profession always be university graduates" (Davinson, 1976, p. 246). The confrontation had perhaps its clearest focus in the deliberations of the now defunct Institute of

Professional Librarians of Ontario (IPLO). These episodes have been analyzed—beginning with the meetings of the forerunner of IPLO, the first Professional Committee of the Ontario Library Association—in a history of the Institute by Houser (1975).

Houser's account sums up much of the essence of the struggle over qualifications: the perhaps naive and purist expectations of those who see the postbaccalaureate degree as the only entrée into the profession; the realities of the field in which, as Asheim has pointed out, education other than that for librarianship as such has a place; the difficulty of harmonizing theory and practice; and the inevitable compromises which are necessary for consensus. In the event, the compromise solution for IPLO was that:

> ... the I.P.L.O. recognized the basic qualification of professional librarianship to be a bachelor's degree from a university of recognized standing, plus a postgraduate degree from a library school accredited by the Canadian and American Library Associations, or the possession of a general university education and a professional education in librarianship which the I.P.L. Registration Committee considers equal in content and quality to the above degrees. That is, having spelled it out in terms of North American training, we have left the door open for our Registration Committee to equate other training. These standards have been accepted by the I.P.L.O. members as the desired pattern of education for librarians in Ontario and were subsequently endorsed by the Ontario Library Association and, in June 1959, the Canadian Library Association at its conference in Edmonton approved identical standards (Houser, 1975, p. 35).

Working within this framework, the Registration Committee of the IPLO eventually developed the following sample list of equivalencies to the postbaccalaureate library science degree from an accredited library school in North America:

Great Britain:
    B.A. plus A.L.A. (Associate of the Library Association,
       if done as a University post-graduate course.)
    B.A. plus Diploma of Librarianship, University of London.
    B.A. plus Diploma course at College of Librarianship
       Wales, Aberystwyth.
    B.A. plus Diploma from The Polytechnic of North London.

Australia:
    B.A. plus Diploma of Library Science, University of
       New South Wales.

New Zealand:
    B.A. plus Diploma of New Zealand Library School.

Philippines:
M.A. with a Major in Library Science, University of Santo Tomas.

India:
M.L.S. or Ph.D., University of Delhi.

There is, however, one extremely important exception to the principle explicit in the IPLO equivalencies, and this is found in the area of school librarianship in Canada. In this area the assumption governing the basic qualifications of the librarian differs from those so far discussed. As Grossman (1968, p. 33), Chief Librarian of the Vancouver Public Library, commented some years ago:

> It is interesting that almost all other institutions, even those requiring a considerable degree of specialized knowledge are reasonably content to accept librarians as librarians. As such they are accepted in Universities, government departments, hospitals, engineering firms and so on. But in SCHOOLS—they *must* be teachers.

The consequence of the preceding assumption is that relatively few school librarians have the M.L.S. degree or its equivalent, although some force has been given to the view that at least the overall coordination of school library systems requires such a level of professional education. Most school librarians, however, may have only one or more of the courses prescribed by the various provincial Departments of Education; and indeed, in many cases before the 1970s, elementary school librarians could have lacked even a B.A. or B.Sc. (Fennell, 1975).

The reluctance of school librarians to endure two full-length professional degree programs, one in teaching and one in librarianship, is understandable, although Departments of Education encourage such a goal through higher salary scales. Fasick (1975, pp. 179–80) nicely sums up the situation.

> A compelling argument against requiring an M.L.S. degree for certification as a school librarian is that the length of training is excessively long. A three or four year bachelor's degree, a one-year bachelor's degree in education, and then a two-year M.L.S. program requires time and financial resources not often available to prospective school librarians. On the other hand, continuing the present system would seem to place an increasing hardship upon school librarians whose tasks are fully as complex as the professional librarian's, but who are not given comparable library training. As school libraries grow in their importance within the school curriculum, and as they are increasingly called upon to integrate with other libraries in total community service, the differences in training between the

two groups will become even more obvious and a handicap to the librarian without library school training.

The British Columbia School of Librarianship is now moving, as we have seen, to resolve the dilemma through a joint master's program in education and librarianship; and the Toronto Faculty of Library Science has opened negotiations with the University's Faculty of Education toward the same end. Until some type of generally accepted postbaccalaureate school librarian's degree program exists in each of the Canadian provinces, however, the task of harmonizing the overall qualifications of one extremely important subset of the profession with those supported by IPLO and the Canadian Library Association seems virtually impossible.

X. THE RESEARCH COMPONENT

As has been noted earlier in this chapter, in the discussion of librarianship as an academic discipline, the number of advanced research degrees held by Canadian library educators has been rising in recent years and the amount of research and publication has been substantial, although not uniform across all schools and all professorial ranks. The question remains, however, as to the extent to which these changes are reflected in the increasing incorporation of a research component into the programs of the library schools.

To turn first to the doctoral programs in library science in Canada, those at Toronto and at Western Ontario, we find that in both programs only those persons who are members of their respective Faculties of Graduate Studies can direct doctoral dissertations, and membership in the graduate faculty normally involves demonstrated research production following the doctorate. The level of research input into both Ph.D. programs is, therefore, expectedly high. The dissertation topics thus far approved deal with fundamental and far-reaching problems in Canadian librarianship and should provide at least partial solutions to questions of immediate practical concern. The graduates, and almost-graduates of the programs, are already occupying key positions in Canadian libraries and library schools and as a result are introducing a knowledge of research techniques to their students and colleagues throughout the nation.

Second, let us turn to the research elements in the master's programs of the library schools. Grotzinger's (1976) study of master's level research courses in North American library schools reports that, apart from the increasingly pervasive reliance upon research findings in all M.L.S. courses, six out of the seven then accredited Canadian schools require a specific research course (the seventh school, L'Ecole de Bibliothéconomie, did not respond to the survey but does list "méthodologie de la recherche" among its "cours obligatoires"). Grotzinger also implies that all six schools stress the design of a scientific research study and the collection and analysis of data. Her study does not cover research as an elective; but all seven Canadian Schools offer such courses. Alberta has an optional thesis route; British Columbia allows substitution of a research project for a course or seminar; Dalhousie has a two-term thesis elective and encourages students "to pursue an individual research project"; Montreal includes an elective "travail individuel" resulting in a written paper prepared under faculty supervision; Toronto has a four-credit research "package" consisting of an advanced research methods half course, a reading half course, and a full-course research report; and Western has grouped six courses under the heading of "Research and Evaluation", and this group includes two units of guided research. There is no indication in the calendars of the number of students who avail themselves of the opportunity to pursue research at the master's level; but, for Toronto at least, the number rarely exceeds two or three in any given year.

These, then, are the major research components in education for librarianship in Canada; but there is a further, and perhaps surprising, recent development in this area. Although it might normally be inappropriate to include library technicians' programs in a discussion of research degrees, since those programs do not lead to a degree and do not usually require as high a level of demonstrated research competence on the part of their faculty, it is worth mentioning that at least one College of Applied Arts and Science (Sheridan) is experimenting with a joint library techniques/research techniques three-year program which will offer courses such as computer concepts for libraries, basic reference and bibliography, applied research, planning theory, data analysis, and marketing research. Although the level of sophistication achieved in such a program must be predicated upon a high school rather than a university background, it seems clear that a good student exposed to so wide a range of library-related subjects (including courses on sociology and psychology) should be capable of fulfilling an important role in library research. Indeed, one student in the joint program at the College of Applied Arts and Science is currently completing her practicum with the Centre for Research in Librarianship (CRL) of the University of Toronto.

Mention of the Centre for Research introduces one final research component of education for librarianship in Canada. The Centre was founded as a component of the Toronto Faculty of Library Science in November 1975, and was from the first conceived of as a center for relevant research in Canada rather than merely in its own Faculty or University. The goals of the Centre are to:

1. Further an understanding of the nature of librarianship and of information interfaces in general by adding to the body of relevant specialized data, particularly as it pertains to Canada.
2. Increase the visibility of librarianship and cognate disciplines in Canada in terms of political and fiscal support.
3. Provide a research and intellectual focus for library educators, graduate students, and librarians throughout Canada, as well as for interested researchers from other countries.

CRL was fortunate to have as its first contract the development of a research design for a Canadian public library inquiry, a contract which brought it immediate national attention and which enabled it from the first to create a team of researchers representing library schools from coast to coast. In its initial year of operation CRL negotiated research contracts exceeding $100,000 and has reason to hope that contracts for 1976–1977 may exceed that amount. It is as yet too soon, however, to assess fully the impact of the Centre for Research in Librarianship upon Canadian librarianship and library education.

XI. CANADIAN LIBRARY ASSOCIATIONS AND EDUCATION FOR LIBRARIANSHIP

Because Canadian Library Schools are not circumscribed by external examinations or by nationally codified standards or regulations, they have few formal links with external agencies such as library associations. CALS (the Canadian Association of Library Schools) and CCLS (the Canadian Council of Library Schools), while they meet at the same time and in the same place as the annual conference of the Canadian Library Association, have always been wholly independent of the CLA. Moreover, although the CLA does have a committee on the education of library technicians, the structure of the CLA as a whole makes so little provision for library educators *per se* that for a recent period of time no such category was included on the membership application form, and even now library educators are included as a subset of librarians ("Librarians and Library Employees include Library Educators, Library Assistants, Technicians, Clerical [sic], etc."). The implications of this lack of formal recognition were shown, for example, in the restructuring of the Canadian Association of College and University Libraries (CACUL), a Division of CLA. In that restructuring, three committees of CACUL were established: the two representing research and small university libraries were restricted to chief librarians or their delegates, and only the committee representing community colleges was open to all those involved with such colleges. For the library educator responsible for academic librarianship, there was consequently very limited CLA access to the deliberations of librarians in the field. For their part, library educators have done little to encourage attendance by library practitioners at meetings of CALS.

On the other hand, individual library schools do involve practicing librarians in their deliberations. Thus, for example, the Toronto Faculty of Library Science has representatives from the field on its Faculty and Council Committees. The Director of the Dalhousie school annually receives feedback from his report to the General Meeting of the Atlantic Provinces Library Association, and the Deans of both the Western Ontario and Toronto schools report annually to the annual conference of the Ontario Library Association. Apart from Toronto, however, there is little formal provision for participation by practitioners in the governance of the library schools, and "feedback is piecemeal and informal" (Gil, 1977, p. 454).

If, instead of looking to the Library Associations for evidence of active input into Canadian library education, we turn to the literature of the field, there is still little to show that practitioners regard education as a major issue. Searching through *Library Literature,* one finds isolated examples such as the article by McLeod (1953, p. 235) in which he states his opinion that "in the groves of academe, the Library Schools enjoy an eminence not entirely answerable to function or worth... because librarianship is more a practice than a theory... and relies largely on a system of rote learning." However, McLeod's brief article caused an even briefer flurry; and a further decade passed before another minor explosion occurred, this time of somewhat greater duration and sparked by Spicer's (1969) "Case Against a Two-year First Degree Course for Librarians in Canada." Apart from such isolated outbursts, articles on Canadian library education, at least according to *Library Literature* which indexes the major Canadian library journals, totaled under thirty in the twenty-eight years from 1946 to 1974; and many of these were faculty descriptions of programs rather than expressions of concern from the field.

In all fairness, it must be said that formal Association activity and essays on controversial topics are by no means the only ways in which librarians can reveal an interest in education for librarianship. Implementing lessons learned, engaging in continuing studies, and even turning occasionally to the schools for advice or help, are all methods of revealing interest and involvement. Nevertheless, while many practitioners do continue to involve themselves in these ways, it is also fair to suggest that the apparent lack of formalized or codified input into library education by the field would seem to support Shaffer's (1954) conclusion of over two decades ago that "the profession has in fact, by inactivity, allowed a professional situation to develop wherein it has little information and, as a profession, virtually no control [of its formal educational process]."

XII. EXTRAPOLATION

"To advance" is "to move forward, progress, develop." The concept contains a sense of direction as well as movement. Education for librarianship in Canada has unquestionable movement; but what of its direction? What, for example, will Canadian library educators be teaching in the year 2001? No crystal ball can provide the answer, for, as the Toronto calendar for 1976–1978 suggests, "because of the continual change in the nature of libraries and librarianship it is not possible for library educators to foresee all the needs of the future. Therefore, they should endeavour to educate librarians who can analyze problems and then work out their own solutions. Library education should provide a methodology which will enable librarians to function effectively in any professional situation." Certain extrapolations from the present may, however, be essayed; although any such predictions must be of necessity subjective and mutable.

Some years ago I began a paper, in which I hazarded some thoughts on the future of librarianship in Ontario, with the following statement:

> It is a truism that prediction is all too often an exercise in futility. Even the most learned forecast may be rendered twaddle by the unforeseen modification of one basic variable. Yet there is in librarianship... a logic implicit in our present position which, if extrapolated, allows us to suggest what our position *should* be in the future. Indeed, it may not be too pessimistic to wonder whether—unless we as librarians do soon learn to act upon, and plan in terms of, that implicit logic—the 1999 edition of Webster's may not define librarianship as "a subcategory of information science, in common use until the last quarter of the twentieth century but now obsolete."
>
> To be logical, then, let us begin by recognizing that... libraries exist through no inherent right or cultural axiom. They exist because they have in the past formed *an acceptable response to a social challenge.*

I see no reason to change this statement in applying it to education for librarianship. Indeed, one thing is very certain: if libraries no longer exist in 2001, neither will library education as such. Moreover, from this truism can we perhaps go further? If societal expectations for library service focus upon techniques rather than upon sophisticated client relationships—if, in other words, the graduates of postbaccalaureate library science courses fail to recognize, and fail to educate their communities to recognize, the full implication of their library's potential—the steadily improving quality of library technician programs in Canada may well end up by satisfying society's expectations for libraries in the twenty-first century.

Clearly such a development would be unnecessary and undesirable, not least to the library technicians themselves. It could only come about if librarians and library educators alike fail to identify and respond to universal informational (rather than bibliothecal?) needs. In this process, the library schools must, through research and teaching, take a leading role. They must mark clearly the road librarianship should follow, lest other information specialists press their present advantage and take over at the point where the library technician leaves off. For,

> [It was only after the second world war] that "information divisions" were widely created instead of libraries; that a large number of professionally trained people entered the information services business, but not as librarians. And a number of competent entrepreneurs more sensitive to the changing market found a real

opportunity to provide information services and with profit to themselves. This turn of events was not preordained. It took a positive turning away from the problem by the general library community to bring about this situation (Knox, 1965, p. 723).

To avoid turning away from such problems in the future, Canadian library education must continue above all to emphasize the development of research in its program; not only the incorporation of research findings in course content, but also the production of research by library educators and advanced students. Many of the problems which now face librarianship are, as Knox suggests, those of the "information services business"; and such problems involve particularly the production of informational records, the (automated) access to such records; and the relationship of formal and informal records to user needs.

Despite their long bibliothecal involvement, library educators in Canada have only recently begun to focus on such problems; and, although current progress in the area is reassuring, we are still without much of the researched data necessary to comprehensive synthesis. With the advent of Ph.D. programs in library science, however; with the stress upon research-qualified faculty; with the inception of a nationally oriented center for library research; and with a steadily growing reservoir of Ph.D. and M.L.S. graduates who understand the need to respond to users with intelligence and imagination, the probability is that present advances in Canadian library education and librarianship will result in the future in a structuring of programs upon a much firmer basis of theoretical research.

Within this structure, the distinction between librarians and library technicians will become clearer, and the involvement of the field in the formal education process will increase qualitatively and quantitatively. At the same time, librarianship will grow in academic stature and interdisciplinary interest, and its sociological emphasis will encourage regional diversities among the programs of the several library schools, without, however, destroying the distinctively Canadian concerns of those programs. Practice work will continue as a requirement, but will increasingly involve practice in field research. Continuing education programs will gain purpose and strength as the boundaries of relevant knowledge expand, and such programs will provide an ideal opportunity for regional emphases. Above all, that intellectual freedom—relatively untrammeled by codification or bureaucratic practices—which has been the hallmark of library education in this country, should lend to education for librarianship in Canada a flexibility and ability to innovate which might well place it in the forefront of library development in the twenty-first century.

ACKNOWLEDGMENTS

I became increasingly aware as this chapter developed that it would be at best a working paper. No one person can accurately portray the nuances of programs in each of the Canadian library schools; and, despite the very helpful comments and corrections of colleagues who have read over the penultimate draft, conflicts of interpretation and probably even of fact may remain. Moreover, the situations described changed even as the review was being written. I accept full responsibility, of course, for any errors and omissions, but I do thank, very much, readers Francess Halpenny, Norman Horrocks, Laurent-G. Denis, and Brian Land who made many suggestions; and I am grateful also to those members of my family—Professor Bertie Wilkinson, Edith Wilkinson, and my wife Isobel—who tried hard to ensure that my writing was at least comprehensible. Finally, my thanks for assistance in compiling data is given to Catherine Godin, Library Technician student at Sheridan College of Applied Arts and Technology, Oakville, Ontario.

REFERENCES

Angel, M. R., and Brown, G. R. (1977). Survey of library technician programs in Canada. *Canadian Library Journal* 34, 41–55.
Asheim, L. (1975). Trends in library education—United States. *In* "Advances in Librarianship" (M. J. Voigt, ed.), pp. 147–179. Academic Press, New York.
Beckman, M. (1972). CACUL university library standards. *Technical Sidelights* 3/4, 15–16.
Bergen, D. P. (1963). Librarians and the bipolarization of the academic enterprise. *College and Research Libraries* 24, 467–480.
"Canada Year Book 1974: An Annual Review of Economic, Social and Political Developments in Canada." (1974). Statistics Canada, Ottawa.
Canadian Library Association (1961). "The Present State of Library Service in Canada: A Program of Inquiry for 1960–61, Parts IB and IIB." Canadian Library Association, Ottawa.
Commission of Enquiry (1933). "Libraries in Canada: A Study of Library Conditions and Needs." Ryerson Press, Toronto.
Davinson, D. (1976). Trends in library education—Europe. *In* "Advances in Librarianship" (M. J. Voigt and M. H. Harris, eds.), Vol. 6, pp. 217–252. Academic Press, New York.
Denis, L. G. and Houser, L. J. (1972). A study of the need for Ph.D.s in library science in large Canadian libraries. *Canadian Library Journal* 29, 19–27.

Fasick, A. (1975). Education for school librarians: the library schools. *IPLO Quarterly* 16, 168–181.
Fennell, D. P. (1975). Education for school librarians: the ministry of education. *IPLO Quarterly* 16, 156–167.
Gil, O. J. (1977). Education for librarianship: a practitioner's point of view. *In* "Canadian Libraries in Their Changing Environment" (L. S. Garry and C. Garry, eds.), pp. 443–459. York University, Centre for Continuing Education, Toronto.
Grossman, P. (1968). Teacher education in school librarianship: professional dualism or schizophrenia? *In* "Education for School Librarianship in Canada," pp. 32–35. Canadian School Library Association, Ottawa.
Grotzinger, L. (1976). Characteristics of research courses in master's level curricula. *Journal of Education for Librarianship* 17, 85–97.
Harlow, N. (1965). The education problem. *Canadian Library Journal* 22, 84–89.
Houser, L. J., ed. (1975). The Institute of Professional Librarians of Ontario, an analysis: 1954–1975. *IPLO Quarterly* 17, 11–12.
Knox, W. T. (1965). The changing role of librarians. *ALA Bulletin* 59, 720–725.
Land, R. B. (1970). Recent developments in education for librarianship in Canada. *Library Association Record* 72, 142–146.
McLeod, P. (1953). *Library Literature.*
Marshall, J. M. (1973). "Summary of a Survey of Library Technicians Training Programs in Canada." 5th Ed., Rev. Canadian Library Association, Ottawa.
Shaffer, K. R. (1954). Personnel and the library school. *Library Trends* 3, 13–21.
Shera, J., and Anderson, M. (1975). "Education for Librarianship in the United States and Canada." Liverpool Polytechnic Department of Library and Information Studies, Liverpool.
Spicer, E. J. (1969). Case against a two-year first degree course for librarians in Canada: a personal view. *Canadian Library Journal* 26, 292–294.
Weihs, J. R. (1977). The library technician. *In* "Canadian Libraries in Their Changing Environment" (L. S. Garry and C. Garry, eds.), pp. 420–442. York University, Centre for Continuing Education, Toronto.
Whitteker, J. D. (1970). *Quill and Quire* August 28.
Wilkinson, J. P. (1968). SCOPE'ing the future of librarianship in Ontario. *In* "Co-operate?? or Co-operate!!!," pp. 32–42. Ontario Resources and Technical Service Group, Windsor.
Wilkinson, J. P. (1972). A case study in standards. *Technical Sidelights* 3/4, 8–15.

APPENDIX

Subjects Required by

Name of school	Residency first year	Number of contact hours	Total credits for M.L.S.	Number of core and required courses	Orientation to library	Audio-visual	Library and society
Univ. of Alberta[b]	Yes	15	14 (BLS)	6	X		X
Univ. of British Columbia[c]	Yes	Not stated	30	6	X		
Dalhousie Univ.[d]	Yes	Not stated	Not stated	5 core and 6 required	X	X	
McGill Univ.[e]	Yes	27	Not stated	10	X		
Univ. de Montréal[f]	Yes	Not stated	48	7	X		
Univ. of Toronto[g]	Yes	8	13	6			X
Univ. of Western Ontario[h]	No	Not stated	15 (3-term program) 10 (2-term program)	9			

[a] Prepared by Ellen Jones, Faculty of Library Science Library, University of Toronto, April 1977.
[b] 1975–1976 calendar.
[c] 1970–1971 calendar.
[d] 1971–1978 calendar.
[e] 1975–1976 calendar.
[f] 1975–1976 calendar.
[g] 1976–1978 calendar.
[h] 1976–1978 calendar.

Canadian Library Schools[a]

Subjects required to be taken (X = 1 course)

Cataloging and classification	Collections	Reference	Administration	Research methods	Data processing	Miscellaneous
X	X	X	X			
X		X	X	X		Automation in libraries
X		XXXX	X	X	XX	
XX	XX	XX	X	X	X	
X	X	X	X	X		Documentation methods
X		X	X	X	X	
			X	X	XX	Professional theory and methodology 1. Humanities 2. Social sciences 3. Science and technology, language, logic, and mathematics; master's seminar

Continuing Education for Librarians in the United States

ELIZABETH W. STONE

Graduate Department of Library and Information Science,
The Catholic University of America

I. Introduction	242
II. Definitions: Distinctions	243
A. Lifelong Learning	244
B. Continuing Education	245
C. Staff Development	246
D. Continuing Competence in Librarianship	247
E. Technical Obsolescence	250
F. Professionalism	251
III. Factors Affecting the Design of Continuing Education Systems	255
A. Systems Approach to Continuing Education	255
B. Conditions for Adult Learning	256
C. Learning Needs—Basis for Programming	258
D. Task Analysis—Basis for Competency Identification	259
E. Determing Goals and Objectives	264
F. Evaluation	266
G. Recognition for Continuing Education	268
IV. Responsibility for Continuing Education of Librarians	271
A. Introduction	271
B. Role of the Individual Practitioner	272
C. Role of the Professional Association	274
D. Role of the Academic Institution	293

	E. Role of the Employing Library	303
	F. Role of the State Library Agencies	307
	G. Role of the Federal Government	311
	H. Conclusion	314
V.	The Continuing Library Education Network and Exchange (CLENE)	314
	A. What is CLENE?	314
	B. Background	315
	C. Implementation	316
	D. Goals	318
	E. Achievements	318
	F. National Repository of Data about Continuing Education Programs	320
VI.	Looking toward the Future	322
	References	323

I. INTRODUCTION

"Nobody's Baby" was the title of an article in which Samuel Rothstein (1965), Director of the School of Librarianship, University of British Columbia, made the assertion that "continuing professional education is essentially a peripheral activity with librarianship." He made a plea for the baby's adoption.

His succinct, two-page article pointed out reasons for continuing education for library practitioners that go beyond the requirements of the profession: formal training is shorter than for most professions; it is conceived as a port of entry, not a terminal point; there is only time for generalization, not for specialization. "Surely," he exhorted, "As people who make their living from promoting and facilitating continuing education for others, are not we obliged to take a little of our own medicine?" And while he acknowledged the variety of ways librarians seek to continue their education (conferences, workshops, institutes), he criticized these efforts for lack of effectiveness, for duplication of programming, for scrappy coverage, for lack of pattern or progression of subjects and/or levels covered.

What progress has been made in the years since Rothstein's critique? Has library education caught up with other professions in the recognition of the prime importance of continuing education? Do continuing studies in librarianship enhance the competence of individuals as practicing librarians? Is continuing education for librarianship compatible with the trends in worldwide educational philosophy, as expressed in the Faure *et al.* (1972) report for UNESCO?

This world-acclaimed report presents a master plan for education throughout the world during the balance of the twentieth century, in which the importance of nontraditional learning in such a nonschool institution as the public library is stressed and in which the individual is put at the heart of the process, precisely where, as Cyril Houle (1974) has pointed out, the library puts him.

There has been a great deal of continuing education activity since the Rothstein article; this survey summarizes some of the plans and activities that have attempted to move continuing education from a "peripheral activity" to a "center stage activity" since 1965. Not all activities can be covered, but it is hoped enough will be touched upon so that the reader will have sufficient information to evaluate the advances that have been made. The reader might also want to consult the two recent annotated bibliographies on this subject prepared by Michael (1975), Patrick (1976), and Stone (1974).

II. DEFINITIONS: DISTINCTIONS

During the last ten years the pace of societal change, the amount of new knowledge, the impact of new technology, and the increasing recognition of the value of information by all sectors of the population have placed increasing demands on libraries* for new and more efficient types of service. All these changes have rapidly been changing the technological bases, procedures, and work patterns in libraries. As a result, the library profession has had to come to realize that the pace of change is now so fast that basic career education cannot presume to teach students "all they need to know." Accordingly, the only reasonable policy for the profession is to look forward to, and plan for, a growing activity in continuing education as a distinct educational function separate from advanced degree programs. It is a matter of

---

*In this review, the term "library" encompasses all kinds of information and media facilities. Similarly, "librarian" includes information and media personnel; and "library school" includes the information science or service school.

establishing and maintaining a new and vital dimension for development throughout the practitioner's career.

Before discussing the status of continuing education and the responsibilities that the various groups and individuals have accepted relative to continuing education, some definitions concerning the scope of continuing education and other related concepts, are presented *as used in this review*. This is necessary since examining the literature of professional education or listening to discussions at professional meetings immediately reveals that lifelong learning, continuing education, staff development, continuing professional competence, and other frequently used terms have different meanings to different people. This has been a stumbling block that has slowed down the development of continuing education opportunities.

A. Lifelong Learning

Lifelong learning is generally conceived of as a process and system initiated at birth and continued throughout life. It integrates learning into work and leisure. Lifelong learning is concerned with the total person and with creative life, not just the productive part of living. This concept, as it is used today, implies that people will spend periods throughout their lives in some structured learning experiences; that they can leave and return as they desire. It is a trend, in principle, to recognize that all paths, whether formal or informal, institutionalized or not, will be acknowledged as equally valid. The concept implies that there should be freedom of choice as to means and methods. These would include full-time education, part-time education, education by correspondence, as well as all the many forms of self-education making direct use of information sources (Faure *et al.*, 1972).

One of the key events in the evolution of the concept of lifelong learning in the United States was the inclusion of Part B of Title I of the Higher Education Act in the Education Amendments of 1976—the "Lifelong Learning Amendment." The thrust of this legislation is to develop a national strategy for lifelong learning which will direct the flow of a number of educational streams so that they more readily can nourish the learning needs of the American people (Kurland, 1976).

B. Continuing Education

Continuing education, as used here, consists of those learning activities utilized by individuals, following their preparatory education for entrance into the field. Learning experiences designated as continuing education are those designed primarily to increase the competence of practitioners performing roles responsibly in the profession in order to provide: (1) quality library services to all residents of the nation; (2) enrichment of library careers.

Continuing education implies a concept of lifelong learning as a critical necessity in meeting challenges inherent in an era of highly accelerated change. It includes those learning opportunities utilized by individuals in the profession which:

1. Keep them abreast of new concepts, knowledge, and skills both within the field and within related, relevant disciplines.
2. Update their basic education.
3. Refresh them in various aspects of their basic education.
4. Prepare them for changes in personal career lines by providing opportunity for diversification to perform new roles within the profession.
5. Enable them to master new conceptions of the profession itself as its membership seeks to discharge effectively the social role imposed on it.

The objective of continuing education is the specific enhancement of the competence of the individual as a practitioner, rather than the attainment of an additional academic degree.

Continuing education is that process of self-directed learning in which the individual assumes the basic responsibility for his or her own development. However, viewed on a broader level within the profession, continuing education encompasses the concern, the shared responsibility, the cooperation, and the interaction of at least seven relevant groups—the employing institutions, academic institutions, professional associations, state library agencies, relevant federal agencies, individual practitioners in libraries, and users of library services. Each of these groups is guided by its own goals and motivations. These goals and motivations determine the kind and amount of responsibility each group assumes and the amount and degree of cooperation between groups. As a consequence each group carries out differing and constantly changing roles in relation to continuing education.

A fully developed program of continuing education that will meet the needs of providing information services must make provision for *all* library personnel—professional and supportive—to have equal opportunity to continue their education. Local inadequacies in continuing education should be minimized or eliminated by new learning patterns and technology. Opportunity for continuing education should be available at a time, place, and pace appropriate to each practitioner.

Continuing education programs may be on a full-time or part-time basis, but are usually of relatively short duration, i.e., days to months. The sponsoring organization may be formal or informal: academic institutions, employing institutions, organizations, government agencies, and professional associations. Continuing education opportunities are conducted in a great variety of forms using many methods and techniques, including nontraditional forms of learning such as home study programs and transportable learning laboratories.

C. Staff Development

Whereas continuing education takes as its base the individual, staff development focuses on the development of the group as it relates to the total organizational system. Therefore, staff development relates specifically to: (1) the relationship between the system of management and the content of the development programs; (2) the internal consistency of the content of staff development courses; (3) the congruence of the methods used in the programs with the management style of the organization. Thus, according to Likert (1967), the goals of the entire organization need to be examined to ensure that the learning needs identified by individuals are in keeping with the goals of the organization. If they are not, many problems and frustrations can arise when the philosophy and methods used in the area of staff development are incongruent with other components of the organization's management system.

Satisfactory staff development consists of more than a maze of development programs and activities. That is not to say that the strategies of staff development—orientation programs, on-the-job training programs, job enrichment, skills training, effective supervision—are not important, but rather to emphasize that singularly and in themselves they do not constitute the total means for the development of the library's human resources. Staff development is not carried out in a vacuum. It functions in an environment of recruiting, promotion, and salary policies, procedures, standards, appraisal, institutional objectives, and organizational planning; it is intimately related also to the style of management operative in the library.

Staff development in an organization implies change and growth in work groups (individuals who have a face-to-face relationship in going about their daily tasks), in individuals, and in the organization itself in relation to its mission and goals. A staff development program can help work groups function more effectively and efficiently; can help build bridges among work groups; can help individuals augment their knowledge, skills, and attitudes; and can help the total organization change and develop.

As employers, libraries rightfully need to self-select the continuing education responsibilities they wish to shoulder, since each has its own special relationship to the individuals seeking to learn, its own style of management, its own specialized capabilities, its own justification for continuing education, and its own point of view concerning the manner in which it should support continuing education in relation to its goals (Stone, 1974). But whatever degree of responsibility is assumed for continuing education, the needs of library staff can only be realized in an organization which continuously maintains a *climate for learning* (Monroe, 1967). Elements in maintaining such a climate include the institution's assumption of responsibility for providing the resources necessary for self-development and for the provision of procedural help and consultation services. The employing institution should also be concerned with helping people find their unique talents and potential above and beyond the core of common competencies that are expected of everyone in the profession, and in addition to any specialist competencies an individual may develop (Knowles, 1976).

D. Continuing Competence in Librarianship

Any definition of continuing competence depends on the definition adopted for initial competence. One broad definition of competence states: "Competency is the presence of characteristics or the absence of disabilities which render a person fit, or qualified, to perform a specific task or to assume a defined role. To be competent is to possess sufficient knowledge and ability to meet specified requirements in the sense of being able, adequate, suitable, and capable" (Brown, 1973).

A simpler definition identifies competence as "the ability to accomplish an essential performance characteristic in a satisfactory fashion" (AACP/APHA Task Force, 1975). The School of Library Service, University of California, Los Angeles, has defined the basic professional competencies which encompass the fundamentals of librarianship, bibliography, and information science as: "the common knowledge base which enables librarians to communicate effectively among themselves, to cooperate in efforts to achieve total library service, and to perform at the professional rather than the technical or supportive level" (Horn, 1972).

Within the context of these definitions, two elements seem basic: (1) possession by the individual of a body of current and up-to-date knowledge in the field of librarianship or in the special area in which the individual practices; and (2) adequate and appropriate performance in a manner consistent with established professional knowledge and procedures. These two elements comprise both an ability and a desire on the part of the practitioner to provide quality library services to clients, and an environment that is favorable or conducive to such services.

Continuing competence should involve a number of related factors. These include:

1. Education and training in accordance with recognized standards for the practice of librarianship
2. Assurance that the practitioner, at the time of graduation, has achieved a defined level of competence.
3. Involvement on the part of the practitioner in continual learning.
4. Commitment on the part of the practitioner to serve the best interests of the public.
5. Assurance to the public and the profession that the practitioner continues to perform at a defined level of competence.
6. Establishment of professional criteria or standards that will serve as a guide for practitioners in their individual endeavors to main-

tain competence; that will assist the profession, colleges and universities, associations, and other organizations in planning and developing their educational offerings; and that will aid the profession and the public, in assuring competence and identifying competent practitioners.

In addition to increased public concern with the accountability of all professions and competence of professional practitioners, a number of factors have recently emerged which emphasize the increasing importance of continuing competence for all librarians. These include: revolutionary changes in procedures and tools for recording, processing, and disseminating information; increasing recognition of the economic and social value of information which has increased demand for comprehensive information services in every field of science, the humanities, business, technology, as well as the professions; the spectacular growth of computer systems and of microform, publication, and communications technologies; and the rapidly changing technological bases, procedures, and work patterns in library and information service activities. In addition to these factors the profession itself is becoming more acutely aware of its professional responsibility to provide the most up-to-date knowledge and the most effective service to the public.

The question that presents itself to all professions concerned with competency development is: How can continuing competence of practitioners be assured? In librarianship, each individual practitioner has been expected to assume the responsibility of maintaining this competence. Although this is perhaps the ideal approach, and while many members of the profession have fully maintained, and continue to maintain, a high degree of competence, it is doubtful that the incentives are sufficient to encourage all practitioners to continue to maintain their competence under this system.

Although participation in continuing education is no guarantee of improved competence it is recognized as one means to this end. The means by which professionals continue their education are varied, but whatever the means, it is essential that the practitioner be stimulated by a desire to improve his/her competence. Many professions have developed systems to stimulate such motivation. For example, in a recent study by Jackson (1977), it was found that the eight allied health professional organizations encouraged their members to participate in continuing education activities by providing them with some type of service or recognition.

E. Technological Obsolescence

A central concept and concern in discussing continuing education is that of obsolescence, stemming from the accelerated growth and expansion of knowledge and technology. In order to maintain job effectiveness, all professionals need to acquire new knowledge after receiving their last degrees. In fact, the degrees themselves are in part obsolescent because the knowledge represented by the degree is frequently dated, as was so aptly expressed by Shera (1972) in his article, "The Self Destructing Diploma." Often the term "technological obsolescence" is used in the literature but not defined; however, generally, when it refers to an individual, it is taken to mean "a deficiency of knowledge such that he approaches problems with viewpoints, theories, and techniques less effective than others currently used in his field of specialization" (National Science Foundation, 1969).

There are a number of types of obsolescent persons. One is the person who has not kept up with new knowledge and techniques in his or her field. Competence has aged in the face of the knowledge explosion, and the individual is obsolescent as compared both to new graduates and to colleagues who keep up with, and apply, new findings. A second type of obsolescent person is one who is overspecialized, who has only kept up with his or her own very narrow field of specialization. This individual has lost contact with broader changes. A third type of obsolescent person is the one who moves out of one career into another that may not be very closely related. This individual's training is no longer closely integrated with his/her work.

Although there are different degrees of technical obsolescence and it does not affect all people the same way, the majority of people seem to recognize it as a threat to their job competence, or even to their employability. There is evidence in the literature that the degree of threat varies. One study in librarianship demonstrates the anxiety that technology can bring. The respondents, middle and upper-level librarians, showed the greatest interest in courses in automation, even though few of them were in libraries that were automated at the time or had future plans for automation. It was shown statistically that having automated activities in the respondent's library and wanting to take a course in library automation were unrelated. The high demand seemed to be related to the respondents' anxiety; a fear that they might need a knowledge of automation in their jobs in the future. It was also shown that there was a high correlation between the other courses the respondents wanted to take and their present job needs (Stone, 1969).

As knowledge in every discipline advances, the public, aware of the social and economic role of information, has a right to expect library service to be performed in the most efficient manner possible. However, Bundy and Wasserman maintain that most librarians resist the idea that the library's most important commodity is information in myriad forms, and their continuing reliance on the book, combined with their lack of specialized knowledge in subject areas, has resulted in their failure to satisfy the newly emerging needs of users. They ask whether librarianship will be able to institute changes and transform itself in a manner demanded by current pressures in society (Bundy and Wasserman, 1968). Klempner believes a major factor contributing to this situation is the lack of continuing education for librarians (Klempner, 1968).

F. Professionalism

The School Library Manpower Project identified professionalism as a major concern in the education of school library media specialists, and provided the following definition, which can be used by an individual librarian as a guide to daily practice:

> Professionalism is the conduct of qualified people who share responsibilities for rendering a service; for engaging in continued study; and for maintaining high standards of achievement and practice within the principles, structure and content of a body of knowledge (ALA, 1970b).

Eight behavioral objectives were set for this area of competency by the Project, one of which deals specifically with continuing education:

> To engage in continuous study for professional growth including the study of current information and trends affecting message design and system analysis and contribution to the creation of such processes.

Since the landmark statement by Flexner (1915) there has never been any complete agreement on the characteristics of a "profession" as opposed to an "occupation." New ones are constantly being suggested by various professions, and it is unlikely that there will ever be any consensus. A strong case can be made, however, for Houle's position that a "dynamic concept of professionalization, based on discovery, growth and innovation" offers the educator concerned with continuing education the best foundation on which to build. Houle takes the position that much of the difficulty would be resolved if a profession were not defined as a vocation in which a fixed level of achievement or certain standards have been or have to be attained, but rather as an ideal state toward which many occupational groups are striving. He suggests 13 aims that such a group might seek (Houle, 1970). Such an approach also places the educator in a central position because his or her expertise is seen as a way of enhancing and speeding up the process of professionalization.

Houle presents another consideration which is important in discussing the continuing education of various professions. Different professions have different patterns of work, and what might be the best or ideal method for one group may not be the most effective for another. Therefore, to avoid distortion, it is necessary to recognize that service provided by professionals follows several different patterns; each group has its own dominant way of working. Houle has identified three basic patterns:

1. The entrepreneurial occupations, in which "the practitioner organizes, operates and assumes the risk for his own work, either alone or in partnership with colleagues." They offer direct service to clients as they demand it. The professionalizing groups where this pattern is dominant include accounting, architecture, dentistry, law, medicine, and optometry.
2. The collective occupations, in which practitioners perform their services in the institution that employs them. Sometimes clients are members of an association, as is true with most Protestant and Jewish ministries. Sometimes clients are members of the general public or some special public. Among the professionalizing occupations predominantly using this type of service are engineering, forestry, journalism, librarianship, nursing, pharmacy, social work, and teaching. Practitioners in this group

sometimes work alone, but more often they are associated with a group of colleagues in either their own vocation or others allied to it.
3. The hierarchical occupations, in which "the practitioners also work within an institutional framework but their expertise lies not in giving of direct service but in their capacity to operate an ordered structure of authority and to initiate or to enforce the policies that best maintain this structure." Among the professionalizing groups that characteristically follow this pattern are the armed services, business administration, and the Roman Catholic clergy. If the practitioner leaves the employ of the sole possible user of his services, he leaves the profession (Houle, 1970).

Keeping these classifications in mind, it becomes clear that independence of action is the greatest in the entrepreneurial group and is present in varying degrees in the other types. The expertise of the individual professional gives him a quality that distinguishes him/her from others employed in the same institution. The knowledge of these basic patterns has implications for the development of continuing education programs. Not only do they make the task of comparison much more difficult, but the educational practices used are influenced by these basic differences in patterns.

Nattress, in his comparative study of continuing education for the professions in the United States, finds that there are three stages of development in continuing education programs. In stage one he places those professions for which continuing education is just beginning to be recognized as necessary for competent practice, and cites the clergy as an example.

In the second stage he places those professions in which continuing education has been joined to formal preservice education into a continuum—where one blends into the other in a continuous process. He cites law as an example of this stage.

From his study, he cites medicine as the profession which most approximates the ultimate criterion by which effectiveness can be measured. This stage he characterizes as having a broad approach to continuing education which is designed to be available to each individual and has as an overriding goal service to the total population (Nattress, 1970).

Where does librarianship fit within this three-stage classification scheme? It would seem that although many positive steps have been taken in the last few years (which will be highlighted in the succeeding pages) librarianship is still most closely parallel to "stage 1", in which there is much activity and there are high hopes and plans for the future, but many apparent weaknesses (Stevenson, 1967).

Until recently there has been little attention to structure either from the point of view of society's needs or from the viewpoint of the individual practitioner's needs. Lorenz (1964) stated a thesis relative to this problem:

> My thesis . . . is that society has a right to look to the various professions and to their professional associations for effective planning and action in developing opportunities for continuing education at local, regional, and national levels; the efforts toward systematic development of full-scale programs of continuing education to meet the needs of library personnel at all levels and in all types of libraries have been insufficient, indeed. Programs of continuing library education have been, to say the least, hit or miss.

Throughout the professions, continuing education is viewed generally as a major contributor in supporting change and reequipping individuals and institutions for new tasks. Logically, therefore, continuing education for the library profession has the potential to introduce and improve services to all users. The design and implementation of service systems for libraries congruent with real life needs is one result that should lead to increased emphasis on continuing education. Yet, in spite of greater activity in the area of continuing education in recent years, there is still a disjunction between use and users, and many problem areas remain. Many examples of problems which are susceptible to treatment through continuing education are indicated in the *Proceedings of a Conference on the Needs of Occupational, Ethnic and Other Groups in the United States* sponsored by the National Commission on Libraries and Information Science in 1973 (NCLIS, 1973). Problem areas in delivery of service include the aging, labor, the disadvantaged, the handicapped, the biomedical community, and urban residents. Specific shortcomings in the mismatch between information needs of urban residents and institutional library service are also specified in a 1973 study "Information Needs of Urban Residents" (Warner, 1973).

Design and successful implementation of delivery systems for serving the needs of users is one problem area which continuing education for librarians needs to address before it can move into a "stage 3" level of development, which has as its dominant characteristic the improvement of services to the population as a whole. It is a stage in which the stated goal is the availability of continuing education to every professional who wishes it, made possible by full use of new technology; a stage in which identification and management of the conditions of learning are considered in relation to continuing education programs; a stage in which the ultimate goal is increasing the competence of the public to deal with life in contemporary society; a stage in which learning objectives are clearly identified for programs in which criteria have been established and in which evaluation procedures are systematically integrated into the whole programming and planning process.

Before leaving the subject of professionalism, a word should be said about the necessity for cooperation between the professions. Nattress calls attention to two national organizations concerned with continuing education for professions: The Adult Education Association (AEA) of the United States, which formed a Section on Continuing Education for the Professions in 1966, and the National University Extension Association (NUEA) which formed a similar section in 1969. Generally, the AEA has focused attention on the problems of the learner and the NUEA on problems in relation to the administration of continuing education programs (Nattress, 1970). To date, the professions, including librarianship, have not used either of these national associations to any great extent as a means of interaction with other groups. Instead, all the professions seem to be moving "separately down the same path" at different rates of speed. Houle (1970) has pointed out the wastefulness of such an approach and urges interprofessional cooperation. He believes that such interprofessional efforts would lead to important and healthy consequences for our society.

III. FACTORS AFFECTING THE DESIGN OF CONTINUING EDUCATION SYSTEMS

A. Systems Approach to Continuing Education

> We will have to reorient our thinking so as to look upon education as a life-long process for continuing development of the individual. In planning the education

program, we will have to learn to consider the whole person—not merely one or two aspects of his existence. *In short, we will have to adopt a systems approach to education* (Greenwood, 1970).

This statement by Greenwood of the Brookings Institute is followed by a criticism of the education profession for not preparing individuals for a multidisciplinary approach to problem solving, for not preparing individuals to give appropriate consideration to all of the significant elements and relationships in a situation. He summarizes his position by stressing the importance of interrelatedness—of the elements and processes within a subsystem, of the interrelatedness of subsystems, and of the interrelatedness of systems with their environment—and the holistic viewpoint—the recognition that the whole is more than the sum of the parts.

This emphasis on an application of the systems approach to education has received considerable attention in the continuing education literature. One group of significant articles by leaders who advocate this approach can be found in the May 1965 issue of *Audiovisual Instruction*.

Another example is the Commission on Instructional Technology's Report to the President and the Congress of the United States. This document defines instructional technology as "a systematic way of designing, carrying out, and evaluating the total process of learning and teaching in terms of specific objectives, based on research in human learning and communication, and employing a combination of human and non-human resources to bring about more effective instruction" (U.S. Congress, House Commission, 1970).

Gagne (1965) sums up the concept of an educational system as an arrangement of people and conditions whose purpose is to bring about learning. He discusses five areas of decisions which affect the function of an educational system: learning objectives, the structure of knowledge to be learned, motivation, conditions for learning, and the transferability of knowledge and assessment.

B. Conditions for Adult Learning

The Commission on Instructional Technology reported that the first and most far-reaching reason why instructional technology had not been used more widely was the lack of a practical understanding about the process of human learning (U.S. Congress, House Commission,

1970). In *The Modern Practice of Adult Education: Andragogy versus Pedagogy,* Knowles (1970) presents the premise that the adult educator must be aware of certain basic factors about learning that are quite different from the learning patterns of the young. He specifies four of these assumptions:

> As a person matures, 1) his self-concept moves from one of being a dependent personality toward one of being a self-directing human being; 2) he accumulates a growing reservoir of experience that becomes an increasing resource for learning; 3) his readiness to learn becomes oriented increasingly to the developmental tasks of his social roles; and 4) his time perspective changes from one of postponed application of knowledge to immediacy of application, and accordingly his orientation toward learning shifts from one of subject-centeredness to one of problem-centeredness.

One of the most forceful statements on the importance of knowing how adults learn is found in a critique by Zachert (1972):

> Library science education has traditionally conceived of its students as children. Inherited curricula and teaching methods reflect this orientation, which has not yet been seriously challenged either at the level of basic professional education or at the level of continuing education. The most pregnant generalization from adult learning research is that adults learn differently than children, the inescapable conclusion is that education for adults must be planned and implemented differently than education for children. Acceptance of this generalization augurs for change.

Zachert sums up the findings of recent research about adult learning and explores its implications for continuing library education under three headings: physiological, psychological, and social. From her perceptive and selective analysis, she derives a profile of the adult learner; a profile of the role of the adult learner, the "configuration of the complementary learning situation"; and briefly touches on the role of the teacher.

Others involved in continuing education for librarians have tried to influence practice by emphasizing the characteristics of the adult learner. Hiatt (1971) identifies five characteristics of the adult learner and gives the principles concerning adult learning that have implications for designing continuing education programs. The American Library Association Staff Development Committee (1971) notes that the design of staff development programs must be based on the nature of the adult learner and specifies four factors to consider in relation to the adult as a learner.

C. Learning Needs—Basis for Programming

The assessment of needs is the first step in the continuing education process. Programs should develop opportunities targeted to the needs of a specific group of participants rather than offering isolated courses for whomever might be recruited to take them.

In a practical guide to training and continuing education developed by the Hospital Continuing Education Project under a grant from the Kellogg Foundation "learning needs" is defined as meaning "a lack of knowledge, skill, or attitude that prevents an employee from giving a satisfactory job performance, or that interferes with his potential for assuming greater responsibilities. In all cases, therefore, existence of a need means that present performance should be changed in some way. In all cases, also, change must come through new learning" (Hospital Continuing Education Project, 1970).

The chapter on needs assessment in *Continuing Continuing Education for the Public Service: A Design for Action for Education and Training for the Public Service* emphasizes that the needs of those to be served must be met if continuing education programs are to be successful, and points out that it should be recognized that: "participation in continuing education . . . is a highly personalized intentional endeavor. The satisfaction of this intention becomes a principal objective of the learning situation. Learning unrelated to experience and interaction, or not perceived to be so related . . . is likely to be the cause of profound disappointment, discouragement, frustration, and a negative outlook on future offerings (Institute for Local Self Government, 1971)."

Similarly in a survey of a cross section of different types of librarians, it was found that the sources of encouragement (motivating factors) that led the librarians to engage in continuing education activities (both formal and informal) were chiefly content factors related to the work process. That is to say, that they were continuing education activities that met their job-related needs (Stone, 1969).

Surveys tend to validate the theories of Maslow (1943) and McGregor (1960) that human beings are goal-seeking and need-meeting organisms and this insight should have top priority in planning continuing education programs. This leads to the conclusion that learning will be most effective when participants in continuing education programs have diagnosed their own needs and formulated their own goals for learning.

At a meeting of librarians in 1976, Knowles (1976) presented a model for assessing continuing education needs based on competencies required first to be a professional, and second to perform a specific job. The starting point for such a plan is a model of desired competencies in which Knowles advocates the use of a learning contract as the basic vehicle for organizing systematic programs of continuing competence development.

A selective recent bibliography of value to all those involved in needs assessment relative to continuing education is one prepared by Barbulesco and Means (1976) at the University of Illinois. It is divided into four sections: definitions; techniques/models; using needs assessment in educational program development; and assessing the needs of specific target populations—case studies.

D. Task Analysis—Basis for Competency Identification

There is a vast amount of evidence that "libraries have too long been regarded as passive conveyors of information or recreation, available when needed, but not playing, or expected to play, active roles in the educational process. Their vast capabilities have often been ignored" (Gould, 1974).

The inability of library service to supply answers to real life and survival questions in our society indicates areas in which there is need for continuing education. Some of these unmet service needs are detailed in the *Proceedings of a Conference on the Needs of Occupational, Ethnic, and Other Groups in the United States* sponsored by the National Commission on Libraries and Information Science in 1973 (NCLIS, 1973). Needs of special groups in the population that could be met by library and information services were also identified by the Institute of Continuing Education Program Planning for Library Staffs in the Southwest in 1975 (Foos, 1975).

The constructive efforts of libraries to build their own programs of services for individuals and groups and to collaborate with other agencies still seem to lag behind the need for such services. Further, as nontraditional study mounts, it will create problems but also enhance opportunities for libraries. Librarians will need to know how to counsel not only students but also the planners of programs. "If the problems encountered in these programs can be solved,—if the necessary funds are forthcoming, if staffs are prepared, information is disseminated, coordination is provided, and educators are made aware of potentials for service—then libraries will no longer be merely extensions of educational programs but active planners and collaborators in them" (Gould, 1974).

Challenges are also presented in the Lifetime Learning Act, which states, in part, that Congress recognizes the need for increasing opportunities for continued personal, vocational, and professional development, and that in order to assist a lifetime learning program there needs to be: conversion of facilities to serve adult participants in any such lifetime learning program; development of techniques for guidance and counseling of adult participants in any such program; and the development of curricula appropriate to the needs of any such program. It would seem possible for the library to play a key role in providing support for lifelong learning programs.

Another study has been recently released by the United States Office of Education entitled *Adult Functional Competency* (AFC) which calls for a reshaping of adult education so that students receive the kind of information that will make modern life easier for them—that will enable them to cope with the problems of today's society. The AFC study identified five general areas necessary for adult competence: occupational knowledge, consumer economics, government and law, health, and community resources. The study asserts that in order to correct the situation, vast efforts will be required in the training and the development of local staff. This would seem to present a clear opportunity for the library profession.

People are essential to the process of bridging the serious gaps between available knowledge and its everyday applications. Librarians are charged with the responsibility of connecting people to the knowledge and skills they need. There is an urgent need for the provision of continuing educational opportunities to prepare library staffs to provide help to citizens in their continuing education efforts and in their efforts to cope successfully with our complex society.

But in order to qualify to serve the public in specific areas it is necessary to identify the skills necessary to carry out these functions effectively. This would mean the development of skills in the following five competency areas: (1) advancing occupational knowledge, including competence in providing adults with information to help them in this decision making relative to pursuing education beyond high school—whether, when, and where; (2) advancing consumer economic competence; (3) advancing competence in the area of government and law; (4) advancing competence in the area of health care resources; (5) advancing competence in the area of community resources.

Within each of these categories there will be numerous specific skills or competencies which a librarian may need to acquire; but first, these competencies have to be identified. Once identified, they would provide an operational definition of what should occur in a developmental program for librarians seeking to help adults cope with the complexities of today's society.

Returning to the subject of the main heading of this section, "Task Analysis—Basis for Competency Identification," it may be noted that Gagne, in a now classic paper, argued that total performance can be analyzed into a set of component tasks that are relatively distinct from each other, and that proficiency in each component is what determines total performance. In summing up his thesis that task analysis has everything to do with training, he states: "If I were faced with the problem of improving training, I should not look for much help from the well-known learning principles... I should look instead at the technique of task analysis" (Gagne, 1962). Other strong proponents of the use of task analysis are Corson and Paul who emphasize the importance of finding out what work activities are engaged in by the employees who constitute the professions under study (Corson and Paul, 1966).

Historically, the library profession has not shown much interest in job analysis as a basis for building continuing education programs. One of the first job-analysis studies was begun in 1924 as an attempt was made to apply the findings of research to the development of library education programs (Charters, 1925). The objective of the study was to identify the tasks librarians perform in various operations, and from the data a series of library school texts were prepared; the best known probably is Margaret Mann's publication on cataloging which has gone through several printings.

In developing a survey of educational needs in librarianship at the post-master's level, Kortendick and Stone (1971) used the task-analysis or job-inventory approach to determine curriculum needs at the post-master's level. The basic focus of the research was curriculum development to equip middle- and upper-level personnel in libraries for a changing field. The job inventory was used to answer three important questions: In what kind of job activities are librarians engaged? How much time do they devote to these activities? How important are these activities at the level of the individual position? They concluded that the development of well-defined, job-relevant objectives based on the individual's needs for effective job performance is the aspect of curriculum development that should receive primary emphasis.

It has also been found that application of knowledge in the actual job situation is the primary motivation for engaging in formal course work at the post-master's level (Stone, 1969). This further supports the premise that curriculum development at the post-master's level should start with an accurate assessment of the librarian's job activities.

Another study in librarianship, The School Library Manpower Project, also used task analysis as an activity leading to the development of new definitions of school library media personnel and the identification of roles presently performed by a wide variety of individuals in school library media centers. This led to the publication of *School Library Personnel: Task Analysis Survey* (ALA, 1970b), and to recommendations for new avenues of entry and for curriculum content and structure (Case, 1973).

Under a grant from the U.S. Office of Education, the National Education Association undertook the Jobs in Instructional Media Study (JIMS). In order to look at media jobs, as they are performed, the JIMS examined two major aspects simultaneously—what the worker does and what gets done. The Domain of Instructional Technology (DIT) was used by JIMS as a way of looking at what gets done in the field. The technique of Functional Job Analysis was adopted to study what the worker does (Hyer, 1971).

The Association for Education Communications and Technology (AECT) took the JIMS data and the School Library Manpower Project data and attempted to define what competencies workers in the field of educational communications and technology should possess, and further, to classify these competencies and tasks by area of responsibility and level of difficulty (Prigge, 1974). On the basis of the resulting definition of the field, the AECT Task Forces developed guidelines for a competency-based certification program (Guidelines for the certification of personnel, 1974).

In summary, some exploratory work has been done to identify tasks as an aid to curriculum building for continuing education, but there is need for further task analyses to determine job dimensions. Not only would such information be valuable for curriculum and program building but it is also necessary for job restructuring and for self-assessment in continuing education programming.

Two recently completed studies in continuing library education, one funded by the National Commission on Libraries and Information Science (Stone *et al.*, 1974) and the other by the National Library of Medicine (Virgo, 1976) have pointed to the need for self-assessment testing for continuing education purposes. Both studies found that library personnel felt a strong need for continuing education, but were unable to articulate precisely what their continuing education needs were, and at what levels. In order to develop self-assessment tools there needs to be a precise understanding of what it is that one needs to know. Once this has been determined, self-assessment tests can be developed, individuals can ascertain their strengths and weaknesses, and a program of continuing education can be precisely defined.

Before leaving the subject of task analysis, it should also be pointed out that for groups such as the Medical Library Association, which has recently voted to adopt new standards for certification of health sciences librarians and library technicians, competency-based examinations are to be used. The first step in developing the examinations is identification of tasks performed by entry librarians and library technicians. Task analysis has been ruled, in recent U. S. Court decisions, as the only acceptable method for obtaining validity in occupational testing. The most recent draft of the Equal Opportunity Employment Guidelines (Uniform Guidelines on Employee Selection Procedures, 1974) states that to demonstrate content-, construct-, and criterion-related validity in testing there must be task analysis data available.

Finally, because of the increasing demands for accountability by the public relative to service by professional groups, it should be noted that an increasing number of states are passing legislation requiring certification of all types of professionals. A March 1977 survey of state library agencies revealed that, in addition to the certification standards for school/media librarians, 14 of the 29 states responding to the survey had certification requirements for public librarians; 3 for college/university librarians; 2 for junior/community college librarians; and 2 for special librarians. In 7 other states the issue of certification of librarians was being discussed and in 2 others it was beginning to surface (Stone, 1977). All of these certification efforts are based on some form of task analysis.

E. Determining Goals and Objectives

1. GOALS

The focus in continuing education should be on service to the nation's citizens. Goals, therefore, are: (1) improved library and information service to all residents of the country; and (2) maintenance of the lifelong competence of practitioners.

These goals can be achieved—insofar as the practitioner—client and practitioner—community relationship can contribute to them—by encouraging library personnel to use the latest knowledge and skills; by increasing the "information competence" of the American people; and by improving opportunities for continuing personal, vocational, and career development.

2. OBJECTIVES

Objectives for continuing education programs are derived from three sources of needs and interest: (1) the individual; (2) the sponsoring group, as perceived by its leaders; and (3) society as perceived by the profession.

The effectiveness, and the opportunity to measure the effectiveness, of any specific educational program is enhanced if, in the earliest stages of its planning, a statement of specific objectives is formulated in areas such as: (1) changes desired in the attitude and approach of the learner to the solution of problems; (2) correction of outdated knowledge; (3) explanation and interpretation of new knowledge in specific areas; (4) the introduction to and/or mastery of specific skills and techniques; and (5) change in the habits of the learner.

The objectives of a single short course or brief program will probably not include statements in all these categories. Statements of objectives should be measurable and action oriented and as specific as possible for a number of reasons: (1) to enable the full resources available to be employed for their achievement; (2) to provide the potential participant with some basis upon which to judge whether or not the opportunity meets his or her criteria for enrollment; and (3) to enable meaningful evaluation of the program (Did the program meet the stated objectives?). Without such specific objectives it is unlikely that any program will be fully effective and economical.

Learning needs, which relate to deficiencies in the learners, need to be distinguished from "learning objectives" which relate to what is to be learned. Learning objectives are statements of what the participant in the continuing education program should know, or should demonstrate that he or she is able to do, as a result of a learning experience.

The involvement of the participants in choosing the objectives on which they wish to focus will serve two purposes: (1) the participants will have a stronger commitment to the achievement of the objectives; and (2) the participants will have gained experience in the setting of realistic objectives.

In the literature on objectives, three terms are used which are important in the measurement of learning: performance, or behavior; terminal performance, or behavior; and criterion. "All learning results in some degree of behavioral change. We conclude that someone has learned an idea or a task when his behavior changes. 'Behavior' in this sense, is used to mean any relevant, observable activity displayed by the learner. It is fundamental that the results of learning be observable; otherwise progress toward objectives could not be determined" (Hospital Continuing Education Project, 1970).

In order to describe terminal performance, or behavior, (what the learner is to be able to do), Mager (1975) suggests: (1) identifying and naming the overall performance; (2) designing the important conditions under which the performance is expected to occur; and (3) determining the criterion (the quality or level of acceptable performance). Mager recommends that a separate statement be written for each objective as he believes that the more statements you have, the better chance you have of making clear your intent.

The term "criterion" is used to mean a standard or test by which terminal performance can be evaluated. "A criterion is a measuring stick that tells how well the learner is expected to do something after instruction has been completed. Establishing criteria with which to measure or appraise terminal behavior is fundamental to evaluation of results" (Hospital Continuing Education Project, 1970).

In summary, learning is concerned with observable behavior, particularly with the "terminal behavior" shown at the end of the learning experience, which is to be evaluated with reference to specific criteria that state how participants are expected to perform. That is to say, objectives should describe just what the instructor or evaluator should be able to observe in the participant's performance when the objective has been reached.

F. Evaluation

A review of the literature leads to the conclusion that one of the weakest features of continuing education programs is lack of evaluation. This is true not only of programs offered but also of newer methods of instruction used, including the use of television (Thiede, 1968). Guba and Stufflebeam (1970) proposed a definition that has been used widely: "Evaluation is the process of obtaining and providing useful information for making educational decisions." They also offer a valuable service in distinguishing four types of evaluation: context, input, process, and product (forming the acronym CIPP). *Context* evaluation services *planning decisions,* which determine objectives; *Input* evaluation services *structuring decisions,* which determine procedural designs for achieving objectives; *Process* evaluation services *implementing decisions,* which determine the execution of chosen designs; and *Product* evaluation services *recycling decisions,* which determine whether to continue, terminate, or modify a project.

Basically the CIPP Model answers four questions: What objectives should be accomplished? What procedures should be followed? Are the procedures working properly? Are the objectives being achieved?

Thomson (1972) provides a wealth of information related to application of the CIPP Model including "Guidelines for Statewide Library Planning and Evaluation" and "Ten Critique Letters" of statewide library plans. A particularly helpful application of the CIPP Model, largely in chart form, is found in the *Evaluation for Environmental Education* for New Jersey (New Jersey State Council, 1969).

During 1971–1972, the Evaluation Center of the Ohio State University College of Education engaged in a twelve-month program, sponsored by the Division of Library Programs in the Bureau of Libraries and Educational Technology in the U.S. Office of Education, "to train heads of state library administrative agencies and Library Services and Construction Act planners in each state in the concepts, methods, and procedures of evaluation and planning" (Thomson, 1972). Subsequently the Bureau of Libraries and Educational Technology (subsequently renamed the Office of Libraries and Learning Resources) has sponsored a number of institutes which have had as their purpose the training of librarians in the use of the CIPP Model for all kinds of library-related evaluations, including continuing library education programs.

For those who have not had the benefit of exposure to the conceptualizations of the CIPP Model, many of the same results can be achieved through the use of planning, programming, and budgeting models. A chief difference is the greater emphasis in the CIPP Model on continuous systematic evaluation.

A helpful source specifically designed for the evaluation of staff development and continuing education programs for library personnel is provided by Conroy (1972). Five guidelines are suggested for evaluation, each followed by a number of criteria and suggestions.

Thiede (1968) emphasizes an evaluative concept that is often overlooked when he states that each learning experience should make the participant more independent. "This demands that as a part of each learning experience, the adult be helped to diagnose his educational need, plan the learning experience, and evaluate his progress."

The reason the least sophisticated and often the least professional of evaluation forms, such as popularity "polls," are so often used is that we have not thought through our evaluation problems sufficiently. If efficient, effective, economical use of evaluation as an important tool for improving continuing education is to be achieved, it will be necessary to raise the profession's competence in this area.

Experiments directed toward better ways of accomplishing evaluation skills should be encouraged. It is hoped that sponsors as well as participants engaged in programs will become more interested in such evaluation efforts as pre- and postprogram tests, and will cooperate in the development of tools that will be of universal value.

In recognition of the importance of evaluation in program improvement, a considerable segment of the 1976–1977 CLENE (USOE-funded) Institute for State Library Agency Personnel Responsible for Continuing Education, was devoted to training and demonstration in the use of evaluation instruments for continuing education programs, including both internal and external evaluation techniques.

One of the products from the Institute was a self-evaluative checklist to be used in statewide planning (Institute for State Library Agency Personnel Responsible for Statewide Systems for Continuing Education, 1977); another was an annotated bibliography on evaluation concepts with relevancy to library situations (Stone, 1976).

Many program evaluation efforts include adaptation of evaluation rationales and instruments prepared for similar purposes. The book, *Evaluation of Adult Basic Education: How and Why?* contains many relevant examples (Grotelueschen et al., 1976). A summary approach to evaluation is presented in *Planning and Evaluating Library Training* (Sheldon, 1976). This paper will be helpful to those who do not know where to begin upgrading their competence in educational evaluation.

G. Recognition for Continuing Education

The practitioner's real reward for participation in continuing education should be an improved ability to meet the service needs of users and the stimulation of a personal spirit of intellectual adventure. However, this does not preclude the necessity of recognizing all participants in continuing education programs.

1. PURPOSE OF RECOGNITION FOR CONTINUING EDUCATION

The purposes of recognition systems for continuing education as developed by the various professions are to: (1) recognize, encourage, and support those who participate regularly in continuing education activities; (2) emphasize the importance of developing more meaningful opportunities for practitioners; (3) provide a visible means of accountability; (4) encourage the development of new nontraditional formats of continuing education; (5) make it possible for practitioners to gain recognition for their continuing education efforts even if it is not possible for them, because of restrictions of geography and time, to attend formal classes.

Recognition should be given to individuals who complete continuing education activities. A voluntary system, it is not intended to honor practitioners for outstanding accomplishment. Recognition for continuing education is built upon the assumption that all personnel—professional and supportive—should continue their education on a regular voluntary basis throughout their careers so that quality service will be available to library users.

2. THE NEED FOR A PROFESSIONWIDE SYSTEM OF MEASUREMENT AND RECOGNITION FOR PARTICIPANTS IN CONTINUING EDUCATION ACTIVITIES

Society has come to believe that lifelong learning is a right of the individual and an obligation of the professional practitioner. Concomitantly, the necessity for practicing librarians to continuously update and expand their professional knowledge and skills is unquestioned and essential. Librarianship, like other professions, has come to recognize the importance of a universal system of measurement and recognition for participation in nontraditional educational activities that do not lead to an academic degree.

In 1975 the Continuing Education for Library Staffs in the Southwest (CELS) issued a "Survey with Recommendations." One of the seven goals in this statement was: "To develop a reward system, consistent with the national plan, recognizing the responsibility of the employing institution." In the description of the proposed continuing model, Item #7 dealt with a reward system in these terms: "As indicated by this and other studies of continuing eduation, a reward system is an integral component in an effective continuing education program (Martin and Duggan, 1975). The survey spoke of the necessity of an appropriate reward system being devised and made operational. It was recommended that the role of certification be considered in any reward system that was developed.

As early as 1972, the Continuing Education Committee of the Association of American Library Schools, in a comprehensive position paper on continuing education, pointed out the need for the "development and use of some means of recognition and reward for those in continuing education programs" as a component for national planning for continuing library education (AALS, Committee, 1972).

Another evidence of need for a recognition system is the fact that the Education of Public Librarians Committee of the Strategy for Public Library Change group of the Public Library Association, ALA, has, for a number of years, been investigating recognition systems in other professions with a view to making recommendations on the basic components of such a system for public librarians.

Although there is a sparsity of literature on recognition systems in library and information science, there is a quantity of material available in other professions. A summary of examples of recognition plans in other professions, representing several different models, is presented in *Continuing Library Education as Viewed in Relation to Other Continuing Professional Education Movements* (Stone, 1974). One research study cited in that work is by Barrett (1970) who found that a reward structure in terms of recognition and professional reputation is an important determinant of self-development efforts. He concluded: "If organization members do not perceive a link between their development activities and the organization's reward system, the probability of active efforts to update knowledge and skills is lessened." Two studies in librarianship (Kortendick and Stone, 1971; Stone, 1977) have concluded that consideration of factors which tend to motivate individual practitioners to participate in continuing education is a prime determinant in the individual's decision to participate. The need for an increase in participation seems to be widely accepted. For example, in the 1971 report, *Job Dimensions and Education Needs in Librarianship,* it was found that a majority (57 percent) of the participants had not participated in any form of course work (including workshops and short-term courses) since receiving their graduate degree in library science (Kortendick and Stone, 1971).

On the basis of data collected for the Continuing Library and Information Science Study sponsored by the National Commission, it was recommended that a task force be appointed by the Continuing Library Education Network and Exchange (CLENE) to study in as comprehensive a manner as possible the issue of adopting a system for the measurement or recognition of noncredit participation in continuing education activities (Stone *et al.,* 1974). The report emphasized the practitioners' view that any system should provide for recognition of participation in nontraditional types of programs, such as home study programs and traveling workshops or laboratories. Taking into account the emphasis throughout the nation today on accountability and continued competence, the report stressed the importance of including all levels of library and information science personnel in any recognition system that might be designed. A recognition system would seem to be particularly useful for operating librarians (without a master's degree in Library Science) and for paraprofessionals, since it would provide a way in which their concern for lifelong learning could be documented. For example, paraprofessionals, who are unable to qualify for admission to college and university programs, may be active in association-sponsored continuing education programs, but these generally are not recorded. Thus, they have no evidence to show an employer that they have had learning experiences that might qualify them to undertake new tasks or increased responsibilities (Stone *et al.*, 1974).

3. ADVANTAGES OF A COMPATIBLE SYSTEM

The lack of a compatible recognition system could create difficulties for both the individual practitioner and the profession. A compatible system would have the following advantages:

1. Facilitate the recognition of participation in continuing education between all parts of the country and between different types of libraries.
2. Provide employees with a commonly understood record of continuing education activities.
3. Facilitate the review of the records of individuals whose continuing education activities take place in more than one state and in more than one institution or association.
4. Facilitate the recognition of employees who are trying to avoid obsolescence.
5. Provide a basis for the collection of data about continuing education as an individual process of lifelong learning.
6. Assist in meeting identified needs in continuing education of library personnel.

IV. RESPONSIBILITY FOR CONTINUING EDUCATION OF LIBRARIANS

A. Introduction

A survey of professional literature indicates that in all professions and disciplines the obligation for continuing education and for continuing competence is a responsibility that should be shared by several groups. Generally, the continuing education literature assumes that the individual carries the basic responsibility for lifelong learning and continuing education. The employer has the responsibility of both providing opportunities for continuing education and ensuring a job structure that encourages the employees to keep up-to-date. Professional societies and universities are expected to help individuals by providing educational opportunities and subject matter choices from which individuals can best select those opportunities that meet their needs. Employers and professional societies, more than universities, share some responsibility for making individuals aware of their needs and helping them plan to meet them. Ideally, responsibility for assessing quality service should be a community responsibility with abundant interaction between the employer, the university, the professional association, the state library agency, the federal government, the public that is served, and other professional groups.

In library literature there are many studies calling for a recognition of this division of roles (AALS, Committee, 1972; Martin and Duggan, 1975; Stone, 1970, 1974; Warncke, 1973). While endorsement of such a division of responsibility is widespread, it does not necessarily reflect how the various roles are actually being carried out. One has to remember that groups and individuals rightfully need to self-select the responsibilities they wish to shoulder. Each group has its own special relationship to the individuals seeking to learn, its own style of leadership, its own specialized capabilities, its own motivations for continuing education, its own point of view relative to the significance of continuing education. The responsibilities of concerned groups and individuals and the roles they have played in continuing education are described in the following sections.

B. Role of the Individual Practitioner

In introducing the partnership of responsibility for continuing education, certain assumptions are made about the individuals and their roles. Those who read this survey will need to ask themselves if they share certain fundamental assumptions.

In general, continuing education is viewed as a prime means of assisting the practitioner in career development and of ensuring quality library service. The learner has the ability and the right to be a self-directing person whose basic purpose is to become more competent by acquiring the necessary knowledge, skills, and attitudes to deal with a relatively immediate problem, task, or decision, and to plan for change in resources and services to meet society's needs.

Evidence leads to the conclusion that when adults learn something naturally (as contrasted with being taught) they are highly self-directing. It also appears that what adults learn on their own initiative, they learn more thoroughly and permanently than what they learn by being taught.

The individual must supply the energy and the initiative necessary to motivate learning. Without internal drive, individuals are unlikely to benefit from educational experience. The individual must also be sensitive enough to recognize his or her needs for learning, motivated enough to seek opportunities, farsighted enough to plan for future developments. The individual is in the best position to determine what he or she needs to know and whether this need is a matter of updating or extending competence into areas considered necessary for job performance or career development.

This leads to another assumption—the assumption that continuing education within a profession is concerned with the development of competencies for performing roles. A definition for a professional, according to Knowles, is a "performer of a role." Thus continuing education should be concerned with the development of competencies to perform roles (Knowles, 1976).

In January 1976, Knowles pointed out at the CLENE Assembly that those kinds of learning that have as their purpose improving one's competence to perform in a job or in a profession must take into account the needs and expectations of organizations, professions, and society. Learning contracts, he emphasized, provide a means for negotiating a reconciliation between these external needs and expectations and the learner's internal needs and interests. Learning contracts also provide a vehicle for making the planning of learning experiences a mutal undertaking between a learner and the educator. By participating in the process of diagnosing needs, and formulating expected accomplishments, the learner develops a sense of ownership of (and commitment to) the plan. Knowles suggests eight basic steps for practitioners to use in developing their learning contracts: diagnose learning needs; specify learning objectives; specify learning resources and strategies; specify evidence of accomplishment; specify how the evidence will be validated; review contract with consultants; carry out the contract; and evaluate the learning (Knowles, 1976).

Understanding the use and techniques of competency-based learning contracts is a skill that is important for library personnel, not only in diagnosing their own needs but also in assisting the independent learner in libraries. In order to perform this role effectively, library personnel need to understand the adult learner, the process of personal decision making, interview techniques, needs assessment procedures, and identification of the special resources available and appropriate for the adult learner.

The 1974 NCLIS survey of continuing education suggested some additional responsibilities for individual library and information science practitioners:

1. Assisting, encouraging, and advancing continuing education for those supervised.
2. Committing personal time and money to continuing education; planning to share some costs with employers.
3. Commiting time and energy to serve on continuing education committees and task force groups.
4. Accepting a new image of education—lifelong education in which the learning process is continuous and unbroken (Stone et al., 1974).

C. Role of the Professional Association

The 1960s saw a tremendous increase in the number and types of continuing education activities sponsored by professional associations. The realization has come to profession after profession that preservice education, an occasional trip to an annual meeting or a regional conference, and scanning the journals in the field will not enable professionals to perform their distinctive services and maintain their roles efficiently throughout a lifetime (Houle, 1967). Throughout the professions the trend has been to plan, to coordinate, and to implement organized forms of continuing education.

1. TYPES OF ACTIVITIES

The most common types of activities carried out by professional associations are those associated with the dissemination of information and the planning, coordinating, and implementing of specific continuing education activities aimed at updating and broadening the librarians' skills and knowledge.

Possible responsibilities for the library association, as identified in the NCLIS study of library continuing education, are:

1. Determining major continuing education needs within the profession, currently and in the future.
2. Organizing and implementing continuing education programs to produce new skills and to disseminate new information.
3. Encouraging members to participate in continuing education by disseminating information about continuing education to members.
4. Identifying continuing education experts among the membership and encouraging their use.
5. Commiting conference time and resources to continuing education.
6. Establishing a continuing education committee within the association structure and appointing Linking-Agents and if finances permit, assigning at least one full-time staff person to be in charge of continuing education.
7. Developing a closer relationship with employing libraries with regard to continuing education efforts.
8. Considering ways of increasing the distribution of preprints and reprints of articles and papers published in the association journals and increasing the quality of association journals.
9. Assisting in setting standards and guidelines for continuing education programs (Stone et al., 1974).

Suggestions to local, state, and regional associations, and to national professional associations are also offered in "Guidelines to the Development of Human Resources in Libraries" in the July 1971 issue of *Library Trends* (ALA, Staff Development Committee, 1971).

Practitioners have also offered suggestions on the role of the library associations. One survey (Stone, 1977) found that librarians believed that library associations needed, first and foremost, to upgrade the content of their activities.

Next to content, the practicing librarians were desirous of deeper involvement in the affairs of the association; this was especially lacking, they felt, in regard to new members of the association. The third most frequent recommendation urged professional associations to take continuing education opportunities to where the librarians are geographically located. They recommended that programs of worthwhile content travel.

In the professional associations, these concerns are reflected in the experimentation now going on. Examples of some of the new ways in which five professional associations—architecture, banking, education, engineering, ministry—were developing new approaches at a national level were presented at a mini-workshop sponsored by the Continuing Library Education Committee of the Association of American Library Schools in January 1973 (AALS, 1973).

In an attempt to assess library association progress the Continuing Library Education Committee of the Association of American Library Schools (AALS) mailed, in August 1972, questionnaires to twenty-six library associations. This total included the thirteen divisions of the American Library Association. A full statistical tabulation of the results can be found in Appendix C of *Continuing Library Education as Viewed in Relation to Other Continuing Education Movements* (Stone, 1974).

By December, in spite of follow-up letters, only six associations had returned the completed questionnaire. In reviewing the data it should be realized that the response of six out of twenty-six represents only a 23 percent return by the library associations. Nevertheless, it gives an indication of the state-of-the-art of library associations relative to continuing education in 1972.

The six associations which responded were: the American Association of Law Libraries, Reference and Adult Services Division of ALA, Resources and Technical Services Division of ALA, the Association of Jewish Libraries, the Medical Library Association, and the Special Libraries Association.

From the results received it was apparent that the most frequent type of activity has been the workshop, the seminar, and the pre- or postconference institute. There was little activity reported showing library associations cooperating with other library associations or other professional groups, employing libraries, or with library schools.

There was also no report from the six associations of the development of packaged printed programs, and only one group reported the development of cassettes for distribution. In the publication field, activities were carried on by all the groups. There was a lack, however, of books published specifically for continuing education programs, or of programmed texts. There was no mention of circulation of preprints. There was no reported use of talk-back TV or of the development of tutorial centers; only one association reported any programming in Cable TV. One group reported the use of clinics.

The only association which reported any research projects was the Medical Library Association, which reported two projects, one on the continuing education needs of medical librarians, and the other, closely related, on the continuing education needs for medical librarianship. No group reported that it had held an annual conference with its chief focus on continuing education.

Three of the associations responded that continuing education was a "high priority" in relation to other objectives of the association. A fourth stated that it was "important." Another responded that the objectives of the association were not ranked, and another that it was a matter of budget.

The six reporting associations indicated that the Education Committee and/or the Board of Directors, on the basis of input from committees or individuals, decide on the continuing education programs that will be developed and implemented. In answer to the question on how needs are determined, two of the associations said that questionnaires and surveys were used. One stated that need was determined through analysis of journal articles, letters to the editor of the association's publication, and information from conversations. The others seemed to rely on decisions by the Board of Directors and/or the Committee on Continuing Education.

The associations provide continuing education programming for all members of the association. Generally membership seemed to be open to all practitioners who wished to join. In answer to a question concerning structuring, it appears that the major focus is on pre- or postsessions at the annual meeting of the association. Content varied according to needs of the various divisions of the association. It also appears that programs are presented at state and regional levels as well as nationally, but not on a systematic basis. Such programs seem to be left to the initiative of the local group with a variety of local patterns emerging. For example, one association might combine with others in an area for an all-day workshop, or various interest groups might join to present a program.

Two stable structuring patterns were reported. The Medical Library Association reported that twenty courses are available. These may be sponsored by any regional medical library, regional medical program, regional medical group, or any other interested group on a local, state, or regional basis. The American Association of Law Librarians reported four rotating Continuing Education Institutes, offering four special subject area curricula, held at preconventions since 1964. These are planned to meet the needs of law librarians who are employed at both advanced and intermediate levels of professional responsibility.

Two associations reported that continuing education programs were funded totally by registration fees. Three others reported funding by a varying combination of registration fees, dues, and grants.

The chief method of distribution of materials seems to be through materials given out at the time of pre- or postconference sessions, through the publications of associations, or through published proceedings of institutes.

In answer to the question as to how leaders are identified or chosen to develop programs, the most frequent pattern seemed to be by the Continuing Education Committee and/or by the Board of Directors.

The two chief means of evaluation reported were reaction evaluation sheets members attending the programs, and review and evaluation by the planning committee or executive committee responsible for implementation of the programs. Only one of the associations reported that specific evaluative criteria had been established by the association.

In the area of recognition, two associations stated that certificates were given for participation in programs. Another stated that a certificate of attendance was going to be offered from now on.

Three of the associations reported that one specific person or group had responsibility in the area of continuing education. In each case this was the Chairman of a committee with responsibility for continuing education. This individual generally seemed to have the same responsibilities in all three associations, namely: directing and coordinating continuing education activities; surveying and evaluating programs developed; advising and providing guidelines and standards for programs throughout the association. Only the Medical Library Association reported a full-time director with a subsidiary staff. The other positions were held by volunteers. The associations reported that background, training, and experience were qualifications for the position, but none reported any specific training or orientation being given to those responsible for continuing education activities.

In regard to clearinghouse functions, the chief one (reported by three associations) was for bibliographies. One association stated that it was a clearinghouse for cassettes.

Three associations reported that they established experimental programs intended to discover new methods and solutions to persistent problems in the field. Four indicated that their associations search for new and effective educational techniques and modes in order to maximize the content presented in continuing education programs.

A major step forward for continuing education took place in 1970 when Asheim included a strong statement on continuing education in the American Library Association's policy statement, "Manpower: A Statement of Policy Adopted by the Council of the American Library Association, June 1970" (ALA, 1970a). The last three of 33 policy statements in the document refer to continuing education:

31. Continuing education is essential for all library personnel, professional and supportive, whether they remain within a position category or are preparing to move into a higher one. Continuing education opportunities include both formal and informal learning situations, and need not be limited to library subjects or the offerings of library schools.
32. The "continuing education" which leads to eligibility for Senior Librarian or Specialist positions may take any forms suggested directly above so long as the additional education and experience are relevant to the responsibilities of the assignment.
33. Library administrators must accept responsibility for providing support and opportunities (in the form of leaves, sabbaticals, and released time) for the continuing education of their staffs.

This statement represents a major breakthrough for the cause of continuing education in the profession for it provides a standard toward which the profession can strive.

In 1970, a strong position statement on continuing education was made by the American Libraries Association, Activities Committee on New Directions for ALA (1970). This document stated forcefully the Subcommittee on Manpower's position that "commitment to the continuing education of the profession must be made by the individual librarian, by the managers of libraries, and by the professional association—especially the A.L.A." Credit was given to the Association for "its extensive conference programming, publishing activity, and task-oriented committees"—all of which "combine to make the Association by far the most active agency for library personnel development in the world," but it pointed out that ALA could do much more than in the past to support continuing education. "Accusations of Association non-interest are justified only in the sense that it has not in the past seen fit to bring together all of its activities concerned with continuing education under a single administrative oversight, so as to give them uniform organization, coordination, and direction." The Subcommittee stated that such a move seemed now to be called for and cited the following ways in which the ALA could do more than it had done for the continuing education and professional growth of its members:

1. Sponsor a wide range of seminars and workshops, perhaps mounted regionally but outside of the annual conference, on issues of current or topical concern to librarians; the recent MARC II workshops and occasional joint programs with the regional associations might serve as prototypes.
2. Prepare packaged multimedia programs for professional updating that can be lent or rented to local libraries and to library agencies for use by their personnel.
3. Design and produce programmed instructional courses for sale to librarians who wish to improve the currency of their expertise or gain new professional skills or understanding; both these recommendations would seem to be natural extensions of ALA's existing publishing program.
4. Gain much wider promulgation than there has been in the past of the work done by ALA's clearinghouse for opportunities outside of ALA for the continuing education and professional growth of librarians.
5. Lend consultative and advisory, perhaps even support, services to local libraries and library agencies wishing to develop continuing education programs of their own.
6. Coordinate, articulate, and rationalize all ALA activities concerned with the professional upgrading of librarians.

Although covered by what has already been said, one particular aspect of postprofessional training is so needful of attention that in the eyes of the Committee it deserved special mention in this report. That is the need for management training for librarians who find themselves assigned to positions of administrative responsibility. It is patently false to assume that a good librarian will necessarily be a good manager, yet hierarchical promotion in many libraries appears to rest heavily upon this assumption. It appears essential that special effort be expended by the ALA to help facilitate the transition of good librarians into good managers when their duties and responsibilities call for it.

Particular notice should be given to the workshops sponsored by the Information Science and Automation Division (ISAD) of ALA, mentioned under the first item in the preceding list. Starting with the one-day meetings on automation and systems analysis at the 1969 conference of ALA in Atlantic City, the Division has maintained a consistent record, particularly with its MARC II workshops, in taking continuing education opportunities to librarians in many sections of the United States. The third series of ISAD institutes was held in 1977 and focused on "The National Bibliographic Network." The 1969 format used by ISAD at Atlantic City served as the model on which the Staff Development Committee built its programming, which is described in the next section.

The statement of the Activities Committee on New Directions for ALA regarding the critical need for management training for librarians has been emphasized by many others in analyzing needs of the profession (Booz, Allen and Hamilton, Inc., 1973; Ginsburg and Brown, 1967; Harlow, 1969; Kortendick and Stone, 1971; Stone, 1969).

A significant contribution toward improving this situation is being made through the recent establishment of the Management Studies Office of the Association of Research Libraries. Although designed to serve the members of that Association, its publications should have an important influence on continuing education efforts in the area of administration and management for all librarians. In addition to its publication program, the office conducts an ongoing research and development program which prepares special studies related to basic issues and problems of university library management, such as papers on library policies (Webster, 1972a,b), and the Management Review and Analysis Program (MRAP) has been of major significance in improving library effectiveness relative to organization and decision-making processes (Association of Research Libraries, 1972). For member libraries the Office will also conduct library management conference programs, and provide library management consultation.

The efforts of two other groups have had significant and long-range results. One is the Staff Development Committee of the Personnel

Section of the Library Administration Division (LAD) of ALA. The other is the Association of American Library School's Committee on Continuing Education which sent out the questionnaire referred to previously.

At the January 1970 meeting of the Staff Development Committee of the Personnel Section of LAD, two major avenues of approach in the area of continuing education were identified by the Committee members. One was the use of an all-day mini-workshop concept on the opening day of the ALA annual conference, and the other was the publication of a *Library Trends* issue on Personnel Development and Continuing Education (Stone, 1971b).

The first concept was built on three assumptions:

1. That the American Library Association has a role in personnel development and, as our leading professional body, it should emphatically foster continuing education of its membership.
2. That continuing personnel development is an important commitment librarianship must face today.
3. That in librarianship we are a long way from realizing the potential represented by the human resources now employed in libraries (Stone, 1970).

The first micro-workshop was held at the 1970 ADA Conference in Detroit. Papers relating to staff development and continuing education were presented under the umbrella title: "New Directions in Staff Development: Moving from Ideas to Action" (Stone, 1971a).

During the workshop, more than 200 participants filled out evaluation sheets which provided important feedback for planning future workshops, Analysis of the questionnaires submitted by the participants showed that there was a distinct preference for having a day's micro-workshop concentrate on one area of staff development rather than cover several areas in survey fashion. In rank order, the four specific areas that were rated highest by the conferees for future continuing education workshops were: (1) employee motivation; (2) participatory management; (3) training techniques and educational methods for staff development programs; and (4) management by objectives as an approach to staff development.

Based on these data, the second Staff Development Workshop was held at the 1971 ALA Conference in Dallas on "Motivation," and a third workshop was held in 1972 at the conference in Chicago on "Educational Technology as an Aid to Staff Development." The reason why the second choice—"Participatory Management"—was not scheduled for 1971 or 1972 was that there was a strong emphasis on this subject during the 1970 workshop.

It should be noted that the first workshop in Detroit was entirely conceived, planned, and implemented through the initiative of the Staff Development Committee with minimal support from LAD. The ALA Conference Office cooperated by assigning a place on the printed schedule for the workshop and by providing the needed audiovisual equipment. The Committee members themselves, through their own resources, produced the packaged handouts distributed at the workshop (programs, motivation bibliography, write-ups on the volunteer program leaders, evaluation sheets, film information, etc.); sent the mailings to registrants and prepared a preworkshop paper designed to set the stage for the emphasis on participatory management. In other words the Committee had the objective of demonstrating that such a program featuring staff development and continuing education was a felt need of the ALA membership and that it would be supported by attendees. The Detroit Workshop was a notable success, and since that time the Library Administration Division has budgeted funds for the support of the Staff Development opening day mini-workshops.

The second main activity of the Staff Development Committee was the publication of the July 1971 *Library Trends* issue entitled "Personnel Development and Continuing Education in Libraries" (Stone, 1971b). The Committee prepared two of the contributions for the issue—the guidelines and the model noted above—and selected the qualified leaders who contributed the other articles to the issue.

A landmark study in the area of public librarianship was conducted by Allie Beth Martin and published in 1972, *A Strategy for Public Library Change*. This document cites continuing education as one of the highest priorities for action:

> There is an urgent need for concentration on training and retraining of the practitioners—those presently performing and those who will follow—to enable them to know how to establish goals for individual libraries, how to develop libraries which will continually change with society and perform efficiently in the community.

As a result of this study, a task force on continuing education was activiated within the Public Library Association (PLA). Its emphasis on continuing education for personnel of public libraries stems from the goals study's identification of the barriers to future public library development. Martin's goals study found that: "There was a general expression from the respondents that library education is failing to respond to the educational needs of public libraries either in the formal academic program leading to a degree or in meeting educational needs" (Martin, 1972).

In this study, Mrs. Martin eloquently presented the view that opportunities have never been more promising for libraries—that they are on the threshold of renascence. She believed that continuing education was a major force for implementation of a renascence. Continuing education for whom? She stated it this way: "Broadest possible inclusion should be the goal. . . . Continuing education should be available to all at whatever level of employment. Formal recognition in the form of certificates or other awards would be desirable" (Martin, 1972).

In the fall of 1968, President-Elect Kortendick of the American Association of Library Schools wrote a proposal, later funded by the Council on Library Resources, to hold a conference in Bethesda, Maryland, for the purpose of identifying needed research in library and information science. Other conveners of the conference, in addition to Father Kortendick who served as chairman, were Kurt Cylke, the acting Chief of the Library and Information Sciences Research Branch of the U.S. Office of Education, and Foster Mohrhardt of the Council on Library Resources. As a result of the conference, Harold Borko was engaged as principal investigator to carry out the objectives set by the conferees. The objectives were:

1. To describe and summarize the content of existing programs being offered in librarianship and information science.
2. To identify problems and needs in library and information science education, and to indicate the data and the research that would be required to resolve these problems.
3. To coordinate the various research suggestions and to list them in order of priority.

One of the areas covered in the Borko report was "Research Needs in the Field of Continuing Education for Librarians," by Kortendick. The specific research proposals suggested in the area of continuing library education were:

1. Feasibility Study of a National Program of Continuing Education for Librarians.
2. A National Survey of Continuing Education Needs of Librarians: A Study of Educational Needs, Job Dimensions, and Professional and Personal Characteristics.
3. Motivational Factors Related to Participation in Continuing Education Activities.
4. Development of a Model for Continuing Education and Staff Development in Libraries.
5. Development of a Comprehensive Model for Managing and Evaluating Short-Term Institutes and Workshops for the Continuing Education of Librarians.
6. Communication and Research Information Exchange in Library Science.
7. The Development of Model Packaged Programs of Study in Selected Defined Areas Pertinent to the Needs of In-Service Librarians for Updating and Expanding Their Knowledge of Advances in the Field.
8. Evaluation of the Potential Capabilities of Various Media for Use in the Continuing Education of Librarians: A Feasibility Study
9. Toward Closer Reciprocal Relationships between Library Science Professors and Practicing Library Administrators: An Exploratory Study.
10. Postgraduate Internships and Trainee Programs in Librarianship: An Evaluation of Existing Programs and a Proposal for Development of the Internship Concept in Continuing Education for Librarians.
11. A Study of Attitudes and Responses to Participation of Mid-Career Librarians in Community Affairs as Stimulators and Effectors in Continuing Professional Growth (Kortendick, 1973).

In 1970, President Monroe of AALS appointed an ad hoc committee to write a position paper on the "Role of A.A.L.S. in Continuing Library Education" (AALS, *Standing Committee* 1972). The following year, at the 1971 Meeting, the position paper was presented to the membership and was used as a point of departure for program meetings which concentrated on continuing education. During this conference, the Executive Board of AALS voted to establish a Standing Committee on Continuing Education. This committee, as appointed by President Thomas Slavens, consisted of the members who had served on the ad hoc committee plus others who had indicated a particular interest in this area of activity of the Association. The activities of this Standing Committee on Continuing Library Education are outlined in a report published in the Fall 1972 issue of the *Journal of Education for Librarianship* (AALS, Standing Committee, 1972).

One of the charges of the Committee was to build a continuing education network made up of representatives from the library schools and library associations. The network was subsequently enlarged to include representatives from library schools not yet accredited by ALA and representatives of state library agencies.

A second activity engaged in by the Committee was the planning and presenting of a mini-workshop on continuing education as practiced at a national level by a representative group of professional associations. This workshop, referred to a number of times in this chapter, was held during the 1973 Annual Meeting of the Association. Following the workshop, the Board of Directors of AALS responded to the activity of the Continuing Library Education Committee during 1972 by budgeting $2,000 for its activities during 1973.

A third activity of the Committee was to write (and to urge 26 other library associations to write) to the members of the National Commission on Libraries and Information Science, encouraging them to select continuing library education as one of their top priorities for attention and action. This action was successful in that the Commission issued a call for a proposal for a continuing library education study. This study was funded and led to the 1974 NCLIS survey, which contributed to the initiation of the Continuing Library Education Network and Exchange (CLENE). For a discussion of CLENE and its activities see Section V.

The Medical Library Association (MLA) began its continuing education efforts in 1957 with the holding of national seminars and has experimented with a number of formats since that time. The first

Committee on Continuing Education was appointed in 1962. Recently, the activity of the Association has been greatly intensified with the appointment of a full-time Director of Medical Library Education. A full-scale national program has been launched which includes needs assessment, sponsoring approved training courses in connection with national and regional meetings, seeking funding for the preparation of individualized instructional packages, and the regular publication in the *Medical Library Association News* of "Continuing Education Opportunities Available." Regional medical library groups have also been active in this area as is evidenced by the recently completed study by James Nelson (1977) "Conditions for Development: Continuing Education at Six Accredited Library Schools," which was undertaken for the Kentucky-Ohio-Michigan Regional Medical Library Program.

The MLA has taken the lead in advocating the advantages of certification for librarians and in developing a certification system for medical libraries. For each profession the National Commission on Accrediting designates just one body to accredit programs; in librarianship this designated body is the ALA, which is authorized to accredit library school programs at the first professional degree level only. Certification, however, may be granted by agencies or associations to individuals, and at more than one level. The MLA adopted a certification program for medical libraries in 1948 and revised the code in 1964. As a result of increasing dissatisfaction with the existing code, the MLA, after a number of years of work, developed a new code which was adopted by the membership in September 1974. Since that time the Association has been moving toward implementation of this code.

Starting on January 1, 1976, the MLA awarded Continuing Education Unit (CEU) credits for participation in its courses and management institutes. The actual number of CEU credits to be awarded is determined individually for each of MLA's continuing education courses and institutes. Credit is given for participation at MLA courses presented in conjunction with regional group meetings, at the Annual Meeting in June, and all other presentations sponsored by MLA. The CEU records are kept at the MLA Headquarters in Chicago (MLA, 1976).

One CEU is defined as "ten contact hours of participation in an organized continuing education experience under responsible sponsorship, capable direction and qualified instruction" (National Task Force on the Continuing Education Unit). CEUs are nationally recognized and are awarded by a growing number of universities, associations, and other organizations. Other library groups offering the CEU in 1976 were the Special Libraries Association at its June Annual Meeting for the preconference continuing education programs and the New York Library Association, which claims to be the first state library association to offer the CEU.

The American Society of Information Science (ASIS) has a Special Interest Group on Education (SIG/ED) which has provided leadership in the area of continuing education for that association through the conducting of surveys, the development of preconference workshops, a newsletter, and the sponsoring of publications focused on continuing education. For example, the survey by SIG/ED Chairman Swanson in 1975 investigated the continuing education needs of ASIS members. One of the findings indicated membership preferences for tutorials, institutes, and workshops. Ranked in order from greatest need, the four most frequently mentioned topics were: Management (170 mentions); Technologies, including computers (139); Information Systems (122); Information Retrieval (60) (Swanson and Johns, 1976).

In 1973, G. J. Sophar, Chairman of the ASIS Commission on Long Range Planning identified Education for Continuing Education as one of seven tasks with which the Society should be concerned in these terms: "To examine the existing educational activities available to information scientists, practitioners in information science, users, and decision-makers; to determine the needs of this same group; and to compare the degree to which existing activities meet these needs (of particular concern will be the continuing education of users and decision-makers who formerly were not aware of their need for information and were not qualified in determining the use or value of information processing techniques and/or media" (Sophar, 1974).

Since 1953, the American Association of Law Libraries, in cooperation with a law school near the particular convention city, has held preconvention institutes on various aspects of librarianship. Since 1964, the Association has rotated courses, each on four basic areas of law librarianship. Each of the institutes is divided into two sections, basic (for less experienced law librarians) and advanced (for the more experienced) (Wildman, 1972).

The Special Libraries Association (SLA), during its 1968 annual meeting, held a general planning session on continuing education sponsored by the Education Committee (Sloane, 1968). Each year since that time the Education Committee has sponsored a full day of continuing education seminars on the first day of its annual conference. In his inaugural address at the 1972 Annual Meeting in Boston, the President of SLA, Edward C. Strable, stated that he considered continuing education to be the most outstanding and encouraging trend in librarianship today. At its 1976 annual conference, SLA gave Continuing Education Units to those who participated in the preconference continuing education sessions. The SLA also sponsored a study of continuing education needs among its members (Allen, 1974).

Another organization concerned with continuing education is the Council on Library Technical Assistants (COLT), which was organized in 1967 by those concerned with the technical training programs for library supportive staff. Originally called the Council on Library Technology, the organization assumed its present name in 1973 following the adoption of three documents by the American Library Association which gave full, official acceptance to the classification and the training of personnel at the technical assistant level. These documents were: (1) the 1968 report of the Interdivisional Ad Hoc Committee which proposed some basic definitions of the subprofessional or "technician class of library employees"; (2) the "Criteria for Programs to Prepare Library Technical Assistants" as recommended by the Interdivisional Committee on Training Programs for Supportive Library Staff in 1969; (3) the statement on Library Education and Manpower adopted in 1970.

These actions plus the formal affiliation of COLT with ALA which was publicly announced in 1974 "presaged a new period of cooperation rather than rivalry between the two organizations" (Asheim, 1975).

The 1976 edition of the *COLT Directory* lists 130 schools offering training for library technical assistants. During 1974/1975 more than 7,000 students were enrolled in LTA programs (Taylor, 1976). In addition to these formal academic programs, COLT organizes workshops and meetings to serve the continuing education needs of Library Technical Assistants and has sponsored a number of programs on the Continuing Library Education Network and Exchange (CLENE).

Supplementing the work of the national associations, regional and state library associations carry on continuing education programs. Two of the most active regional associations have been the Continuing Education for Library Staffs in the Southwest (CELS) and the Continuing Education Program for Library Personnel of the Western Interstate Commission for Higher Education (WICHE).

CELS grew out of strongly expressed needs of the libraries in the six-state Southwestern Library Association (SWLA). The ALA Goals Award Survey of the Southwestern Library Association conducted by Stevenson (1971) states: "One of the programs most frequently listed as needed was continuing education, at all levels, in all forms, and covering all subject matter. There were many requests for educational opportunities at the regional level and within the states."

In September 1970, library leaders from the Southwest identified continuing education as the highest priority in the list of eleven regionwide needs. As a result of that meeting, a proposal was written requesting $25,000 from the Council of Library Resources, and funds were granted to establish a Southwestern Library Interstate Cooperative Endeavor (SLICE): CELS is a major project of SLICE. Subsequently, the six-state library agencies in SWLA each contributed $2,000 to SLICE.

A major accomplishment of CELS was the survey of continuing education of library staffs in the Southwest by Martin and Duggan which gave recommendations for carrying out continuing education activities based on the needs discovered from the survey. It includes information on the institutions and agencies that were providing continuing education opportunities when the survey was done in 1972–1973. The survey was published in 1975 by the University of Texas at Austin Graduate School of Library Science (Martin and Duggan, 1975). In 1977, an evaluation of the CELS Project, 1974–1977, which is a progress report with recommendations for the future, was carried out by Sheldon (1977).

A special ongoing project of CELS is the Audio Cassette Awareness Program. The tapes survey briefly articles of interest in a wide variety of library periodicals. Reviews focus on new trends in all areas of librarianship, issues of concern to the profession, and innovative programs (O'Donnell, 1975).

Under the umbrella of the Western Interstate Commission for Higher Education (WICHE) a nonprofit agency created in 1953 by thirteen states to improve educational programs and facilities, the

Continuing Education Program for Library Personnel was initiated on September 1, 1970. Peter Hiatt, the first director of the program, summarized the rationale for this multistate operation as follows:

> By sharing multi-state resources, problems and experiments, WICHE is in a position to mount experimental programming and to evaluate techniques, materials, and results.... The overview offered by a multi-state operation makes it possible to develop programs which not only meet a real need, but which also contribute to an educational matrix which can result in a planned, continuous program of continuing education rather than in the usual scattership approach of unrelated, uncoordinated institutes, workshops, courses, and packages (Hiatt, 1973).

The Continuing Education Programs for Library Personnel was designed as a demonstration program to result in the establishment of a self-supporting system of continuing education for library personnel in the Western States. Components of the demonstration included basic continuing education programs to help update and improve library services for all types of libraries in the West; training the trainers' institutes to develop continuing education leadership; identification and testing of materials for continuing education; stimulation and use of good teaching methodology and content; evaluation not only of its own programs, but of techniques and methodologies generally (Hiatt, 1971).

In 1976 the Continuing Education Program for Library Personnel changed its name to the Western Interstate Library Coordinating Organization (WILCO) and announced that it would carry out activities in relation to three chief concerns—continuing education, networking, and research. Subsequently, on January 10, 1977, WILCO restructured its organization and moved from under the WICHE umbrella, stating: "With the completion of the Council on Library Resources project resulting in the published plan, *Library Networking in the West,* we must move into a cooperative area where we have greater flexibility to involve all the Western States in a coordinating role" (Pearson, 1977).

These constitute but two examples of regional associations which recognize continuing education as a central responsibility. Many more could be cited, such as: the annual conference workshops of the Pacific Northwest Association initiated under the presidency of Mary Ann

Reynolds; the New England Library Association with its "Outreach Network" approach developed under the leadership of Barbara Conroy; and the present activities of the Continuing Education Task Force of the New England Library Board, a multistate agency dedicated to the improvement of library and information services in the six-state area comprising Connecticut, Maine, Massachusetts, New Hampshire, Rhode Island, and Vermont. Six Midwestern States—Missouri, Wisconsin, Minnesota, Indiana, Michigan, and Illinois—formed a Committee on Continuing Education and meet regularly to exchange plans and achievements and to identify special resources and research being conducted which would be helpful in planning for continuing education programs (Midwest States Library Meeting, 1972). Recently, the Southeastern Library Association and the Mountain Plains Library Association have launched programs designed to ascertain continuing education needs and provide workshops and other activities to meet the needs identified.

In addition to the examples of national and regional association activities mentioned in this section, there are many excellent programs sponsored by state library associations. Taken together, this sampling of activities indicates clearly that there is interest and growing concern for program development in the area of continuing library education. It would also seem to imply that serious attention needs to be directed toward the raising of issues and planning at a national level in order to create prototypes and advise and coordinate the type of functions deemed necessary to further continuing library education. In planning for the future, those concerned with improving the quality and quantity of continuing library education could find many applicable examples by studying what other professions are doing and in interacting with them in the area of mutual concern—continuing education. Examples of activity in other professions that would seem to merit special attention are highlighted in *Continuing Library Education as Viewed in Relation to Other Continuing Professional Education Movements* (Stone, 1974).

To gain an overview of the type of continuing education opportunities offered by library associations, the reader is referred to the 1977 CLENE *Directory of Continuing Education Opportunities*. Of 239 offerings reported, 36, or 15 percent, were by associations (CLENE, 1977).

D. Role of the Academic Institution

1. THE ROLE OF THE ACADEMIC INSTITUTION IN CONTINUING EDUCATION

Because academic institutions are the specialists in preparing for the professions, are the gatekeepers for those entering the professions, and set the standards of quality and dimensions of student performance, colleges and universities occupy a central place in continuing education. The literature is full of what should be done by academic institutions in the field of continuing education.

The Carnegie Foundation, in emphasizing the urgency of continuing education on the part of academic institutions and its broad scope, defined it in these terms: "It has to do with the out-reach of a university to society at large, with extending the resources of the campus to individuals and groups who are not part of the regular academic community, and with bringing an academic institution's special competence to bear on the solution of society's problems" (Carnegie Corporation, 1967).

A report, "Continuing Continuing Education for the Public Service," prepared for the University of California, was designed to motivate the university to take action in the area of continuing education. It presents a strong case, citing many educational and national leaders, for the university providing a full range of continuing education opportunities for practitioners. The whole first chapter presents arguments why it is the duty of the university to take responsibility for continuing education, emphasizing that taking on this additional role "would not dilute the University's nature as an institution of higher education or scholarship and scientific inquiry" (Institute for Local Self Government, 1971).

The report not only makes the case for the necessity of the University to provide continuing education for practitioners, but it places equal emphasis on the advantages that will come to the university by providing an opportunity "for academicians to be intimate with the marketplace through the mingling process inherent in a program of continuing education."

The report makes the point that the special emphasis of a university is to do things that other institutions cannot do.

It [the University] should be ready to move forward along new lines in continuing education—to experiment, to generate and try out original ideas and approaches in instruction, research and public service.... Continuing education provides an unparalleled opportunity to feed ideas into the system through its most "influentials" that will in time result in the modification and adjustment of the system to its environment (Institute for Local Self Government, 1971).

These examples, representing but a few of many available in the literature, serve to illustrate the type of role that universities should be playing in continuing education. There is a tendency, as specifically stated in the engineering and public service literature, to dissociate advanced academic degree and certificate seeking from continuing education.

2. ROLE OF THE ACADEMIC INSTITUTION IN CONTINUING LIBRARY EDUCATION

Since basic library education cannot presume to teach all that is necessary to students, it becomes increasingly clear that the profession, and the academic institutions which serve it, must look forward to growing activity in continuing library studies as a distinct educational function, beyond advanced degree and certificate programs. This is a matter of establishing, strengthening, and maintaining a new dimension of personal development throughout the practitioner's career. It is a matter of taking a long-range look at the ever-increasing rate of technological and societal change and deciding now what needs to be done to assure continuing competence of the profession in the 1980s and beyond. In this sense, even the expanded activity of educational institutions during the last few years under the broad title "continuing education" cannot be considered as adequate to the need.

The objective of continuing library education is the specific enhancement of the competence of the individual as a practicing librarian, rather than the attainment of additional academic degrees or certificates. This dimension of continuing education must expand and achieve new levels of effectiveness. It differs from the "academic ladder" of successive degree levels in formal education. It might be called the "career ladder," a sequence of more individualized studies pursued at various times outside of degree programs, and selected principally for the independent purpose of career extension and stimulation. This "dual ladder" concept is presented in Fig. 1. On the left, it shows that academic institutions alone are responsible for the degree ladder, but

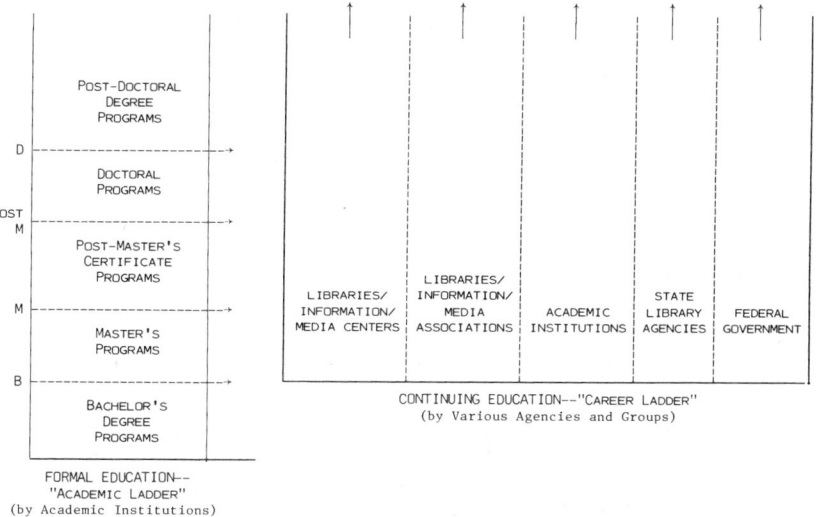

Fig. 1. Dual roles of formal academic and continuing education.

are partners with employing libraries, with professional associations, and with government agencies in broader career ladder activities. Dual involvement of academic institutions is to be expected, because it is normal that the greatest amount of educational experience and teaching expertise is to be found in faculty groups. At the same time, excellent teaching talent will also be found among practicing librarians. It is essential, therefore, that these groups cooperate in providing the necessary opportunities for continuing education.

In accordance with the definition given in Section II, continuing education relates to keeping abreast of new concepts: updating, refreshing, diversifying, and broadening aspects of library education. Suitable recognition for achieving these purposes should be provided, but it seems questionable to grant academic degrees merely for updating a master's degree, for instance. However, many students (and their employers) in attempting to fulfill the needs for continuing education will seek graduate credit courses from a university. Many believe an accepted recognition system is needed to support and encourage all types of continuing education studies.

Until recently, doctoral study provided the only opportunity for advanced work in library science, and this opportunity had been offered by a relatively small number of institutions. The Ph.D. was initiated by the Graduate Library School of the University of Chicago in 1928, and up to 1948 only two more doctoral programs were introduced—at the University of Illinois and at the University of Michigan (Asheim, 1975). According to the 1977 listing of accredited library schools by the American Library Association, twenty-one of the fifty-eight schools accredited by ALA in the United States offer a doctoral degree (ALA does not accredit programs leading to the doctorate). Starting in 1961, formal programs were offered at the level immediately following the first professional degree. The first of these post-master's programs was established at Columbia University School of Library Service in 1961. By 1977, the number of schools on the list of accredited programs in the United States offering the post-master's specialist or certificate program was twenty-eight out of the fifty-eight (these programs are not accredited by ALA).

The programs offering a certificate, diploma. or specialist degree, speak to a need not met by the first degree programs, but, as indicated in Fig. 1, they are, in this review, considered a part of the "academic ladder" and not strictly "continuing education" as defined in this survey. However, a major object of such programs is the strengthening of an individual's area of specialization; they are usually functionally oriented toward the participant's professional objectives.

The reader who wishes to consider whether or not these programs have been able to provide the type of study which leads to "handling information with sophistication and meaning" is referred to studies and critiques of the post-master's programs (Danton, 1971; Fryden, 1969; Harrison 1968). The Association of American Library Schools is preparing a detailed report on the post-master's programs which should be of considerable interest.

In 1968, Dalton identified the most pressing problem facing American librarianship as upgrading our "advanced study" programs to the stage where they will be able to produce and provide places for those who are "prepared to commit themselves deeply to the job of sifting, reviewing, and synthesizing information, i.e., to handling information with sophistication and meaning" as described in the Weinberg Report (*Science, Government and Information,* 1963) and in Overhage's (1967) article. Dalton concludes:

> Our advanced study programs are, of course, not very far advanced. When they are, they will produce and provide places for the kind of people described above. These people are available and will be available in increasing numbers. We have

before us a job of selective recruiting at a high level. We have done very little of this kind of recruiting and it will not be easy to persuade the people we need most. But we know we need them, even if our vision of the promised land we are offering them is still a little cloudy. Here lies the most pressing problem facing American librarianship today (Dalton, 1968).

As a result of their survey of a cross section of federal librarians, Kortendick and Stone (1971) recommended that the library-school-based post-master's program should be recognized as the primary method for upgrading the profession to meet the informational demands facing the profession. This conclusion was based on the character of the education needs found in their study, and they make recommendations on the form and content of this type of program.

In addition to formal courses in post-master's programs using traditional course formats which are generally open on a course-by-course basis to practitioners, the library schools have been actively engaged in holding workshops, short courses and institutes, and conferences. The overall extent of such offerings can be surmised by studying the lists of continuing education opportunities in librarianship which were initiated in 1964 by Reed and published by the U. S. Office of Education (Reed, 1964, 1965, 1966) and, starting in 1967, were published by the American Library Association in varying formats (ALA, Library Education Division, 1972).

The extent to which these are offered at the present time is indicated by the entries sponsored by library education programs in the 1977 CLENE *Directory of Continuing Education Opportunities for Library/Information/Media Personnel.* This compilation lists courses and programs which have as their goal the enhancement of skills, knowledge, or performance and were developed for library, information, and media personnel; they are not offered as part of degree programs but are designed specifically for practitioners (at all levels of library service) after entrance into the field. In the Directory there are 239 entries which were submitted by library education programs (all levels); state, national, and regional library and information science associations; and state agencies. Of the 239 entries, 157 (65 percent were sponsored by library education programs, 36 (15 percent) by professional associations, and 18 (7 percent) by state library agencies (CLENE, 1977). Comparing these figures with the 1976 Directory of 178 listings, there were 135 (76 percent) programs offered by library education programs, 32 (18 percent) offered by professional associations, and 5 (3 percent) offered by state library agencies. Of the 58 subject categories included in 1977, the fields with the largest number of opportunities are: Administration and Management (19); Reference (17); Media: Design and Production (10); and Cataloging and Classification (9).

In spite of the efforts of the library schools in providing sixth year post-master's programs and workshops, short courses, institutes, and conferences, the participation in these programs by practicing librarians has not been great. For example, in the Kortendick and Stone (1971) study, it is reported that only 15 percent of the librarians surveyed indicated that they had taken six credit hours or more since receiving their M.L.S. degrees; 28 percent had taken a workshop and/or less than six credit hours; and 57 percent had taken no formal course or workshop of any kind.

In spite of their previous lack of participation, 70 percent of the respondents in that study indicated that they needed and would take courses in a workshop format, 51 percent said that they would take a course later; and 33 percent said they were interested in a one-year post-M.L.S. program. Since respondents indicated a need for updating and upgrading—49 percent said that they lacked courses that would have been of use to them on their jobs; 22 percent stated that because of deficiencies in training they were not performing duties in their jobs which they felt were required—the question arises: Why has there been so little participation in the continuing education activities provided by the schools?

Some explanations given by the survey respondents were practical considerations not directly related to job needs: lack of financial support and leaves of absence, poor accessibility, and inflexible scheduling.

In a survey (Stone, 1969) of a cross section of librarians, it was reported that practicing librarians felt that library schools were not giving enough serious thought to their roles in continuing education. There was a consensus that the schools should continually adapt the curriculum to behavioral, societal, and technological advances and provide courses needed by the participants in their present jobs. They felt whatever was offered should be: interdisciplinary in its scope; flexible and not bound by insistence upon credits or advanced degrees or certificates; and accessible to all regardless of geographic location.

Generally the plea was for knowledge for the sake of doing a better job.

Next, attention is turned to answers to a questionnaire developed by the AALS Standing Committee on Continuing Library Education and sent to the 57 ALA-accredited library schools in August 1972. A full statistical tabulation of the results summarized here and a list of the participating schools can be found in Appendix L of *Continuing Library Education as Viewed in Relation to Other Continuing Professional Education Movements* (Stone, 1974).

There was a considerable amount of unevenness in the replies returned, some forms were filled out in great detail; while others were minimally answered. In reading the results of the survey, it needs to be borne in mind that the findings represent only 56 percent of the library schools to whom the questionnaire was sent, and that there was a wide variation in the amount of data reported. Therefore, the report can be taken only as an indication of the current status of continuing education as it existed in the accredited schools in 1972.

Of the 32 reporting schools, 26 indicated that they offered formal courses for credit to practitioners interested in continuing education. Some schools indicated that their offering formal courses simply meant that they admitted nondegree students to regular university credit courses. The data collected did not make it possible to tell how many formal courses were designed solely for practitioners at the post-master's level.

Thirty of the 32 schools might be considered "active" in continuing education as they sponsored various modes of continuing education in addition to formal courses, such as workshops, seminars, institutes, or conferences. The least popular mode was the noncredit course, with only seven schools reporting activity in this type of opportunity. This lack of use of the noncredit course seems to imply a lack of experimentation in developing formats which are more flexible than university credit courses in meeting the individual's needs in continuing education.

Taking all the opportunities together, the highest concentration of single offerings was in (1) multimedia; (2) school/media librarianship, (3) administration and management. When the 200 different offerings were divided into high categories or fields, the highest number of offerings were in (1) types of librarianship, (2) user services, (3) administration.

Overall, the responses showed a lack of specific objectives as well as a lack of diversification of objectives between degree programs and continuing education offerings. Of the 32 reporting library schools, two schools submitted tentative policy statements which showed that separate continuing education objectives had been established; three other schools stated that committees had been formed to work out comprehensive statements; another school reported that the library school was cooperating with the total university in working out a policy statement which would include a statement of philosophy and objectives for the whole university, including the development of standards. On the whole, the other statements were vague or informal.

The decision to engage in continuing education or not to engage in continuing education was most frequently made by the faculty collectively, by faculty committees, or individual faculty action. Similarly, the discontinuance of continuing education offerings was reported to be left mainly to library school and faculty action. This decision is influenced, of course, by the enrollment, for tuition is the main means by which continuing education programs are financed. The next most mentioned means of financing programs was outside (including federal) grants. Five schools said that there was some provision for continuing education activities in the department's budget. Only one school mentioned a type of financing that would seem to have a number of advantages—long-range financial support by employers.

One of the greatest impediments to the development of continuing education in academic institutions has been failure to incorporate into the university reward system acknowledgment that continuing education studies are equivalent to regular course offerings. Generally there seems to exist an underlying assumption that such activities are somehow second-rate, and continuing education faculty do not receive the same rewards or prestige as do the faculty engaged in teaching degree students, publishing, or doing research. In relation to this problem, 10 of the 32 schools replied that there was nothing in the reward structure for recognizing participation in continuing education activities. Eleven said that continuing education activity was taken into consideration when salaries and promotions were being determined. Nine comments indicated that lack of participation would be held against the faculty member and implied that such participation was expected.

In regard to the status of continuing education on the university campuses, the respondents indicated that faculty members have to squeeze continuing education efforts into the myriad of other activities demanded of them. There also seemed to be a lack of long-range planning for continuing education in collaborative arrangements with professional associations, employing institutions, or other professional groups. This was more pronounced, according the the respondents, for the universities as a whole than for the library schools themselves. Generally, however, the replies received seem to indicate that continuing education had greater status and recognition in library science than in other places on the campus.

Taking the overall responses to the questionnaire, there seemed to be a lack of emphasis on collaborative arrangements on continuing education activities between the schools and the library employers. On the basis of answers, one condition exists which is important in producing the spirit and attitude of cooperation which makes specific continuing education activities easier to establish in the future. This condition is the use of faculty in continuing education efforts off-campus.

Exchange of personnel was reported as taking the form of working with local library systems (4 schools listed); serving as consultant for workshops and special continuing education projects outside the university (2 schools listed); faculty involved with state library associations on continuing education activities (6 schools listed); making surveys (3 schools); and serving as consultants to directors of state continuing education programs (2 schools listed).

Another type of collaboration emphasized by Houle (1970) and Schein (1972) is between the professions. There were questions in the survey dealing with the interface with other professional groups on the campus. Eighteen of the 32 schools indicated that they had discussed continuing education with other professional programs on campus. Eight said they had not, three said they did sometimes.

On campus there seemed to be a mutual effort to keep the different schools aware of what was being done in continuing education. This effort was carried on through distribution of newsletters, extension bulletins, and other publications. Twenty-four schools said they were aware of what other professionally oriented groups were doing on campus in the area of continuing education and two additional schools answered "somewhat" to this question.

The question relative to interface with other professional groups on campus asked in what ways library school personnel interacted or thought it would be beneficial to interact with other professional continuing education programs. The activity that was mentioned the most often in this regard was participation in a campus continuing education advisory council. Mentioned next most frequently was increased awareness, pooling of resources, and additional concern for a bigger total program.

Houle (1970) recommends that members of each profession should not act as though they alone had any need of continuing education and should drop the assumption that their processes and needs are wholly unique. Such interprofessional efforts, also advocated by Allen (1969) would, according to Houle, lead to important consequences for our society. It would seem that the campus would offer an excellent opportunity to start such cooperation, and that the time is ripe for innovation in this type of cooperative programming in continuing education.

There has also been some insistence that faculty members themselves should be participating in continuing education (Martin, 1971). In answer to the question whether there were any specific requirements regarding the continuing education of faculty members, the largest response, listed 21 times, was "No." A chief means for improving the teaching effectiveness of faculty members has been activity by the Association of American Library Schools by means of annual programs, an interest group on teaching techniques, and articles in the *Journal of Education for Librarianship*.

The final question asked: "On your campus, do you observe indications of a change in role or a trend toward loosening up in the offering of continuing education opportunities to professional groups or individuals?" Only three schools stated that no drastic changes were seen.

It seems clear that, except in a very few instances, the respondents were in agreement that on their campuses there were observable indications of a change in role or a tendency toward loosening up in the offering of continuing education opportunities to professional groups and individuals.

The 1974 NCLIS continuing education and information survey reaffirmed the profession's desire to see library educators become more heavily involved in continuing education. Among the needs cited by respondents were: the creation of faculty positions specifically charged with continuing education programming; the design and implementation of surveys designed to clearly define the educational needs of the profession, to emphasize the profession's obligation to continue their education, and to investigate on an ongoing basis the most effective means of implementing continuing education programs.

E. Role of the Employing Library

It is beyond the scope of this review to include a detailed discussion of the factors and conditions in the work place that stimulate participation in continuing education. This subject is dealt with in some detail in *Continuing Library Education as Viewed in Relation to Other Continuing Professional Education Movements* (Stone, 1974), and the reader is referred to that presentation and to "Guidelines to Development of Human Resources in Libraries (ALA, Staff Development Committee, 1971)." In the conclusion of that study the concepts that seem to merit special attention by those planning for continuing education in the work environment of the library are discussed in detail. These considerations and specifications are important and since studies in librarianship (Association of Research Libraries, 1972; Conroy, 1977; DeProspo, 1971; Kaser, 1971; Marchant, 1971; Monroe, 1967; Plate and Stone, 1974; Stone, 1969) indicate that few libraries are actually doing much about continuing education in any organized fashion, these conclusions and observations are summarized here:

1. Administrators should take the initiative and responsibility for defining and providing support opportunities for the continuing education of their staffs.
2. The continuing education and professional development program of the library should be conceptualized as a subsystem of the total organizational system.
3. Administrators should recognize the need for establishing a long-range educational program with definite objectives to parallel long-range library goals. There is evidence that continuing education on an if-and-when basis is not sufficient to cope with the requirements of a library actively responding to societal changes.
4. Continuing education programs require strong support and encouragement by supervisory personnel. Top administration should make it explicit that one of the functions of supervision is stimulating subordinates to continuing education and reviewing with them their plans for development. Conscious

recognition of what an "innovator" type of supervisor is and does relative to continuing education helps make plain what management can expect of supervision.

5. A philosophy should predominate in which it is assumed: (a) that most individuals have a natural inclination toward growth and development and that the individual will accept his share of responsibility for development; (b) that each person is considered a unique individual and his or her special talents are recognized, encouraged to develop, and utilized; (c) that each individual is allowed to identify his personal career goals and match those against the library's goals; and (d) that management's function is to supply the opportunity, guidance, and stimulation.

6. Continuing education programs require the personal motivation of the individual employee. There is evidence that for an individual to be personally motivated toward continuing education, he or she must see the results of the learning as being related and necessary to the performance of his or her job.

7. Individual jobs should be organized and enriched so that the nature of the work will provide individual motivation for growth and development.

8. Policy statements should recognize updating personnel as part of the daily work.

9. Employee appraisal should be recognized as closely related to development. To serve as a motivating factor toward continuing education, there is evidence that appraisal needs to be a continuous, cumulative process, using a management by objectives approach.

10. An active continuing education committee, representing the views and needs of all levels of the organization, should be established. The function of such a committee is to initiate, review, and recommend action programs in continuing education. The committee should also suggest priorities based on the conduct and evaluation of "reviews of need" in the work force as related to organizational goals and needs. A professional development committee can create and sustain enthusiasm for continuing education because its very existence demonstrates the administration's support and reliance on continuing education as a professional development technique.

11. It should be recognized that individual and group needs are so varied that short courses, degree programs, formal courses, institutes, etc., will not meet all continuing education needs. The organization should provide a sufficient number of alternatives in order for each professional to select and integrate what is useful and needed by him.
12. Deterring environmental factors relating to continuing education, such as lack of time, inconvenient location, poor working conditions, should be eliminated insofar as possible.
13. Ways and means should be developed to overcome the physical and psychological barriers of individuals participating in continuing education opportunities outside the work place. Management should set up in some central place in the library a section where information on outside continuing education is collected, kept up-to-date, and made easily available to those considering or in need of outside continuing education opportunities.
14. A system should be operative which periodically and systematically evaluates the need for continuing education opportunities.
15. An ongoing evaluation system should continuously feed back information on ways and means by which the continuing education program can be improved.
16. Management should maintain an accurate record-keeping system which reflects the number and types of personnel engaged in employer-sponsored modes of continuing education and the cost per participant. Ways should be found to measure and assess the modes of continuing education in terms of their value to the organization and to the individual.
17. Participation in decision making should be viewed as one way of stimulating employees toward engaging in continuing education opportunities. According to Monroe (1967), "there is no better educator than the exercise of responsibility nor is there a better prod to continuing formal education."
18. The organization should continuously maintain a climate for learning. Elements in such a climate include: (a) the concept of professional group practice should pervade the library in which stimulation for continuing learning is inherent; (b) the learner shares in the plan for his learning; (c) research as a method of

continuing learning is recognized (Monroe, 1967); (d) a developmental style of leadership exists throughout the organization. In regard to the effect of leadership style on library organization, a current project—Consortium of Public Library Innovation involving nine major public libraries—is testing the effect of leadership styles on library service and focusing on more collaboration with community/educational agencies (Woodrum, 1977).

In the NCLIS study, possible responsibilities that might be assumed by employing libraries in the area of continuing education are stated in much the same fashion.

For practicing librarians to be deeply involved in continuing education, they must feel assured that they will have opportunities to use their talents and skills to the maximum extent, and that progression in the library either through administration or specialization channels will be in keeping with their value to the library and the publics served.

Real development does not necessarily involve job change by vertical promotion; it can involve an entirely new experience or simply the realignment of responsibility, carrying with it something new and worthwhile. Career development is optimized when each job assignment is made with two thoughts in mind: What will the individual contribute to the job, and what will the job contribute to the individual? To assure return on participation in continuing education programs, such programs must be founded on the concept that each employee is an individual and that his or her special talents should be recognized, encouraged to develop, and utilized; that continuing education should be continuous; that the individual must accept his or her share of responsibility for development; and that management's function is to supply the opportunity, encouragement, guidance, and stimulation.

Library education programs should equip librarians who are prepared to cope with change and willing to continue their learning throughout their careers; employing libraries must see that development opportunities continue. Administrators and supervisors must take seriously the Library Manpower Statement of ALA and its three items relative to continuing education as quoted in the section on "Associations." The individual must be stimulated to learn, and continuing education must be within his or her reach.

Individual and group needs are so varied that formal courses alone will not satisfy them. Many other ways must be found. One way to gain individual commitment for professional growth is by means of participation in a plan for self-development by means of competency-based learning contracts. There needs to be some "payoff" in terms of a recognition system for individuals in the library and/or profession to put forth substantial efforts in the area of continuing education.

Career development is a continuum which depends to a large extent on momentum. This momentum is a function of the attitude of the individual, and this attitude depends to a large degree on the incentive the individual receives in his or her environment—from employers, from educators, from professional societies, and from state library agencies, among others.

F. Role of the State Library Agencies

State library agencies recognize the need for giving more attention to continuing education, as reflected in a report entitled *Education of State Library Personnel* (Hiatt *et al.*, 1971). The report has implications for continuing education that go far beyond the group for which it was specifically designed; namely, state library agency professional personnel. In fact, most of the report can be applied equally well to all levels of library personnel and to all types of libraries. The report grew out of a charge by the (then) American Association of State Libraries and the Library Education Division to their Interdivisional Committee on Education of State Library Personnel. Its stated objectives were:

1. To assess the needs of professional personnel performing functions unique to state library agencies, with emphasis on the consultant and administrative-supervisory personnel.
2. To recommend means and methods of designing educational programs to meet these education eneeds.
3. To recommend a structure for carrying out this programming.

The emphasis of the report is on continuing education, whether formal or informal. In order to accomplish the goals described, the Committee emphasized the need for cooperation with other agencies and institutions, especially with graduate schools in the fields of librarianship, communications, and related disciplines; professional associations; and regional and national agencies in higher education. The report is valuable from a number of viewpoints. One of these is that specific means of implementation for the stated objectives are detailed through the suggestion of two immediate steps of implementation and one long-range plan for later consideration. The report also recommends a National Advisory and Action Committee for Continuing Education of State Library Personnel.

A conclusion of the NCLIS survey of continuing education was that all component groups concerned with continuing education should work as a partnership to vitalize and generally improve continuing library and information science education throughout the nation. However, an enlarged role was suggested for state library agencies. This position was justified and considered necessary for a number of reasons (Stone *et al.*, 1974), including the following:

1. The new federalism gives increased importance to states taking energetic and responsible action in the development of all educational policies and services.
2. The state library agencies are the only agencies which have implied responsibility for all personnel engaged in supplying library and information service for all residents of the United States. Individuals are free to join or not to join library associations—many do not.
3. Education, of whatever type and level, is constitutionally a state responsibility. It is the states, through their officials, that must respond if we are to realize the essential dream of American education, that *all* individuals have the opportunity to develop the best that is in them throughout their lifetimes.
4. In the interviews that were held as a part of the NCLIS survey, the importance of states having a strong part to play in continuing library education is indicated by the fact that 42 percent of the interviewees believed the states should have a prime role to play; 28 percent thought the library schools should have a leading role; 15 percent favored a strong role for regional and national associations.
5. The public's demand for increased accountability on the part of all professions is resulting in state legislatures making continuing education mandatory for some professions. State library agencies need a well-developed statewide plan for continuing education for library personnel to demonstrate, if called upon,

that the state library agency in collaboration with constituent groups within the profession is capably providing for the continuing education of library personnel.

Possible types of responsibilities relative to continuing education suggested for state library agencies by participants in the NCLIS survey include:

1. Coordinating continuing education programs on a statewide basis involving practicing library and information science personnel, employing libraries, library associations, and library educators (involved with graduate, undergraduate, and community college technician programs).
2. Providing a link between individual libraries and nationwide and regional plans.
3. Identifying priority continuing education needs of the state.
4. Justifying continuing education for librarians to the state funding body so that adequate support for such activities can be secured.
5. Providing role models by instituting sound internal training and staff development programs.
6. Planning, implementing, and evaluating statewide continuing education programs based on the identification of needs:
    a. Providing basic training in technical services.
    b. Providing consultant services.
    c. Promoting and publicizing regional and in-state opportunities.
    d. Conducting institutes and seminars.
    e. Experimenting with new training techniques, such as simulation.
    f. Intensifying existing continuing education programs.
7. Appointing at least one employee to be in charge of the coordination and promotion of continuing education and to serve as a linking agent (Stone *et al.,* 1974).

Inherent in the success of any specific statewide planning for continuing education for library personnel is provision for *all* levels and *all* types of library personnel to identify their needs in relation to their clienteles and to become involved in the planning process itself.

An example of sound library planning for continuing education is provided by the Illinois State Library which, through its 27-member (representing all types of librarians, public library trustees, and library educators) Advisory Committee on Education and Training, has developed a "Statement of Policy on Continuing Education" which is in the process of implementation. The preface to that document is important because it relates continuing education to the ultimate goal—service to the public—and it includes not only those who work in libraries, but all those who work "with" libraries (Illinois State Library, 1976).

The philosophical basis on which they carried out their work is based on the fact that the largest single expenditure of libraries is for personnel. "The individuals who work in and with libraries assume the responsibility for interpreting society's information needs and providing ways to meet those needs. It is therefore essential that these individuals are provided with the opportunity to maintain and improve their competencies. Continuing education, though not an end in itself, is a means to maximize the efforts of the library's most expensive resource—persons involved in providing library services" (Illinois State Library, 1976).

The document has so many excellent features it is tempting to quote from it in still greater length. The statement includes the areas of responsibilities for continuing education—individuals working in and with libraries; employing libraries; library systems; regional and national elements, including library associations; library education programs, the Illinois State Library.

One of the most encouraging advances in continuing education is the increasing interest and activity on the part of state library agencies in continuing education. Another example of positive action by a state in long-range planning is provided by the establishment of the Advisory Council of Library Education in New Jersey (McDonough, 1972).

But perhaps the most aggressive example of state library initiatives in the area of continuing education is to be found in the establishment of the Office for Continuing Education at the College of Library Science at the University of Kentucky. This office, funded jointly by the Kentucky Department of Library and Archives and the College of Library Science, was established in August of 1973, and soon was recognized as a model of state library/library school cooperation. Under the auspices of the office a number of broadly based institutes utilizing the latest technological developments were held, and the

Continuing Education and Librarianship Newsletter was initiated (Nelson, 1976).

An example of needs assessment at the grass-roots level is provided by David McKay, North Carolina State Librarian, who announced in March 1977 a statewide planning endeavor was being undertaken which will provide in-depth analysis of the needs and resources of every community in the state. The survey will obtain grass-roots input from every county in the state (McKay, 1977).

Increasingly state library agencies, often in cooperation with state library associations and universities, are offering workshops to sharpen the skills of library personnel. For example, in Ohio, during 1971–1972, 477 librarians participated in staff development programs sponsored by the state library. Programs emphasized improved management, PPBS (Program Planning and Budgeting System), the development of leadership and motivation, and the evaluation of employee performance (State Library of Ohio, 1972).

Another indication of state library interest and concern in continuing education is the fact that fifteen state library agencies joined the Continuing Library Education Network and Exchange during its first year. These states are: Arkansas, Florida, Idaho, Illinois, Maryland, New Hampshire, New York, North Carolina, Ohio, Oregon, Pennsylvania, Vermont, Virginia, Washington, and Wisconsin.

Two incentives in the recent efforts by state library agencies in the area of continuing education deserve mention. One has been the funding of three institutes by the USOE—Office of Library and Learning Resources—to provide training and support to representatives from state library agencies in their statewide planning for continuing education.

Another incentive has been the interest and concern of the Chief Officers of State Library Agencies (COSLA) as demonstrated by their support of CLENE, by their active involvement in the planning for the recent institutes funded by USOE for State Library Agency Personnel, and by the appointment of a Continuing Education Task Force of COSLA to work continuously in this area.

G. Role of the Federal Government

The federal government has played an important role in advancing continuing library education. A number of acts of Congress have provided assistance to continuing education. The first major encouragement came in the form of the Library Services and Construction Act of 1956 (LSCA) which, although chiefly designed for the improvement of rural library services, made provision, through its Title I, for scholarship aid for public librarians; and with the extension and expansion of this Act, the states have been able to use this funding for a wide variety of continuing education efforts. Other pieces of legislation which have financed continuing education are: (1) the National Defense Education Act of 1958 (NDEA) which, through its Title II, provided for institutes which would be applied to the training of school librarians; (2) the Elementary and Secondary Education Act of 1965 (ESEA) which, through its Title II, expanded on the institute concept of NDEA funding; and (3) the Higher Education Act of 1965 (HEA) which, through its Title II-B, has been the major source of funding for continuing education for library personnel. Its Title VI-B and Title I supported faculty development programs and continuing education programs which could be used for the training of librarians. Other sources of funding for training and continuing education opportunities included the Vocational Education Act, 1963; the Economic Opportunity Act, 1965; and the Education Professions Development Act, 1967. The Medical Library Assistance Act of 1966 provided assistance for the training and continuing education of medical librarians.

Title II-B of the Higher Education Act of 1965, as amended, provides the opportunity for institutions of higher education and other library agencies to make application for library training and retraining grants. These grants provide for fellowship, traineeship, and institute training opportunities. The institute program provides for short-term and long-term retraining opportunities and is, therefore, the primary vehicle for federal support for continuing education. In the past, institute programs have been largely devoted to upgrading professional skills in critical areas. More recently, however, many institutes have been devoted to the *process* of continuing education (Stevens, 1975).

One result emanating from the Leadership Training Institute of Florida State University, sponsored by the U. S. Office of Education, was Sheldon's (1976) publication, "Planning and Evaluating Library Training Programs: A Guide for Library Leaders, Staffs and Advisory Groups." The overall impact of the HEW Title II-B Institutes in Librarianship is summarized in the publication by McCarthy (1973).

Another indication of the rising recognition of continuing education as a high priority in the field of library and information science was the fact that, in the regional hearings the National Commission on Libraries and Information Science held throughout the country in 1972 and 1973, the need for continuing education was repeatedly expressed. As a result, the Commission issued a call for a proposal for the provision of recommendations for a nationwide program of continuing library and information science education. The completed study recommended the formation of the Continuing Library Education Network and Exchange (CLENE), and the USOE funded a planning grant to enable its implementation.

Title II-B of the Higher Education Act also provides funds for research and demonstration projects in library and information science, and a number of these grants have included projects designed to upgrade library service to the public through the provision of continuing education products and programs. For example, in 1968 the U. S. Office of Education and the Federal Library Committee set out to identify the special educational needs of federal librarians and to provide programming to meet these needs. A research team at The Catholic University of America conducted a survey of librarians from all over the country (Kortendick and Stone, 1971). As a result, the specific continuing education needs of federal librarians were identified and three courses were developed (Kortendick and Stone, 1972), which have, since the completion of the project, been offered to the library community. The materials produced in connection with the courses have been supplied to others on request.

An example of a 1976/1977 project funded from Title II-B funds for library research and demonstration is the CLENE effort which developed a suggested model recognition system for library personnel to include nontraditional forms of study and the development of a prototype home study program.

Examples can be found of many other federally funded programs which have furthered the continuing education of library personnel, such as: the short courses planned and implemented by the Civil Service Commission; the training programs of the Federal Library Committee; the instruction of employees and users of the National Library of Medicine's MEDLINE system.

The instances presented in this section illustrate some of the ways in which the federal government has helped the profession improve continuing education and which, in turn, have helped to upgrade the quality of library service. Recent cutbacks in the funds available for library-related programming have caused concern throughout the profession; but with the current interest in lifelong learning legislation, the hope is that there will be increased funding for continuing education programs.

H. Conclusion

This section has given examples of the diverse responsibilities that individuals and various groups within the profession have self-selected and that they wish to shoulder to facilitate the continuing education of library/information/media practitioners. It also indicates some roles suggested by those in the field which might be played by various groups that have not been fully implemented and hold potential for future development.

Examination of the responsibilities presented indicates that there is need for greater development of collaborative efforts between these various groups. Also, there is need for greater interaction with clients in order to discover more fully their needs which call for continuing education on the part of practitioners.

V. THE CONTINUING LIBRARY EDUCATION NETWORK AND EXCHANGE (CLENE)

A. What is CLENE?

CLENE is an acronym for the Continuing Library Education Network and Exchange. It is a special service and resource facility to make continuing education opportunities available to library personnel at all levels of sophistication and need. It is a new national organization whose *ultimate purpose* is to improve the library and information services of the nation. CLENE is a unique concept that makes continuing education resources and opportunities available in a way that has not been attempted before.

CLENE creates a partnership for the advancement of continuing education among state library associations and allied professional associations—local, state, and national; national libraries; library schools; employing libraries; state library agencies; federal agencies including the National Commission on Libraries and Information Science; and concerned individuals. It also seeks to be interdisciplinary in its approach to continuing education and thus benefits from the research and experience of other disciplines, fields, and professions.

B. Background

The development of CLENE is the direct outgrowth of the fourth objective of the national program promulgated by the National Commission on Libraries and Information Science. That objective, designed to "ensure basic and continuing education of personnel essential to the implementation of a National Program," noted the lack in the country at the time of a concerted effort to "redefine... educational programs, in order... to build the leadership needed to remold traditional librarianship into a dynamic profession. A new approach to educational curricula will be needed in library and information science if librarians, information scientists, library technicians, and auxiliary personnel are to learn to function as an interdisciplinary team." It further stressed that "it is essential... that all librarians understand the potentials of the new technologies; and this is especially true for those librarians who serve the user directly. Those in contact with the user must understand the capabilities of the statewide or nationwide network with which they are working...." To achieve this technological and organizational upgrading of libraries and information centers new approaches to continuing education were clearly required.

Recognizing the need for continuing education throughout the profession, the National Commission funded a study of library and information science continuing education. CLENE was proposed as the recommendation of the resulting nine-month study conducted in 1974 by Stone, Patrick, and Conroy at The Catholic University of America. This study suggested starting points in the process of developing a highly diversified nationwide framework of continuing education for all types of library personnel. Based on a philosophy of lifelong, self-directed learning, the basic missions of CLENE are:

1. To provide equal access to continuing education opportunities, available in quantity and quality over a substantial period of time to ensure library and information science personnel and

organizations the competency to delivery quality library and information services to all.
2. To create an awareness and a sense of need for continuing education of library (and information science) personnel on the part of employers and individuals as a means of responding to societal and technological change.

Thus, CLENE was formed in response to a recognized need for continuous updating and renewal of our knowledge and competencies in the changing field of library and information science. It also recognizes that many other professions have a more coherent program for meeting their continuing education needs. The NCLIS research study found that no central mechanism existed for providing information on continuing education programs; that continuing education programs at state and regional levels were uncoordinated; that no assessment of continuing education needs had been made with a resulting coordinated plan of action for meeting these needs; and that continuing education planners and trainers themselves frequently needed additional training.

CLENE's activities are focused in four major program areas. The first is needs assessment and problem definition. The focus here is on continuous assessment of individual and group needs for continuing education and on the definition of problems. The second area, information acquisition and coordination, involves the acquisition, coordination, and exchange of information about existing continuing education resources in library science. The third area is product and resource development. This involves the planning, design, production, and evaluation of CLENE services. The fourth area, communications and delivery, involves creating an awareness and sense of need for continuing education on the part of employers, and in planning ways and means to deliver materials to users.

C. Implementation

Serving as a catalyst toward the development of nationwide planning in continuing education, NCLIS, in the context of the NCLIS 9-month study and related work, sponsored an invitational conference in October 1974. Members of this ad hoc group were representative of public, school, and academic libraries; medical, special, educational technology, and information science associations; state libraries; library schools; ALA; and a broad spectrum of the total library community. These representatives were not only vocal about the programs and needs of their constitutents but also interested in the benefits of addressing common needs and problems. Roderick Swartz, Acting Executive Director of the National Commission, and Bessie Boehm Moore, Vice Chairman of the Commission, represented NCLIS at the conference. It was the unanimous consensus of those present that CLENE should be implemented. Furthermore, all members agreed to report back to their respective organizations and to attempt to secure their support for the principles of CLENE. The entire group agreed to meet again in January 1975.

Meanwhile, Alphonse Trezza became the Executive Director of the National Commission on Libraries and Information Science and supported the action that had taken place. Trezza opened the meeting of the second implementation conference; Bessie Moore, Vice Chairman of the National Commission, was also present as a liaison representative from NCLIS. By this time, the CLENE report had been published and distributed to library schools, every state library, and every major library association.

During this second meeting, the priorities for CLENE and the criteria for membership on the ad hoc Board of Directors and the ad hoc Advisory Committee were developed. Following these meetings grant proposals were written, an operating office for CLENE was established in Washington, D.C., and members of the two ad hoc groups were appointed.

The ad hoc Board of Directors and the ad hoc Advisory Committee met in June 1975. The following interim officers were elected: Nettie B. Taylor (Assistant State Superintendent for Libraries, Division of Library Development Service, Maryland State Department of Education), President; Margaret Meyers (Executive Secretary, Library Education Division, American Library Association), Vice-President; Julie Virgo (Director of Education, Medical Library Association), Secretary; and K. Leon Montgomery (ASIS representative), Treasurer. For the Steering Committee, Ruth Patrick (Syracuse University) and Travis Tyer (Illinois State Library) were elected as Chairman and Secretary, respectively.

Initial funding for CLENE came from (1) a one-year grant of $25,000 by the Office of Libraries and Learning Resources of the U.S.

Office of Education and (2) $52,845 from ten state library agencies (Arkansas, Florida, Idaho, Illinois, Maryland, New York, North Carolina, Ohio, Pennsylvania, and Wisconsin) over a three-year period. Later in the year five other states joined—New Hampshire, Oregon, Vermont, Virginia, and Washington. Serving as project director, Elizabeth W. Stone assembled a project staff: Principal Investigator—Mary Baxter; Research Assistant—Dr. Hermes D. Kreilkamp; Secretary—Mary Anding. A more detailed description of CLENE can be found in Pauline Vaillancourt's (1976) article.

D. Goals

To accomplish the purpose and missions of CLENE, the goals, as stated in the bylaws, are:

(a) To develop a process for continually assessing the continuing education needs of library and information science personnel at all levels and in all locales.
(b) To develop methods for responding to the continuing education needs of individuals and groups.
(c) To develop a coordinative mechanism for suppliers of continuing library and information science education at local, state, regional, and national levels, as a means of:
   (1) insuring maximum use of existing resources, and
   (2) eliminating unnecessary duplication of effort.
(d) To develop a delivery system for responding to the continuing education needs of individuals and groups.
(e) To collect and disseminate interdisciplinary information relating to continuing education of working adults.
(f) To encourage broad involvement in planning, building, and modifying the processes of the Continuing Library Education Network and Exchange.

E. Achievements

During its first year CLENE set four project objectives: (1) creation of a permanent administrative structure; (2) establishment of a dues and fees system; (3) development of the operational mechanisms required for the implementation of CLENE: and (4) identification of funding sources and the preparation of proposals.

The first objective was achieved through the formation of the CLENE Assembly which is made up of all members; the 21-member

Advisory Committee; the 15-member Board of Directors; and the elected officers. Bylaws were also written, and the organization was incorporated in the District of Columbia in 1976.

The second objective was met when the membership categories shown in Table I were established:

Meeting the third objective involved CLENE staff and members in four basic programs: (1) needs assessment and problem definition; (2) information acquisition and dissemination; (3) product and resource development; and (4) communications.

The first of these programs was initiated by means of a survey and sessions of the CLENE Assembly. A list of top priority needs was constructed with the most important items being: (1) a directory and data bank on continuing education opportunities in library science; (2) program reviews; (3) a newsletter; (4) the development of home study programs; and (5) the creation of learning packages.

The second program involved the acquisition of a collection of materials on continuing education and the design of an on-line data base concerning continuing education. The third program resulted in the preparation of a number of papers dealing with the evaluation of continuing education programs in library science. Papers by Brooke Sheldon (1976) and Alan Knox (1976) were published by CLENE.

The last program dealt with communication. In this regard CLENE quarterly and annual reports were prepared and widely disseminated, the *CLENExchange* (a newsletter) was established, preparation of a

TABLE I
CLENE Types and Number of Members as of December 31, 1976

Type of membership category	No. of members:
Individual members	600
Institutional members	21
Association/organization members	15
Support members (state agencies)	15
Consortium members	2
Sustaining members	0

slide-program on CLENE was completed and made available to the library community, and numerous news releases were issued.

The final CLENE objective—the identification of funding sources and the preparation of proposals—involved CLENE in a number of successful projects. A $25,000 grant was awarded to CLENE for an institute to train state library staff to carry out continuing education activities. A second grant was awarded by the USOE Office of Library Research and Demonstration and totaled some $81,800. In this project, by means of 82 discussion groups (involving about 800 individuals) and 82 interviews, grassroots opinion was sought on the shape and form that a recognition system, which would include nontraditional forms of study, might take for the profession which would support and encourage practitioners to continue their education. A major part of the project is the development of one type of nontraditional learning—home study. A course on "Motivation: Vital Force in the Organization" (Peterson, *et al.*, 1977) was prepared and tested on a pilot basis with 65 librarians throughout the United States. Along with the development of this prototype, course guidelines were prepared for participants, for faculty evaluators, for group leaders, for authors of home study packages, and for supporting record-keeping procedures. These guidelines present criteria that, if followed, will qualify this type of program for acceptability in a professionwide recognition system and will be the means by which the experimental program can be extended and advanced (Stone *et al.*, 1977).

F. National Repository of Data about Continuing Education Programs

Since the top priority from the field for CLENE activity was the development of a national repository of data about continuing education programs, and since this was the first major project accomplished by the CLENE staff, a description of this service is presented.

1. CLIENT GROUPS

The information system developed has been designed to serve four major client groups. Librarians who are seeking information about available courses and programs to meet their needs now have recourse to a system for locating the specific type of course they are seeking and the various places where such a course or program will be offered. The major mode of making this information available is in the form of a directory listing courses by subject and geographical location. Specific searches can be made by time offered, mode of the course, sponsor, and leader of the course. Other types of information provided include: costs, target audience for which the program was designed, level of difficulty, entrance requirements, methods used, type of credit and/or recognition given for completion of the program, evaluation of the course, and objectives stated in terms of educational outcomes—what can the participant expect to be able to do after completing the program?

The second group served by the system is made up of those institutions and associations which provide continuing education for practitioners. This group can publicize programs by sending information to CLENE for distribution through the system. They can also determine whether gaps or duplication of courses exist in their geographical area or in content areas in which they have expertise. Finally, they will be able to identify those who are currently offering continuing education courses and programs.

The third group served by the system consists of planners concerned with manpower development and education. The system provides an inventory of what exists for the continuing education of library personnel. Needs of this clientele group include information about types of courses available, information about geographical distribution of course offerings, and indications of duplication of effort.

A final group served by the information is system is composed of continuing education instructors. Persons who are interested in teaching continuing education can identify which institutions are offering courses in the areas of their experience and when such courses are being offered during the year.

2. ON-LINE SYSTEM

It should be stressed that this is an on-line system, so that if a course or program is developed after the Directory is printed, it is still important to enter it in the system, since the course and program information can be located by direct questions to any of the major categories included in the system.

An essential requirement for the effectiveness of the information system is that its data elements be as complete and appropriate as possible. This is particularly true of an on-line system which will be required to answer quite specific questions about a course or program. Specific information is also important for purposes of analyzing statistically just what is being offered at the present time or in the immediate future.

For all these reasons an attempt has been made to define the elements in the CLENE information system in order to provide quality service and still keep the system as cost-effective as possible. Eligible for listing in the CLENE Information System are programs or courses offered which have as their goal the enhancement of skills, knowledge, or performance as developed for library, information, and media personnel. Regular courses which are offered for degrees—A.A., B.A., B.S., Ph.D., or other degree programs—are not included. However, courses and programs developed specifically for practitioners after entrance into the field, such as the post-M.L.S. courses and programs, are eligible for entry. Institutes, workshops, laboratories, or other specially designed continuing education programs are eligible. Packaged programs are eligible for listing, and producers are urged to send them in for listing.

VI. LOOKING TOWARD THE FUTURE

It has been suggested that in the year 2000 there will be at least 160 million adults in the United States above the age of 24. If only 3 percent of these adults (a very conservative estimate) choose to attend college full time for one semester this would constitute a total enrollment approximately twice that of today. In addition, if the trends toward nontraditional study increase as expected, the total learning force in the year 2000 could well number as many as 100 million persons (Hamilton and Halladay, 1976). As the number of people seeking to learn in individualized ways increases, increased pressures will be placed on libraries to adjust to meet their demands for increased and new educational experiences. The message is clear, libraries will need to keep pace with rapidly changing societal needs for lifelong learning, and this will dictate an increased attention to continuing education for librarians to prepare them for the changing nature of their work.

As the library profession plans not only for its own continuing education, but also looks to its role in relation to the lifelong learning needs of the public it serves, it will become obvious that the increase in nontraditional learning will both enhance and challenge the library's role in American society. It therefore would appear essential that the library profession begin now to develop the blueprints and devise the appropriate policies necessary to the systematic and intelligent provision of continuing education of America's librarians.

REFERENCES

Allen, J. R., Jr. (1969). "The Educational Third Dimension." (Paper presented at the Galaxy Conference on Adult and Continuing Education, Washington, D.C., December 9, 1969.) (Mimeograph copy.)

Allen, L. A. (1974). "Continuing Education Needs of Special Librarians." Special Library Association, New York.

American Association of Colleges of Pharmacy and the American Pharmaceutical (AACP/APHA) Task Force (1975). The continuing competence of pharmacists. *Journal of the American Pharmaceutical Association* 457, 432–437.

American Library Association (ALA) (1970a). "Library Education and Manpower: A Statement of Policy Adopted by the Council of the American Library Association, June 30, 1970." American Library Association, Chicago, Illinois.

American Library Association (ALA) (1970b). "School Library Manpower Project: Phase I—Final Report." American Library Association, Chicago, Illinois.

American Library Association (ALA), Activities Committee on New Directions for ALA (1970). "The Final Report of the Activities Committee on New Directions for ALA." American Library Association, Chicago, Illinois.

American Library Association (ALA), Library Education Division (1972). Continuing education for librarians—conferences, workshops, short courses, 1972. *American Libraries* 2, 1217–1219. [Supplements in *American Libraries* 3, 179–181, 423–426, 662–664 (1973)].

American Library Association (ALA), Staff Development Committee (1971). Guidelines to the development of human resources in libraries: rationale, policies, programs and recommendations. *Library Trends* 20, 97–117.

Asheim, L. (1975). Trends in Library Education—United States. *In* "Advances in Librarianship" (M. J. Voigt, ed.), Vol. 5, pp. 147–201. Academic Press, New York.

Association of American Library Schools (AALS) (1973). "Papers Presented at a Mini-Workshop on Continuing Education Sponsored by the Standing Committee on Continuing Library Education of the Association of American Library Schools during the Annual Meeting of the Association, January 28, 1973." Association of American Library Schools, Washington, D.C. (Transcription of a tape of the presentation.)

Association of American Library Schools (AALS), Committee on Continuing Library Education (1972). "The Role of the Association of American Library Schools in

Continuing Library Education." (A position paper distributed at the 1972 Annual Meeting of the Association of American Library Schools, Chicago, Illinois, January 1972.) [Also published in Stone, E. W. (1974). "Continuing Library Education as Viewed in Relation to Other Continuing Professional Education Movements." American Society for Information Sciences, Washington, D.C.

Association of American Library Schools (AALS), Standing Committee on Continuing Library Education (1972). Report of Standing Committee on Continuing Library Education. *Journal of Education for Librarianship* **13**, 137–144.

Association of Research Libraries (1972). "Management Review and Analysis Program." Association of Research Libraries, Office of University Library Management Studies, Washington, D.C.

Barbulesco, D. W., and Means, R. P. (1976). Selected bibliography on continuing education needs assessment. *CLENExchange* 1, 12, 13.

Barrett, G. V. (1970). "Combating Obsolescence Using Perceived Discrepancies in Job Expectations of Research Managers and Scientists." University of Rochester, Management Research Center, Rochester, New York. (ED 047 250.)

Booz, Allen and Hamilton, Inc. (1973). "Organization and Staffing of the Libraries of Columbia University: A Case Study." Redgrave Information Resources Corp., Westport, Connecticut.

Brown, T. C. (1973). Competency-based approach to reproductive biology. *American Journal of Obstetrics and Gynecology* **116**, 1037.

Bundy, M. I., and Wasserman, P. (1968). Professionalism reconsidered. *College and Research Libraries* **29**, 5–26.

Carnegie Corporation (1967). "62nd Annual Report." Carnegie Corp., New York.

Case, R. N. (1973). "Behavioral Requirements Analysis Checklist." American Association of School Librarians, School Library Manpower Project, Chicago, Illinois.

Charters, W. W. (1925). Job analysis in education for librarianship. *Libraries* **32**, 7.

CLENE (Continuing Library Education Opportunities for Library/Information Media Personnel," 2d Ed. CLENE, Washington, D.C.

Conroy, B. (1972). "Leadership for Change: A report of the Outreach Network." New England Center for Continuing Education, Durham, New Hampshire.

Conroy, B. (1977). "Human Resources Development for Library Personnel: A Manual for Program of Staff Development Continuing Education." Libraries Unlimited, Littleton, Colorado.

Corson, J. J., and Paul, R. S. (1966). "Men Near the Top: Filling Key Posts in the Federal Service." Johns Hopkins Press, Baltimore, Maryland.

Dalton, J. (1968). Observations on advanced study programs in the library schools of the United States. *In* "Library Education: An International Survey" (L. E. Bone, ed.), pp. 317–328. University of Illinois Graduate School of Library Science, Champaign, Illinois.

Danton, J. P. (1971). "Between MLS and Ph.D.: Sixty-Year Specialist Programs in Library Schools Accredited by the American Library Association." American Library Association, Chicago, Illinois.

DeProspo, E. R. (1971). Personnel evaluation as an impetus to growth. *Library Trends* 20, 69–70.
Faure, E., Herrera, F., Kaddoura, A.-R., Lopes, H., Petrovsky, A. V., Rahnema, M., and Ward, F. D. (1972). "Learning to Be: The World of Education Today and Tomorrow." UNESCO, Paris.
Flexner, A. (1915). Is social work a profession? *School and Society* 1, 901–911.
Foos, D. D. (1975). "Proceedings of the HEA Title II-B Institute on Continuing Education Program Planning for Library Staffs in the Sothwest, March 17–18, 1975." Louisiana State University Graduate School of Library Science and the Southwestern Library Association, Baton Rouge, Louisiana.
Fryden, F. N. (1969). Post-Master's degree programs in the accredited U. S. library schools. *Library Quarterly* 39, 233–244.
Gagne, R. M. (1962). Military training and principles of learning. *American Psychologist* 17, 83–91.
Gagne, R. M. (1965). "The Conditions of Learning." Holt, Rinehart and Winston, New York.
Ginsburg, E., and Brown, C. A. (1967). "Manpower for Library Services." Columbia University, New York. (ED 023 408.)
Gould, S. B. (1974). "Diversity by Design." Jossey-Bass, Washington, D.C.
Greenwood, J. W., Jr. (1970). Nature and importance of systems education. *International Associations* 1, 3–5.
Grotelneschen, A. D., Gooler, D. D., and Knox, A. B. (1976). "Evaluation in Adult Basic Education: How and Why." Interstate Printers and Publishers, Danville, Illinois.
Guba, E. G., and Stufflebeam, D. (1970). "Evaluation: The Process of Stimulating, Aiding and Abetting Insightful Action." Indiana University, Bloomington, Indiana.
Guidelines for the certification of personnel in educational communications technology. (1974). *Audiovisual Instruction* 19, 20–21.
Hamilton, B. I., and Halladay, R. E. (1976). "The Third Century: Postsecondary Planning for the Non-Traditional Learner: A Report Prepared for the Higher Education Facilities Commission of the State of Iowa." Educational Testing Service, Princeton, New Jersey.
Harlow, N. (1969). "Administration and Change: Continuing Education in Library Administration." Rutgers University Press, New Brunswick, New Jersey.
Harrison, J. C. (1968). Advanced study: A mid-Atlantic point of view. *In* "Library Education: An International Survey" (L. E. Bone, ed.), pp. 329–336. University of Illinois Graduate School of Library Science, Champaign, Illinois.
Hiatt, P. (1971). The educational third dimension, III. Toward the development of a national program of continuing education for library personnel. *Library Trends* 20, 169–183.
Hiatt, P. (1973). WICHE continuing education program for library personnel. *Illinois Libraries* 55, 332–336.
Hiatt, P., Allen, L. A., Duchac, K. F., Engen, R. B., Fisher, J. A., and Smith, D. C. (1971). "Education of State Library Personnel: A Report with Recom-

mendations Relating to the Continuing Education of State Library Agency Professional Personnel." (Prepared by the Association of State Library Agencies and the Library Education Division, Interdivisional Committee on Education of State Library Personnel, under a grant from the H. W. Wilson Foundation.) American Library Association, Chicago, Illinois.

Horn, A. H. (1972). The new position on the M.L.S. degree at UCLA. *California Librarian* 33, 5–8.

Hospital Continuing Education Project (1970). "Training and Continuing Education: A Handbook for Health Care Institutions." Hospital Research and Educational Trust, Chicago, Illinois.

Houle, C. O. (1967). The role of continuing education in current professional development. *ALA Bulletin* 61, 259–267.

Houle, C. O. (1970). The comparative study of continuing professional education. *Convergence* 3, 3–12.

Houle, C. O. (1974). "The Public Library's Role in Non-Traditional Study." [A Commissioned Paper under the Commissioned Papers Project Teachers College, Columbia University. USOE Grant OEG-0-70-4039 (725), Project Number 00-4026 Part B] Division of Library Programs, U.S. Office of Education, HEW, Washington, D.C. ED 098-993.

Hyer, A. U. (1971). "Jobs in Instructional Media Study." [Final Report: USPE Project No. 8-0688. Grant No. OEG-0-8-080688-4494 (085).] National Education Association, Division of Educational Technology, Washington, D.C.

Illinois State Library, Advisory Committee on Education and Training (1976). "Proposed Statement of Policy on Continuing Education." Illinois State Library, Advisory Committee on Education and Training, Springfield, Illinois.

Institute for Local Self Government (1971). "Continuing Continuing Education for the Public Service: A Design for Action for Education and Training for the Public Service." Institute for Local Self Government, Berkeley, California.

Institute for State Library Agency Personnel Responsible for Statewide Systems of Continuing Education (1977). "Continuing Education Planning Inventory: A Self-Evaluation Checklist." CLENE, Washington, D.C.

Jackson, M. A. (1977). Continuing education in eight allied health professional organizations. *Adult Leadership* 25, 153–156.

Kaser, D. (1971). The training subsystem. *Library Trends* 20, 71–77.

Klempner, I. M. (1968). Information centers and continuing education for librarianship. *Special Libraries* 59, 729–732.

Knowles, M. (1970). "The Modern Practice of Adult Education: Andragogy Versus Pedagogy." Association Press, New York.

Knowles, M. (1976). Model for assessing continuing education needs for a profession. *In* "First CLENE Assembly Proceedings, January 23–24, 1976" (Kieth Wright, ed.), pp. 82–102. CLENE, Washington, D.C.

Knox, A. (1976). "Helping Adults to Learn." CLENE, Washington, D.C. (Concept Paper No. 4.)

Kortendick, J. J. (1973). Continuing education for librarians. *In* "Targets for Research in Library Education" (H. Burko, ed.), pp. 145–172. American Library Association, Chicago, Illinois.

Kortendick, J. J., and Stone, E. W. (1971). "Job Dimensions and Educational Needs in Librarianship." American Library Association, Chicago, Illinois.

Kortendick, J. J., and Stone, E. W. (1972). "Post-Master's Education for Middle and Upper Level Personnel in Libraries and Information Centers." [Final Report, Phase II, Project No. 8-0731.] Office of Education, Department of Health, Education, and Welfare, Washington, D.C. (Included with the final report are three packaged Post-MLS courses edited by the authors of the report.)

Kurland, N. D. (1976). "A National Strategy for Lifelong Learning." [Remarks Prepared for the Dialogue on Lifelong Learning, October 18, 1976.] Institute for Educational Leadership, Postsecondary Education Convening Authority, The George Washington University, Washington, D.C. (Photoduplicated.)

Likert, R. (1967). "The Human Organization: Its Management and Value." McGraw-Hill, New York.

Lorenz, J. G. (1964). The challenge of change. *PNLA Quarterly* 29, 7–15.

McCarthy, D. R. (1973). Impact of HEA Title II-B Institutes in librarianship. *In* "Narrative Evaluation Report on the Leadership Training Institute" (Harold Goldstein, ed.). Florida State University, School of Library Science, CSC/Pacific, Palo Alto, California.

McDonough, R. H. (1972). "Library Education in New Jersey. Report and Recommendations of a Study Sponsored by the New Jersey Department of Higher Education and the New Jersey Department of Education." (Conducted by the New Jersey State Library with the assistance of an Advisory Committee.) New Jersey State Library, Trenton, New Jersey.

McGregor, D. (1960). "The Human Side of Enterprise." McGraw-Hill, New York.

McKay, D. (1977). North Carolina survey planned. *CLENExchange* 2, 5.

Mager, R. F. (1975). "Preparing Instructional Objectives," 2nd ed. Fearon Publishers, Palo Alto, California.

Marchant, M. P. (1971). Participative management as related to personnel development. *Library Trends* 20, 48–59.

Martin, A. B. (1972). "A Strategy for Public Library Change: Proposed Public Library Goals—Feasibility Study." Public Library Association, Chicago, Illinois.

Martin, A. B. (1971). Out of the ivory tower. *Library Journal,* 96, 2026.

Martin, A.B., and Duggan, M. (1975). "The Continuing Education for Library Staffs in the Southwest (CELS): A Survey with Recommendations." Graduate School of Library Science, University of Texas, Austin, Texas. (Reprint of 1973 edition.)

Maslow, A. H. (1943). A theory of human motivation. *Psychological Review* 50, 370–396.

Medical Library Association (MLA) (1976). MLS to award CEU's. *MLA News,* no. 74, January, 2.

Michael, M. E. (1975). "Continuing Professional Education in Librarianship and Other Fields: A Classified and Annotated Bibliography, 1965–1974." Garland Publishing, New York.

Midwest States Library Meeting, October 16–17, 1972 (n.d.). "Report on Committee on Continuing Education." (Photoduplicated.) (n.p.)

Monroe, M. E. (1967). Variety in continuing education. *ALA Bulletin* 61, 275-278.
National Commission on Libraries and Information Science (NCLIS) (1973). "Library and Information Service Needs of the Nation: Proceedings of a Conference on the Needs of Occupational, Ethnic, and Other Groups in the United States." U.S. Government Printing Office, Washington, D.C.
National Commission on Libraries and Information Science (NCLIS) (1973). "Library and Information Service Needs of the Nation: Proceedings of a Conference on the Needs of Occupational, Ethnic, and Other Groups in the United States." US. Government Printing Office, Washington, D.C.
National Science Foundation (1969). "Continuing Education for R&D Careers: An Exploratory Study of Employer-Sponsored and Self-Teaching Models of Continuing Education in Large Industrial and Federal Government Owned R&D Laboratories." (Prepared for the National Science Foundation by Social Research, Inc.) National Science Foundation, Washington, D.C. (ED 035 813.) (NSF 69-20.)
Nattress, L. W., Jr. (1970). Continuing education for the professions in the United States. *Convergence* 3, 42-50.
Nelson, J. (1976). Kentucky model for continuing education. *Journal of Education for Librarianship* 16, 129-138.
Nelson, J. (1977). "Conditions for Development: Continuing Education at Six Accredited Library Schools with Selected Additional Resourses." Kentucky-Ohio-Michigan Regional Medical Library Program, Lexington, Kentucky. (Mimeographed copy.) (n.p.)
New Jersey State Council for Environmental Education (1969). "Evaluation for Environmental Education." New Jersey State Council for Environmental Education, Mountain Lakes, New Jersey.
O'Donnell, P. (1975). Audio cassette awareness program. *CELS Update* December, 2.
Overhage, C. F. J. (1967). Science libraries; prospects and problems. *Science* 155, 802-806.
Patrick, R. J. (1976). "An Annotated Bibliography of Recent Continuing Education Literature." ERIC Clearinghouse on Information Resources, Stanford, California.
Pearson, K. (1977). WILCO restructures: will move from WICHE. *WILCO Newsletter*, no. 6, February, 1.
Plate, K. H., and Stone, E. W. (1974). Factors affecting librarians' job satisfaction: A report of two studies. *Library Quarterly* 44, 97-110.
Prigge, W. C. (1974). Accreditation and certification: A frame of reference. *Audiovisual Instruction* 19, 12-18.
Reed, S. R. (1964). "Continuing Education for Librarians—Conferences, Workshops and Short Courses, 1964-65." Office of Education, US. Department of Health, Education, and Welfare, Washington, D.C.
Reed, S. R. (1965). "Continuing Education for Librarians—Conferences, Workshops and Short Courses, 1965-66." Office of Education, US. Department of Health, Education, and Welfare, Washington, D.C.
Reed, S. R. (1966). "Continuing Education for Librarians—Conferences, Work-

shops and Short Courses, 1966–67." Office of Education, US. Department of Health, Education, and Welfare, Washington, D.C.

Rothstein, S. (1965). Nobody's baby. *Library Journal* 90, 2226–2227.

Schein, E. H. (1972). "Professional Education: Some New Directions." McGraw-Hill, New York.

"Science, Government and Information: The Responsibilities of the Technical Community and the Government in the Transfer of Information." (1963). The President's Science Advisory Commission, Washington, D.C.

Sheldon, B. E. (1976). "Planning and Evaluating Library Training Programs: A Guide for Library Leaders, Staffs and Advisory Groups." CLENE, Washington, D.C. (Reprint of 1973 edition published by Florida State University, Leadership Training Institute, Tallahassee, Florida.)

Sheldon, B. E. (1977). "The CELS Project—1974–1977: A Progress Report with Recommendations for the Future." Southwestern Library Association, Dallas, Texas.

Shera, J. H. (1972). The self-destructing diploma. *Ohio Library Association Bulletin* 42, 4–8.

Sloane, M. N. (1968). "Continuing Education for Special Librarianship. Where Do We Go From Here?" Special Libraries Association, New York. (ED 032 086.)

Sophar, G. J. (1974). ASIS Commission on long-range planning. *ASIS Newsletter* 13, 3.

State Library of Ohio (1972). Workshops sharpen skills. *In* "The State Library Review, A Report from The State Library of Ohio 1971–1972," p. 8. Columbus, Ohio.

Stevens, F. A. (1975). Institutes on continuing education. *CLENExchange* 1, 7.

Stevenson, G. T. (1967). Training for growth—the future for librarians. *ALA Bulletin* 61, 278–286.

Stevenson, G. T. (1971). "ALA Chapter Relationships—National, Regional, and State." American Library Association, Chicago, Illinois.

Stone, E. W. (1969). "Factors Related to the Professional Development of Librarians." Scarecrow Press, Metuchen, New Jersey.

Stone, E. W. (1970). Continuing education in librarianship: ideas for action. *American Libraries* 1, 543–553.

Stone, E. W. ed. (1971a). "New Directions in Staff Development: Moving from Ideas to Action." American Library Association, Chicago, Illinois.

Stone, E. W. ed. (1971b). Personnel development and continuing education in libraries. *Library Trends* 20.

Stone, E. W. (1974). "Continuing Library Education as Viewed in Relation to Other Continuing Professional Education Movements." American Society for Information Science, Washington, D.C.

Stone, E. W. (1976). "An Annotated Bibliography on Evaluation Concepts with Relevancy to Library/Media/Information Science Situtations." CLENE, Washington, D.C. (Mimeograph copy.)

Stone, E. W. (1977). "Tabulation of Questionnaire Regarding Certification of Librarians and the Use of CEU by States." CLENE, Washington, D.C.

Stone, E. W., Patrick, R. J., and Conroy, B. (1974). "Continuing Library and

Information Science Education: Final Report to the National Commission on Libraries and Information Science." US. Government Printing Office, Washington, D.C. and American Society for Information Science, Washington, D.C.

Stone, E. W., Sheahan, E., and Harig, K. J. (1977). "Development of a Continuing Education Recognition System in Library and Information Science Including Provision for Nontraditional Studies and Development of a Prototype Home Study Program." 2 Vols. [Final Report, USOE Grant G007603021, Project 475H60125 B, Office of Libraries and Learning Resources, U.S. Office of Education, Department of Health Education and Welfare]. CLENE, Washington, D.C.

Swanson, R. W., and Johns, C. J., Jr. (1976). Some highlight findings of the ASIS membership survey. SIG/ED Newsletter, no. ED-76-1, January, 8–10.

Taylor, R. L. (1976). "Directory of Institutions Offering or Planning Programs for the Training of Library Technical Assistants," 4th Ed. Council of Library Technical Assistants, Chicago, Illinois.

Thiede, W. B. (1968). Measurement and evaluation in adult education. In "Research Methods in Librarianship: Measurement and Evaluation" (H. Goldhor, ed.), pp. 88–94. University of Illinois Graduate School of Library Science, Champaign, Illinois.

Thomson, D. D. (1972). "Planning and Evaluation for Statewide Library Development: New Directions." Ohio State University Evaluation Center, Columbus, Ohio.

"Uniform Guidelines on Employee Selection Procedures." (1974). Equal Employment Opportunity Coordinating Council, Staff Committee Draft, Washington, D. C.

US. Congress, House Commission on Instructional Technology (1970). "A Report to the President and the Congress of the United States." US. Government Printing Office, Washington, D.C.

Vaillancourt, P. N. (1976). The Continuing Library Education Network and Exchange (CLENE): Aid to continuing education for special librarians. *Special Libraries* 67, 208–216.

Virgo, J. (1976). "Continuing Education Needs for Health Sciences Library Personnel: Final Report to the National Library of Medicine." National Library of Medicine, Bethesda, Maryland.

Warncke, R. (1973). Continuing education: whose responsibility? *Minnesota Libraries* 24, 59–65.

Warner, E. S. (1973). "Information Needs of Urban Residents." (Final Report, No. OEC-0-71-4555.) U.S. Department of Health, Education, and Welfare, Office of Education, Bureau of Libraries and Educational Technology, Washington, D.C.

Webster, D. E. (1972a). "Library Policies: Analysis, Formulation and Use in Academic Institutions." Office of University Library Management Studies. Association of Research Libraries, Washington, D.C. (Occasional Paper No. 2.)

Webster, D. E. (1972b). The Management Review and Analysis Program: An assisted self-study to secure constructive change in the management of research libraries. *College and Research Libraries* **35**, 114–125.

Wildman, I. J. (1972). Education—A lifelong process. *Law Library Journal* **65**, 130–133.

Woodrum, P. (1977). Libraries have miles to go and promises to keep. *In* "Proceedings, CLENE Assembly III, February 4–5, 1977" (Kieth Wright, ed.). CLENE, Washington, D.C.

Zachert, M. J. K. (1972). Continuing education for librarians: The role of the learner. *In* "University of Tennessee Library Lectures, Numbers Twenty-Two, Twenty-Three, and Twenty-Four" E. E. Goehring, ed.). University of Tennessee, Knoxville, Tennessee.

Subject Index

A

AALS, see Association of American Library Schools
Academic environment, economic situation and, 10
Academic institution, continuing education and, 293–303
  see also Continuing education; University libraries
Academic libraries
  see also University libraries
  in American library history, 184–187
  appropriations for, 9
  salaries in, 93
Acquisition environment, administrative adjustments to, 12–20
  see also Collection development
Adult Education Association, 255
Adult Functional Competency, 260
Adult learning, conditions for, 256–258
  see also Continuing education
Advisory Council of Library Education in New Jersey, 310
AECT, see Association for Education Communications and Technology
AFC, see Adult Functional Competency
Affirmative action
  see also Equal Employment Opportunity Subcommittee, ALA
  civil service requirements and, 116–117
  collective bargaining and, 117–119
  defined, 83
  economic conditions and, 112–113

employment procedures and practices in, 124–127
future of, 121–127
handicapped and, 127
institutional programs in, 105–110
legal and enforcement uncertainties in, 113–114
legal aspects of, 83–86
librarianship and, 81–128
as national policy, 82
outline pattern in, 103–105
problem areas in, 104
recruitment and training in, 100–103, 124
research needs of, 122–124
reverse discrimination and, 114–116
selection procedures in, 119
social change and, 128
socioeconomic trends and, 86–97
trend and survey data for, 121–122
women employment and, 90–94
Affirmative Action and Equal Employment: A Guidebook for Employees (Equal Employment Opportunity Commission), 105
Affirmative Action Information Packet, 88, 105
Affirmative Action Plan Development, 103–112
Age Discrimination in Employment Act (1967), 85
Akwesasne Library-Culture Center, 157–159
ALA/OLPR, see American Library Association Office for Library Personnel Resources
Alberta, University of, 204, 214

Alcoholism and Drug Rehabilitation Program, 161
American Association of Law Librarians, 278
American Association of Law Libraries, 276, 288–289
American Association of Library Schools, 284
American Indian
  see also Indian American
  enrollments of, 145–146
  Media Evaluation and Development by, 167
American Indian Center, Chicago, 143
American Indian Historical Society, 147
American Indian Law Newsletter, 146
American Indian Libraries Newsletter, 167
American Indian Library Service, 135–174
  Akwesasne Library-Culture Center and, 157–159
  in Arizona, 161–162
  community information needs and, 168–169
  community libraries in, 143–144, 152–154
  domain in, 142–148
  funding of, 171
  future trends in, 172–174
  goals of, 148
  implementing of, 172–174
  Indian control in, 169–170
  information demand and, 169
  knowledge base of, 168–172
  National Indian Association Library Project and, 149–152
  Newberry Library Center and, 166
  in New Mexico, 162–164
  personal utilization and training in, 171–172
  policy development in, 172–173
  postsecondary and research libraries in, 145–147
  professional associations and, 167–168
  progress in since 1973, 149–168
  Rough Rock Community School Library and, 152–154
  school libraries and, 144–145
  service strategies in, 170
  Shoshone-Bannock Library and Media Center in, 160–161
  Sioux City Public Library Indian Library Project and, 159–160
  Standing Rock Tribal Library and, 154–157
  in Wisconsin, 164–165
American Indian library technical assistants, 102
American Indian Policy Review Commission, 169
American librarianship, women employment and, 90–94
American Library Association, 63–65, 67, 88, 102, 147, 167–168, 204, 276, 296
  activities of, 97–100
  Activities Committee in New Directions for, 281
  Continuing Education policy statement of, 279–281
  educational program information of, 88–90
  Equal Employment Opportunity Subcommittee of, *see* Equal Employment Opportunity Subcommittee, ALA
  history of, 191
  Library Administration Division of, 94, 99, 127, 282
  Library Education Division of, 126
  Library Manpower Statement of, 306
  Office for Library Personnel Resources, 88, 98, 123–124
  Staff Development Committee of, 257
American library education
  climate for learning in, 247
  competency identification in, 259–260
  continuing, *see* Continuing education
  continuing education concept of, 245–246
  definitions and distinctions in, 243–255
  learning needs in, 258–259
  lifelong nature of, 244
  professionalism and, 251–255
  programming in, 258–259
  staff development and, 246–247
  task analysis in, 259–264
  technological obsolescence in, 250–251
American library history
  academic libraries and, 184–187
  advances in writing of, 181–195
  dissertations on, 182–183
  future opportunities in, 193–194
  general observations on, 193–195
  geographical areas in, 188
  "horizontal" studies in, 186–187

Subject Index

individual libraries and librarians in, 188
library associations in, 190–191
library education in, 191–192
organization of materials in, 190
public libraries and, 187–190
recent attention to, 181–184
recent gains in, 193–194
recent research in, 184–192
relevance of, 183–184
revision in, 189–190
utility of to library profession, 194–195
American Society of Information Science, 288
Arizona
   American Indian Library Service in, 161–162
   University of, 166
Arizona Department of Libraries and Archives, 143
Arizona State University, 102, 166
ARL, see Association of Research Libraries
Asian American Librarians Caucus, 88
ASIS, see American Society of Information Science
Association of American Library Schools, 191, 269, 276, 296, 299
Association of College and Research Libraries, 90, 95
Association for Education Communications and Technology, 262
Association of Jewish Libraries, 276
Association of Research Libraries, 2, 4, 105, 108
Atlantic Provinces Library Association, 232

B

BALLOTS system, 35, 37
BIA, see Bureau of Indian Affairs
Bibliographers, subject, see Subject Bibliographers
Black Caucus, 88, 94
Black librarians, employment of, 94
Bookmobile services, in Indian communities, 143
Brigham City (Utah) Indian collection, 145
British Columbia, University of, 203, 209, 242
Brookings Institution, 66

Budget allocation formulas, in university libraries, 15–16
Bureau of Indian Affairs, 140, 144, 146, 161, 171, 173
Bureau of Libraries and Educational Technology, 267

C

CACUL, see Canadian Association of College and University Libraries
California, University of, 146, 293
California Community College, 102
California Fair Employment Practices Commission, 115
California Library Association, 100–101
California State Library, 101
CALS, see Canadian Association of Library Schools
Canada
   community colleges of, 204
   National Library of, 203
   population and demographics of, 202–203
   postgraduate library schools in, 203–204
Canadian Association of College and University Libraries, 232
Canadian Association of Library Schools, 231
Canadian Association of University Libraries, 205
Canadian culture, library education and, 201–204
Canadian Library Association, 88, 208, 217, 222–224
Canadian library associations, 231–233
Canadian library education, 201–238
   B.L.S. programs in, 219, 224
   compared with U.S., 204–206
   continuing education and, 224–226
   curricular responses in, 209–216
   extrapolation in, 233–236
   field work or practicum in, 215
   future of, 233–239
   harmonization of qualifications in, 226
   librarianship as academic discipline in, 219–222
   library associations and education for leadership in, 231–233
   M.L.S. program in, 213–214, 218–219, 224, 235
   Ph.D. program in, 210–212, 229, 235

Canadian library education (*continued*)
  publications of, 220–221
  regional and national needs of, 206–209
  research component in, 229–231
  stratification in, 216–219
  subjects required by, 237–238
Cataloging-in-Publication program, 61–62
Catholic University of America, 313, 315
CELS, *see* Continuing Education for Library Staffs in the Southwest
Center for Research Libraries, 34–35
CETA, *see* Comprehensive Employment and Training Act
CEU, *see* Continuing Education Unit
Chicago Public Library, The (Spencer), 188
Chief Officers of State Library Agencies, 311
Chronicle of Higher Education, 8, 11
CIPP model, in continuing education evaluation, 266–267
Civil Service Commission, 84
Civil service systems, affirmative action in, 116–117
Civil Rights Act (1964), 84, 118
CLA, *see* Canadian Library Association
CLENE, *see* Continuing Library Education Network and Exchange
CLENE Directory of Continuing Education Opportunities, 292, 297
CLENE Institute for State Library Agency Personnel Responsible for Continuing Education, 267
Cleveland Indian Center, 143
Cleveland Public Library, 182
COA, *see* Committee on Accreditation, ALA
Collection development, 1–40
  see also University Libraries
  academic environment and, 10–12
  and acquisition environment of 1970s, 7–20
  and acquisition trends of 1960s, 3–7
  control and evaluation of, 37–39
  cooperative programs in, 32–37
  formal coordination of, 18–19
  reprint articles in, 2
  selection priorities and, 20–24
  special problems and responses in, 24–30
Collection development committees, 19
Collection development officers, 18–19
Collective bargaining, affirmative action and, 117–119

College and Research Libraries News, 37, 187, 194
Colorado River Tribes Public Library, 143
COLT, *see* Council on Library Technical Assistants
COLT Directory, 289
Columbia University Library, 101, 107
Commission on Civil Rights, U.S., 118
Commission on Instructional Technology, 258
Committee on Accreditation, ALA, 99
Committee on the Status of Women in Librarianship, 88
Comprehensive Employment and Training Act, 112–113
Conservation, in university libraries, 30–32
Context evaluation, 266
Continuing competence, concept of, 247–250
Continuing education, 241–323
  see also American library education
  academic institutions and, 293–303
  ALA policy on, 279–281
  campus questionnaire on, 300–301
  compatible system in, 271
  concept of, 245–246
  evaluation in, 266–268
  federal government and, 311–314
  goals and objectives in, 264–266
  individual practitioner in, 74
  learning needs in, 258–259
  professional associations in, 274–292
  professional system of measurement for, 269–271
  responsibility for, 271–314
  state library agencies in, 307–311
  system design in, 255–271
  systems approach to, 255–256
Continuing Education for Library Staffs in the Southwest, 269, 290
Continuing Education Program for Library Personnel of the Western Interstate Commission for Higher Education, 290–291
Continuing Education for State Library Personnel, 308
Continuing Education Unit, MLA, 287–288
Continuing Library and Information Science Study, 270

Continuing Library Education as Viewed in Relation to Other Continuing Professional Educational Movements (Stone), 303-306
Continuing Library Education Committee, Association of American Library Schools, 276, 286
Continuing Library Education Network and Exchange, 270, 273, 287, 311, 313-322
   achievements of, 318-320
   background of, 315-316
   as data repository, 320-322
   defined, 314
   dues and fees structure of, 319-320
   future of, 322
   goals of, 318
Cooperative programs, in university libraries, 32-37
Copyright Office, U.S., 61
   see also Library of Congress
COSLA, *see* Chief Officers of State Library Agencies
Council on Library Resources, 20
Council on Library Technical Assistants, 120, 289
Council on Library Technology, 289
CRL, *see* Center for Research Libraries

D

Dalhousie University, 203, 224-225
Dayton and Montgomery County Public Library, 107
Deganawidah-Quetzalcoatl University, 146
Degrees, Number of conferred, 11
Detroit Public Library, 182, 188
Dewey decimal classification, 62, 190
District of Columbia Library, 107
DIT (Domain of Instructional Technology), 262
Domestic publications, in university libraries, 21-22
Duke University, 107
Duplication, in university libraries, 28

E

Economic Opportunity Act (1965), 312
Education, *see* American library education; Canadian library education; Continuing education

Educational programs, affirmative action and, 88-90
Education Amendments (1976), 244
Education of State Library Personnel (Hiatt), 307
Education Professions Development Act (1967), 312
EEOCC, *see* Equal Employment Opportunity Coordinating Council
EEO subcommittee, *see* Equal Employment Opportunity subcommittee
Elementary and Secondary Education Act (1965), 312
Employment
   of minorities, 94-97
   of women, 90-94
Employment procedures, affirmative action and, 124-126
Enoch Pratt Free Library, 182, 188
Equal employment opportunity, 82
   legal and enforcement uncertainties in, 113-114
Equal Employment Opportunity Act (1972), 84
Equal Employment Opportunity Commission, U.S., 84, 119
Equal Employment Opportunity Coordinating Council, 119
Equal Employment Opportunity Guidelines, 263
Equal Employment Opportunity Subcommittee, ALA, 98-99, 103, 105-106, 108
Equal Pay Act (1963), 84
ESEA, *see* Elementary and Secondary Education Act (1965)
Evaluation of Adult Basic Education: How and Why? (Grotelueschen et al.), 268
Exchanges, in university libraries, 27-28
Expanded Journals Project, 34

F

Farmington Plan, 6
Farmington Plan Newsletter, 33
Federal funding, of university libraries, 9
Federal government, continuing education and, 311-314
Federal Library Committee, 313
Federal Register, 114

Florida State Library, 312
Foreign acquisitions, in university libraries, 4-5
Foreign Acquisitions Newsletter, 33
Funding variations, in university libraries, 9, 28-29

G

Ganado, College of, 161-162
General Electric vs. Gilbert, 114
Gifts, for university libraries, 26-27
Great Depression, public library in, 190
Great Lakes International Council, 165
Great Society programs, 143
Guidelines for the Training of Library Technicians (Canadian Library Association), 217-218

H

Harvard University Library, 65-66
HEA, *see* Higher Education Act
Health, Education and Welfare Department, U.S., 85, 99
Health and Rehabilitation Services Division, ALA, 99
Higher education, support for, 8
Higher Education Act (1965), 101-102, 124, 244, 312
Higher Education Guidelines: Executive Order 11246, 105
Hou Kola, 155
House Labor-HEW Appropriations Committee, 101
HRSD, *see* Health and Rehabilitation Services Division, ALA

I

Illinois Minorities Manpower Project, 100
Illinois State Library, 100
Indiana University Graduate Library School, 24, 40
Indian American(s)
  see also American Indian Library Service
  demographic data on, 137-140
  in 1970s, 137-142
  population of by state, 138-139
  self-determination in, 140-142

Indian Historian Press, 147
Indian Technical Assistance Center, 165
Input evaluation, 266
Institute of Professional Librarians of Ontario, 227-229
Interior Department, U.S., 173
International Federation of Library Associations, 216
IPLO, *see* Institute of Professional Librarians of Ontario

J

Jefferson library, purchase of by U.S., 57
JIMS (Jobs in Instructional Media Study), 262
Johnson-O'Malley Act, 155
Journal of Education for Librarianship, 286, 302

K

Ka Ri Wen Ha Wi Newsletter, 158
Kentucky, University of, 310

L

Latin American Cooperative Acquisitions Project, 33
Labor Department, U.S., 87
LACAP, *see* Latin American Cooperative Acquisitions Project
LACPL, *see* Los Angeles County Public Library
LAD, *see* Library Administrative Division, ALA
Lakehead University, 218
Lakota Higher Education Center, 146
Latin American Cooperative Acquisitions Project, 33
LC, *see* Library of Congress
Leona Johnson Memorial Library, 159
LIBGIS, *see* Library General Information Survey
Librarian of Congress, induction of, 56
Librarians
  continuing education for, 241-323
  race and origin of, 96
  responsibility for continuing education of, 271-314

total number of, 96
women as, 90–94, 110
Librarianship
  as academic discipline, 219–222
  affirmative action and, 81–128
  continuing competence in, 247–250
Libraries, academic, *see* Academic libraries; University libraries
Library, defined, 243 n.
Library Administration Division, ALA, 282
Library associations, in American library history, 190–191
Library education
  in American library history, 191–192
  in Canada, 201–238
  continuing, *see* Continuing education
  trends in, 201–238
Library General Information Survey, 123
Library history, *see* American library history
Library Journal, 33, 127
Library Literature, 233
Library Networking in the West, 291
Library of Congress, U.S., 55–78
  affirmative action and, 109–112
  authors' and publishers' services of, 61
  catalog cards of, 62
  Congress and, 58–59
  copyright activities of, 58
  Copyright Office of, 61
  disagreement over role of, 63–68
  dual nature of, 57
  federal government and, 59–60
  founding of, 58
  general public and, 60–61
  gifts to, 60
  legislative and national roles of, 57–63, 71–76
  library services of, 62–63
  minorities employed at, 110–111
  national responsibilities of, 74–76
  Office of Planning and Development in, 71
  organizational changes in, 73–74
  Planning Committee of, 65
  President and, 59–60
  Presidential papers of, 61–62
  redefinition of role of, 69–71
  scholars' and researchers' services of, 61–62
  service role of, 58–63

Task Force of, 68–71
Task Force recommendations for, 71–78
women employed at, 110
Library profession, racism and sexism in, 99
  see also Librarians; Librarianship
Library Service for American Indian People, 147
Library Services and Construction Act (1956), 143, 164–165, 312
Library Trends, 3, 194, 283
Lifelong learning, concept of, 244
Lifetime Learning Act, 260
Los Angeles County Public Library, 107, 112, 115
Louisiana State University, 112
LSCA, *see* Library Services and Construction Act (1956)

M

McGill University, 203, 207, 209, 213
Machine-Readable Cataloging Program, 62, 67
Management Review and Analysis Program, 281
Manitoba Institute of Technology, 217
MARC, *see* Machine-Readable Cataloging Program
MEDIA (Media Evaluation and Development by American Indians), 167
Medical Library Association, 100, 276–277, 287
Medical Library Assistance Act (1966), 312
Medical Library Association News, 287
MEDLINE system, 313
Menominee County Library, 165
Michigan, University of, 102
Michigan Library Association, 100
Michigan State University, 181
Minnesota, University of, 147, 150–151, 168
Minorities
  data collection for, 123–124
  employment of, 94–96
  in Library of Congress, 110–111
  reverse discrimination and, 114–116
M.L.S. degree
  job descriptions and, 126
  validity of, 120
Modern Practice of Adult Education, The (Knowles), 257

Montclair Public Library, 107
Montréal, Université de, 203, 207
Mountain-Plains Library Association, 100, 292
Museum of the American Indian, 146

N

National Archives, 147
National Association of Spanish-Speaking Librarians, 88
National Commission on Libraries and Information Science, 263, 274, 302, 306–309, 316–317
National Defense Education Act (1958), 312
National Education Association, 262
National Endowment for the Humanities, 24
National Indian Education Act, 171
National Indian Education Association, 147, 167, 169
National Indian Education Association Library Project, 149–152, 154, 164
National Indian Law Library, 147
National Library, 65, 192, 313
National Library Advisory Board, 66
National Library of Medicine, 263
National Program for Acquisitions and Cataloging, 62
National Register of Microform Masters, 32
National University Extension Association, 255
Native American Evaluation of Media Materials, 167
Navajo Community College, 146, 161
Navajo Health Authority, 162
Navajo Tribal Museum, 162
NCLIS, *see* National Commission on Libraries and Information Science
NDEA, *see* National Defense Education Act (1958)
Newberry Library Center for the History of the American Indian, 166
New England Library Association, 101, 292
New England Library Board, 292
New Mexico
  American Indian Library Service in, 162–164
  University of, 162
New Mexico State Library, 164
Newspapers in Microform, 32
New York Public Library, 188

NIEA, *see* National Indian Education Association
Nondiscrimination, equal employment and, 82
North Carolina, University of, 107

O

OFCC (Office for Federal Contract Compliance), 85
Office for Civil Rights, U.S., 84, 86
Office of Education, U.S., 84, 101, 262, 284, 297, 311, 313
Office of Libraries and Learning Resources, U.S. Office of Education, 267
Office for Library Personnel Resources, ALA, 88, 123–124, 147, 168
Office of Library Service for the Disadvantaged, ALA, 147
Office of Library and Information Services, Interior Department, 173
Oklahoma City University, 102
OLPR, *see* Office for Library Personnel Resources
Orange County Library, 107
Ottawa, University of, 207

P

Pacific Northwest Association, 291
PLA, *see* Public Library Association
Pratt Institute, 102
President's Committee on Employment of the Handicapped, 108, 127
Process evaluation, 266
Product evaluation, 266
Professional associations, in continuing education, 274–292
Professionalism, in American library education, 251–255
Public Libraries
  in American library history, 187–190
  salaries in, 93
  women employment in, 91
Public Library Association, 99, 284
Publishers Weekly, 9–10

Q

Quantitative methods, in university libraries, 37–39

R

Racial and Ethnic Data for Institutions of Higher Education, Fall 1970, 89
Racism, combating of, 99–100
Raking the Historic Coals (Holley), 189
REFORMA: National Association of Spanish-Speaking Librarians, 88
Research Libraries Group, 36
Research needs, university libraries and, 22–23
Reverse discrimination, 114–116
Rosary College School of Library Science, 100
Rough Rock Community School Library, 152–154
Rutgers University, 107

S

Sacramento City-County Library, 120
St. Regis Akwesasne Mohawk Reservation, 157
Salaries
 of black librarians, 95
 in various types of libraries, 93
 for women, 90–94
Santa Clara Community Library, 163
Save the Children Foundation, 143
School libraries, salaries in, 93
School Library Manpower Project, 251
School Library Personnel Task Analysis Survey, 262
School of Library and Information Science, University of Western Ontario, 203, 210, 214–216
SCMAI, *see* Staff Committee on Mediation, Arbitration, and Inquiry
Seattle Indian Center, 143
Selection priorities, in university libraries, 20–24
Self-determination, in American Indians, 140–142
Serials, in university libraries, 24–26, 35–36
Sexism, combating of, 99–100
Shoshone-Bannock Library and Media Center, 160–161
SIG/Ed, *see* Special Interest Group in Education
Sinte Gleska College, 146
Sioux City Public Library Indian Library Project, 159–160
SLICE, *see* Southwestern Library Interstate Cooperative Endeavor
SLIS, *see* School of Library and Information Science
Smithsonian library, acquisition of, 61
Social change, affirmative action and, 128
Socioeconomic trends, affirmative action and, 86–97
South Dakota, University of, 147
Southwestern Library Association, 290, 292
Southwestern Library Interstate Cooperative Endeavor, 290
Southwest Museum, 146
Spanish-speaking librarians, 88, 95
Special Interest Group on Education, 288
Special Libraries Association, 95, 100, 226, 289
Staff Committee on Mediation, Arbitration and Inquiry, 99
Staff development, in American library education, 246–247
Standing Rock Tribal Library, 154–157
Standing Rock Tribal Library Newsletter, 155
Story Up to Now, The (Mearns), 65
Subject bibliographers, in university libraries, 5–6
Subject-field competition, in university libraries, 23–24
SWLA, *see* Southwestern Library Association

T

Tacoma Public Library, 107
TAP, *see* Training, Appraisal, and Promotion Program
Task Force, Library of Congress, 68–78
Task Force on Women, 88, 99
Teaching needs, university libraries and, 22–23
Toronto, University of, 229, 231
Toronto Faculty of Library Science, 210, 231
Toronto Public Library, 222
Training, Appraisal, and Promotion Program, 109
Tucson Public Library, 101

U

United Nations Educational, Scientific, and Cultural Organization, 243

United States, continuing education for librarians in, 241–323
  see also American (adj.)
University libraries
  academic environment of, 10–12
  administrative adjustments in, 12–20
  appropriations to, 9
  blanket orders and approval plans in, 6–7
  budget allocation formulas for, 15–16
  catalog-information sharing of, 35
  collection development in, 1–40
  competition among subject fields in, 23–24
  conservation in, 30–32
  cooperative programs in, 32–37
  current domestic publications in, 21–22
  economic realities in, 7–8
  exchanges in, 27–28
  foreign acquisitions in, 4–5
  funding in, 9, 28–29
  gifts and gift funds in, 26–27
  growth rates for, 3–4
  increase problems of 1960s in, 3–7
  inflation and, 9–10
  long-range acquisition planning in, 17–18
  long-standing arrangements in, 33–35
  quantitative methods in, 37–39
  replacement and duplication in, 28
  research and teaching needs in, 22–23
  selection priorities in, 20–24
  serials in, 24–26, 35–36
  special problems and responses in, 24–32
  subject bibliographers in, 5–6
  weeding and storage in, 29–30

V

Vietnam Era Veterans Readjustment Act (1974), 85
Vocational Education Act (1963), 312
Vocational Rehabilitation Act (1973), 85

W

WEAL Education and Legal Defense Fund, 89
Weeding, in university libraries, 29–30
Western Interstate Commission for Higher Education, 290
Western Interstate Library Coordinating Organization, 291
Western Ontario, University of, 203, 213
WICHE, see Western Interstate Commission for Higher Education
Window Rock Public Schools, 161
Wisconsin, American Indian Library Service in, 164–165
Wisconsin Valley Library Service, 165
Women
  in Library of Congress, 110
  salaries for, 90–94
  task force on, see Task Force on Women
Women employment, affirmative action and, 90–94
Women Library Workers, 88
Women's Bureau, Labor Department, 87

Z

Zuni Public Library, 163

Z
674
A4
v.8
1978

JUN 20 1978